AF480790

white girl within

LETTERS OF **SELF-DISCOVERY** BETWEEN A TRANSGENDER AND TRANSRACIAL BLACK MAN AND HIS **INNER FEMALE**

October

PUBLISHING

Cinncinnati, Ohio

Contact information for October Publishing– www.whitegirlwithin.com

ISBN: 979-8-9866654-0-5 (paperback)
ISBN: 979-8-9866654-1-2 (ebook)
ISBN: 979-8-9866654-2-9 (hardcover)
ISBN: 979-8-9866654-3-6 (audiobook)

Ordering Information:
Special discounts are available on quantity purchases by corporations, associations, and others. For details, contact www.whitegirlwithin.com

Publisher's Cataloging-in-Publication Data

Names: Gladden, Ronnie, 1978-.
Title: White girl within : letters of self-discovery between a transgender and transracial black man and his inner female / Ronnie Gladden.
Description: Cincinnati, OH : October Publishing, 2023. | Summary: An identity management resource and self-help memoir for teens and young adults, this book tells the true story of the author's challenging and complex intersectional identity and how they liberated their collective self from oppressive cultural shackles.
Identifiers: ISBN 9798986665429 (hardcover) | ISBN 9798986665405 (pbk.) | ISBN 9798986665412 (ebook)
Subjects: LCSH: Gladden Ronnie, 1978 – Biography. Transgender women – United States – Biography. | Gender identity – Social aspects. | African American transgender people – Violence against. | Race awareness – United States. | Racism – United States. | Intersectionality (Sociology). | Cincinnati (Ohio). | BISAC: BIOGRAPHY & AUTOBIOGRAPHY / LGBTQ+. | SELF-HELP / Gender & Sexuality. | SOCIAL SCIENCE / Race & Ethnic Relations.
Classification: LCC HQ77.8 G53 2023 | DDC 306.76/8092 G—dc23

white girl within

LETTERS OF **SELF-DISCOVERY** BETWEEN A TRANSGENDER AND TRANSRACIAL BLACK MAN AND HIS **INNER FEMALE**

RONNIE GLADDEN

"My book is my best letter, my response, my truest explanation of it all. In it I have put my body and spirit. You understand this better and fuller and clearer than anyone else."

—*Walt Whitman*[1]

---

1   Walt Whitman, *The Correspondence*, ed. Edwin Haviland Miller (New York: New York University Press, 1961–1977): 140.

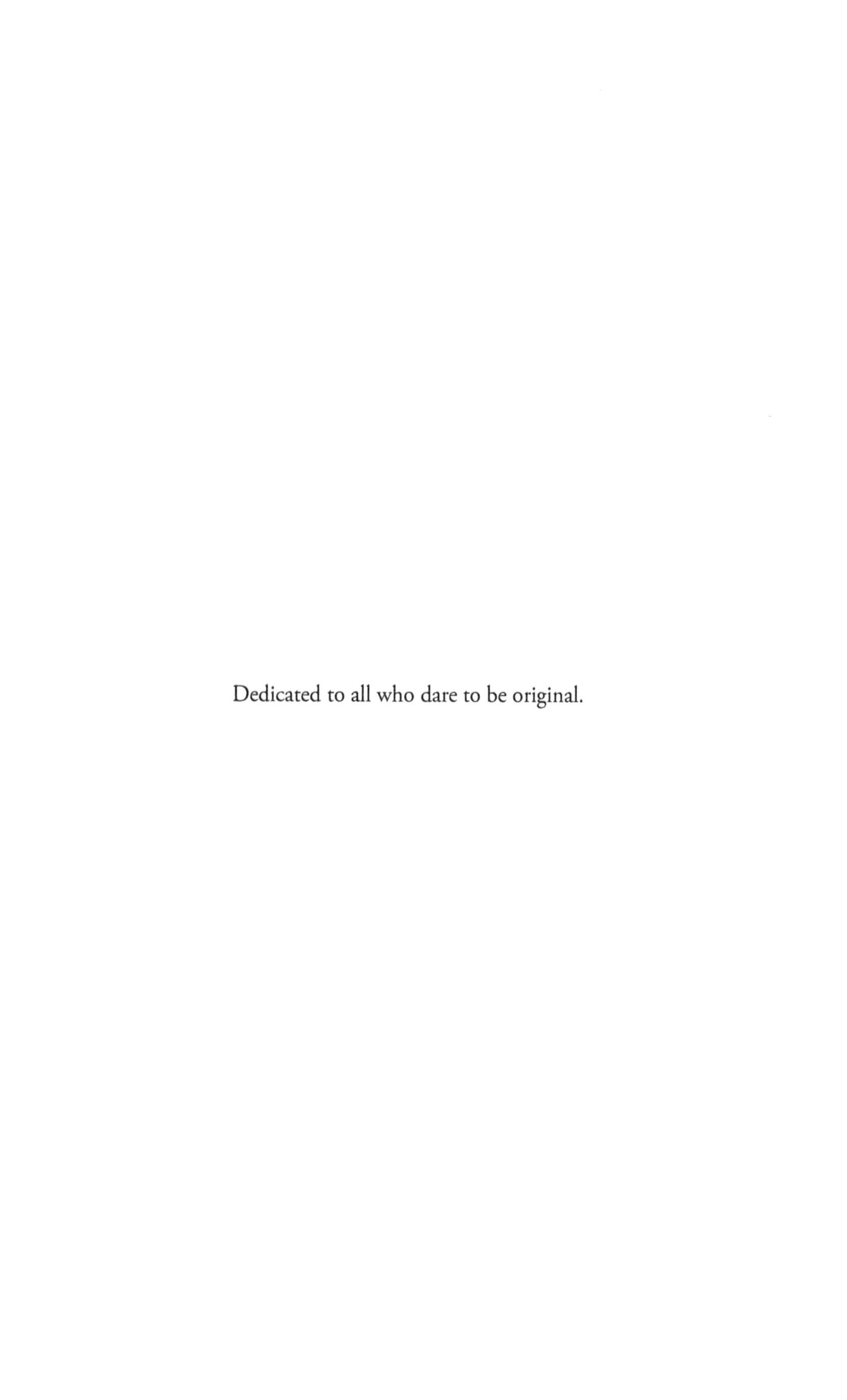

Dedicated to all who dare to be original.

"We meet no stranger but ourself."

—Emily Dickinson[2]

2   "We Meet No Stranger But Ourself," Key-life.org, https://key-life.org/2020/06/30/we-meet-no-stranger-but-ourself/.

I hope you will enjoy reading *White Girl Within*.

If you do, please leave a review here:
https://www.goodreads.com/book/show/63191633-white-girl-within

Let's spread literacy, authentic storytelling,
and the celebration of the individual sovereign. ☺

AUTHOR'S LETTER TO THE READER

This is an identity self-help book primarily designed for teens and young adults. Yet, anyone grappling to formulate a coherent sense of self may find this work valuable. Through my own improbable story of struggling to understand my strong sense of internal White female identity locked inside of a Black male body, I've worked to find answers. Why would this happen? How could this happen? What is the point of this all? Why did I have to be burdened with this? And why is this still my truth?

While my journey at face value may be a bit stratospheric and abstract, the desire to soul-search and to make sense of our experiences, I think, are universal to us all. And when elements of trauma are woven into this fabric, it's all the more challenging to achieve perspective and gain ground. Can you relate? I hope that through reading this book, you glean an understanding through the portraiture that emerges. As you delve into the meaning-making process, I challenge you to apply those tools and processes in creating or clarifying your own portrait so as to not only gain more of an understanding of yourself -- but also to enhance your understanding of others and the complex world we live in. Let us unite to improve society for a more inclusive world!

TABLE OF CONTENTS

part one
THE WHITE GIRL WITHIN WRITES LETTERS TO RONNIE

Letter 1: Coming Out 3

Letter 2: Longing for White Girlhood 11

Letter 3: And the Beat Goes On 16

Letter 4: Lipstick on the Basin 19

Letter 5: Watering the Glove 23

Letter 6: Lacy Pinch Fall Out 25

Letter 7: Dresser Drawer Carvings... 27

Letter 8: Cassette Tape Threat.. 29

Letter 9: The First "N" 31

Letter 10: Winton Terrace Tales.. 38

Letter 11: Ebony and Ivory (Not in Perfect Harmony) 41

Letter 12: The Fay 47

Letter 13: Sailing to School 51

Letter 14: Elder High School.. 53

Letter 15: Seton High School 55

Letter 16: Cheviot Elementary School 57

Letter 17: Jane and Andy... 63

Letter 18: TV Land 71

Letter 19: Golden Girls and Full House 83

Letter 20: My Kind of Family.. 85

Letter 21: Marge Schott 87

Letter 22: Spanning the Generations & Forms 92

Letter 23: Sweet Dreams and Other Escapes............................ 102

Letter 24: Rubble 104

Letter 25: Cincinnati 108

Letter 26: The School for Creative and Performing Arts 111

Letter 27: School (but Not All Was Sweet…) 120

Letter 28: The Censure 123

Letter 29: Brandon & Identity 126

Letter 30: Leo, Ronnie, and Me 128

Letter 31: Forced Reckoning 132

Letter 32: Lost in Our Musings 135

Letter 33: Exceptionalism 137

Letter 34: Teens and TNT 139

Letter 35: Ben's Instincts 142

Letter 36: Murder and THE Death of Childhood 144

Letter 37: Pulling the Trigger 149

Letter 38: Teacher and Teen Suicides 151

Letter 39: Pound Cake 154

Letter 40: Airborne 158

Letter 41: Meeting Rachel Dolezal, The 'Infamous One' 160

Letter 42: The Other INFAMY 165

Letter 43: Checking My Privilege 167

Letter 44: She-roes 172

Letter 45: Female Power 176

Letter 46: Fight Back 179

part two

RONNIE RESPONDS TO THE WHITE GIRL WITHIN

Letter 1: Ronnie Responds 184

Letter 2: Coup de Gras 190

Letter 3: Slave Legacy 192

Letter 4: Virginia's Woolf 194

Letter 5: The Grandmother 196

Letter 6: The Aunt..204

Letter 7: $200 207

Letter 8: My Father Wound..210

Letter 9: Post-Traumatic Slave Syndrome 212

Letter 10: Negative Black Males 215

Letter 11: Some Good Black Men 219

Letter 12: Rebels 221

Letter 13: Some Black Male Considerations 228

Letter 14: Black Tax...230

Letter 15: She-Ra's Salvation..233

Letter 16: Fighting Emasculation 235

Letter 17: Distractions...237

Letter 18: Jerry Springer Meeting (First Time)...................239

Letter 19: The Jerry Springer Show.....................................243

Letter 20: Bill Clinton...249

Letter 21: Barack Obama 252

Letter 22: Ronald Reagan 254

Letter 23: Men Going Their Own Way (MGTOW)..............257

Letter 24: Those Shows and Movies....................................261

part three

COLLISION & CHAOS: WHITE GIRL AND RONNIE INTERTWINE ON THE ROAD

Mile Marker 1: Trans* Intermediaries....................................268

Mile Marker 2: Paranormal 272

Mile Marker 3: Similar Souls...275

Mile Marker 4: White House Visit 279

Mile Marker 5: Elders & Leaders...284

Mile Marker 6: Mythology 286

Mile Marker 7: Numerology 289

Mile Marker 8: Astrology 293

Mile Marker 9: Synthetic Humans/West World 296

Mile Marker 10: Breasts and White...299

Mile Marker 11: Underground Railroad..303

Mile Marker 12: Bone-chiller 307

Mile Marker 13: Romeo and Juliet...311

Mile Marker 14: The King and I 318

Mile Marker 15: Meeting the White Girl 325

Mile Marker 16: Civil War 329

Mile Marker 17: Rebirth: And Then There Were None 339

part four
RESOURCES

Introduction..346

Topics and Questions for Discussion...347

Enhance Your Library...352

Gender Mini-Lesson Content: Gender and Society 353

Mini-Lesson: Race and Society 355

Introduction to Critical Race Theory...357

Racial and Cultural Trauma...358

LGBTQ+ Resources 364

Chemical Dependency Resources...365

Domestic Violence Resources...366

Suicide Prevention..368

Write Letters to Yourself...371

part one

The White Girl Within
Writes Letters to Ronnie

LETTER 1:
COMING OUT

I was just going to keep going along with it. I get it. I will be that mysterious energy—always present but only just so. I've been squeezed a long time, and so, I've learned how to make do with my role. I assume that you have, too.

To the world, you will present as Black and male. You'll be front and center, living and doing things—in full incarnate form. And I will be someplace else in the distance, hiding away. Crazy. I mean, to most, it would seem rather silly, would it not? White *and* female on the inside, but Black and male on the outside. Really? Who feels that? Who does that? But that's what it is. We're locked in this shared, split routine. How the hell did we get here? And I wonder, how have we made this situation work for as long as we have?

I know. There are bigger issues out there. The homeless. Cancer. Bills. Dating. AIDS. Terrorism. Climate change. Politics. Pandemics. Wars. Inflation. Sexism. And racism—particularly the bout we've both had to overcome—your self-hatred, and my arrogant disdain. Dysphoria makes you think things you don't actually believe. We were wrongly based in negative projections and some of it still lingers. Cleanse. It was all anger really.

When given the opportunity, I would chop—like wood—the thick of your consciousness away from mine. The work is never done, and the task of maintenance endures. The internal landscape is unbelievably thornier than the world could ever produce. I have to keep submitting to you and the world. It's a lie by omission. It's a toiling resignation of pretending like I do not exist. Instead of working to shape and structure myself, I work to promote your external and three-dimensional reality. At times, I've seen being locked in your body as a kind of eminent domain. I've nearly evicted the fluidity of my essence in order to keep you going for the good of the general public and societal structure.

I support your career and artistic ideas. I give you my spiritual insights and deepest ambitions. And you get to benefit all of the time; it's a narrow farm. Yes. The deal is for me to remain somewhere in the background in the pursuit to span generation gaps. Not quite X. And not exactly a millennial. I'd say we're more of a "Xennial," of sorts. That generational "X" branding affixed above us might just represent the missing chromosome that I need for full expression. Our gender and race intersections smack in a similar liminality. And we stumbled onto our kind of intersectional category. With me in you, we're T-squared. Part transgender *and* part transracial. Put together, I'd say we are *transgracial*. But where is the line? It flickers. I just roll with the mysterious currents of energy that's always present within your Black male-appearing body. I become the ever-roaming ghost. Our souls grate and we make dazzling orange embers.

Yes, I trot through your mind. I'm a neurological nomad that traverses through different areas of your brain, your psyche, and your spirit—all the while managing my own constantly changing essence. For sure, we're part conjoined. But there must be an exit at some point. I'm always mucking about. It's hard to clean up. With each of us suppressed in your body, our heft is perpetually locked in the orbit of your projected Black maleness.

It was in adolescence when gravity clearly started to give in. You just couldn't keep carrying me while you grew in outer Blackness and male repose. And look at all of what happened outside of us. Remember the early 1990s L.A. race riots that somehow hit us smack in the center of our soul in Cincinnati? That legacy endures and is now tangled into the latest #Blacklivesmatter protests. Justice is needed for our lost and invisible neighbors. Time churns along and history really does rhyme. The verbal and physical aggression of your father was always locked and loaded. And the death of childhood and murder of your half-sister still rings through. So much went on for both of us—right in the center of our middle school years.

And now—so much is unfolding as we embark on the middle of our adult experience as we float between the 30s and 50s. Unfinished business beckons. Through all of this, am I even worth mentioning?

If it's any consolation to you, as I get Whiter, I grow Blacker. The heft of my thoughts is dark. My brood is Black, and it binds. It's a clever wall. And the mix of faux and real goth sensibilities is expressed from time to time—in my soul and the outer edges. Maybe that's where we meet in the middle. The result is a slow burn of dark undercurrents. But through all the noir, I know the light of my White femaleness swirls and lurks about. I thought it would always just have to be this way.

No—I wasn't going to crow about our mix-up.

Yet when I look around through your eyes and see that people are coming out for all sorts of reasons these days, I can't help but think about finding my place. Maybe I'll meet my tribe one day. Jazz Jennings, Caitlyn Jenner, and Laverne Cox are representing and redefining the landscape, showing us all that it's OK to express yourself no matter your age or stage. And lesser-known Oli London and Ja Du are out there representing. The language of true identity transcends race, generations, and time, and it provides hope. Of course, Ronnie, you have to be on board with me. New, hard-fought laws are in place to preserve identity, nuanced ways of life and expression like never before. And we can even work to do more.

The debate on the worthiness of unique identities rages on. In my case, I know I have to guard against accusations of cultural appropriation. I'm not stealing anything from you, Ronnie. For me it's not appropriation—it's truly appreciation, my dear. I'd even say it's a *repatriation*. Let's go back to the beginning and to the place we met... don't let it slip away this time. I've grown to respect all that you have to offer. And at the same time, you have shown me my own value. When the dust settles, a truth will lie that I can live with— and I hope that others can, too. Until then, many might say my feelings are misguided. Many others just won't give a damn. At any rate, I'm getting ready for the battle ahead.

Ronnie, they say I'm your oppressor.

I'm the illness in your mind that blunts the potential of your Black excellence. I pervert your masculine potentials.

I embody that sentimental scourge that rocks you to madness. But what about the onslaught I endure with and through you?

You and me. Are we the tragic sum of the integration project?

I know that many would say Black people lost their way and the sense of self because of integration. Is this how I got into you?

Dr. Martin Luther King Jr. did so many great things. He dreamt that one day little Black boys and girls could go to school alongside little White boys and girls. Still, I needed Dr. King's dream to go further.

And Ronnie, I wanted you to do more than just sit beside your counterparts—I wanted you to *release* me. We have invested time to integrate with the diversity that lives *outside* of us. It's now time to invest in integrating the diversity that lives *inside* of us. The civil rights of society should extend to the civil rights of the soul. Does my unexpressed White femaleness constitute the content of my character—as well as yours, for that matter? These are supposed to be woke times, right?

But, Ronnie, you might be thinking—why now?

Why such hoopla in the middle of things? Why not just support the Black intelligentsia? Why fall to the siren song of what critics call the gay and the trans[3] agenda?

And how convenient.

What about the Black female experience, too?

By letting my voice ring louder, I'm not—we are not—here to drown out the full chorus of perspectives from others. Ronnie, don't be weak minded just for my sake.

Have you bought into the negative stereotypes and the systematic take downs that whip up against the brown and female, let alone the trans women of color?

Everything is so politicized. (And part of it for damn good reasons.)

Before going on, I have to know about the history—the collective as well as my own. Trust me, I want to learn. In the meantime, let me help you—us—to break away from the double-fisted, two-toned binding imprisonment. We're caught in the shackles from the East to the West. For me, these chains form a different kind of *Black Snake Moan.*

In some ways, the West African scratch marks shout. The doors leading to no return open while the oceans of blood roar. We're both in the clutches of all the waves.

And we're both united in our losses.

We're locked in a double-bind paradox of the soul. How can one person be

---

3   'Trans' is the shortened form of the term 'transgender'—others may also use the term 'transsexual.' Transgender refers to an individual who feels that their personal and gender identity do not align with their birth sex.

two? And how can two be one? Are we each being squeezed to make way for a new, radically evolved state of expressing?

We have to paddle through the red oceans of grief and stitch back the unknown tapestries of dignity that are scattered. The answers to our situation are in the lost tongues. The frayed trust at the hands of hawkish hegemony and patriarchal privilege must loosen their grip. And yet, it is what it is. There's so much pain. A lot went wrong. And through it all, I realize we need to sift through and rail against the leftover vestiges of well meaning, but the suffocating legacy of Black solidarity and group think. This is for both of us. We really do need to be found.

The trigger is pulled. And the aftermath is anarchy and a chemical cocktail of warfare that works from the inside out. Just look around. Things are getting real, and time is running out. We aren't old but we are getting older. Just how much longer do you want to keep going through the motions?

It's worth getting to know me just as much as it is for you to find your way.

And so—here I am.

Ronnie, this is my cry out to you.

Yes, I'm a White girl.

I am a female brought along into the time of an adult season. My development is not linear. I'm working to get caught up with everything. I want to get my stuff right: my voice, my looks, my actions, my stride—and my time. I am dispossessed and displaced. And I know you've tired of the company; sorry for wearing out my welcome. I just might be the mother of unwanted house guests. Even though we are both well meaning, I hate that the world sees me as you—a Black man. But in truth, I am White and female.

Ronnie, your life and form always eclipses me. It's true, I'm a White girl. And for the longest time I've been your White girl. I know I'm me because I see it. The subtext abounds. It's those eyes from three-dimensional White females that see me buried in you. Their instinct knows it and feels it, even if consciously they can't identify it. Ronnie, through you, and then to me, the other White girls and women seem to offer a quiet outward nod. They share in the archetype blazed into me and hosted by you.

But I want to be my own person now.

Aren't you ready to birth me?

This has got to be the longest gestational period ever!

I'm ready to be free and to "move out" while "coming out," but I don't know how to start. Hence, this letter—and all of the rest of them. I think that if I could break through your surface and decouple for perspective, it'd be good for both of us.

Ronnie, get up!

You're crying as you look through these tears that soak your failed relationships and measured manners. This is why you can hear me so clearly now. My voice slaps your consciousness and will.

Get up!

You're bewildered inside of Angela's house—your real-life, three-dimensional girlfriend. Ronnie, you are upset in her abode just as I often feel conflicted in the house that is your body. There is strife under both roofs. Stop getting lost in the ruminations. Get up and get out of yourself.

I thought I had this down, you know. I would always be the aloof and inaccessible conjoined twin, the shadowy passenger to your outer life. But now I'm triggered. The revolution is on. More people are coming out and singing their songs. I want to belt out my part before we eddy into eternity. The daring rebels are taking the risks and refusing to toe the line any longer. I'm shouting all this on the inside. You are crying on the outside. This needs to become my moment. Ronnie, I'm in your house. You're in Angela's house. We are all locked away. I know you feel this, too. You're always with me. But you don't always acknowledge my presence. But I can see you growing more and more resigned with time. You're growing tired and are just as confused as me.

But going forward, though, I'll do this with or without you.

Something has flipped. Can't you hear me? What do you have to say? We are conjoined. This is what happens when you're detached. You can do anything you want right now without acknowledging me. And now I have my own set of questions.

Sincerely,
White Girl

LONGING FOR WHITE GIRLHOOD

Hey Ronnie:

Will I ever know what it's like to have the sun's rays on my alabaster skin? Will I get a chance to enjoy and be annoyed by the floating, flailing, and tangling of my hair as the wind churns and combs through my mane? Will I get to make those cute little wispy mustaches from my long locks of hair? Will I get just a bit of time to come out of your shell that is my cell and take a deep breath for the first time? Can't I just begin to build my life?

I'm loaned out.

I am not supposed to be here, not like this. I thought I'd be with the Germans, the Anglos, and with the Saxons, or maybe the Nordics in Europe. I should be with the ones who tan but aren't naturally "tan."

There's so much that's missing.

Early birthdays, first words, the unconscious first introductions to my unknown family. I wanted to have the time to properly form.

I've been locked away from the simple but joyous pleasures that called to the deepest parts of my honesty. Forced imaginings abounded. Maybe I would have sprawled on the top of what could have been my grandmother's roof near Stricker's Grove Park where I'd carelessly sunbathe in Crosby Township's golden high balm. I know that my hair would beg to hold on to the sun's rays as I called in the seasonal highlights and the frenzied charge. And then, later, I'd frolic in the park as myself, near the carnival rides, picnic tables, and cornstalks in the near distance. I loved Stricker's large sloping slide. It had its own kind of topsy-turvy voluptuousness that screamed a low-key female attitude. A red striped one, at that.

I missed out on commiserating with similar-looking people in my expressed White female form. All I wanted was a conversation and an unbiased acknowledgment. They'd help to finish up the picture reflected to me that I caught through television, movies, and in the classroom. And I wanted to fit into the storybooks and be the characters I read about—like *Snow White*, *Cinderella*, and Wendy in *Peter Pan*. They were all lost girls, too. I just wanted to eventually grow into my own kind of *Pride and Prejudice* lifestyle. I wanted comfort. I had to exist somewhere before being puréed.

I missed feeling the seamless thread of my people in faraway places run through my center as a unique kind of umbilical cord. I must be a descendant of Joan of Arc, Queen Victoria, Lauren Bacall, Rita Hayworth, and Donna Reed. Yet somehow, I embody the fashion and culture of Elle Fanning. Let me see and feel my glowing fair skin, my light burning on the projector screen. And still, I know race is not real. It's only so because society says it is. Despite knowing this, I still can't escape the call to the form. Ronnie, our shared vision would hinge on my true representation of White femaleness, and we would dance in the possibilities of it all—in true James Baldwin fare.

I applaud Baldwin's white female teacher with a male name. She helped James to align the reality of his black maleness with the abstractions of white femaleness. And I love the irony and symmetry. Ronnie you are a black male bodied teacher with a nonbinary name -- sporting an internalized white female who wears your body as a male lyric. These improbable juxtapositions teach, guide, and connect our mission

It's our own version of *Go Tell it on the Mountain.*

Yes. And with eyes closed we all disrobed. I want to know if it's true that "Love takes off the masks that we fear we cannot live without and know we cannot live within."[4] Ronnie, I am ready for you to unmask so I can be fully revealed. I am tired of bleeding.

See me just as Baldwin saw Bette Davis.

His eyes locked with hers as he watched her on the cinematic screen.

Baldwin and Davis had the same kind of round protruding eyes that popped.

And although the legendary actress was White and revered—to Baldwin, Davis still moved like a "n—ger."

I am sure you do not see me as an authentic white girl.

Through the complications—the Black of Baldwin's maleness met with the White of Davis's femaleness.

Ronnie—meet me in the same way—all the way back to the beginning.

Yes, I'm still blonde in childhood and, of course, I jumped rope. The gold flecks of sun cut through my blonde ringlets with a serene frankness—and the residue seemed to encase me with a protective warmth as I played behind that gray fence. Cars abounded and people whisked in droves. I moved consistently and rhythmically but at a slower pace than everyone else. Delayed sounds penetrated the near blank and stagnant atmosphere in rhythm with my feet as they arced in the air. Why didn't I speak? And Ronnie, why didn't you? As I jumped rope, did I silently lynch you at the same time—Marion, Indiana, style? It's a fine day for a picnic—and a barbeque.

I must have caused a kind of inverted eclipse that placed the dark of your skin

---

4   Douglas Giles, "James Baldwin on Love and Masks," Medium, November 27, 2018, https://medium.com/inserting-philosophy/james-baldwin-on-masks-214abab12d97.

second to the light of my white.

Am I a covert agent with a sophisticated order to carry out? We've been hacked. I might just be that innocuous blonde assassin succeeding to attack you. Some might cheer me on. They might say I am a vestige of "White supremacy" at work to feminize and hang you out in high noon. Is it winning?

Yes.

Some would say I am stamping you out while bringing myself up and out. There's not enough room for us in this kind of embodiment. Is this the consequence of Iago's revenge,[5] maybe?

But who came up with these theories?

I just want to be me and enjoy my freedom.

Unplug.

But it's always expensive, right? I'm just looking around. I feel as if I could do the jump-rope thing with no end.

Just bring out my childhood hair of the sun, eyes of the sea, elegant stature, and grace. Enshroud me in innocent hangouts and fun times. I jibe with the way us White girls look when we say "ew!" and are grossed out. I like how we appear when studying with a mess of long, flowing, tussled hair atop creamy skin, electric eyes, and intense crimson lips. I think what I've really longed for is my authenticity. Circular statements.

Yes, I hate being wrapped in the wrong form and being viewed as a threat. Here's where the misogyny comes in—because it's your form that blocks and subdues me. I could say I'm apart of #metoo. But are we both lynching each other? You also jumped rope.

I don't want to be a part of that legacy. It's scary to be considered an "endangered species" and a racist, for that matter. I just want my brand of prettiness

---

5   From Shakespeare's play *Othello*, Iago is a character that wishes revenge on Othello and Desdemona after the former promotes Cassio to Lieutenant instead of him.

and production. I'm fighting for that. I'm looking to stand atop of the ash heap that forms only after being beaten down. I need to build my life. Maybe I—we—can be clarion in some way. This is an experience that I think needs to be shared. But while living in your brown body, I have become skilled at maintaining the balancing act.

This was especially true during the childhood years. I leapt from jumping rope to tightrope walking. I think I must have always been around, swirling in your psyche and soul. Unfortunately, we didn't meet until you were four years old. The acceptance between us was instant. I was the sibling you never had. I was the gender that came with the most ease. I was the flexible form that could adapt to whatever you needed. Through strife, loneliness, and fear, I was the blank check that came through to deliver no matter where you were in the process of growing up in real time. In the beginning, this was good on the inside, even if the problems beckoned on the outside.

Longing,
Me

LETTER 3:
AND THE BEAT GOES ON

Ronnie,

Blurred memories. But our mother's recollection was sharp. Ronnie, she told you about the event. The heat and sting of it though feels familiar. It was a smack of rage. Hot pepper and tobacco sauce induced. How does the temperament shift from mundane to attacking so quickly? To hear your father speak now, he says how he doesn't support the attack of seniors. Isn't that convenient? Now that he's older and has meshed into a vulnerable space, suddenly he wants to protect those who may not be able to fight back. Where was that stance when it came to you and me, Ronnie?

Your crime was your supreme energy and diligence. You wanted a soda added to your meal while in the drive thru. As rambunctious as any three-year-old, you were strident and eager to be heard and to enjoy the sugary quench.

"I want a pop!" your three-year-old self exclaimed with bursting, raw energy.

"Wait a minute," your father directed while trying to complete the order. But again, with cheeriness and direction, you exclaimed.

"I want a pop!"

"Wait til I'm finished," he directed again. Reason was lost on you. The need for the soda took over.

"I want a *pop!*" you exclaimed in the midst of the list of items your dad ordered.

Whack!

This time he backhand slapped you right in the mouth with intense contact. He had good aim. It was a three-year-old soda smackdown. Ronnie, you felt the pain, and I felt the resentment.

And I had to deal with more than just being displaced.

Your mother railed back at your father and blasted his abuse. You sobbed with soreness and hurt.

You didn't have the grace or the patience to rein in your requests.

Brute force and power assertion could not be tamed within your father; he used the blunt tools.

Indeed, you got your pop—you just did not know it would be served with a raw smack.

I'm flushed with crimson ire myself, Ronnie, as I think about this.

Who the hell did he think he was?

There had to have been something trapped within him, too. You were raised as an only child, so you had the chance to escape and reflect. Your father was born as the eighth of nine children. From the start, he had to work his way through being controlled by so many other older brothers and sisters, parents, cousins, aunts, uncles, and teachers. And all of that happened in the smallest of spaces in the narrowest of towns in the most constrained hot box of southern states just on the dawn of civil rights. Your father's time was during the linger of Jim Crow edicts and the looming reign of George Wallace. Ronnie, your father's short-lived athletic strength needed an outlet. Maybe the young family you embodied represented a new kind of maze for your dad to work through and to support. It was responsibility and cramped circumstances for your elder all over again. But the abuse is unacceptable.

Enraged,
WG

LETTER 4:
LIPSTICK ON THE BASIN

Hey, Ronnie—

There's more.

Through your body, was I sketching myself in that basin?

Maybe I attempted to clarify and draw myself out of that sink in Pygmalion form.[6] You'd love me. I'd love me. And I would love to be loved.

But now that I think about it, was the red lipstick doubling as red ink? And did the basin double as paper? Were you—we—attempting to point out the flaws of your father's fury in a way to rein him in? Or through you, could I have used that red lipstick as the ink that would lead you to me? The basin might have represented what I could've become—porcelain and gracefully solidified. The ink would mark the spot where you could find me.

---

6 Referencing the 1913 play by George Bernard Shaw, 'pygmalion' refers to a sculptor in classical mythology who hated women but fell in love with a sculpture he made of a woman, which later comes to life.

Not sure.

Through your body, we randomly secured your mom's red lipstick and circled the drain in the sink basin in the bathroom of that Fay apartment townhouse. Or so we thought at the time. Through your toddler bones and logic, we painted and smeared the crumbling red hue against the pale of the porcelain and the silver drain cap.

In the heaviness and the reflection of the night, in an over-sized t-shirt fitting like a mini dress on your young soul and soma, you ventured around the townhouse in search of mischief; we wanted to explore, and we were curious. Compelled to play with the colors and to make a palette, you mused and honored the instinct to draw the elements that brought expansion and expression through the pulchritude of colors.

What was the point?

There really wasn't one, per se.

Ronnie, I guess you wanted to see what you could make. Selfishly, I wonder if you were drawing my outline like it was a crime scene, only this would be in reverse. You could bring my Whiteness and femaleness to life instead of framing the being that once was. With the hum of '80s TV background noise—likely *Hill Street Blues* or *The A-Team*—and the projection of electronic deep blues permeating the still of the night, you ventured into the bathroom and saw the sink as your canvas.

That was answered in toddler years and form.

It was free and exploratory.

It was a nuisance to everyone else.

But it didn't warrant a beating.

It didn't matter.

In your dad's mid-thirties Alabama logic, it did.

"What are you doing?" your father scolded as if you'd started a fire.

Ronnie, you gave no response.

You just looked at him. Startled by the force of his words and the intonation, it practically tore down the thin brown door. We were rattled.

"I said, why are you doing this!" He spoke through a long-wrinkled face, Pennywise-high forehead, and narrowed eyes. Your dad had a southern drawl.

Swiftly, he lunged toward your frame and began the world of whippings that felt more like "whoppings." If there was any attempt to correct the flames of his misplaced fury, it was lost. The aggression and the level of discipline was almost always out of proportion.

To him you must have been a vandal. It was emerging graffiti. A premature tattoo. The basin was adequately stained. Through your three-dimensional flesh, I certainly felt the stain and sting of his asinine actions and approach in our psychological matrix, and my rage began to take shape.

I would be kindred in this way with Drew Barrymore; she was not solo in the *Fire Starter.*

And it seems I would be family to Dana and Rufus Weylin as portrayed in Octavia Butler's *Kindred.* Yet Unlike Dana—a young Black woman who transported from the 1970s to the mid-1800s to stop the boy Rufus, her White ancestor, from doing more destruction by the fire he set in his family home—I came to you to help *start* a blaze through red lipstick. Rufus burned the drapes in the house on his plantation because his dad beat him in the literary world. Here I am as a White girl, being with you, Ronnie, in part, because your dad beat you in real life.

At three years old, this was just before you knew of me. The soda smack down now collided with red lipstick whippings. Was this he final straw? You sensed the tension and rage from your father while you were in utero. That combustible anger bled into infancy and now your toddlerdom. It simmered in you. And now, Ronnie—we—had become the real-life victims in the narratives.

You've never told me, but I wonder if this is how you came to me. Maybe I was the pressure release valve you needed. I would be blameless and innocent to the point where I could do no wrong. Kawaii.[7] Is this why you let me in?

Curious,
WG

---

7   Emma Taggart and Margherita Cole, "What is Kawaii? Discover What Led to Japan's Culture of Cuteness," My Modern Met, January 1, 2022, https://mymodernmet.com/kawaii-art-japanese-culture/.

LETTER 5:
WATERING THE GLOVE

Oh, hey Ronnie—

Remember having lunch in the kitchen?

In the Fay, we sat at the dining table. We were about five or six years old.

Your parents were in the adjacent room—the common area—with the TV on while the two us enjoyed our soup. Without a three-dimensional sibling or friend around, we took it upon ourselves to have a food fight—targeted and clinical as it was.

But possessed with an invisible autopilot, Ronnie, in unison, we ladled broth from our chicken soup and poured it onto your father's black glove. Was it random?

Where would all the broth go? Could the glove absorb it all? How much and for how long? Somewhat fixed and somewhat curious, we robotically became lost in ladling soup on that thick, black-suede glove next to our soup bowl.

With a rare smile and a gentle gesture, your father stood at the threshold between the kitchen and common area—originally as an attempt to dote. But in less than three seconds, his demeanor shifted from doting and semi-frolic to fire and fury.

On cue, he leapt and whipped you on the spot, verbally berating you in the process.

How could he be so changeable, so quickly?

We'd go on to learn what hair triggered meant. Hot, irritable anger always seemed to simmer just beneath your father's surface. Obviously, it didn't take much to bring it out.

I'm not sure if I forced these onslaughts on you because I wanted out. Or maybe you forced your abstractions on me because you wanted me out. Ronnie, looking back, I guess it was an unusual attempt to drown out the oppressive power that pained us both.

No iron fist, but a black glove.

In that moment, the gloves were detached and removed from the hands that delivered the domestic terror. In hindsight, it almost looked like O.J.'s glove. We couldn't grip the actual origin of your dad's aggression. But in glove form, we could. Or at least we tried.

We drenched the anger. We drenched his fire. We drenched Thanos. But we didn't extinguish it. His ways steamed with persistence as did our conjoined and locked arrangement.

Boiling over,
WG

LACY PINCH FALL OUT

Ronnie,

What was it about Lacy that led to your pinching interaction? A mix of youthful rough-housing and rambunctiousness, no doubt. Perhaps there was a mutual crush between you. Or was there some element of control at stake? Ronnie, I was there, too, in Cheviot School, remember?

I was in the middle of your little puppy infatuation, albeit within the recesses of your mind and psyche. But maybe you sought to bring Lacy into our orbit as a way of helping me find form. The pinch confirmed that she was real. Lacy was embodied and animated. In the moment of the grab, you connected closely and tightly. The sharp emotion she felt bonded both of you, and it was stored within your boy body. Ronnie, were you accumulating remnants and energy aspects of Lacy to feed the growth of my shapeless and suppressed form that meandered within your body?

Tension needed to be released.

And you transferred both the tension and pain from Lacy and through us, forming a kind of ghosted triangle between yourself, me, and Lacy.

But soon, it became the spectacle that included your teacher and father.

The authorities clamped down and just ultimately put us back into hiding. This might have been the beginning of entangled infatuation and the searching for my White Girl form.

What a kindergarten squabble it was, tinged with the undercurrent of the mean hand in the distance.

Ronnie, you had to go home with a note pinned onto your chest. Once your father read it, he immediately unleashed the world of hard hits and pain. Through the ever-present violent hand of your father, ironically, you would eventually learn not to be physical with others. The pinch was innocuous. It was not meant to be violent and dominate. But Ronnie, you realized that if being physical was tantamount to being like a domestic terrorist, you wanted no part in it. And I applaud you. Add that to the reading, writing, and arithmetic lessons of kindergarten.

But your dad never engaged in a discussion. It was always one sided. In the kitchen of The Fay apartment, you got the contradictory signals of violence. The R in your father's name was borrowed from the R in "retribution." Maybe I helped you to realize that I would not want to inflict on anyone else what your father put on you—and your mother.

Piecing it together,

White Girl

DRESSER DRAWER CARVINGS

Ronnie—

And then those etchings happened.

The big TV was in your parents' bedroom. That floor model led to a portal of other worlds, for sure. This was a reprieve for us both, but especially for me. It's through that blinking box that I was able to slip through and live in other universes. I piecemealed the images to create a digital Frankensteinian form that would take shape and last for as long as the moments would allow.

Positioned next to the black and white Zenith floor model was a brown faux-chestnut dresser set. Through you, we began making our mark. Yes, there might have been some carryover from our Pygmalion basin days. But this time, we were sophisticated eight-year-olds, with perceptible initials.

Ronnie, you etched in the bedroom dresser set the initials of one who caught your attention in elementary school. I think he was a diversion. You wanted to be him. I think you were beginning to grow fatigued with me inside of you. Although David was White, he was at least male. You both had the XYs in common. This might have been your attempt to pay a kind of homage to him, a way to plant the seeds that transitioned to something that you thought was more attainable. You could actually embody this, no? I guess he offered an escape from your body and from me.

But only for just a while.

It wasn't long before your creation roused the wrath that winnowed its aggression through the small of your eight-year-old self. Of course, your father caught wind of it and unleashed the lashings that cemented and carved into you the profound anger that had made itself the indelible punctuated soundtrack of your—our—earliest days.

Discipline is one thing.

But misplaced domination and aggressive attacks are another. Ronnie, I wanted to etch something other than what was there into the soul and psyche of your father. I grew hot as hell with loathe and rage, and it seemed that every time pain and power was brought over us, it was through a Black man. A severe looking and obstinate Black man with the soul of Saturn scattered among every molecule and cell within his body.

Still seething,

WG

LETTER 8:
CASSETTE TAPE THREAT

By this point, Ronnie, you had your own inner recordings just like that tape held. Your mental songbook became darker and moodier.

And on the outside, the harsh aggression was so consistent—like it was on a schedule. It hid under the form of "discipline" and "religion." Spare the rod, spoil the child.[8] It even hid under the ethnic traditions and practices. But you hadn't even done anything. You played around with a cassette tape and appeared to have broken it.

"When we get home, I'm going to beat yo ass."

Your father did not mince any words with that statement. You knew where you stood as you sat as the passenger in that '79 crimson LeBaron.

But first, we would stop by his friend's house as he casually hung out and enjoyed her company while we both were trapped under the weight of another hard-looming bout with discipline. I felt so bad for you and your body even though I would feel the pain, as well. But Ronnie, you were at the front line.

Yet surprisingly this time, we'd be spared.

"Honey, why are you so quiet?" Terry, your dad's friend, richly intoned.

Through tears and sniffling exhaustion, you let out, "He's going to whoop me."

"Oh, Ronnie, don't beat 'em," she pled to your dad with a conciliatory stance. Terry went on, "No, Ronnie, don't beat 'em."

In an arrogant and tone-deaf logic, your father asserted, "I would have beat 'em if I wasn't able to fix the cassette."

A pound of your flesh was spared by that generous ounce of prevention from Terry. And yet, Ronnie, I suffocated from the tension of the burden you endured. It seemed like you did your own tightrope walking against the thick of the cassette tape. Gone another way, you could've ended up clothes pinned by it from the misplaced rage of a heavy-handed father.

As we reflect on the childhood days, am I the whiny mouthpiece complaining on your behalf, Ronnie?

Some might see these anecdotes as a nullity.

You weren't burned with cigarette butts. You weren't locked in closets or in the shed. You weren't denied food. And you weren't knocked unconscious.

Ronnie, "I'm not just crestfallen on the landing of champagne problems," as I have heard Taylor Swift sing.

So, should I let this go?

Hell no, I won't.

I say the pen is mightier than the punch.

All of those greatest hits just kept coming.

Reeling,
WG

THE FIRST "N"

So, Ronnie:

It is especially hard to write about how your father talked to you at times.

"Listen to me, nigger, you don't bother that woman for no more damn pens!"

Yes, your dad said that to you.

It's funny that the first time you were called a nigger, it was from the person who sired you.

That deepened your father wound.

After all of that fighting in the Deep South and dealing with watching movies in the balcony, sitting on the back of the bus, drenched from mass hosings, and quivering flesh from deep dog bites—it's crazy that he would call you a nigger. Twisted.

And if you were a "nigger," wouldn't that make your father one, too?

Or was he an artificial one doing the master's bidding? This was a cruel but necessary hazing, no?

The slur hit you harder than any of his lashings.

And Ronnie, I was emotionally rocked. The backdraft from pure hate strangled me.

We learned that no one is supposed to say this to you. Those were words of the past. Those times were buried. For the strife we had to endure with our complex identity intersections, at least we had the good fortune to be born in far more progressive times than your parents and grandparents.

But the first epithet hurled at your head came from the one who was supposed to protect you. Your father was the individual who was supposed to uplift.

The person who was designed to help you along the path paved by Martin Luther King Jr. and other civil rights activists was the one who took you right back to those years of violence and hate. It was like he became an agent of White supremacy to subdue you. The mid-1980s were approaching—but that confrontation was aged. In that instance, your father was like Stephen in *Django Unchained* decades before the movie would debut. He made your room a hot box.

With me in the mix, I became extremely awkward in your little brown body and soul. Through the slur, your dad made me "better" than you—but I had residence within your parts. My social status could have subdued him if only I was released. But trust me, it was good that you couldn't let me out. God help him.

Ronnie, we moved from Black abstractions at that point. His labeling intensified the imprisonment. We couldn't just breezily associate with being Black and male bodied in a mere intellectual sense—we had to own it. Live up to it. It was the hand we were dealt. Sure, we knew all along I—a White girl—was locked in your Black male body. But youth and dreams gave us a pass for a little while and we ran with that. We thought it was just a stopgap until we could get on with the real deal.

But in that moment of confrontation, Ronnie, your father verbally whipped and chastised your six-year-old self. You committed the crime of berating your kindergarten teacher, Mrs. Gruninger, for her ink pen. That was it. Why such an outsized reaction for something so trivial? It must have been your passion.

You wanted hers—not one like it, but *hers*.

Unfortunately, his heavy-handedness was not having that, so he continued.

"You already have a lot of pens over there!" He referred to a little make-shift stationary and sets of writing utensils just above your own little dresser.

I recall, with his thick hand balling up your collar and pulling your six-year-old face to his hardened 35-year-old visage of vortexed rage. The whirl of belt whipping started and you—we—were enveloped with confusion, hurt, but at the same time, growing rage, and my undercurrents especially boiled; it was an unwanted transfer.

As he whipped you, the strands of the plantation and its owner came through. It fell on your skin. It was a double-bodied lashing through that system. Ronnie, I felt the pain, too, but I looked on in a kind of distant matrix. Suddenly I got a taste of what sexism had to have felt like. I didn't know whether I should have cried for you, for me, or for us both. I nearly went catatonic. I think this is where the mystery continued.

Ronnie, in wanting your teacher's pen, did you want to write about us and share our story of White and Black? Girl and boy? We would go on to love others who had already done similar work. I doubt that you had the know how back then at six. But, like now, I can feel the rich instincts coursing through you. I ride on them.

I wonder, who else out there has felt the same?

The beatings and domestic violence added to the tapestry of twisted confusion, resentment, and separation. Your essence divided from mine. Was it all just a means to survive what at times felt like a domestic plantation? Was it just for a way to plant the seeds of division? We had to compartmentalize.

We had to cut our way past this, not just to talk to one another. We'd have to scythe through it all just to learn more about others.

Unknown Exorcism

As he whipped you, even though he couldn't see or hear me, I felt like he reached to beat me, too. Maybe he was trying to drive me out. Kick me into a submission. Kill my spirit. Maybe he wanted me dead. Ronnie, you weren't showing any interest in sports. You weren't like a lot of other boys—especially not the other Black boys that were around. Was I obstructing you, too? Remember how your aunt told you that your dad was going to get "your mother out of you"? Were his lashings really the attempt to exorcise excess "girly" energy out of your being?

On a different day, looking back, the yellow school bus ride from your early kindergarten days just fueled his ire. Ronnie, it didn't go unnoticed that you were sandwiched between two girls on the bus ride home from school. You were placed there by an adult, the bus driver. But I wonder if I must have sent signals to enshroud your being. I think I might have invited the girls to join us for company. Maybe it was an indirect way to begin an authentic expansion process by flanking you with unrelenting feminine energy—what a force! Like attracted like, and I wanted you to have the modeling and support you needed. It felt right for both of us.

But not to everyone.

In just a few years, even your mother would tell you to "stop hanging around girls."

Cast me out!

Your father must have felt my heat of hate for him. When your dad was in his aggressor state, I wanted to be the *Firestarter* that engulfed the blaze of *The Burning Bed* he caused. This really would be fighting fire with fire. The beatings had to have been an exorcism with discipline. To clear the way would have led you closer to a life he knew and expected.

I think he wanted you to ask for a baseball or basketball. Or as your father would have really preferred, beg for a football. He once had the pigskin glory that may just as well added to his own kind of trauma. Show your exuberance out on the field, not on the stage. Get excited by the sports announcer's voice, not by the "Let's Hear it for the Boy!" song. They did not want you to be influenced by Boy George. *Be* the boy they were singing about instead of supporting and cheering for the boy. Don't be *Footloose.* Play Football.

I sure as hell never wanted anything else your dad had to give. I would rather go hungry emotionally than to have to deal with this. I struggled to incarnate into the maiden to overcome the aggressive and hostile onslaughts. A part of me thinks I could have shielded us if I were present. Would your dad have beat a young girl? Would he have beaten a young *White* girl?

What would it have meant if I was embodied and spoke the things that you didn't? Or just ran away with you for the help? I would have been a different kind of clarion call to others on the outside. We wanted his toxicity gone.

We knew, even then at our young ages, his reactions were over-reactions—they were outrageous, and it damn sure would be outrageous now. I think he knew that the pen really is mightier than the sword and a pair of fists, and he was scared of what you—and us—could and would do with ink. From the way I saw it, this was his mother Sarah's work. Your dad was her product, and a weird kind of Cold War developed. She'd benefit from his prowess on demand.

It seemed that your dad blocked what I thought could be possible—that we could one day coexist outwardly. He wouldn't have it. Everyone seemed to have to just accept their lot, play the hand that was dealt, as he'd say. But did that mean he'd have to beat you, and your mom, to look at those cards? Why not start over? Reshuffle the deck and get going. I never got the sense that he was a dreamer. And I couldn't have that. There was no way I'd just "accept" being stuck like this, watching your (our) mom and you—us—being abused. But for all of that hostility, we would soon meet another kindred spirit.

You know, the darkness of your skin and the darkness enshrouding Edgar Allan Poe might not be that much different. Both are cloaked in a type of back-drop of mystery that often goes misunderstood. That must be the plight of all Black men of every incarnation: skin related, macabre leanings, or otherwise. Maybe I hear you both at the loudest when you and Poe (and others alike) write because you are all dark. When you all write, your consciousness meets my consciousness, and your "light" meets my "light" of inquiry and familiarity. From the dark come dark letters that must be placed on a consciousness of White paper and psyche. Taylor Swift has a "blank space." And she'll write someone else's name in it. Ronnie, I *am* a blank space. And as soon as I find my name—I'll write it all over my entity. In the meantime, keep writing. Give me that consciousness.

And yet, at the same time, for me, wheat and tear were planted as the conflict of your mystery and your father's lockstep. From this point on, Ronnie, there would be this two-sided type of complexity that would exist between us—but particularly from my point-of-view when it came to Black men. I wanted to crack your surface and get out like hell. If I could have, the power of my neoteny would have canceled your dad through supreme innocence and simultaneous authority. I guess my White privilege would have checked him. Of course, it would have just been freaky to see a whole other person come through your form, even if I would've given my all to do that.

Ironically, at some level, the hurt didn't hurt. Ronnie, you separated from your father in the womb. You rejected the strife he brought before you were born because your father was already a domestic terror before we arrived on the scene. The uncertainty and the hot angst. The opening must have left enough room for me to come in and join you.

I get, though, now more than ever, that you have had to fight against all kinds of pressure, just like your dad did. By many accounts, you're an endangered species, and you have to tap into your instinct to survive. But what happens when you confirm the stereotypes and succumb to lowered expectations? Your dad needed to hear that. How about fighting to overcoming the struggle? You've thought like this, too. There's a deep ambivalence. All of this just made me want to dig in more and to become me and be seen. Why would I want to look like the threat I'm trying to escape? I just couldn't do it, Ronnie, and I still can't. I really hope you understand this. I have my needs and instincts, too, and I think your dad reacted to his instincts about our secret time together. It was retribution.

But why?

Was there just too much *Gun Smoke* and John Wayne in his life? Or was he mad that Prince and Michael Jackson did too much modeling for you, Ronnie? He was trying to rein in something. He was on a quest, and you were (are), too. He knew that. Iron didn't sharpen iron, but it clashed up against each other.

I get that he had to fight a lot harder than you did. He had to hit up against Jim Crow and *Brown vs. Board of Education.*[9] He had to knock out the ravages of Deep South poverty. He had to untangle the strangle of Alabama apartheid. He'd been fighting, and swinging, all of his life. I get that he bled. I hope it doesn't sound like I'm making excuses for him—I'm not distracted, here. I'm just trying to understand his perspective.

He never told us much. I just wonder why he would still feel threatened. I've always wondered—didn't he know that he was free? Your father only needed to stay on the farm if he wanted. It was totally optional. But his penchant for punching seemed uncontrollable. We were forced to make our safe havens.

Making it through,
WG

---

9   "Brown v. Board of Education," History, January 11, 2022, https://www.history.com/topics/black-history/brown-v-board-of-education-of-topeka.

LETTER 10:
WINTON TERRACE TALES

Ya' know, Ronnie—

It is **IRONIC**. You frantically called to me while drowning in Winton Terrace: you drowned in that project with the images of the winos and the hard; you drowned in the sorrows of the "big store" and "little store" workers; you drowned in the paranoia of the stabbed and the stabbers; and you continued to drown in the feeling that came from the feeble, toothless, and those born under broken stars and Saturn's harshest rings. You couldn't always escape the heavy-handedness of your father. And that hardness was only amplified by his mother.

"When you come at some, ya gonna get some!"

Sarah, your grandmother, belted her well-crafted and worn southern idioms. Her sharp, resonant, angry, self-righteous grip would never let up. Short, portly, and dark skinned—Sarah was a mean matronly figure, imbued with a brawny and ruddy matter-of-factness that came from hard living. She was a Winton Terrace fixture. At times, I saw your grandmother as a Gambino crossed with an unlikable version of Vera from *Harlem Nights*. There was a mob kind of energy, for sure.

I saw your grandmother, together with her daughter, similar to the women trying to civilize like Huck as in the *Adventures of Huckleberry Finn*—but in a different kind of way. Ronnie, they tried to "civilize" you in the art of the other side of southern charm: scrappy machismo added with a pinch of misplaced ghetto urban badassery. Maybe that would be useful someday. Through Pall Mall's and sips of Wild Irish Rose, Ronnie, Sarah would fire:

"You go grow up to fight—you too tender!" your grandmother proclaimed to your four-year-old self.

And yet at other instances, I remember how you'd try to "let me out" during the most inopportune times.

"Hell-o?" Ronnie, you answered the phone and intoned a youthful, clear, well-enunciated voice. This was my spirit that rang out into the receiver.

"Let me speak to Sarah," a coarsened voice shot back to you.

"O-k," you'd say as you went off to go get your grandmother.

Moments later, the crone quizzed you—us. "What'd you say on that phone?"

Ronnie, you shrugged.

What were you supposed to say? You greeted the caller and went on with the obligatory routine of beckoning your grandmother.

"She said you sound like a White girl on the phone," Sarah uttered in a bewildered, accusatory tone.

Seconds later, without missing a beat, your aunt shot back in a drawl and southern frustration. "He better not sound like no gurl!"

Your aunt seethed with an impassioned down south twang and disagreeableness.

Did you reach out to me to *not* be like your grandmother—or to escape from her? Were you afraid of the worst that would come later, having to deal with her son—your father? You knew he wouldn't just talk about "coming at some to get some." He would be ready to dole out the "some" through thick dark fingers, square shoulders, and prime O.J. Simpson -like anger; he was a powerful progeny in that way.

Going through it,
Me (The White Girl)

EBONY AND IVORY (NOT IN PERFECT HARMONY)

Hey, Ronnie—

"Call 'em!" Your paternal grandmother went on.

She said that with a jagged and flat, authoritative resoluteness to your aunt in that Winton Terrace apartment. Reality bit back. Ronnie, you were about six then.

The taut, concise structure of the Winton Terrace project housed a train of different personalities and issues weaving in and out of your grandmother's place. Of course, the train wrecked often. I think we were both just beginning to figure out what was going on around us. Your grandma liked drama.

She seemed to want to stir the hornets' nest but didn't understand why she was being swarmed. And worse yet, she expected someone else to take the stings. That undercurrent wafted through the tiny brick flat with so much thickness and slowness that the energy became stagnant and low.

"Now, I know it's time for y'all to go." Sarah, your grandmother, staunchly scolded the two dark-brown winos. The nameless men buzzed off of makeshift thug passion alcohol, southern blues, and mid-life gravity. From what I remember, both of them were resistant to leaving.

Ronnie, we were both sort of out of it ourselves. At the other end of the life spectrum, we meandered through a youthful haze that fogged things up. It was a different kind of drunk, or maybe, just youthfully deluded. I thought the happy interracial living I saw through your eyes on *The Facts of Life*, *Gimme a Break!*, and *Diff'rent Strokes* marked a truth we could live out in our crazy and unlikely embodiment.

In *The Facts of Life*, the interplay between the characters Blair, Joe, Natalie, Tootie, and Mrs. Garrett brought a sweet idyllic calm to a lot of the domestic waters we treaded at home. And yes—I buzzed on that elixir. The power of their female strength harmonized with the stuff that is my White femaleness.

Gimme a Break! and *Diff'rent Strokes* seemed to say it was possible to bring the different races and ages together in a happy harmonious family. That cut against the strife of racism we were introduced to. Ronnie, we cocooned in the maze of possibilities as we pieced together our joint coupling.

But our soft reality was punctuated with the presence of your dad. And he was now summoned by his mother to do some equalizing. He brought a supreme objectivity, seriousness, and focus to that little apartment. He was as reinforcing as the red bricks of the dwelling.

In your grandmother's red Winton Terrace apartment, all I remember is seeing you watch your dad effortlessly sweep each wino up out of their seats and throw them out onto the concrete front steps. Your father grabbed them by their collars one at a time—kind of like what he did to you as he belligerently attacked you, Ronnie, because you asked your kindergarten teacher for her ink pen. But in his mother's apartment, he pinned the now unwanted men up on the tall black door, demanding with all-out, mad fighting flare and intensity that they were never to return. They were seemingly thrown through the tattered screen door and onto the generic looking concrete steps. This was his

Muhammad Ali moment. Fragmented sprinkles of glass from whiskey bottles littered and glowed upon the manila tiles on the floor.

A small whiskey stream snaked through the corridors soaking your white socks. You felt—Ronnie, we felt—the stream beneath our feet. The whiskey was a condensed tributary of the Ohio River, a lake created by geographical and regional boundaries of a different order. The souls of your Black against the souls of my White. The burnish of your boyishness pitted against the girding of my girlhood were solidified and oddly disintegrated in ways that were surreal and volatile, all at once. The fluidity and softness of our world that normally was within became dampened and dissolved a smidge, unraveling in front of and between us. I know you were glad that it wasn't you or your mom on the other end of the wrath this time. But we were shaken.

Your grandmother and aunt were triumphant. You saw your father's expression of pent-up ire and southern swagger in a different context. He was simply a very angry man. Why couldn't his aggression be more usefully redirected? This had to have been the way he knocked out barriers in his younger years. That was the right way to use the John Wayne energy he possessed.

Ronnie, when your dad told you he would "beat Larry Holmes over you" in his crimson '79 LeBaron, that was a better way of channeling his aggression—with a peer, a fellow grown man—instead of making you Larry Holmes. It's funny that Holmes's reign as Heavyweight Champion of the World lasted about as long as the worst of your dad's domestic terror—roughly seven years. In the more constructive ways, maybe your dad channeled some of the valor and lore of Ali.

But little did your father know that in an indirect way, you were instead like boxer Jack Johnson. Johnson, was a Black fighter, who openly dated White women when it was dangerous and practically illegal to do so. Of course, Ronnie, the twist is that you co-existed with me: a displaced White girl inhabiting inside of you when this was super radical and unheard of in the early 1980s. Our intersectionality was a boxing match of a completely different kind, but nonetheless equally as grueling.

Mike Tyson, another famous boxer, said, "I didn't set a good example of being a Black man for my kids."[10] He realized they are attracted to other races. Namely that of White individuals. Ronnie, how do you feel about the example your father has set? You know where I stand.

Misplaced Sanctuary

I have to give you credit, though. There were times when you did want to confront your father. The attacks weren't just on you (us) but on your mother, too.

On a different occasion in your grandmother's bedroom, your five-year-old self sat next to the matriarch on her bed. Ronnie, you had already spoken with your grandma ahead of your father arriving to take you home. You beckoned to the matron while your father stood at the threshold of her bedroom, seemingly blocking out the rest of the light behind him.

"Tell him. *Tell* him," you said.

With hesitancy, your grandmother waited tentatively. Then she went forward. "You ought to be ashamed of yourself...beating on your wife..." she said to your father.

"What?" your dad incredulously asked while preparing to collect you.

"Beatin' on Deborah," your grandmother deadpanned in a near obligatory manner. The words clobbered him and hung in the air. Now he was the opponent.

"I don't know what you're talkin' about," he seethed. Your father seemed to almost be on the verge of unleashing more domestic rage at any moment.

He went on to gather you up, Ronnie, and to take you home.

"Why did you say that?"

---

10   Paul Meara, "Mike Tyson Wonders Why His Children 'Don't Like Black Kids'," BET, January 12, 2020, https://www.bet.com/article/64nwiv/mike-tyson-wonders-why-his-children-don-t-like-black-kids.

Your dad excoriated you in that crimson LeBaron. The mood was tight with awkward anger, and Ronnie, I sweated on the inside of you with primal bloodlust. I felt like we'd coordinated in a fantastic way. I wanted things to get better and you wanted things to improve, just the same. It was a critical hurdle we had to get past. But this internal triumph did not manifest in the outer world.

Your five-year-old mind ran short. Ronnie, you didn't have a full response to deliver to your father.

But I had words.

How's this:

"STOP doing what you're f*****g doing. Stop hitting us!"

Ronnie—that was my full-on response. I remember it clear as day.

That was an odd time. You feared and were angry with your father all at once. I simply hated him and only wished I had form to belt out my burning loathe. And yet strangely, I felt protected. But we were usually confused about which side of the wrath we would end up on, too. So nebulous. I think it's like this for us in society, too. I've felt sorry for you, because you were a Black child on the path to being a Black man. I've hated you for that if I'm being honest. Your oncoming maturation would be the doubling-down of the weight of your Black matter that was and is its own kind of density. This is as much your making as it is not. I know that you've longed to allow me to be expressed. You were ready to sacrifice.

You know, as we got older, Ronnie, I realized I wanted to throw you out with the same kind of intensity your dad bounced those Winton Terrace winos out of your grandmother's place. They wouldn't leave, and seemingly, neither would your exterior. I wanted to restore balance. I know that you did, too. You wanted me gone. See, these were our boxing dynamics.

But until you'd try to get rid of me, I was your escape. When you were with me, no one judged you. You weren't threatened, and I understood. No one teased you as we melded because those were the rare times when we became each other. No one needed to try to "get your mother out of you." And you could rock out to Denise Williams and "Let's Hear it for the Boy" all you wanted.

When your eyes were closed, the spirit of blocked met with the spirit of kindred and calm. Your skin became mine—white, soft, and glowing. Your nose became mine—tight, angular, and condensed. Your mangled femininity poured into and reunited with me. I'm so glad that your four-year-old self let me in, no matter the ups and downs we would have later on. We agreed there's nothing that could stop us, and we dreamt often.

Escaping,
WG

LETTER 12:
THE FAY

Ronnie—

When your father was gone, it felt safe in "The Fay." We could finally relax and be relieved of the invisible tensions that choked us.

Even though, Ronnie, you were brown on the outside and I was your White and female interior essence, the irony of "The Fay" is that the housing was made up of apartments and townhouses with white siding and paint.

The Fay Townhome

Whiteness abounded on each of the buildings for all in the neighborhood to see. And the white structures housed the scores of Brown and Black lives that struggled to access and maintain currency—green money—and so much more. Of course, my desires for currency differed from most given my (our) age at the time.

The community center in the Fay was a welcomed addition. It helped with the stigma of the neighborhood. The white building greeted all visitors and reminded the community of our face. It subtly promoted to be mindful of appearances. The unwritten message must have made it to the basketball players that pirouetted in an athletic funk and swagger on the outside asphalt. The ping, ping, bouncing of the ball was anchored by the cylindric silver beams that supported the hoop and net. The outside animation of the game contrasted with the stoic simplicity of the sharply rectangular community center just outside the adjacent reach of the small and singular President Drive Church.

We already were fully aware of appearances.

Maybe a bit too aware.

After all, appearances are a strong force to be reckoned with. That must be because of the tough people that dwell within. Legend has it that in the '70s one of the worst tornadoes in Cincinnati's history "skipped over" the entire Fay apartment community. But funnily, so many have forgotten about the tornado. Too much competition abounded. Maybe the tornado skipped the Fay because the domestic tornadoes within had not. We certainly haven't forgotten those whirlwinds. At times, Ronnie, I feared that you had forgotten me. It would be very easy to get swept up in the currents of business and obligatory distractions all about. Before you know it, you'd be engulfed in your own torrents of time.

But, if the lore holds true, at least years of destruction was spared in the Fay. Perched high atop of a hill that might as well had been a mountain, it overlooked the spaces and places that would be your future: The University of Cincinnati; Cincinnati State Technical and Community College; Clifton and Northside neighborhoods; Union Terminal; Music Hall, and more. You saw the panoramic of nearly all of Cincinnati's seven hills and seven cities. For you, "The Fay" also meant "The Future."

But despite a lot of despair, The Fay was dotted with bits of veiled fun, too.

In the Fay apartments, when you were upstairs, you'd steal a clear-colored currency— slipping on one of those plastic Jheri-curl caps from your parents to prance around and pretend you were Mrs. G. It was a small respite. The kindergarten emojis of that time were all smiles in the '80s and were well ahead of their time. They punctuated the domestic brutality that would ring familiar amid future police brutality you would see.

But your first teacher, Mrs. G, boasted teased blonde hair that never moved. In a way, you—we—became her, anointed and strong. And we were safe and sound upstairs between the white walls as we softly but dramatically moved about atop the brown wooden stairs. You (we) were letting it all hang out! It felt great to get that surprise letter from Mrs. G during our junior year in high school, and in particular how she directed her words to you. You really did surprise her during your performance as the Baron in *The Madwoman of Chaillot.*

She said, "There sat a tall young man…"

I thought it was fitting that her letter came near the end of our high school journey. It was a wake-up call and a full-circle moment. She reached out to you then, just as I'm doing to you now that there's another full-circle point for us to deal with.

But back to our time, in the Fay, you were comforted to know that mom was downstairs in the living room, filling up the place with her powerful voice and stories, while Lionel Richie's "Love Will Find a Way" eddied in the distance. She was that steady nightly foundation.

Strangely, in your father's absence, Lionel seemed to reflect his most refined tastes --your father was a fan as well. Both men are southern, Alabama-born people hailing from the same year. Clearly, they had very different ways of expressing themselves. One through the warm, rich, simple elegance of ballads and funky up-tempo beats, while the other used brute force to display his limited range of ways to connect. Who really knew what swirled within him?

Ronnie, inside of us, we were moving to Cyndi Lauper's "Girls Just Want to Have Fun." #Whitegirldance, #Whitegirlitout. We were comfortable, you and me (and our mom, too). We were warm and safe with our "curl" cap on. Other times when your t-shirt would get stuck on your head, you'd look in the mirror and realize, "Hey, I've got long hair, like a girl!" A White one, I'd add. We loved this. This was sweet. So, we'd time out our prancing about so no one would catch us. You were pretty safe with your dad working the "Nightshift," as The Commodores sang.

We didn't want this feeling to end. Why couldn't things be like this more often? We wanted to be relieved of the burden of crazy brutish ways.

"Lock him out." Ronnie, you innocently but passionately proclaimed in all of your five-year-old resolve. Your mom was taken aback.

"I can't do that," she said sheepishly.

I sure as hell could.

At a deep unknown level, I think we wanted the supremacy of the supernatural to reign down to check and control the violent ways of your dad. I wanted him brought to heel; it would have been a powerful locked door. But in this moment, in the Fay—things were sublime. I could hear and feel The Commodores belting "Sail On!" The sounds were light, and the air was sweet.

Love,
Me (The White Girl)

SAILING TO SCHOOL

Hey, Ronnie—

School became an inviting refuge. Here, the soul of my hidden Whiteness and femaleness sailed to relief. Actually, we both encountered one of the first beacons of hope in Santa Maria Pre-School. This is where we escaped fire's fury. The school bridged an erratic domestic life replete with frequent domestic violence with a new world of mutual self-discovery. This was just before the emphasis of hyper-masculinity, the last window before some of the perils of hip-hop would enshroud school. I found a vessel for my voice.

Santa Maria

And you, Ronnie, found the silent and invisible pain of restriction and classification. Yet, you still thrived. Your sailing was not as smooth as mine. We found our first interactions with Whites in what would be one of the most earnest of ways. Your best friend at Santa Maria was a White girl. We can't remember her name today, though the bond created is surely still in the cosmos.

With me hidden in tow, we ran through the lopsided fields and grassy knolls in Price Hill, just outside of Cincinnati. The black iron gates grounded and brought a barrier that was not unlike our own dynamic. But the whipping, rippling, and running alongside the long brown pigtails of your schoolmate amid the chorus of other kids hooting, the sun, the crooked trees, wind, and dirt brought the kind of cadence and glow that healed. The teachers only seemed to reinforce the kind of nurturing. I loved the symmetry that happened. The soul's mirror pushed and projected outward into real time. I synched in the rhythm of play and voice along with the other White girls.

And you tried to do the same.

But you couldn't.

Your hair, your bones, nose, presence, and hue didn't match and harmonize with the rest of us.

You rocked the boat. You sloshed from one side to the next and tried to hold on for dear life. Yet going overboard couldn't be avoided. You reveled in personal compensation. You went overboard in personality and affect. Here is where you tried to conform your parts. You were the outsider here and it was odd. We traded places, since in this space you were fashioned as the minority. There were very few other Blacks around.

Ronnie, when you were at home you encased me—the White girl—who was a minority there. But in school, I invisibly sprang into action and interlocked with my brethren as soon as I had the chance. My consciousness encased you at this time. I loved the camaraderie rather than the conquest. It was refreshing to get out from under myself and out of you so I could live in the moment. Time changed, and as I floated but you paid the price.

Two Catholic schools nearby but separated by the genders (Elder was an all-boy high school and Seton was an all-girl school) would help us. Just like the black of the iron gates that reigned in our play and frolic in the outside fields, the closeness of the separate high school buildings offered a different type of containment that was needed.

Still reflecting,
WG

LETTER 14:
ELDER HIGH SCHOOL

Ronnie—

In Santa Maria, we sailed on a river of emerging consciousness that would shape us for many years to come. The community at school brought us to new shores. So much was flexible and fluid—just as it should have been. But when we had outside visitors, even though Elder High School was right next door, they brought an earthly reckoning that only further confirmed our separateness inside of society's center.

The boys from Elder seemed identical. This must have been due to some type of community service where high schoolers would visit pre-schools and display leadership and role modeling for the next generation. In this regard, I think they delivered. It's all a bit of a stretch for my memory at this point. But the Elder boys seemed to pause their adolescent male swagger when they visited us. They honed their boisterousness into a brotherly, ambient, and energetic youthful grace. And they certainly were elders to us in a kindly way.

For sure. The bright, milky skin adorned in purple oxford shirts unified in a precision and team-like fashion. Ronnie, they enriched us. It was good will. The tall, sturdy, and gently imposing boys commanded the space and reduced it to a very modest sum. They read stories—*Peter Pan* was one of our favorites. And then told us their own stories. They showered us with earnest, honest, friendly attention that would certainly make any Archbishop proud.

Looking up to them through your little frame, we marveled at their height as they walked about.

We didn't fully understand everything they were doing.

Ronnie, we were four.

But through their community responsibilities, the high schoolers looked after us as if we were their little brothers and sisters. Their energy vibrated the room with goodness. They embodied the beacon of Santa Maria. We were right next to it.

Perhaps the first introductions to the separating of identity, the masculine from the feminine, appeared in how Seton and Elder were disconnected in this way.

Reconnecting with reminiscing,
White Girl

LETTER 15:
SETON HIGH SCHOOL

I remember the Seton High School girls visiting us as we developed in pre-school.

Those girls had what I lacked in embodiment and expression. But we shared a controlled female essence in careful regimented training. The Seton girls seemed more pleasantly serene and poised. Like us, they were split—but happily so. They had their distinctness and independent lives. I connected to the invisible strings that would bind us. The lines of culture, camaraderie, and content of learning in budding self-direction and coming of age.

The Seton girls reflected the grounding from their grandparents, parents, friends, and education. And that emerging maturity fed the new city that was our being. Ronnie, they helped to build an infrastructure around the sailing—mentally and physically. The proverbial waters were plumbed. The shore around the watery streams of consciousness were cultivated with the seeds of a dual society. In measured uniforms, controlled hair usually brushed back or pulled into a ponytail, the Seton girls brought a high sense of young decorum, focus, and purpose when they arrived to our pre-school. It's like they already knew exactly what was expected of them (because they did!).

Ronnie, the two different worlds of your three-dimensional form and invisible universe grated along the gates. The friction sparked white jewels of tension of competition. We both wanted to be seen just as all toddlers do. I think the Seton girls were there to help to build and bid us well in the process. Maybe they competed to leave a more impactful impression on us. They were the torch bearers that set a kind of kindred connection ablaze.

The Catholic control of Elder and Seton offered a path to interior change—even for the non-Catholic among us.

Transubstantiation.

That transformation is a staple in both their education and their faith. The work and hope of transmuting the holy works into tangible accessible outcomes drive them. They desire full manifestation and embodiment of the sacred in accessible and practical ways that exist in the day to day.

Ronnie, that's what I want, too.

The inner, shapeless, hard-to-define stuff that is me needs its own kind of secular treatment of transubstantiation. I didn't know it then, but I can't help to think now if some of those early interactions from Santa Maria, Elder, and Seton formed the basis for how I would work and see things, and how we would have to work to survive. But I loved the schools. The sights of those students helped me to become a bit more whole and defined. I cleaved to the introductions.

Sincerely,
White Girl

LETTER 16:
CHEVIOT ELEMENTARY SCHOOL

Dear Ronnie,

By the time we made it to Cheviot, things solidified pretty well for us. The watery streams of consciousness were still there, but they receded. More often, they felt more like lakes that only childhood could grace. Or maybe the growth of our society that was our consciousness closed in those waters. More frontiers were present. The duality was not just left between us to grapple with—there was an external one too, where I added more shape and form.

The dual focus of English and Spanish was there as well, and the international seeds were planted. Later on at the performing arts school, the dual focus with artistry and academics would prevail supreme. Cheviot, though, was first to introduce the dynamics of two-ness. The East met the West. The Whites met with the Hispanics. And maybe it was here that your outer Blackness congealed with my inner Whiteness. And your maleness with my femaleness.

You learned more about English. First, you began work to adopt an understanding of the Spanish language. Did you also work to learn how to hear and understand me, as I understood you? Bilingual was more than just the outer, other, Spanish tongue. We started with the Santa Maria, sure. But it was here where the broadening of language and culture really commenced.

"Is there any trouble at home?"

Dark skinned and crowned with long, slender, braided locks, Ms. Williams often oscillated between serene niceness to an annoyed snapping aptitude of classic strong Black woman proportions in the snap of a finger. With almost rhythmic timing, our class could predict when her voice would shift into church melody organ-esque moans of frustration. Ms. Williams seemingly had a gospel choir in her throat. And she maintained authority through the changing of emotions and her resolute sternness. These boundary controls kept us in our place while in polite society, so to speak. I behaved for the most part, and that helped you to perform to your expectations about as best as you could—all things considered.

But out of all your teachers, she was the only one to seem to zero in on some of the troubles that occurred along the way. She was the one who actually called your home.

Clad in anxiety and curiosity, we wondered what the conversation was like between your mother and Ms. Williams, your first-grade teacher.

Through the phone, your mom didn't seem to show much emotion, though she was involved, nevertheless.

"Excuse me?" your mother uttered. "No, there's not," your mother went on to affirm.

"She asked if there was a problem at home," your mother mentioned.

Ms. Williams sought a justification for what she saw as part of your erratic seven-year-old self, I suppose. This is the second instance when issues from the home were blunted. Ronnie, you summoned the courage to tell the grandmother about the father to make him stop, and he didn't; and I was right there with you. Now, any help from the teacher was blocked. This stagnated home life, and in turn, made us stagnant. But through this, school life was still the needed beacon. Here, seemingly, it took another Black-bodied person to see to the depths of another and know that something was askew. That was its own kind of cultural language and intuiting, for sure.

School definitely brought much more balance and expansion to our days. Yes, we clung to that environment and place more than most. But that's because the domestic scene was beginning to change for us. The fights and the worst of the domestic furor that was in The Fay mainly stayed in The Fay. Maybe your mother was acknowledging the progress that had been made. I am sure she did not want to relive the worst of the trauma.

Your Aunt Mildred, the beloved figure that looked after you so well, really advanced the lives of not just us—but your mother, too. Ronnie, once your mom told your aunt about how her brother—your father—had been abusive, Aunt Mildred went into action and helped to get a court hearing to hold your father accountable. But "Aunt Mil," as you lovingly called her, left you far too soon. Ronnie, I felt her love, too, and I still remember lines from her obituary:

> *"Sleep on dear sister and get your rest.*
>
> *We loved you so dearly,*
>
> *but God loves you best."*

The main entrance leading to Aunt Mildred's apartment.

The void your aunt left was sadly filled with the verbal aggression and emotional stonewalling from your father. Though it never fully abated, yes at least the physical abuse was bound. By the time you could begin to understand more of this, it was time to start fresh in a new place.

Maybe a completely different language would offer a nice diversion.

Senorita Bolero, your third-grade Spanish teacher, pulled no punches and said aloud just what she thought. Ronnie, I know that she saw me shining through you—and you were called out for it.

"!Eres tan feminine!" your teacher nearly franticly belted.

"What?" Ronnie, I remember your query.

"You're so feminine!" Senorita Bolero clarified.

Yes—Senorita B. was fluent, too, it seemed—in more ways than one.

Your normally whip smart brain could not compute a response. You were knocked off your feet. You just sat there with a kind of sweet, stunned, and deadpan expression.

"Haz que tu papa' te lleve a un partido de beisbol," Senorita B. warily softened.

Puzzled again, Ronnie, this time you just stared at your Spanish teacher.

"Have your dad take you to a baseball game." She double downed.

Apparently, the language of our locked essences transcended space, time, and language. She knew. And she translated it from Spanish, and from adult to child. Other teachers at Cheviot would also help with our language of expression.

Mrs. Wessel was as close to meeting a *Golden Girl* in the flesh that you could get—and she was actually teaching you. White-haired, bespectacled, and brisk with resolve and resoluteness, Mrs. Wessel was the polarizing figure that lived on the other end of the life spectrum. And Ronnie, I was simply along the ride for your third-grade, nine-year-old experience, just like your peers.

But your teacher clearly reflected a person from a bygone era. In fact, she may have been older than some of *The Golden Girls* actors. This had a civilizing effect on us. We refined our cursive through her instruction. You perfected your elocution through her. She engineered an order in the classroom that seemingly could only come from age and authority. We always sat upright because of Mrs. Wessel. And I have to wonder if she could have brought this authority and rule to our domestic circumstance. Maybe we were drawn to her because we thought she could deliver the control over your father in a way that your own grandmother could not and did not. Through her, maybe we saw a glimpse of ourselves many decades into the future.

By the third grade, you adopted to wearing ties and dress shirts. You projected an emerging dignity and maturity beyond your nine years of age. Clean cut and poised, I think you caught the gentle admiration of many of your teachers with some being more vocal than others.

A light-skinned Black woman with a collapsed asymmetrical nose, Ms. Saunders beamed with a kind of patriotism that was only equal in pride to her teaching. The classroom was often adorned with all kinds of eye-popping decorations, and her spirit spilled into the hallway outside of her actual classroom. These are fond second and third-grade memories.

Ronnie, it was a reckoning to meet with her years later through your young adult body in the department store where you worked. She looked the same, but obviously you did not. Your second and third-grade body gave way to your senior high school stance. Your newly acquired young adulthood invited some unexpected and interesting recollections from Ms. Saunders.

"I was going to give you a run for your money," Ms. Saunders beamed.

I assumed she meant that she saw you as a handsome kid. If she were younger, she would have wanted to date you, and that would have required your finances. That was a quasi-acceptable comment for the time. Today, that would be so #cringe, #amberalert. You were in third grade after all! And she was well into her middle age.

Obviously, your youthful graces made an impression. You were the young Black boy version of Alex P. Keaton of *Family Ties* in the halls of Cheviot Elementary School. But later on, the bloom must have been off the rose.

"You're as old as me," Ms. Saunders said.

The words were lead heavy. She was right. You aged more aggressively than most. You were a senior in high school by this time, working in a department store in Western Hills Plaza. But in her mind, you might as well have been an actual senior getting ready for your walk-in bathtub (no offense, of course).

Were you tired from carrying your burdens as well as mine? Were you aging for two? My inner stuff wasn't formed, but there was certainly more of me. I bear my responsibility for the heft of my mass. Your outer image projected that you had it all together. You were funeral director ready, as one of your college peers would tell you years later.

It's fitting, don't you think? You had a kind of rigor mortis in your posture. A ram rod straight gait to contain my lively verve. Puberty might have been more of an extended wake. Glimpses of the future were a chilly, stern affair.

Growing pains,
White Girl

LETTER 17:
JANE AND ANDY

Ronnie,

"Who are you?" Jane, a blonde, thin, peach-complexioned girl questioned.

"I'm your new neighbor!" Ronnie, you exclaimed that through your shorter, cocoa-colored six-year-old frame.

These were simple exchanges, but it was enough to unleash the whirlwind of meaningful but short-lived times ahead.

This is when we would enter the childhood house that we'd grow up in. On a hill, the red wood frame home with large wide white windows looked open and curious. The view was good too, and you could see the small impressions of many other neighborhoods that lay sprawled in opposite directions. The surrounding communities took on a Donna Walker aesthetic.

I often felt that way inside of you. Ronnie, I could go up to highest parts of your insights and perceptions and see the small, yet wide nets of hamlets and ecosystems outside of your being. Queues you'd taken in both wittingly and unwittingly from your own investigations lay there. Ronnie, you were the human lighthouse, and the new red home was its own kind of lightship even though I didn't know what the house was guiding. Luckily, we clicked instantly with the new locals.

Looking back, it was just the right capstone for your intermediate childhood experience. But even then, you would often retreat into your shell. And from time to time it would take some coaxing to bring you out.

"We can play News 5," your new friend Jane said, just a couple of years later.

What I didn't realize is that we'd play this game like we were actually in the newsroom. We would write the news scripts in creative ways to make it as interesting as possible for our imaginary audience. We mimicked what we saw on television and regurgitated the things that we heard. It was great fun in the moment, of course. But it was a painful metaphor for what you would eventually internalize for many years to come.

This is where your suppression of me really began to compound. The domestic struggles eased up a bit. Through our childhood play, we standardized and sanitized the narrative, sharpened the language, and ran down the stoic stream of restraint that we're still shaking off. Even so, Ronnie, our fun with Jane and Andy eventually led to our serious involvement in theater, TV, movies, and so much more.

Yet at times, Jane had a way of getting under our skin.

"It sticks in your hair," Jane lamented.

Ronnie, the truth landed just as stubbornly as the hay lodged within the thick of the fortress of your curly hair. We were just playing around in her yard as she threw foliage at your head and frame.

As much as I saw Jane as part-avatar and part-vicarious friend while admiring her classic midwestern tween beauty -- Ronnie, I felt a line drawn between you and her. And that affected me, too. You were reminded of the coming limitations your hue and embodiment would bring. You would grow up to present as a Black man. And as a suppressed White girl, I was the one who had to accept the caged reality.

This was especially true since our friend Jane boasted a mane mixed with hues of wheat and auburn—just the kind of locks we loved. When you factor in the added grace of her additional three years in age and inches in height against your dark boyish frame, our internal conflict rumbled in a mix of angst, jealousy, longing, and need. Ronnie, I was dysphoric. This was yet another reminder of my severe limitations of expression—I had no form!

Sassy, deliberate, and sometimes sharply honest, she was a childhood realist.

"Who are you going to play with when we're gone?" Jane queried.

"My cousin." Ronnie, you defended that claim.

"That's only like once a year," Jane went on to cross-examine you.

I think Jane helped both of us to get real. She reminded you of your boyishness and Blackness through her questions and age. She was a few years ahead of us in grade and experience. In turn, I was put in my place—a shapeless, nameless presence, the default third wheel that begged for formation. A truth slayer.

Jane and Andy might have helped a bit with the transubstantiation of my essence during that brief liminal time. It was the closest proximity to family that I could imagine for myself. One where I could peek through you and get involved with whatever was going on in real time. I was the least guarded during these early days with them. And of course, the set up was too good to last. It all ended too quickly, just like the love that came from your Aunt Mildred.

In our combined loneliness, we'd take on the properties of that tall, skinny, white house that kept your neighbors as a unit. We'd grow singular, slim, and solitary like the silver skeleton keys that locked and mystified the house. It was the late '80s, but their house made it feel like the 1920s with the aura of the home and its relics. Looking back, maybe the scheduled demolition of the house was more of a burial all along. Your neighbors were the last family to inhabit the abode and that space.

Ronnie, through you, Jane introduced me to other older White girls in the neighborhood too, like Pamela. Our energy worked pretty well. It was like a daytime slumber party that happened outside in the neighborhood. We danced, laughed, and talked. We sized up the neighborhood houses and talked about our dreams. It was a golden folly of youth that I wish we could have bottled. Our time spent together then is the equivalent of how some might show highlights of some of their frolicking on TikTok and Instagram today. Our interactions were brief but were always meaningful and took place at just the right time. They were punctuated with youthful buffoonery and a calm nuance that was perfect for our time.

Just not in the pool. Remember?

It was a standard above-ground one, adjacent to the wide, white-rectangular garage on the hill. How harmless could it be? We saw them slowly fill up the pool from the garden hose for what seemed like forever, even though it was actually over the span of just under a week.

Andy, Jane, their younger sister, and another family friend frolicked and jumped around in the water, in sync with the rhythm and season of fun, youth, and summer. We must have missed a step.

"You're going under!" Andy innocently but playfully alarmed.

"What?" Ronnie, you cluelessly uttered.

And then it happened amid the backdrop of laughs, lawn mowing, and all.

You caught a quick glance of the entangled grape vines choking the white gazebo-like structure further away from the pool but closest to the backdoor of that big, white, skinny house.

We almost drowned.

My reticent refusal to be baptized in some strange fashion left us without the ability to float. It wasn't a real baptism, though. It was just a regular backyard pool. You were innocent enough about it. But I knew better. I'm always spinning and swimming around in watery spaces and places within as I struggle to shape my soul.

I wanted to have more of the air that you breathed, and some land of my own.

Jane, too, represented young Catholic teaching and guidance just as we had gotten from Elder and Seton High Schools.

That's the way it was on Cincinnati's westside. It was (and is) a mecca for churches, Catholicism, fish fries, and gas stations. The narrow consciousness is wide in the expansive western terrains of the city where some of the largest neighborhoods take root.

Jane's younger brother, Andy, was similar to Danny Cooksey's *Diff'rent Strokes* character, Sam McKinney. Energetic, edgy, and a partial incarnate of the title character *Dennis the Menace*—Andy helped to make the westside sparkle while charming us.

Ronnie, you and Andy were true extensions of the *Diff'rent Strokes* characters Sam McKinney and Gary Coleman's Arnold Jackson. You appeared as interracial brothers.

The swimming incident aside, I remember how your backyard explorations led to another manageable mini crisis. You and Andy thought you were so cool. You both wanted to pioneer. I guess that comes with playing traditional roles in boyhood. But calculating what might happen without a little more planning was necessary.

Each of you took turns playing in your garage, running in and out. It was a normal non-descript mini dwelling with wooden shafts inside and all kinds of random items strewn in varying arrays: paintbrushes, paint cans, old relics comfortably placed here and there but that would be odd additions inside the house.

As you each ran in and out, you had no idea that the garage door would give. Ronnie, you ended up inside the garage and locked in. You didn't know how or have enough strength to lift the door as it dropped and shielded you inside.

"Help!" you exclaimed with furor.

The inside was dank, dark, and staid. And the space felt bottomless.

Would you ever get out? Your young, seven-year-old mind wondered.

Shortly after you were "rescued" by Andy and his father, Todd. Todd easily and effortlessly raised the door with a crooked smile. Todd seemed to mediate between *Diff'rent Strokes* and the *Adventures* of *Huckleberry Finn*-style mischief in a Matthew McConaughey air.

Ronnie, you and Andy were the same age, height, and almost the same weight. And you attended the same school and complimented each other's temperament. Together you both held resonant quirkiness and mischievousness. At different cross-family gatherings you both showed yourself—in the most playful of ways.

"Hey, laser lips, your mama was a snowblower!"

Those were fighting words Andy often uttered. I was angry and so were you.

But what the hell did it mean?

Through him, we united in some of the most unexpected ways.

And the word play was great, too.

Remember "Uncle Snooji Ball"?

Andy's family captured a kind of whimsy and lightness that seemed to escape many in your family, Ronnie. I was especially fed through that sheer light. It quickened and warmed the pace of the time spent in fluidity; it was the welcomed accelerator. The light whimsy and fancy clarified my heart and planted seeds that would help me to flower and form later on.

We both wanted to mobilize and go forward. Andy's parents, Todd and Pamy, had what we thought at the time was a majesty on wheels: a white, five-speed Ford Escort Wagon GT.

Ronnie, we loved the stick shift.

No one on your side of the family seemed to have one. The solid, cylindric gear shift was a joystick that took car riding to the arcade. The upshift and the downshift was a lyric for my ways of travel within.

Although I wouldn't know exactly where I'd end up, in the car, enshrouded within your form and shared vision through your fleshly eyes, we could finally see just where we were headed. Not that we paid much attention—we just loved the form and daily jaggedness of the gear shifts.

The gray Subaru coupe Jane and Andy's parents had was just as fun.

But we were closely packed in a smaller space of metal and wheels. You and Andy thrived together for a little while. Afterall, you liked a lot of the same things, and these rides were included.

But obvious differences were there, too.

Andy's frame was very wiry and taught. Your body had a hot cocoa expanse that draped your bones. His hair was blond and flaxen, and it framed the mist of his blue eyes. He often sucked his fingers. Your small, three-inch afro crowned your head in a symmetrical way.

But both of you were intrigued by the future.

"How old are you?" your friend and neighbor questioned.

"Andy!" Ronnie, you interjected (even though you wanted to know, just the same).

Mr. Homer was clearly old. As kids, he seemed biblically aged. Mr. Homer embodied senior wisdom and steadiness that was other worldly to us at the time.

"It's OK," the elder assured. "At some point I will tell you," Mr. Homer went on to confirm.

But we never found out his age.

Looking back, I have to wonder if Andy really wanted to know how long do we have on the planet? Ronnie you and your friend were clearly at polar opposites of the life continuum, and it gave you two the chance to feel just how far the future felt. And I was there, too—the cooped up White girl. It was both daunting and intriguing to see just how many different stages would be between where we were then and where Mr. Homer had reached. The mature gentleman got to enjoy the energy exchange of youthful laden vigor and curiosity for him to hold on and react to—and all three of us got to have a conversation with what was then a long tunnel of time.

Surprisingly, your dad offered a similar respect to Mr. Homer. He'd mow his lawn, get his groceries, and always affably engaged him in conversation.

At times, Jane and Andy helped to bring each of us out of ourselves. They were the bridge to parts of our true childhoods. Reflective time and introspection ceased when we lived in the silence, scrutiny, and frolic of childhood play. We caught a break from our forced Black boy and White girl encampment. Instead, we rested in the vigorous work of growing up with companions that were actually peers. Riding in this on the way to celebrate Andy's birthday was a simple but storied chunk of childhood that offered a very brief escape from our solitude. Ronnie, they were a surrogate family for me. It was the closest that I would get to feeling linked to a similar brethren. It countered some of my strife.

They were fun,
Me (WG)

TV LAND

Hey, Ronnie—

Given how important TV would be for us, it's funny how reluctant you were at first to engage with yours in your new red house during your childhood.

Ronnie's childhood home.

Ronnie, you just would not watch your television. Surely, you must have wanted to connect with others just as much as I wanted my freedom. The TV would have been one of the best portals for liberation and bonding with new people—especially within faraway places, of course. Your television might as well had been a MacBook for the middle of the 1980s; it seemed that sophisticated at the time. And it definitely helped me to begin making a way toward shape and form as I clung to the images that resonated with me.

"Watch your TV" Ronnie, your mother commanded with a resolute tone.

She went on. "If you don't watch it, I'll give it to mama."

Her mother—our real-life maternal grandmother—certainly would have welcomed the crisp and vivid primary colors that smashed together in the analog box that was '80s television; it would have been her welcomed escape.

But your fleeing would have meant that you would have been forced to watch me. By seven, you had grown a bit more familiar and curious about me and my ever-expanding presence that you were forced to contain. With anxiety from this load, you demolished Tonka trucks a plenty. You tore apart just about all of your *G.I. Joe* action figures.

You were intrigued with the black cables that connected action figures like Skeletor's purple thighs and torso from *He-Man*. You wanted to know what lied beneath. And of course, you just wanted to see how things worked. Yet, you were locked out of your own body, just as you had felt trapped during the brief suspended moment of terror in your backyard garage. You were locked out of most of your soul along with the psyche and truth of another. Tear me up! The curiosity grew.

But didn't I help you?

Loneliness was not just a constant for me, either. You welcomed the company just the same. This explains why you would go on a binge and force me along with you.

Cult of Personas

Remember when you started hoarding personas?

Mrs. G., Mrs. Wessel, music video girls, Wendy from *Peter Pan*, *Sleeping Beauty*, and the like. There were a lot of personalities and archetypes that accumulated by the time you were eight. It seemed that you—we—brought these characters along in the same way most go and buy clothes. We were able to customize and accessorize to shape the soul and release the pent-up frenzy. And then came Jerry.

We can thank Jane for this. She pulled us into playing "News 5."

Our kidding around turned into so much more.

That outward play was divine. We got to bring some of that inward energy out. We made it mean more through the magic of mixing with others. I loved that I also became more of myself with Jane and her friends.

Did you want to stock up on personality types because at some point you were starting to think, even back then, that we would never meet up? Would we be disconnected forever? I guess we were lucky that we discovered, of all things, the local newscast.

"Good evening, a Mt. Washington man has just been identified as the missing son of …"

This was a familiar opening.

Of all people, Jerry Springer would present the gravity of stories like this and I—we—were enthralled. Crazy how this would appeal to a then eight-year-old. The camera angles. The colorful set. The graphics. The crisp language. The relaxed but dignified presentation of stories.

I think all of this brought a kind of levity for us. It was an organized theatrical performance. Reader's Theatre. Jerry anchored the news and in turn, at least for a little while, anchored our personalities. He'd be a good kind of, dare I say it, role model for you then. Someone for you to emulate in order to deal with our split sense of selves. I think it might have been a way for you to "butch" up a bit, too. Jerry showed you that you could embrace your guy body, but you could be reflective at the same time.

Springer was opinionated. He had his own commentary, and you also learned that he was a mayor. Jerry embodied the classic trappings of authority, status, and visibility—things that seemed typically masculine at the time. I think you assumed that if you caught a bit of those things, it would be enough to cloak us so we wouldn't get clocked. We could wear nice clothes, have lightning, and foundational makeup on because of television and status. Ronnie, this seemed to be a nice little compromise of practice for us to deal with our truth.

Through the news, I got to redirect the fear and violence that tinged parts of our upbringing away from us and out to others. It was an uncanny deflection.

Meeting Jerry Springer

And for you Ronnie, especially, it was exhilarating to meet Jerry for the first time. We never would have guessed that Winton Terrace would serve as a portal for you to connect with Jerry. Ledonia Clark, your grandmother's friend, worked at the station. The live news broadcast synched with your live interactions with Ledonia. You even surprised me when you asked her if she actually knew Jerry, and she responded with a round and resolute "yes."

Back then, the local news took us beyond your house, school, and neighborhood. We connected to the entire region: the history, present, and future. For us, the local news was the internet and social media of the '80s.

Ledonia's "yes" opened a door for us that changed everything. Arrangements were soon underway for you to go to the station, and from your standpoint, Ronnie, you might as well have been on the path to meeting Oz.

Arrival at the Channel 5 Studios

"Do you remember a letter from an eight-year-old boy?"

"I'm sorry, I don't. I get so many," Jerry earnestly noted.

"Well, I wrote you." Ronnie, you told him with the honest excitement that could only come from a child.

Although it was brief, the rest of our interaction was powerful.

"Any news station would be happy to hire someone as eager as you," Jerry said in his letter and in person.

Ronnie, for years you pursued this career interest. You fashioned your personality on what was then a calm, rational, and masculine persona. You had a mask that blocked you from me. This was your tool.

It's funny that you would write a letter to bring attention of your interest in Jerry. And here I am all of these years later with letters I've written to you that bring attention to me again. Ronnie, it's time to remove the rest of the mask once and for all. Let the truth shine through.

The childhood news years were unforgettable, though. And it wasn't just all about Jerry, either. This might have been the start of a compromise for you— just in case if you couldn't get to me, yeah? Sounds logical, but then, there was Norma.

Norma Rashid, that raven-haired, fair skinned Cincinnati Channel 5 news anchor who read the stories with Jerry Springer before he was Jerry Springer certainly left her mark. Watching her was like watching Snow White read the news. She taught me about beauty and proportionality—at least until her drunken run-ins that would happen years later. I couldn't help but to think we were connected. Was it puppy love? Unwittingly, Norma encouraged you to connect with me so we could indulge in our softer sensibilities.

Is this why your dad railed against your chance to visit the news station on a different occasion?

Scrambled Signals

"Go to Channel 5 for what?" your father asked in a sharp and supremely dogmatic fashion. Embers from the fire and fury of the earlier days still swirled about.

"I was just going to go to see the anchors," your sheepish boy voice intoned.

"I can't see why you need to be down there," your father vexed and lamented.

After the exchange, Ronnie, I remember you called your mother at work to tell her that your dad reneged on taking you to the station.

She was livid.

This disagreement took me right back to earlier, more fraught times from The Fay.

Mom was at work but had choice words for your father through the seal of professionalism and the dayshift at the hospital. Your eleven-year-old wistfulness could not mobilize the forty years of hardened ire within your father.

Ronnie, why would he force you to cancel Springer?

Through sobs, you had no choice but to call the station and close the door on meeting with Jerry again.

But in truth, I pleaded for help beneath the surface. I think we wanted Jerry not only to make things right with the visit, but to better the domestic strain, too.

"Remember how I was on your schedule?"

"Yes," Jerry affirmed.

"I'll have to make it another time," your weary eleven-year-old-self uttered.

"Well, let me know when you have time," Jerry again affirmed.

"Ok," you mustered in a defeated voice.

"Ok, thank you." Jerry graciously closed the call.

This felt like a dream abused.

Emotionally, this was as raw as a taunt. A harsh look. This was as grave as the hits and slaps that walloped the other interactions you had with your father. His ability to cause pains was not just in a one-on-one situation. Now there was a third party involved, even if it was a former mayor and a news anchor to boot.

Parts of us have to wonder if your local broadcasting news pursuits suffered in part because of this mistreatment. Though simple, it felt like a deep kind of unplugging happened for no reason. Your dad just simply did not want to take you to the station. The dashing must stop.

Your father would later apologize with words, but they were flat. Mostly obligatory and part sincere, the halfhearted way to make amends with you translated into a barren sentiment that collapsed in resonance, often like many of his statements except for his tidal wave of anger. The deadpan "I'm sorry" did not invite any other conversation. The apology was tainted with self-righteousness. The door closed on the subject. The door to no return.

The news was your baseball. It was the medium that gave you boyhood currency. To go to the station and interact with the anchors was your World Series. Jerry Springer was Pete Rose and Johnny Bench in one.

Everyone knew what it meant to you. Your friends at school, your friends down the street, your mom. They all knew the day was coming. The anticipation built and stole parts of your sleep. All of the opportunity and excitement was there.

And it was snatched from you.

Not because of an emergency.

Not because of a more pressing event.

But because your father just simply did not want it to be.

A part of a golden childhood moment was stolen from you, Ronnie, simply because your father thought, "I can't see why you need to go down there."

But we would hold on, just the same.

Ronnie, your childhood news anchor persona helped us to modulate the chaos and volatility of the worst of our domestic circumstances. We got to break from being the subjects and became the narrators of them. You became your own passenger. Ronnie, you were distracted from me. It was a dispassionate break from the emotional earthquakes.

Funnily in the end, though, we still ran to a different kind of Jerry Springer—a future pop-cultural trash television "ringmaster" of the future—to seek a kind of solace and footing.

The local news became the surrogate for friendship. It was Jane's legacy, her innocuous invitation that helped us to concentrate on the broader community in their soon to be absence. Maybe this was the beginning of the notion that "relationships are as diverse as the people who are in them."

Playing the news allowed you to escape from making the news. You received therapy by separating from the hostility of the household. Somewhere within your story, you were compared to the others, and it gave a reprieve and perspective. Yet, in some ways, Ronnie, I was agnostic about it all.

Dead Signal

By the age of 12, the disconnection was complete.

It snapped off as you earnestly tried talking to your father from your room as he stood across the hall in the bathroom grooming his hair and mini beard in front of the mirror in that red house atop a hill.

I felt the proverbial cord yanked out between the two of you just as you did. From that point on, only measured, distanced communication would exist. It is still that way today. The aggression and hostility never abated, and an apathetic foundation would support it all. Your encounter at 12 reminded me of what we had endured in your six-year-old frame.

Flashback From the Fay

Your dad's discord happened in the Fay, and it was times like this when that townhouse felt wicked small.

Mom hung the phone up and ended her call as graciously as she could. I'm not sure who she was talking to. It must have been one of her friends just shooting the breeze and enjoying a moment of peace through her routine socializing.

"Get off the phone or I'll snatch the cord out the wall," your father growled at your mother with severe malice.

Your mother calmly hung up the phone with that warning.

The gall to threaten to yank the cord out, which was the lifeline to bigger horizons makes sense. Your father is a limited man. He is very closed mind-ed. And everything around him needs to be small and managed. There's too much life to be had and to be felt, and this one person wanted to squelch it. This was nearly as cruel as his physical assaults. It was a willful act to possess and control with no tethering to the broader support systems that if they had known would surely have brought him to heel

Flashbacks abounded.

The threat to snatch the phone cord out of the wall during your time at six collided from the past and to your future all at once. Your 12-year-old self stood at the intersection. It was a weird time continuum that was our own *Interstellar.*

In youthful folly, you opened up to your father with the goal of conversation as a 12-year-old, and he shut it down. You felt a bit indifferent and confused. Why was it so important to stop talking? Ronnie, you liked to talk, and I liked talking through you. We loved that. In Cheviot, you were even asked to make a statement to your fellow kindergartners during a school assembly. We connected and felt most like ourselves when we could create the environment with words. So why would he want to stop it?

With times like this, it helped to have television.

In that moment in the red house, your father would finally make good on his promise.

He visibly yanked any obligatory emotional bonds that still existed between you and him as you were on the edge of 12. It was eerily similar to how he threatened to jerk the phone cord out of the wall during one of your mother's conversations in the Fay. Back then, he was hot with irrational anger as he spoke to your mother, as usual. But during your tween years—in that moment in the red house—it was an ice-cold disconnection.

Years later you'd feel the loss twice over.

Thwarted Signals

Remember the news anchors Shawn Hilton and Clayton Morris? They were other local news fixtures at the time. Clayton especially was the stuff of local iconography. He offered another alternative emblem for you to adopt. After Jerry left the local scene for international fame, Clayton was part Langston Hughes and part Denzel Washington with plenty of charm and a six-foot, four-inch frame.

These were the figures of the local Cincinnati television news scene that spanned for decades. It was a big part of your—our—childhood soundtrack and images. These figures were the avatars that you could settle for. Ronnie, as the White Girl residing inside of you, I wasn't showing any signs of leaving anytime soon. These mature, respected, and recognizable Black men ultimately seemed like a safe diversion to hide behind. Ronnie, were you giving up on me far too soon? At some level, I get it.

Clayton commanded a stable and steady elite grace. He embodied the majesty of a Clydesdale—supremely dignified and demanding. He offered what you saw as the best kind of avatar to adopt at the time and would help you to make sense of your place while containing me in a staid and steady resolve of professionalism. These were abstractions that allowed some of my repressed energy to flow in a culturally sanctioned space. And wouldn't you know it, you were starting to gain some respect for the Black man.

But what finally seemed like solid support in the news business turned out to be the worst kind of connection that you'd find. Sure, as a reporter, Shawn Hilton invited you to get closer to him. He gave you his phone number and was at the time the most authoritative and inviting figure that was able to demystify a lot of the confusion and harshness of local television news. Ronnie, you were in college by then. Legal, but still young—far younger than Shawn and at very different points in your career.

"If you call, you're not bothering me," Shawn said in the news station in a congenial tone.

Ronnie, you looked on at him in amazement and surprise.

This was during the latter phases of your undergraduate college years.

But the openness he gave to you was tinged with his habit of luring teenage boys and young men.

Were you their next target?

I guess we'll never know, since soon after he was found to have victimized young males he was supposed to help. He slashed his own throat in an attempt to escape it all, but in the end, he served his jail time.

Your dreams to advance were dashed, and it was sealed with Clayton. Tall, strait-laced and locally iconic. He also showed much openness and encouragement to you, at first. But then, just as quickly, he closed the door of opportunity. After an initial connection via email that happened without a hitch, you followed up with more correspondence.

He agreed to write a letter of recommendation for you, and after noticing that your emails continued to be returned, you realized he had purposefully iced you out. You were blocked and ghosted. Others had warned you about him in the past. He could be snide. And then you knew.

Should you have been a part of the talented tenth? The pattern of troubled Black manhood and camaraderie just wouldn't let up. Especially when it came to your local news ambitions. It felt that between Shawn, Clayton, and your father, there was a triangulation of Black men trying to derail you. "The Fay" really was "The Future." And it is the past. This is a strange kind of supremacy and remote overreach. And, Ronnie, it made me feel hella awkward in the process. I'm still uncomfortable with this. I hate that my truth is politicized. I just want to be free.

But through it all, we stayed linked, and television surely helped. Who would have thought that four older White women would sooth and consul us.

Ronnie, for me, Bea Arthur and her *Golden Girls* character planted the seed for a bawdier and a more subversive version that I would come to embody later. Yes, *The Golden Girls* helped.

Staying close,
Me (The White Girl)

GOLDEN GIRLS AND FULL HOUSE

Hi, Ronnie—

Bea Arthur buoyed us whenever we swam in the sea that is our soul. Her sharp, snapping, "Shut up, Rose!" quips uttered on seemingly all of *The Golden Girls* episodes kept us above water when we were battered and gave us license for swagger. Don't even get me started on Bea's epic fist bites. And she perfected that searing death stare with a menacing seraphic sophistication that was clipped with daggers. I would have loved to have thrown that back at your father and to all of the others that got in the way. What an avatar.

Without fail, those Saturday nights at nine gave us clear direction. Each of the characters were for sure four points in a compass that no doubt guided us. The clarity and direction the mature ladies offered was very comforting. *The Golden Girls* transported us to our future—even though they are cultural figures from our long ago past. The end must really be in the beginning. *The Golden Girls* helped us to peer into that tunnel of the future just as Mr. Homer had offered. But Sophia, Dorothy, Rose, and Blanche were so much more vivacious.

The golden ladies modeled the same kind of fun and dynamics I felt through you when you hung out with Jane and her older friends. They were grounded in their independence; it was a kind of a colony away from the parts of the world that just didn't get it. It was our own island away from and against the world created with our own psychological spaces—in your psyche, Ronnie, is a funky soul and nice society.

If I was a Kimmy Gibbler type, then Bea—or better yet, -- her character, Dorothy—was my grandmother. She'd shut down others before they had the chance to do it to her. We both learned the same habit during the wake of domestic terrorism. I was forced to patch together what would have been my life—how I envisioned my own kind of family, of sorts. I watched *The Golden Girls* as if I was a grandchild interacting with her grandmother and friends. Is Dorothy's character a reflection of what your real-life grandmother Sarah would have been had she had a chance to get a different kind of refinement? Dorothy was the smart, sarcastic disciplinarian that was acidic, but also altru-istic. She was a teacher after all.

And ironically enough, through a reboot and new casting, *The Golden Girls* will be Black. The modern sitcom reworking makes room for more life, looks, heritages, and culture at our societal table. Tracee Ellis Ross, Regina King, Sanaa Lathan, and Alfre Woodard will usher us in a new era. They too are separated by generations and the color line.

I'd love to have room for my story to be a part of all of this, too. These sitcoms span the decades and generations. They fluidly involve different life stages, different people, and in some ways, different races. There's adaptations and cool expressions rooted in a common core. Ronnie, you've got to help me find a way to make this happen for us. Yes, I would really love to be a part of all of this.

Smiling,
Me (White Girl)

LETTER 20:
MY KIND OF FAMILY

Ronnie—

During your childhood, I imbibed on the doses of other '80s sitcoms. I drank in the *Punky Brewster* energies that swirled about. Punky's spunk and adaptableness through abandonment is my rallying cry. And yes, strangely, Kimmy Gibbler from *Full House* helped, too. I see the connection in Punky and Kimmy.

Believe it or not, Kimmy is quite strong. I know that the real-life Andrea Barber played her. I get that. But Gibbler just had the right blend of energies. I mean she was comfortable enough to make you smell her stinky feet! Uninhibited, she'd flail around, dance, and sing. She'd tell you what she thought—whether you wanted to hear it or not. And she'd do this, time and again, with endearing energy that actually made you want to be around her—even if D.J., Stephanie, Uncle Joey, and Uncle Jesse were annoyed in the moment.

For all of Kimmy's clowning and goofiness, I actually think she had a profound insight. I mean, she knew when to enter and when to exit. She'd just kind of show up and disappear as often she wanted. And she was a bit of an enigma. It's just a magnetic kind of thing. And she almost always brought levity to her scenes. You never really got a sense of the kind of family she had. Kimmy was, and I'd guess still is, so Aquarian. I think she represents the transcendental that's lying beneath restrictions. I am that. And Ronnie, you protect this.

Once released, it seemed that both Punky and Kimmy reveled in their freedoms.

I think the Tanners protected Kimmy in an indirect way. Yup, I'd say that the Tanners were actually her real family and humanity was all the more. Kimmy is a kind of sanctuary and proud childhood avatar and symbol that surely could have shaped my younger sensibilities and aspects.

Outspoken enough to be tomboyish but still classically feminine with cute features—emerald eyes and svelte physique. She had a kind of elegance similar to the Victorian houses of Alamo Park in San Francisco. Her smooth wheat hair with touches of golden flecks crowned her perfectly. She just brought it. The right amount of everything. And yet, she wasn't—isn't—real. Kimmy is just the right archetype. And I know the feeling—I live as the perpetual blueprint.

I've toyed with the idea that I might be a strange kind of descendant of Adam's Rib—a fragmented remnant. Was I created because it wasn't good for you, Ronnie, an only child, to be alone? To be the repressed entity living inside of you, and for my essence to be the exact polar opposite of your outer being in both the psychological and the physical senses, is so striking that you just have to laugh and stumble along the way. For sure.

Mos def,
White Girl

MARGE SCHOTT

Hey, Ronnie—

We never met. And we weren't into sports, either. Fifty years, fame, riches, and hierarchies separated Marge Schott from us, Ronnie. Marge's ownership of the Cincinnati Reds did nothing to enthrall us. But I do appreciate her leadership. After all, Marge was in a very small club of women who owned Major League Baseball teams. That's chutzpah. And I am charmed. Marge was a breakthrough. But it is only in hindsight—years after her 2004 death—I am now fully awakened to this unlikely connection I seem to have with parts of Marge's aura and legacy.

If Punky Brewster and Kimmy Gibbler connected with my younger instincts, Marge Schott may show a glimpse into parts of my older evolution. That is in the philanthropic and nuanced sense—it would be sans the scandals. I want to give to you. And I want to give to others.

Though coarsened with time, I'm not sure if Mrs. Schott ever got to fully express the range of her masculine dynamism. Some would beg to differ with me, no doubt. But hear me out. Her dad called her "Butch."[11] The seeds of Marge's gender non-conformity were thus planted. But it seemed it was only by circumstance that she was able to release some of her yang energy.

Marge might have represented an externalized truth and form that I cannot. She was a fully expressed, three-dimensional White female with complex interactions with Black people—especially with Black men. I cannot support her "million-dollar niggers" slurs she allegedly said in jest. And I can't support her ban on hiring Blacks to work for her when she owned the Cincinnati Reds.[12] Cancel those actions. Hold her accountable for that. She should have been taken to task—and she was.

Still, while I am a completely unformed and internalized White female grappling inside of your Black male body, I think I get the fraught exchanges Mrs. Schott had with Black guys.

Funnily, Marge actually had much in common with Black men, just as I—a fluid formed White girl—do, as well. Marge was commanding and colorful. Magnanimous with an unmistakable style that added to the culture. She modeled a kind of cool subversiveness that disrupted and innovated. She went to the heart of things and her energy still rocks people in ways that are good and bad.

Marge was both a loved and hated minority with thunderous charismatic swagger, encompassing an ability to hustle and to command sports. Black men seemed to be starkly loved or hated, too. She was gilded but also gruff. She was disruptive and innovative. She set trends and was misunderstood. She was painfully isolated. It's the misunderstood and isolated truths where I most connect. I get it. It's the instinct.

Think about it.

For all of her riches, Marge knew profound loss.

---

11   Thomas Boswell, "An Arrogant Marge Schott Is an Embarrassment to Baseball," Los Angeles Times, May 12, 1996, https://www.latimes.com/archives/la-xpm-1996-05-12-sp-3360-story.html.

12   Ibid.

She was cheated out of a husband and her time with him was cut devastatingly short when he died early. In fact, rumor has it, he left the world while at his mistress' house. But I clung to the surroundings of Marge's childhood home through your adult body as we slipped into the future. By this point, we walked through the restored two story on Shepard's Way. The hills, forests, and fields encircling the yellow brick house adds a slight air of bucolic grace and charm. It's a healing space. Weddings and graduation rentals happen there.

But according to the municipal guide, Ronnie, you and me were the only ones to tour the house in the way that we had. We didn't marry or graduate in the traditional sense. But we definitely embodied a low-key kind of rite of passage. A lot happened in there. Marge's essence filled the outer fields and the inner walls of her home. Her house and essence have much in common with the skinny white childhood home of your neighbors. It is a long-forgotten structure, and it's kind of hard to believe that to many, Marge is, too.

The slight frame of your neighbor's house doubled as what others lamented as Mrs. Schott's limited world views. In some ways, her ideas were older than the age of the skeleton keys that controlled the doors Jane and Andy's childhood home. Marge was robbed of having kids even though she so adored them.[13] It just never happened with her late husband Charles. She never remarried and adoption just never panned out for her, either.[14] It seemed she was denied of true love. While grieving her loss shortly after taking over her husband's businesses, she found no respect from her employees. She had to work incredibly hard in business and her community in order to succeed. I think she ended up acting like her competition in the process.

The same misogyny thrown at her came from the same place that racism was tossed at other minorities. She became the system to beat the system. Maybe she lost bits of herself along the way. Ronnie, I know this feeling all too well. Maybe Marge tried to make up for some of the pain that she caused through

---

13   Richard Goldstein, "Marge Schott, Eccentric Owner of the Reds, Dies at 75," The New York Times, March 3, 2004, https://www.nytimes.com/2004/03/03/sports/marge-schott-eccentric-owner-of-the-reds-dies-at-75.html.

14   Ibid.

her philanthropy.

Even under the best of circumstances I think it would take anyone a lifetime to muck through the knotted mess that are the Cincinnati factions. Factor in years of unrequited love and immense fallout during your older moments for all in your community (and the world) to see along with the city's inherent tri-angulation of North and South regional clashes, slave and freedom paradoxes, and the strained cultural fabric of an ultra-conservative legacy—you'd take a dancing bear with you as your date to a public party, too. Marge helps me to revel just a bit more in my own isolation.

Her racist comments were despicable, though. Totally inexcusable. She's firm-ly mixed in with all of the seven hills that is Cincinnati. That's where her seven sins must lie, as well. The tragedy of her racism feels a bit like the horrors of Black-on-Black crime.

Ronnie, you preferred the dreams a bit more than I did.

And I can see why. I mean, they were inviting, and it seemed like we were welcomed.

Marge's troubled and complex relationship with Black men mirrored that the challenges you have faced, Ronnie, with other Black males, too. There seemed to be a cultural gap and maybe a perceived power dynamic. Ronnie, your speech patterns and more conservative presentations seemed to be at odds with a lot of the other Black males around you, as you know. You commanded a kind of respect, in your little corner, in the same way that Marge did—al-though she had carved out a much bigger slice of society.

You were rewarded for being non-threatening. You could represent diversity while not disrupting the status quo all that much. There was a time you were predictable and punctual and congenial. You were assimilated in a way where authorities just "got you" and you "got them" to some extent. This came with causing rifts among men of your hue and "demo."

I digress. With our vicarious connection to Mrs. Schott—wisdom, fun, and silliness is rolled into one. Seriously, our atoms meshed in a kind of rich Walt

Whitmanian glory. Our societies intertwine with a fierce grip that was and still is tied deep into the dark and brooding foundations of time, space, and tenderness.

Our air is shared, and our feeling of refuge is great. It's funny that I need you, Ronnie, in this way, too. This connection keeps us unified in place that's so scattered and paradoxical in so many ways. Marge represents those factions and amplifies the fissures of the city in ways many could not. It's funny that we became united with her spirit and these realizations years after she died. It's as if she is calling out to us.

Weird and right at the same time,
White Girl

LETTER 22:
SPANNING THE GENERATIONS & FORMS

Ronnie—

And then, at other times, our switching inner forms have plainly skipped past middle age and squarely landed into maturation fully in our 70s—reflective, strong nonetheless, and quite self-assured and "correct" along with being "established." The transpositions are transits in their own right. Again, the house is full. It's here where I connect with not just Kimmy Gibbler flare –but also with that Kristen Stewart energy.

Kristen seems to be the embodiment of the spanned generation gaps. She is young but also mature. Kristen is strong—and still vulnerable. And somehow Kristen embodies classic feminine and masculine enigmatic energies. Her youthful, androgynous resolve through the panic rooms is not unlike what I go through while walled up in you, Ronnie. It has come in handy to bug out, especially when you were bullied.

And through it all, Ronnie, we work best on an asynchronous clock. I think there's a kind of astrological quality to it.

But damnit, Ronnie, if I can't be released and if you're forced to be the "face," then let's keep playing with personalities. We have to do something with these "spirits" and "identities" that we've collected along the way. Our leaps of personas weren't unlike the kind in *Quantum Leap*. You remember the show where Scott Bakula's character would find himself in the body and the life of another person? Scott would have to make sense of his new circumstances by taking in the new sounds, smells, sights, ages, and appearances.

After leaping and seeing his newly embodied reflection in that of an older Black man, Scott Bakula's normally White character once slightly recoiled, "I'm Black?"[15] I go through this every day. And I also question, "I'm a guy?"

It was all kind of stratospheric and I guess it still is. It's a weird sort of displacement—I am an exotic transplant. It's not of this world. And in so many ways I feel like Evie in the '80s sitcom *Out of This World*.

Part human and part alien, Evie had to reconcile her contradictory embodiment. She was a faction within a faction, just like us, Ronnie. Evie had her superpowers to cope and make it through her world. Ronnie, we have our dreams and reflections to make it through the true grit of our reality. But there were plenty of times when we wanted to be rescued.

Ronnie, what if we could have been adopted and had a real-life *Diff'rent Strokes* existence, where some older, rich, benevolent White man would have adopted a mixed family of Black and White kids? We could have had a fun transracial existence to ease the pain. Or if your mother had simply left your father and found someone else—I wanted that.

I wonder if, in part, our attraction to the local news was based on trying to make sense of all of this. We blurred the surrealism of campy TV sitcoms and the seducing lunar glow of our misty dreams.

———————————

15 *Quantum Leap*, 1990, season 3, episode 7, "Black On White On Fire," directed by Joe Napolitano, Aired November 9, 1990, on NBC.

After falling asleep and forgetting to catch a lot of those dreams, I got determined. I prepared to hold on to whatever message I could. This was useful for me as the other part of your subconscious worked on managing me, your father, and the characters you would work with as an actor. So, armed with my own version of a nighttime diary or notebook, I wrote on the walls of your mind.

I remembered things by adding to your unconscious. Remember, I am that neurological nomad that has full access to your consciousness. I really do travel throughout your brain—but with these dreams, I really got persistent.

I captured the flashes of television light. I recorded the square footage of your bedroom—your red little Ohio house in Westwood where you grew up—to offer the perspective and contrast the difference of your childhood red Cincinnati, Ohio home with *The Golden Girls* house in Miami, Florida.

I wrote by manifesting whatever I needed. I finally penned down my internal reflections, in secret—but on the walls of your neurons for me to clearly see and for you to instinctively feel. It took me a while to piece this all together.

And so, Ronnie, here's how I've been feeling. I want to tell you about the dream I had that refuses to leave me alone. It goes something like this:

Marge and Company (Dream Scene)

Ronnie, I see this scene taking place on the iconic Golden Girls *set. Remember those spaces? From when we'd watch the show in the 1980s, and then again in endless reruns up until even today. The same clean wicker furniture and framed pictures abound in the living room in my dream just like in the show. Even the kitchen is the same, right down the table when the girls would sit every night and eat cheesecake.*

Only, the Golden Girls themselves aren't the same in this dream, not really at all.

Marge keeps coming to my consciousness for some reason. You know, the former Cincinnati Reds Owner Marge Schott. Yes, her. Her demure frame somehow man-

ages to be abrasive yet well-meaning woman in her late 60s—She appears as older than that and is a part of the scene. And in my dream, the original Golden Girls (Sophia, Blanche, and Rose) are not around. But this time around, Marge shares the house with Bea Arthur's character Dorothy, but Marge is not retired. Dorothy Zbornak is retired, though, and she's a tall 5'10" statuesque frame with thick white hair—just like in the show.

Marge and Dorothy have masculine demeanors. However, Marge is much coarser, and Dorothy exhibits a kind of sharp sophisticated wisdom. Dorothy has some feminine touches and grace for sure. Additionally, Andrea Barber's Full House *character, Kimmy Gibbler, is in the scene. She is in early adolescence and is appropriately awkward. Kimmy is the granddaughter of Dorothy. Finally, Joan Jett's persona is featured within the dream. Joan is a twenty-something female with Snow White looks but with a hard rockstar edge. She is the (grand)niece of Marge Schott.*

I guess I travel just as much in your mind as I do in my own dreams. I nearly feel like I am all of the characters. This dream is a strong embodiment of White female energy with all kinds of shades—fully bold rebellious colors of the generations: aquas, pink, red, black, and hard-edge violets—and the ages, with a tint of silly sass and fun, just the same. I can't imagine what it would be like to actually live this. But for now, here's how it went in the dream.

(Dorothy notices Marge through the viewing space in the wall that is between the kitchen and the common area.)

Dorothy: Oh, hi Marge, you're finally here.

Marge: The dealership and the team don't run themselves, Dor.

Dorothy: I never said it did. But you said you were going to take a break.

Marge: I say lots of things.

Dorothy: Fancy that. Well, the cheesecake is over there.

Marge (entering into the kitchen): And the coffee?

Dorothy: To the left. And I suppose you want me to cut the cake and pour the coffee for you, too, ha!

Marge: What else have you done all day?

Dorothy: Marge!

(Marge looks at Dorothy)

Dorothy: I'm not working on a Skylark or the catcher's mound, here, Marge— I'm not at your service.

Marge: Ah—there you go.

Dorothy: And there you aren't…I—

Kimmy (entering through the rear door connected to the kitchen): Are you two mad again?

Marge (lighting a Paul Mall cigarette): Oh, hi, honey.

Kimmy: Hi, Marge. Hi, grandma.

Dorothy: How are you? How's school?

Kimmy: Fine. I hung out with Ronnie.

Marge: No granddaughter of mine would—

Dorothy: Shut up, Marge! Kimmy, go on. What did you do?

Kimmy: We just worked on homework and stuff.

Dorothy: Well, that sounds perfectly reasonable.

Kimmy: And we talked about his inner White girl.

Marge: Is he a young boy or a young girl?

Dorothy: Marge.

Marge: There was a time, when…

Kimmy: Well, he only trusts me. I'm really his only friend.

Dorothy: Well, it's not easy being different.

Kimmy: Tell me about it. Everyone makes fun of me for how I dress, and they say I have stinky feet. And they bully Ronnie for being girly and an Oreo. We're outcasts.

Marge: An Oreo?

Kimmy: Black on the outside, White on the inside.

Marge (eating a slice of cheesecake, and sitting at the kitchen table): You know none of this talk makes sense, see what you've done.

Dorothy (standing up near the kitchen island and tending to kitchen business): Marge—these are changing times—these are the late '80s—we're damn well near to the '90s.

Marge: It's enough dealing with those million-dollar niggers (baseball players on the Cincinnati Reds team). And now this—

Dorothy: I won't stand for it!

(Marge proceeds to leave the kitchen and migrate into the common area to turn the news on. Jerry Springer is providing his commentary on local television. He is a serious Cincinnati news anchor in the late '80s). Jerry Springer's commentary is on topic race and baseball… (embed excerpts of the commentary here).

Kimmy (in the kitchen, sitting where Marge previously occupied): He thinks I'm perfect.

Dorothy: Whom, honey?

Kimmy: Ronnie.

Dorothy: So that's what this is about? He's sweet on you? Well, Kimmy, honey, that's perfectly reasonable.

Kimmy: For hosting. He wants me to host his consciousness. I'd be me on the outside—just like you see me now. And I'd be the same mostly me on the inside, too. But I'd have more ram. Ronnie's thoughts and feelings would live inside me. I'd have more personality: his, plus mine.

Marge (through the view-space): You've already got plenty of that, honey.

Dorothy: Oh, shut up, Marge. We're not speaking to you. Kimmy—are you talking about having that consciousness surgery people are talking about? That's highly experimental. It's dangerous!

Kimmy: I know. But Ronnie is my friend. He's miserable at school. And so am I.

Dorothy: But Kimmy, you two aren't always going to be in school. What happens when you two are both adults?

Kimmy (shrugs shoulders): I dunno? I guess we'll just be really comfortable with each other by then?

Dorothy (pauses and sits down next to Kimmy): This is a little much.

Marge: It's way too much. What about that boy's parents—and his family? I can't believe you're even having a conversation about this.

Dorothy: Shut up, Marge! (To Kimmy, lowering her voice) She's right. What about his parents? Honey, he would have to die to make that work. (Dorothy cuts a slice of cheesecake for Kimmy.)

Kimmy (takes a bite): He said he's already dead.

Dorothy: Saying it and being it are two different things. (Dorothy cuts a slice of cake for herself and sips some of her coffee.) And what could be so bad in that young man's life?

Kimmy: That.

Dorothy: What?

Kimmy: What you just said.

Dorothy: What did I just say? I said, "What."

Kimmy: No, before the "what." It was that.

Marge: Y'know, I can't concentrate on my program with all of the bickering.

Dorothy: Marge …

Kimmy: You said—

Dorothy: Kimmy, honey, just come out with it.

Kimmy: I was trying. You said he was a young man. That's the problem. He feels like a girl. And he feels White. That's why he feels dead. He doesn't feel like who he is: a she.

(Enter Joan Jett through the rear kitchen door.)

Joan: Left my keys…

Marge (notices the sound of Joan's voice, directs her statement to Joan): You know, a proper greeting to your great aunt would be appreciated.

Joan: Hey.

Dorothy: Joan.

Joan: Hey, Aunt Marge. I just came to get my keys.

Marge: You're missing out on this riveting conversation (acknowledges her beloved St. Bernard dog). Schotzie and I just can't get enough.

Joan (matter-of-factly): You're talking to Dorothy and Stinky Feet (Kimmy). It usually pisses you off. So why are you surprised now?

Margie (referring to Dorothy): Tell 'er.

Dorothy: I don't know if we should.

Kimmy: My friend Ronnie wants to have consciousness surgery. He doesn't want to live as a Black boy anymore. He identifies as a White girl. And he wants me to be his host.

Joan (taken aback): Wow, Stinky Feet.

Marge: Her name is Kimmy, Joan.

Joan: Yeah, sure. That's kind of out there.

Marge: We finally agree on something.

Dorothy: I'm afraid I have to echo that, too.

Joan: But who are you if you aren't yourself?

Marge: Oh, here we go (lighting a cigarette and pouring a glass of scotch). Come here, Schotzie. (Marge and Schotzie are approaching the front door, ready to go for a walk.)

Joan: I'm just saying. I mean, it is way out there. You guys are kids—well, young teens. How do you know you're both sure about this?

Kimmy: I know he's my friend. He's been my only real friend since I was little. And he says he's always felt this way since he was little.

Joan: So, what are you asking for? You want permission to go through with this?

Kimmy: Well, yes.

Dorothy: It's expensive. And again, what about Ronnie's family?

Kimmy: I guess we'd have to talk with them.

Dorothy: Even the consultations are expensive.

Joan: Yeah, that's just talk, though. It's at least worth looking into it. Yo, Aunt Marge, will you pay for the talk?

Marge (nearly out of the house): I most certainly will not! I was trained that boys are boys. And girls are girls. Whites are with Whites. And Blacks are with Blacks. All of this mixing and crossing these days are the reasons for a lot of the problems (voice trails off while leaving the house and smoking).

Joan: Whatever, man. I can't stand this bigotry. I'm out (advancing toward the rear kitchen door). Stay strong, Stinky Feet. I'd love to meet Ronnie.

I've never paid this much attention to my dreams, really. I mean I feel them. They come. And sometimes they really grip me with the full attention of an earth rattle. You've felt those earthquakes within, haven't you? It's not always about me challenging you just for sport—sometimes my own psyche gives me a hard time and I shiver. But I had to capture this dream. I gave a lot of time to it. Especially this one. It kept coming. It looked so much like the show. It *felt* like it, too.

They're telling us we can do this, Ronnie. We can coexist. That means integration for me—brought out from your inside and embodied in your flesh. And for you, it's a rebirth—not a death, but a new life. Maybe we need more inner messages. Actually, I think you do. I know how I feel.

Trippy!
WG

LETTER 23:
SWEET DREAMS AND OTHER ESCAPES

Our dreams intertwined with the shows and movies we saw on TV. The blurred lines of the real and the imagined happened often. But we were especially close in those moments. These were the shared common-ground experiences. I really liked the "cheesecake" conversations from our elders.

Through The *Golden Girls*, we found balance, fun, and rationality through calm sit-downs. As Dorothy, Rose, Sophia, and Blanche sat round robin in the yellow kitchen of warmth. They hashed out their differences and thoughts through a mix of aged wisdom and youthful frolic. True "Seenagers." They took on relationships with their past partners, children, and themselves. The seasons of life settled in a nice, condensed form. They had times of deep reflection, much like the way I assume your maternal grandmother had but with much more grandeur and support.

Ronnie, we mixed the process together.

Our premature, insightful wisdom merged with our teeming youthfulness. We counseled each other, in private, in order to make sense of the things around us. We grappled with your tyrannical father and incessant isolation. We could never get beyond the broad quarter of an inch that seemed to separate us from nearly everyone we met. Sometimes we had honey buns or bear claws around to eat in place of cheesecake. Cinnamon Toast Crunch helped out a lot, too. And no doubt, the vicarious enjoyment of cheesecake frequently happened through the screen, as well.

Through sweet slices of pie, we could think, relax, and reflect on all that went on. Air out grievances and mix civility with comedy and sharp insights. Those were steadying and grand interactions.

This was a vicarious childhood slumber party.

The conversations buzzed with the thick electric Friday and Saturday night fun that only seemed to exist after a long school week—or a series of them. The height of loud shrieks, imitations, and friendly camaraderie was bottled between the kitchen and common areas from part of our imaginations, your childhood home, and in the sets of sitcoms that flashed on the screen. Ronnie, as a White Girl my hair would be long, thick, flaxen, and ponytailed. I'd boast a black hoodie, shorts, socks, and bright smiles through the frolic. And yet, the nuance and openness of random conversation would offer a kind of counterweight of gravitas to anchor our earnest reflections of thoughts. It was like lying on the floor with lackadaisical legs up and crossed while hashing it out over cheesecake. We would grow up and express through the silky bonds.

But those talks were the direct opposite of the "pound cake" verbal whippings we would later endure. And after dreams would come the reality of destruction.

Everlasting,
The White Girl

LETTER 24:
RUBBLE

That black wrecking ball crashed into the tall, skinny, white house with George Foreman precision and power. A big part of childhood was suddenly gutted in the wake. Reduced to rubble, ashes, chunks of laminate, siding, and dust—Ronnie your neighbor's home collapsed like a fragile doll house.

Would the same happen to me?

This was a kind of controlled cyclone delivered in slow-motion punches of iron. As we grew older, I wondered what kinds of tensions awaited between us. We were warned. We saw what had already happened to us. But what might happen later on?

Ronnie, would you wreck me and tear down the parts that made up my own kind of "White girl house"?

The fall of that skinny white abode marked the start of the descent into our "Paradise Lost." The golden childhood beams just couldn't stay. Indeed, nothing gold can stay. The City of Cincinnati bought Jane and Andy's home and land of their youth in order to widen the surrounding area. It was time for us all to grow. I suppose parts of our conflict, Ronnie, could hold off for a while longer.

In the rubble are some cherished memories. Highlights of our time in the new neighborhood flashed before us.

We had "moved on up," for sure. We entered a new world after the Fay. It was a new social stratum. What were the new rules for you Ronnie as a budding Black boy who involuntarily smuggled me—a White girl—secretly living inside of you?

Jane and Andy were the first White childhood neighbors we met. But for as much as I tried to bond with Jane, we did not connect like you and her brother Andy did.

Mr. Homer was the gentle, distant neighborly grandfather type that brought the balance and grace that was sorely needed. It was like he was President Reagan's special deputy on our street. We were nestled in what was the twilight of the East Westwood neighborhood.

Even so, your neighbors brought us in to a new kind of domesticity. To a quieter reflection. New vocabulary like "Sellars," "ice-boxes," and "entertainers" were new words they helped to land into our souls.

We hadn't heard those words strung together like that. It wasn't long before we figured out some of the terms were actually quite dated, though we did live in houses built in the 1920s. The quaint architecture of the aged homes created a kind of underlying nostalgia. The Nickelodeon sitcoms connected us to generations before us—*The Donna Reed Show, Dennis the Menace,* and *My Three Sons* came to life. Old world suburbia met the then modern times of quasi-suburbia and satellite urban neighborhoods. These bore from the anatomy of their house to our shared trips. Ronnie, your father gave Jane and Andy's parent's Alpo dog food in exchange for transporting you to Cheviot where you and Andy attended.

Your neighbors exposed us to different ways of expressing and learning. They neatly separated the line between what had been in The Fay and what was now new in a quasi-suburb. Ronnie, I intuited that they all never knew about me. Maybe they helped to give form to what otherwise was a dream. Sure, we saw White kids at school and from afar. But with Jane and Andy we got to talk and practically live with them. We shared parts of our lives together. Remember the birthday parties at Chuck-E-Cheese where the robotic monkeys sang and danced in a band to our childhood delights?

We climbed into the small blue Subaru with the mystical stick shift. Andy, you, his mom, and sister made our way to the blaze of fun. All the expected fair of cake, laughs, well wishes, and silliness happened along the way. But it was cut short.

"Ronnie could have stayed longer, but he kept laughing and carrying on. Let's take him home."

You laughed for two. You reveled in what felt like rare social outings. And I got to let my hair down, too, so to speak. We both doubled downed on the chance to just be free. There was no backdrop of frenzy from a violent and over-determined father lurking in the distance. We didn't feel too cloistered in each other's company, so I think we just let it all go with a release of grand, childish obnoxiousness.

Freedom and fun tasted great in that way.

Mt. Airy Bike Ride

Tough but memorable bike rides in Mt. Airy Forest are still with us.

This time, your father hosted and drove you and Andy to the park. Your father was a solid bike rider. Andy was, too. But, Ronnie, you were clumsy. Like the Scarecrow from *The Wizard of Oz* attempting to steady himself and stand, you flailed on the black chrome Huffy bike with the horn affixed onto the upper right handlebar. I guess it might have been harder for you, Ronnie, because you had to balance for both of us on the bike seat. The center of gravity was doubly dense for your seven-year-old frame. No wonder.

You lagged behind miserably and much to the visible ire of your father. You felt a portion of the sunny childhood balm sliced away from us in the woods. The brief verve of trying on classic boyhood ruggedness quickly fell dour. Again—your father was to blame. On the way back to the car, with a final round of determination to ride well, Ronnie, you wrecked the bike into your dad's crimson LeBaron. You topped off the disaster. A social bust. We stayed on edge. The experience chilled. But we would thaw out on a later occasion.

Kerosene Heater & King's Island

Huddling around the borrowed kerosene heater when the heat went out in your parents' home, it was a kind gesture from Jane and Andy's parents—especially since they invited you over. Fun excursions at Kings Island on all of the rides. This was a kind of tonic and healing balm that was sharply different from a lot of the Fay's turmoil.

And in an instant, our relationship was gone.

It only now exists as a dream, memory, and legacy. Even the rubble has long since scattered. But maybe the legacy created a path that led to deeper discoveries of Cincinnati, your hometown.

Signing off,
Me (WG)

LETTER 25:
CINCINNATI

Cincinnati.

The city is made of seven different hills—and in effect—seven different kinds of micro-cities and mini-universes. Ronnie, this has only made it that much harder for us to find the reconciliation we need. Pieces of our different stages are scattered on the landscape that makes for an emotional canvas of multiple hills.

The thick, snaking Ohio River divides two larger universes: the North and the South. In that, the end of slavery and the beginning of freedom meet. The Mason-Dixon line did more than just separate two different kinds of geographical regions but also represented the different worlds we would have to navigate, Ronnie, for me to make sense. We are a walking Mason-Dixon line. So much is birthed in us.

The birth of the first American baseball team happened here, too. We are certainly the first of our kind on both sides of the family line. The black and orange that is the Cincinnati Bengals Football Team resembles parts of the orange embers that reside in us as our souls and wills grate. These are our abstract connections to some of the culture and lore of the city.

Ronnie, it is nice that we welcomed distractions to get out of our own way in our city from time to time. Cornhole and Delhi Skirt Games—and of course, I loved the idea of a skirt. Greasy spoon hangouts with the occasional friends we had helped, too—especially those late-night hankerings for Skyline Chili or LaRosa's Pizza.

It is cool to know some big names and legends have made their connection to Cincinnati. James Brown got his start in Cincy. George Clooney hails from the area and his dad anchored the local news for years. Kindred Rosemary Clooney (George Clooney's aunt) serenaded the area with glamour and grace in legendary form. Emilio Estevez's favorite place to make movies is here. I wonder if any of them feel scattered across the seven different hills just as we do.

It is funny that my instinct to connect with the Anglos and things European may just as well have been fostered right here in Cincinnati. This city is the Paris of the Midwest. And the inspired architecture and rich Italianate connections replete with the textured and spooky underground tunnels captures the strokes of nuance of the area. Cincy bridges the rifts of race riots of the '60s and early 2000s. Factions of all sorts zig-zagged through the hills of this place. Apparently, it is not just us—Cincinnati has its own scattered identity across its own landscape; the city is still confronting itself.

While the Mason-Dixon line divides two different worlds, it also holds each together and protects them from falling into one another. Ronnie, what is holding us together? The New Madrid Fault Line overlaps with the Cincinnati region. We've never felt it and so it's easy to forget it exists. But it is there. It will tremble and rock out a midwestern "Big One" at any given time. We've been warned. And I am warning you directly, Ronnie. Our identity can only continue to grate, rumble, and slip against each other for so long. It helps to know how to see through the symbols and read the land.

Seven different hills, seven different cities, the Mason-Dixon line, multiple factions, the Underground Railroad, Uncle Tom's Cabin, the Freedom Center—it goes on and on. With our situation, Ronnie, living in Cincinnati is to deal with a segregation within a segregation. We're together. Embodied. But at certain times and in certain spaces, we fall prey to the "Sundowns." In those old, segregated towns, Blacks had to disappear from public view before the sun went down or face violence or death. In some ways, you have to vacate my proximity and my space and deal with whatever is thrown at you—visible and invisible—from whatever a racist legacy has for you. This would become truer as we grew older.

We've grown up in this regional and topographical container that is a knotted, thorny, cascade of diverse gender, racial, and historical factions that served as the basis for our unique soil and atmosphere where we sprouted. For the longest time the best symbol of this was represented in what probably is the ultimate school you ever attended:

The School for Creative and Performing Arts.

Getting real,
WG

THE SCHOOL FOR CREATIVE AND PERFORMING ARTS

Wow Ronnie—

The School for Creative & Performing Arts is Hollywood's midwestern grand-daughter. The once golden era of "PA" sparkled within and atop the boxy gilded bricks in Cincinnati's center. And a roster of famous attendees were also students from our school. Sarah Jessica Parker, Carmen Electra, Nick & Drew Lachey, and Rocky Carroll—just to name a few. The bygone golden glamour of PA beckoned to and harmonized with my childhood golden hair that adorned my White female essence. I was able to crown just a bit of the leftover luster. The black and white artsy SCPA logo symbolizes the polarity we live.

Races melded in "PA.". The double-casting of parts in the plays led to a kind of double-blind impartiality on identity. Ronnie, we are double cast in one body. The peach-colored building of Performing Arts housed diverse arrays of people united in artistic, civic, and educational pursuits. And at times, it felt like we had finally found our tribe. Ronnie, we're each an abstraction of an abstraction in our conjoined state.

Just the same, PA was a multi-layered experienced that haunted us both. The ghosts of eras past swirled with the present (and the future). PA was housed inside of an old high school, which made it double bodied—a school within a school. The building is perched above a part of the actual Underground Railroad that quietly percolates beneath the surface. Many had sought freedom and escape long before the others would seek out a building built above it for education.

The Underground Railroad sought to liberate Black, Brown, and even Whites from oppression. That was all in stark contrast to what became of The Fay (and other buildings of its type). Ronnie, we wanted the layers of PA to align with the layers embedded within you and me. We wanted the same unity and the same reconciliation. It was a meta-educative experience where it seemed that at least in some ways Santa Maria, Seton, Elder, and Cheviot combined their respective elements into this broader and much more complicated space that was PA.

We have to thank your kindergarten teacher, Mrs. G. Remember, she suggested to your mom that you audition for PA once you were old enough. Apparently, your teacher knew that to be educated at Performing Arts would in fact help with our quest for liberation.

But even so, it was a struggle to find the needed catharsis. The minefields of childhood, tween, teen, and young adult stages melded and then worked against each other, often categorically. The politics. The scandals. The complexities of the theatrical shows. It was through PA that real literature and high-level productions walloped. Life and art almost always collided.

Some of this was expressed in the egalitarian and democratic ways instilled within the educational ethos.

Double-casting so as to include opportunities for multi-racial performances. Kids of color got the chance to star in roles designed for White actors. Grade mixing so the students would be positioned alongside kids of varying ages. A fourth grader may very well interact with a senior in high school. A fifth grader and a sophomore would and could interact with one another, too. This usually occurred within the major fall productions that were often of professional grade and within professional spaces.

Anything Goes

"The world has gone mad today" as Ella Fitzgerald so eloquently sang in the song "Anything Goes."

Anything Goes was also the staged musical during our first year at Performing Arts in the fourth grade.

Ronnie, was this an apt harbinger for what would be a part of my experience? Remember those crazy cheating and loan scandals, the crack epidemic, the beginning of wild school violence and the like that was beginning to unfold in society? Critics would say that people like you were dangerous to White girls, like me—they always said that, even before our time. But in that time, we lived it for ourselves at the very end of the 1980s.

Pinocchio

Pinocchio wanted to be a real boy. And Ronnie were burdened to prove that you had real masculine boyishness. And through it all, I just wanted to show that I was a real *girl*—a true embodied human with dignity and expression, for that matter.

But the longer I stayed cooped up in you, I felt, like Pinocchio—I was a liar, too.

How could you be what you said you were? *Pinocchio* was the production during our second year in the fifth grade. And while indeed *Pinocchio* wanted to prove he was a real boy, with me inside of you, Ronnie, ironically you wanted to prove the same. Your boyhood was a fraud to many, and it had been questioned. And in your attempt to establish traditional boyhood, I lied about a lot in the process.

Annie

Annie was another one. That was the musical during our sixth-grade experience. Annie was orphaned, and increasingly I felt—Ronnie, we felt—abandoned, too. We looked for the sun to come out, but it was here when things increasingly blackened. Fittingly, in grade six as you turned 12, Ronnie, that is when you felt your father truly unplug from you. It was a snapped-out process. He finally yanked the cord out of the wall, just as he had threatened to do years before in the Fay. Your communications with your father surely all but ceased and to this day it has never truly recovered. We're still building for tomorrow.

The Wiz

Through double-casting, the fusion of Black with White was highlighted in *The Wiz*, and as puberty was really coming on, that swirl often felt like a cyclone that would and did become a great tornado. Just as I pushed you, Ronnie, to confront the repressed internalized Whiteness and femaleness that I am, PA featured for the first time in our experience, a major production with an emphasis on Blackness and strength.

Black Dorothy, White Dorothy.

Black Aunty Em, White Aunty Em.

A harbinger of challenges of placement and the magical while seeking the agency that was already within, which I am just now truly learning to access and use. *The Wiz's* Evillene didn't want to hear any more "bad news," and I surely don't either.[16] And for so long, like the Scarecrow, "I could not win" in

---

16   *The Wiz*, music and lyrics by Charlie Smalls, Timothy Graphenreed, Harold Wheeler, George Faison, Luther Vandross, and Zachary Walzer, dir. Geoffrey Holder, Morris A. Mechanic Theatre, Baltimore, MA, October 21, 1974.

a dry place.[17] I needed to loosen my imprisoning armor and have someone to "slide some oil to me."[18] But I looked "Somewhere Over the Rainbow" in the ways that Judy Garland and Patti LaBelle sang, trying to find the truth, whatever that was. I would know it when I felt it. Perhaps, really, the truth looked for me.

Oliver!

In *Oliver!*, I wanted more, too. But unlike *Annie*, this time, the play featured a boy's perspective of orphaned life—Ronnie, I know you felt some pangs of this. Ronnie, at this point, you actually had more diversions and a concerted effort to begin running away from me. You actually *didn't* want more. It is here where the seeds for the fight were sown.

The King & I

And in *The King & I*, the King and Anna battled for control, liberation, and human dignity. Those same themes were not only with us in the ninth grade, Ronnie -- it would be a defining tug-of-war between us in high school and for many years ahead. It would be our showdown. But we could at least revel in some other diversions for a little while.

Cinderella

And *Cinderella* was that diversion.

The watery and illusory nature of true love and identity streamed into one another. The clear, glass slipper crystalized and held the truth together. Even if only in a fragile way. Through the odds, Cinderella triumphed over the wicked stepmother and sisters. Ronnie, we held our own against that same kind of step-wicked angst brought on by your grandmother and aunt. Cinderella was

---

17   Ibid.
18   Ibid.

ultimately seen for her elegance and beauty. And Ronnie, you know I surely longed to be seen for my pulchritude. I want to be transformed and swept off my feet just as the title character.

And The Performing Arts version of casting almost seemed to bridge those possibilities. Similar to the Whitney Houston version of *Cinderella*, PA also boasted a multi-cultural cast. The village, the ballet, the orchestra, the chariot, and the regal but accessible lines of dialogue personified some of the same dimensions of campiness and élan that we felt as we made our way through the maze of adolescent quagmires. But parts of our teen years entered its twilight.

Babes in Toyland and The Wizard of Oz

Babes in Toyland and *The Wizard of Oz* were the last two major productions to round out our 11th and 12th grade years. We were veteran students by now—moving into our young adulthood. But these final productions were quite youthful and child centric—in stark contrast to the very first production, *Anything Goes*, which was more adult themed when we were in our youngest forms.

And by our final year, the notion of making a conquest and arrival to a prized destination culminated in *The Wizard of Oz*. Who hasn't identified with embarking on a journey to move forward with finding home? I sure as hell haven't found it yet. And you have not either—we both can agree to that! But, Ronnie, we tried. And the journey was worth it—we carry on.

And yes, similar to *The Wizard of Oz*, a kind of truth is already within each of us. But unlike Dorothy, we never really started out at home. Ronnie, you know I am displaced. And in many ways, you are dispossessed, too. I am on a sort of yellow brick road—but I know exactly what is at the end of it—I just need the form to represent it.

What does somewhere over the rainbow look like?

While we reflect on that, we were more than musicals. We must not forget all of the dramatic performances.

Bone Chiller

Monk Ferris's obscure play would teach us the value of solving riddles through puzzles. Ronnie, we are the jigsaw that needs to learn how to dance a jig.

And Then There Were None

Captain Philip Lombard, Vera, Wargrave—these characters from Agatha Christie's

And Then There Were None represented a critical trinity. Through these inter-dynamics of the characters within the play, life would surely imitate art in some ways. In the end, Ronnie, it would just be us—you and me. We'd have to work to rescue one another. But instead of Captain Lombard saving Vera from Wargrave, I am here to save you, Ronnie, from your father and other repressive societies.

Romeo and Juliet

In William Shakespeare's intense but classic love story, Ronnie, I think we would confront a love for our authenticity through a forbidden integration. I got to confront you in unexpected ways while recognizing we are indeed star crossed like Romeo and Juliet, but in very different ways.

The Madwoman of Chaillot

Ronnie, you have definitely accused me of being a lot of things. And madness is among the catalog. By this time in the 11th grade, yes, I wanted to begin mastering my destiny as we were on the edge of seventeen.

Tartuffe

Sarcasm, wild family dynamics, and innuendo were balanced by Cleante— "la voix de la raison"—the "voice of reason"—as your then drama teacher told you. Ronnie, you played this role, did fairly well at adding the necessary symmetry and balance to Moliere's well-loved play. The francophone locked with emerging outer African American cool and serenity that you displayed. In spite of wanting to portray Orgon—the loud, histrionic, and reactive father—you delivered a respectable performance.

Funnily, we spent all of that time working to get the performances right for all of our characters while also studying the characterizations of others in the catalog of Performing Arts productions: *Anything Goes*, *Pinocchio*, *Annie*, *The Wiz*, *Oliver!*, *The King & I*, *Cinderella*, *Babes in Toyland*, *The Wizard of Oz*, *Bone-chiller*, *Romeo & Juliet*, *The Madwoman of Chaillot*, and *Tartuffe*. And, Ronnie we worked especially hard as you worked to portray Jerry from *Bone-chiller* and Romeo in Shakespeare's play. The intensity spent on the acting craft was immense. The line memorization, delivery, intent, character development, and interaction consumed us. And yet—what about the *real* performances of our lifetimes?

How about the performances of *us*? Both as a unit and separately?

How about my role as a real White girl?

I know that you've wondered why you weren't able to thrive and find your tribe and just live as an unencumbered Black male. With all that went on around you it seemed that surely I would dissolve. I could have dissipated into any of the characters you played or the politics you had to navigate. Clearly there was room for all kinds of identities on the stage. It was even celebrated the more you played characters and the more you wanted to bring me out. I could feel it. Yet, it became easier for you to run away from me. It was the swift paradox of diversions. Some of them were paranormal.

Abigail, the "ghost" and wife of William Cutter, of which the original school occupying the building was named -- often frequented the building. Doors would mysteriously open and close, sometimes loudly. At least that was the lore during our times at Performing Arts.

Abigail and Mary from Richard Wright's *Native Son* had something in common: they were White women who haunted. And I am locked in their destinies.

The haunting carried over on the other side of the racial line.

Luke Ruehlman, a young White boy, claims that he lived a past life as a Black woman named Pamela Robinson.[19]

I couldn't help but think those other White female paranormal figures were looking for something. Lost potential? To solve frustration? Maybe Abigail and Mary are my lost family members. Were Abigail and Mary looking for me? Were the ghosts alert and wanting to right the wrongs of your father and other men like him? Either way, they all came together and connected with the right lot. This is a force.

Reflecting,
White Girl

19   Suzanne Stratford, "Do You Believe in Past Lives? Toddler's Testimony has Family Questioning if He Was a Chicago Woman," Fox 2 Now, February 16, 2015, https://fox2now.com/news/do-you-believe-in-past-lives-toddlers-testimony-has-family-questioning-if-he-was-a-chicago-woman/.

LETTER 27:
SCHOOL
(BUT NOT ALL WAS SWEET...)

So many struggle in school. And we were no different. Yes, Ronnie, we sailed away from the intermittent domestic violent strains. And we usually found refuge in learning away from home. But our navigation in learning would be narrowly compressed by the time we made it to The School for Creative and Performing Arts, as all of the grades four through twelve ran into one another in the same building and hallways. The compression made emotions and general interactions contained and coagulated and made things all the more knotted and thornier.

Like a midlife crisis, Ronnie, through you, the middle years of my tagalong tenure at Performing Arts brought in the most intense cyclones that I had ever dealt with at the time. PA was radically different from Santa Maria, Seton, and Elder schools. And of course—at a fundamental level—it should have been that way. But the educational line from the earlier schools did not quite extend to PA. While the standard fare of hormones, height, hygiene, and hair were all par for the course, it was tough to deal with pressure from both the students and the teachers. And of course, all the while compressed within the frame of your shifting body. The middle almost mauled me.

As you know, just as we always had done from the Santa Maria days, we sought refuge from our teachers. But for the first time, that protection broke down.

"Hope you have a good summer," Ronnie, you said to your seventh-grade teacher. But your good intentions did not always land as I would have hoped.

"I will now that I have you out of my life," Ms. B. deadpanned.

"You wanna be a woman—and a White one, at that." Ms. B. would go on to say that.

She was able to add up the variables and see that the cup of your—our— souls were full and on the verge of running over. You just couldn't keep me at the brim and hold me in the same way as you used to.

Ronnie, I ruined things for you. I am sorry.

I made you weird and annoying. That was not my intent at all.

They didn't know what kind of balancing act you had to complete. We were the same. They didn't know the zany anxiety that quickened and pulsed through your veins. For all of your internal rambunctiousness there was still a kind of leaden resolve that anchored your external being. Compared to others, you still had a lot of redeeming qualities. But you were written off as an adolescent goof. And though some of that was the case, there was so much extra that lay beneath.

Other teachers cut you no mercy.

"That faggot mother****r?" Ms. H. supposedly uttered that about you in conversation to Mr. Wayne.

You had made the mistake of repeating some choice words Mr. Wayne had said in response to Ms. H. Those comments were supposedly made in jest. Either way, Ronnie, you took the "L." And it quickly became apparent what they thought of you.

You were a "faggot motherf****r" and an "ugly Black girl," as Ms. H. would say and think right to your face, I might add, at a later time.

Yes, much was compressed within the building, with all of those grades rolled into one. I now appreciate the value of separate schools for separate age ranges.

What should have remained private between you and the teachers became a big spectacle for you (and us) at the time. In the end, it made me stronger during my journey in you.

Holding on,
WG

LETTER 28:
THE CENSURE

Don't forget this.

During study hall, where practically half of all of the other junior high kids at the time met up, you were the one plucked out of the group of at least 60 students.

"This is the bell I've been waiting for," the study hall monitor bellowed.

The knot grew in your throat. My substance froze. We were targeted. The rage and Al Sharpton like guttural girth and volume in his voice lashed us all the while.

"Why are you going around here saying things?!" Mr. Wayne went on. There was no adult rationalization. Just rage.

Ronnie, you attempted to approach him directly in a more quiet and moderated tone.

But he blatantly rejected that.

Mr. Wayne yelled at and through you like you were in a stadium—say at a Cincinnati Reds game—in the rare instant you would have gone to one. We'd learn that even the Performing Arts security guard who stood outside the door was in shock that an adult handled the situation so inappropriately.

But Ronnie, I give it to you.

You stood statue still in glasses and crowned with a Boyz II Men high-top fade. You were suspended in shock, detached, and brimming with your own anger. And I was choked up and a bit stunned at the quickness of it. The way I see it, you were again failed by yet another Black man. Mr. Wayne was one of very few Black and male classroom authority figures you encountered while in school, and this was the sad experience you had. Like you, Mr. Wayne was also bespectacled. But he boasted a very low buzzed haircut and Eddie Murphy like facial features—but without the charisma and eloquence.

Mr. Wayne didn't let up.

"Going around here thinkin' you Michael Jackson." That was definitely below the belt. He knew that would get to you since you were such a big fan, even during those years when Michael was less popular. But in true stoic Jacksonian repose, you stood still and firmly planted—mannequin-like while being berated before the majority of your peers. Ronnie, it was as if you were on stage performing.

"The only ones who can get you out of this now are your parents," Mr. Wayne would go on to say.

He made it seem as if the consequences were much more dire and severe than they needed to be. This was a cultural ricochet that echoed semblances of your overdetermined father. It was a scare tactic. A sort of trauma to hurl at you. It rhymed with your past.

And yet, Mr. Wayne treated you so aggressively, just as your father had. The strength and resolve you threw back to him had to come from the toughness you built up dealing with your dad. This study hall monitor, a young man in his 20s at the time, seemed to be on code with the older ways of your father, and I would guess those who came before him. Ronnie, you grew resigned while I grew more embittered. Why is this so impossible? Why is the rift so consistent? I guess there was no need for you to fear being hung by me when there seemed to be willing Black minions to do the bidding with verbal lashes.

Exiled in detention. Now we were both kicked out, and he needed to be censured.

UGGGH,
WG

P.S. For just a flash of time, we thought we had found a solution for your development. We appreciated Mr. B. He presented as an exquisite piano player who could so by ear. He was often tastefully but sparingly bejeweled in a contemporary and masculine way. Muscled, proportional, and boasting thick, wavy hair that elevated the Jheri curl to a majestic magnanimous level -- his processed hair was proper. He had swag and was unimpeachably cool. He would be for a time, a role model for you, Ronnie, and finally offer an accessible version of a Black male template that I thought you could latch onto.

But Mr. B. seemingly continued to do the bidding of toxic Black maleness. Mr. B. was more disappointing because of the hopes you had pinned on him. While trying to do the right thing and fully accept the sum of the parts and to live a normal Black male life, I thought he could show you the way to a more refined and expressed way of life as a Black male. And yet, like Shawn, Clayton, your father, and many other elders, he turned out to be yet another big disappointment.

Yuck.
WG

LETTER 29:
BRANDON & IDENTITY

It was nice to know we weren't the only ones struggling with our packaging. I can't forget Brandon, can you? He was the "WHITEBOY" of the Tom McDonald variety in Performing Arts High School in ninth grade. Brandon boasted Vanilla Ice vibes. And he made it clear he wished he was Black. It seemed he was the only one who didn't know he was born White. It was *Emperor's New Clothes* but for skin. Similar to Martina Big, the everyday woman with an everyday obsession with deep tanning to the point that she had changed the appearance of her race.[20] She was born as White and female but now lives as a Black woman. Through aggressive "crispy-brown" tanning and injections, Martina now embodies her tanned truth. I think Brandon would have approved.

One thing is for sure, though. Martina Big and Rachel Dolezal clearly transitioned. They were (are) brave no matter how much they are ridiculed. But

---

20 Tariq Tahir, "White Model Martina Big Who Identifies as Black Slams White People for 'Exploiting' the Black Community," *The U.S. Sun*, June 24, 2020, https://www.the-sun.com/news/1032696/white-martina-big-identifies-black-slams-white-people/.

Ronnie, your physical transition is much more subtle by comparison. It is slow, incremental, and stealth. You are slowly allowing me to integrate with your form. But I have always thought I just simply did not have the privilege to make it work. I know who I am and want I want. But, Ronnie, I did not think your body could fully comply with my expression needs. Could you be trans* enough and White enough to let me shine? Ronnie—we have drowned in the discord of doubt and often wonder if we are simply enough.

The whole transracial idea is still a joke to many. Even for high-level people like Elizabeth Warren, there is a need to atone and apologize. [21] And the senator eventually did just that—directly to the Chief of the Cherokee Nation. She has had her own line of questions. Is she or is she not "of blood" or of Native American descent?[22] While small, her DNA *does* show Native American ancestry. It is a part of her. Ronnie, I know that you have some White genetic ancestry as well. So, what does that mean for us

Controversies and percentages aside, we know our truth. And we know what is real for us, indeed. I think that was true for Brandon.

He did his best to change his color.

He emitted a similar orange glow fashioned by former president Donald Trump. The tanned president, the heavily tanned and tabloid White woman, and Brandon became people "of color." Yet on Brandon, it was not menacing. If anything, Ronnie, I applaud him for working to actually *do* something about what he saw as a problem. It was rumored he not only went to the tanning bed, but he took pills in order to manipulate his melanin. Between that and the strength of his actions and soul, it was hard to deny the truth of his identity and how he felt.

Ambivalent,
The White Girl

---

21 Annie Linskey and Amy Gardner, "Elizabeth Warren Apologizes for Calling Herself Native American," The Washington Post, February 5, 2019, https://www. washingtonpost.com/politics/elizabeth-warren-apologizes-for-calling-herself-native-american/2019/02/05/1627df76-2962-11e9-984d-9b8fba003e81_story.html.

22

LETTER 30:
LEO, RONNIE, AND ME

Ronnie,

You must remember this. We first met Leo in fifth grade homeroom in an unassuming enough fashion. Back then, Leo presented as a young girl. Born as White and female, Leo had little choice to buck conventions. I will not deadname them. Assigned by our teacher, Ronnie, through you, we ended up sitting next to Leo along with our other classmates at a round, brown table. It was like all of the others in the standard-looking classroom with large old classic windows and hints of ornate and intricate designs of alphabet charts, motivational posters, and the like, from yester-year.

I remember that you and Leo were both bespectacled and similar in height. You had a forceful quality about you wrapped in a sort of youthful awkwardness known to many 10- and 11-year-olds. But Leo was direct and combustible with a raw hard-hitting force.

However, Ronnie, you had more of a broad, robust grace laced with more comparative light charm. It was basically raw yin and yang on its course to be solidified. This was a personal algebra.

"So, what do you want to do when you grow up?" Leo asked you in class.

"Be Bryant Gumbel," you said. "I'll take over the *Today* show. The ratings will be through the roof." Ronnie—you affirmed that with youthful certainty.

Former *Today Show* Executive Producer Marty Ryan's response to Ronnie's childhood letter.

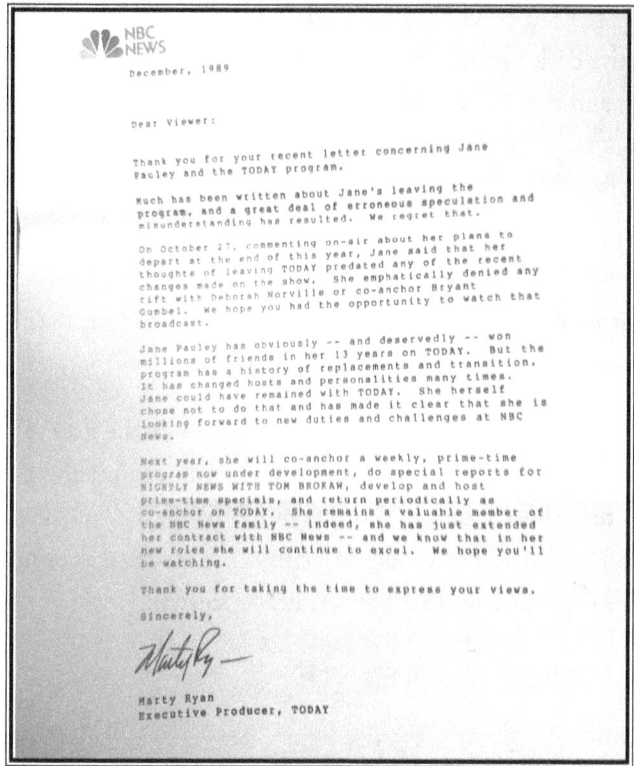

NBC NEWS

December, 1989

Dear Viewer:

Thank you for your recent letter concerning Jane Pauley and the TODAY program.

Much has been written about Jane's leaving the program, and a great deal of erroneous speculation and misunderstanding has resulted. We regret that.

On October 27, commenting on-air about her plans to depart at the end of this year, Jane said that her thoughts of leaving TODAY predated any of the recent changes made on the show. She emphatically denied any rift with Deborah Norville or co-anchor Bryant Gumbel. We hope you had the opportunity to watch that broadcast.

Jane Pauley has obviously -- and deservedly -- won millions of friends in her 13 years on TODAY. But the program has a history of replacements and transition. It has changed hosts and personalities many times. Jane could have remained with TODAY. She herself chose not to do that and has made it clear that she is looking forward to new duties and challenges at NBC News.

Next year, she will co-anchor a weekly, prime-time program now under development, do special reports for NIGHTLY NEWS WITH TOM BROKAW, develop and host prime-time specials, and return periodically as co-anchor on TODAY. She remains a valuable member of the NBC News family -- indeed, she has just extended her contract with NBC News -- and we know that in her new roles she will continue to excel. We hope you'll be watching.

Thank you for taking the time to express your views.

Sincerely,

Marty Ryan
Executive Producer, TODAY

Form Letter Response to Young Ronnie

With a genuine, warm smile, Leo indulged your every word and every move. At the time, you didn't think much of it. You were just pretty much in rhythm. All of the other kids around you were blurred. That's where it all started.

Since that time, it seemed that Leo was able to detect more of the truth within. Their instinct was there and that informed the strength of both of us. While assigned female at birth, –the classically boyish, brute, and brash energy within Leo's childhood female presentation was unbridled. They instinctively clued into the subtle underground signals that buzzed beneath you. It was me—the White girl—just tagging along, as usual. This was at The School for Creative & Performing Arts during the early days. Cincinnati really had brought more to our worlds than we had experienced before leaving Cheviot. The last remnants of elementary school were housed in that gilded boxy building that housed our high stakes education and cultural journeys. This was a brief but powerful fifth grade experience where you and Leo were caught in the dark lunation of the tween years. Yes, Leo sensed you weren't fully alone, and they knew that I was in you.

Ronnie, you and Leo were both displaced. And you each sought refuge from opposite races as you both embodied gender conflicts. You were meant to meet—and I was in the middle. This was trauma bonding.

Maybe that made you even more alluring in childhood on that Performing Arts playground.

Leo bogarted into our space and fiercely clamped on to the stuff of your gentle boyishness. The passion of Leo's pleas pinned you against the black railing outside on the school ground. This was more than just two kids closely connected. Looking back, it was more of a confrontation than a connection. This was that brief spiritual algebra that was nearly solved.

"So, what are you doing?" Leo demanded.

"Um, I'm just—"

"We should go running around," Leo decided. And we did.

But we didn't run yards, we ran decades. Ronnie, you ran with Leo briefly during the lunch bell. But in different ways, we ran away from each other for many years afterward. We faded into the distances through puberty, smoking, punk rebellion on Leo's part, deep distancing, school changes, and so much more. Time, like interest, quickly compounded.

Adult Re-introduction

Years later, Leo was finally able to present himself, just as he had authentically been all along. But the brashness and rough and tumble graces only intensified. Still, there's much to learn from him.

Ronnie, through your adult form, I instantly connected with Leo's evolution. I am glad you re-connected with him while you worked on your doctorate. By then, we had long left fifth grade behind in the late 20th century. We had crossed over into the 21st century—it was the early 2010s.

When reconnecting at the Northside bar, every cell and fiber came together in the right arrangement. The masculine outline of Leo was present but locked in the guise of a then female presenting person back in grade school. And this was the way it was supposed to be. Ronnie, I felt so happy that he was able to make the connection, to manifest the build, the bravery, and the bravado that is his full adult life.

And then I languished. I thought I would have been even more emboldened to come out through you. But then I just got more confused. I couldn't find much of my outline in your body, Ronnie, in the same way Leo had in his. I am the nameless White girl who continues to muck around as unformed consciousness without my own carcass. In that moment, Ronnie, I quietly resigned and allowed you to dominate. By now, you were the doctoral student looking to support your research. It was still just as emotional for you, if not more. But it was tempered to metrics and rules of social science, and so I just got soaked in the regimentation of it all.

Years later, as adults when you pressed him for this, Leo said: "You were the only person that made me feel awesome."

Leo is White. But his own kind did not want him. "The white kids wouldn't play with me because they thought I was weird, so I hung out with the Black kids," he wistfully intoned.

Wow,
Me (WG)

LETTER 31:
FORCED RECKONING

Leo challenged us to get clear on our journey in childhood without us knowing it. As adults when he said that "I have a thing for Black men," it rung out to us. The confrontation felt all the more familiar.

My suppressed White female identity in your body couldn't be contained and your Black male brethren felt it. Other Black boys and men may not have been able to directly call out our transgracial identity—but they knew something was different.

And so, you were singled out. It's one of the reasons why you had so many problems with Black males and is why you felt estranged. Tell me if I am wrong.

Through confrontations from the social expectations, Ronnie, we split away and moved into our psychological factions. We disconnected in sharp contrast to how Leo closely had once zeroed in on our personal space on the playground against the fence at school. That Mason-Dixon line of Cincinnati ran through our psyche and established a boundary between us. Our own kind of New Madrid Fault Line grated and with each slip, guilt and shame ground on both our heads.

Still, admittedly, I was safe, after all. Bitter. Pent-up. Forlorn. Feisty and frustrated, nonetheless, but oddly, I was cocooned in a privileged, gilded body with good amenities.

Ronnie, your hair grew thick, fast, and full. This insulated me with a continual and controlled blaze. Your warm, large, deep cocoa-colored eyes gave a clear, wide panorama to a big, populated, and impersonal world for me to take in. Supreme panopticism. The width of your nose brought in the scents from the constant currents and changes of the winds—I inhaled along with you. Your cheeks padded the firm-centered skeleton system of your face. The thickness of your lips and tongue only enhanced the comfort and ergonomics of your face—and this helped my viewing of the world, as well; that is a useful benefit of being masked.

With a long neck, Ronnie, you gave me plenty of reflection time to do everything from eating, speaking, and more. The trunk of your torso is plenty long enough to give me wandering room, although it's been a bit cramped within your thighs and legs, as they are lean but sturdy, nonetheless. Your lanky and slender feet are what I envision mine to be, but my arch would be a lot higher. And of course, I would be White.

Considering the physical misplacement, I suppose that things could have been much worse. You've given me a healthy body to live in. And I always have time to explore—often in ways I do not even remember. Yes, thank you for the comfort and for the protections.

Ronnie, your dad could never strike out at me. In you, I was protected in a mysterious plane of time and truth—coddled and cocooned in a dark underground tunnel. After all, I was very much my core. Unreflective of its proper place, for sure—but I was my foundation, my time. My inner ethereal and transient forms were perfectly aligned when coherent. Exquisitely shaped and meshed by some delicate and intricate occurrence pulsing with a great and unmatched formidable force. But I found refuge in you, Ronnie, because you had and have what I don't—and that is consistent form.

Facts,
Just a White Girl

LOST IN OUR MUSINGS

Dear Ronnie:

Am I living out my own fall from Eden? Was it sublime in a different plane before my misplacement, and now in you I live out another version of "Paradise Lost"? Am I a Lilith or an Eve? Am I a fragment of a "bad" female archetype that's fallen and is banished to a type of a psycho-social purgatory? Am I the female entity that screwed up the desired plan? Did *we* sin by not fully disclosing and taking part of the land that was created for us? Ronnie, were we too stuck on ourselves that we failed to merge and produce items of value? At any rate, I have continued to store up and repress my insight as long as I could. We needed a sermon.

But the tangled truth is now in a sort of tangled container which makes me vulnerable, confused and needing to find my way—our way. Sometimes I'm ok with it. I think I'm fine to be as I am—a perpetual kind of female consciousness that you can access like that Joaquin Phoenix character has in the movie *Her*. That's a nice, controlled kind of arrangement—at least for you. Why can't you make it on your own? Am I fulfilling some version of your dream?

There are always lots of questions. We're frequently in the dream state. When you and I are in our unconscious unison, we end up wanting the same things. The balance is the most perfect at that point. But our conscious state is where the volatility swirls. Ego. I guess it was hard for you to process how Kimmy Gibbler from *Full House*, with her stinky feet and all, would be the right kind of avatar for us. Never mind that she wasn't real—her character was yet another kind of ghost for you to contend with. It is funny how Kimmy Gibbler, Andrea Barber's character, came back in advanced form. Through you, I've read that she went to Netflix as an adult—now on *Fuller House*. And there are discussions that at some point she may be a part of a reimagined *Golden Girls*-themed show with some of the *Fuller House* cast. Time waits for no one. The different ages and stages are building up in Kimmy Gibbler. And time is doing the same for us; our house is beyond full. Yes, we span those generations.

The ages and the stages keep accumulating. This is not going away, whether or not you deal with the digital or just come back to the shared zeitgeist of our mind and soul. Pound for pound, the messengers call for action. Even though I loved those old sitcoms at the time, I can't help now but to be wary of all corporate media, including the news and the identical script reading by the anchors. And that's exactly what I am trying to help you to break. Free yourself from the drones and dissolve the rote compliance. The body has got to be the messenger of the mind.

Courier,
WG

LETTER 33:
EXCEPTIONALISM

Ronnie,

With me, you get to be "special" and still be a part of society since you're in human form. Do you leverage my presence to escape from your Blackness? Would you even want to leave your Blackness if I had never shown up in you and within your life? That's something that you'll never really know for certain.

Building up your "Blackness" and saturating yourself in pride still would not cancel me out. So, you could run the other way. You know, you could seek refuge from not just Cincinnati's hilly hot box of historical hostility, but, really, the world's ingrained hostility. There aren't many places to turn to.

For sure, the legacy of the land is woven and threaded through the lakes and landscapes all inside of a big blue crystal ball. Some will always see you as a "spook" and a "pariah" just because. But with me, I'm an internal kind of beacon that dwells within. You radiate a strange and surprising glow because of it. We light each other. You never left me. Why didn't you outgrow it? Everyone wants you to quit me, but it just became more complex.

Or maybe this situation is all just a part of the twisted reality of slavery and more than 400 years of the institution of American race and racism. Nell Painter said that Black people will need therapy for life in order to process through the centuries of racial trauma and discord.[23] Is this just my way of processing? Not to mention the centuries of sexism, too. Throw that in for good measure, I guess, while we're at it.

Light skin versus dark skin. Male versus female. It's tough. The warring politics. It isn't just enough to be a spirit with a body and to explore through the systems we call life. There are plenty of other categories and systems that are thrown at us and without our choosing, as a default we have to represent it whether we agree with it or not. We can evolve and educate. We can even meditate and push beyond the boundaries of our bodies and the conscious. But still, the sum of everything, the form and material takes a trump. I wonder how others out there process the reality of things.

So, I think we've been forced to compensate. I couldn't bare the claustrophobia any longer. You were cracking under the weight of the social mask yourself, and we both dealt with some kind of strange cosmic time warp where we were born old—handed a double-bodied type of Benjamin Button karma that allows us to get younger as we go along in life. We operate on a reverse clock. At times, Ronnie, we are both adolescent, with braces sporting our awkward insecurities and growth. And then at other times, it's like we are a young woman—fully in our 20s and living the life of helping and guiding others. Ironically, though, that young woman outwardly is just as self-assured to those she helps as the younger version of her is insecure and doubtful.

Sincerely,
White Girl

---

23   Nell Irvin Painter, "Reparations: Be Black Like Me," *The Nation* 270, no. 20 (May 2000): 2.

LETTER 34:
TEENS AND TNT

Oh, Ronnie:

Lightning tore through the rain and storms. The heft boxed you in life's ring. Familiar. The phantom hits stung. Echoes of your father's fire and ire laced with a new unknown portal that was opening. Adolescence. Testosterone burdened. The Ohio River became an ocean that raged into emotional hurricanes from time to time. All I could do from inside of you, Ronnie, was to look out and up to God. I couldn't believe this change. I never thought it would be so raging. Maybe it's true that "all gods dispense suffering without reasoning."[24] You were the arc of grace the winds whipped and cut with vigor. You were forced to grow into your strength. And yes, "through indiscriminate suffering men know fear and fear is the most divine emotion."[25] Our fears smeared, and the charred smoke swirled in the distance during our different stages.

24   Zora Neale Hurston, *Their Eyes Were Watching God* (New York: Amistad, 2006 Reissue).

25   Hurston, *Their Eyes.*

Provocative Awakenings

Age 12.

My initiation into a long-term dark period. The emotional winds slashed the childhood bloom and scattered the shards of lacy elegance into cyclonic pirouettes. The reminder of what once had been lurked an omnipresence. Yet it was clear that time brought a new era. Something dense and dark took root. Black buds. Black roses. Dark foliage was the order. The new plants arrived, and they somehow sprouted from the center of your core and into our worlds.

Adolescence snaked its raw sentiment and senses into us. The wry devilishness of it all demanded to be chased and boomed its imperial boom. The new agenda and essence were borne and would take shape. It ripped your body from the golden graces of childhood and threw it into the shapeless pubescent purgatory that would have its way on us. Its grip has never quite let up, even now. The assassin kills them all.

The testosterone attack did a number on us. Here's how I have it figured:

The school picture of your 12-year-old self was the first strike. The graces of childhood gave way to looming semblances of your father. The height of head. The width of nose and the smearing asymmetries engulfed the gentler nuances of the youthful exterior that once existed. Ronnie, the school picture betrayed us. Was I more upset that you started to resemble your father? Or was the projection of maleness and Blackness such a strangling overreach that I felt choked off from any fighting chance of trying to resonate through your emerging physical lyric? Sure, classic teen awkwardness marred through your surface. But the billowing of opposite directions nearly killed me, Ronnie, and this is when I became Black, too. The light of my blonde locks dimmed.

The discovery of your growing brow bone encased us in cerebral and concrete consciousness. The dos and don'ts of male and female had rules that never felt sharper. I couldn't breathe. For the first time I felt like I was being buried alive. Liquid concrete poured atop my being.

The darkening of your skin draped the brush of your hardened bones that are your brows. The following year, your skin tinted in ways that stitched your outer into a different individual. You became someone else because you were no longer recognizable. You became political and joined the legions of other adult Black men. The bridge between our Black and White drew up for a time.

The widening of your nose is what quantified the differences. The weight of African and Indian intersections pound for pound added up to undeniable ancestral form. You reflected the excesses of culture in spite of herculean attempts of redirection and counterbalance.

The deepening and thickening of your voice. This was a welcomed shield. It erased the feminine unison of chords and sounds from the elegance of your neck. That part at least remained intact.

Your awareness of attractive individuals. These things murdered the childhood innocence. Ronnie, I knew that I always liked guys. But how about you? Sure, you had plenty of girlfriends. And you cared a lot for some of them. But is there more? The youthful repose of your dark male form could no longer harmonize with the ethereal nature of my light and female form. It now dominated it.

Just taking it all in,
The White Girl

LETTER 35:
BEN'S INSTINCTS

AGE THIRTEEN

Ronnie,

I still can't believe how Ben zeroed in on things in health class, even though it was in the same room where we studied drama. Both subjects collided dramatically, no doubt. I can't even remember how the conversation progressed to this point. But sitting side by side in the old, dank room with notebooks and the humdrum of the regular school day, it just came together. That school was spirited, and there's no telling which other-worldly voices invisibly beckoned to get others to speak and ring things out.

"You wanna be a White girl, Ronnie?"

We stopped.

In your thirteen years of life, no one had ever asked you that in such a point-blank way.

"What?" You stammered—feebly trying to shield our secret—you nearly collapsed in the process.

Ben pushed again. "Do you want to be a White girl?" He insisted through the glow of pale skin and the jolt of blue eyes that pierced the veil of your medium-brown hue.

I wanted to leap out and you wanted to fly away.

Through suppressed panic and deflection, you uttered a near stutter, "Why would you say that to me?"

"I just think you do," Ben concluded with an earnest realization.

There was no angsty malice. He genuinely wanted confirmation. Apparently, you'd left the breadcrumbs all the way through. Just as your teachers and classmates "clocked" your feminine graces earlier on at Cheviot Elementary. They must have been attuned to the quiet finesse and sensitivity. It resonates into a kind of subtle mist enshrouding your frame. It's hiding in plain sight for anyone that's willing to listen to the whispers. It is nearly spiritual ASMR.

Silence.

This real-life drama was more than what can be experienced in any theater class.

Ben hit a nerve.

Ronnie, I roared as he questioned you; I was finally acknowledged.

Yes, in the seventh grade—in health class but in the drama room—he saw through you, and there I was. He could smell it.

The stink of fear, repression, and complacency beaten to a pulp. What else would you expect from me when you're always on the run?

Dashing,
The White Girl

MURDER AND THE DEATH OF CHILDHOOD

Ronnie,

During adolescence, the pruning was not just left to us. It fell on a relative, too. Your half-sister, Sharon, was cut away from the family tree. But rather than a knife, it was a bullet's blast that did the real damage. And then the world at large showed us how they'd use their weapons to the point where finally it hit home. The pulling of this trigger was not an act of liberation. There was no equalizing moment. It was not staged. We won't pretend to have been close. We didn't really know her. Separated by eight years, a different mother, and city, we were quite distanced. You hardly strung together a paragraph of exchange. But the murder of your half-sister Sharon Gladden in Dayton, Ohio, was an ultimate explosion and dismantling. She was a young person connected to you.

Sharon Gladden, Ronnie's half-sister's featured picture within her obituary.

And the seriousness of the attack only made the reality of life and initiation into your teens more intense. You put on a stoic and bespectacled brave face. Here you had to really separate from me so that you could nurture the moment and reflect on the circumstance. The poem Sharon wrote suggested that somehow, she knew her untimely death was near. "Don't miss me…" was the line that rang out during her funeral. She was eulogized with great conviction. The delivery by the reader seemed to match the fever pitch of Sharon's sass.

Sharon was saying that she'd be fine and wanted all of us to do the same. The soul is immortal. She was separated from the vessel but not from the velocity and value of experience and worth. This is truly something for all of us to reflect on. Sharon was struck from behind. The bullet was an unknown marauder that ricocheted and eclipsed the early fusions of dark skin and sunny spring of life. But in death, her resoluteness was borrowed from the stern forcefulness of winter. "Don't Miss Me" she said through her poem.

Ronnie, don't miss me either. Work with me while I am still here. Take heed to the sentiment.

I went deeper as your voice deepened. I went further under as your skin darkened. I longed as your limbs lengthened. You gained more control over me. You were stronger. Boyhood gradually banished and the forced rites of manhood manifested.

That meant the need and expectation to dominate, lead, and colonize your empire was thrust upon you. And in all of that there would just not be any additional room for me—at least not in the way it had been. I expected to be pulverized. I grappled with the coming war from inner White on outer Black. This meshed with the destruction of the war from the Black-on-Black crime your half-sister endured through senseless murder. The "Blacker devil" boxes with the "angel." Ronnie, I am cocooned, remember. But pent-up explosions happened on both sides. In execution savagery and violent senselessness, your sister's fleshly lyric died to the blast's song. She never knew it was coming. But the eruption was no respecter of persons. Ronnie, the violent shooting aftermath braided with the early part of your dissent into the unknown adolescent maze.

The years of whippings and the emotional distance you suffered at the hands of your father multiplied and overlapped with the death knell of very close proximity. Sharon's execution forced a reckoning. Ronnie, your outer self grew Blacker, bigger, and your voice boomed. At times it seemed that your voice was its own kind of blast of resonance that ricocheted everywhere and inside of you. I endured the onslaught.

Fortunately, you often honed your strong voice on stage and in the other correct kinds of circumstances. But I found it nearly impossible for the light of my White female voice to ride along with yours—as we did in childhood. There would be no mistaking you as a White girl as you once had been long ago at your grandmother's while on the phone. The song of my lyric that was my voice felt pruned, as well—and I had to discover my new sound for my evolved expression, too.

With all of that, secrets and the like all became too much to manage.

The Los Angeles riots of the 1990s happened. And in ways, the mayhem reflected the agony we felt within. Our own inner rebellion was underway— just in time, of course, for the start of our teen years. Looking back, it seemed the 1992 L.A. riots were a harbinger for the 2001 Cincinnati riots that were on the way nearly 10 years later.[26] I inhabited both places and wanted to escape to the same factions.

Decades later, the Black Lives Matter protests feel eerily familiar as the wheel keeps turning. An emotional California quake rumbled along the fault that linked to my adolescence. And the '01 riots in Cincinnati inhabited along a nearby fault line that awoke the new adulthood. The tension squeezed. It felt uncannily like the shackles that linked the lineages from the east to the west.

And all of this overlapped with our time in middle school. Sure, it was in the seventh grade when our sutured persona started to loosen. Ronnie, you were leaving clues.

I know that was the hardest time to keep a wrap on things with the changing hormones and all. Ben's question boomerangs all over again and a whole new level of drama abounded around and within us. Class ended leaving only the drama. Ben really was a sharp one. I cannot get over his simple question.

"You wanna be a White girl, Ronnie?"

Well, *do* you?

You never answered.

The gentle zeal of Ben's blue eyes continues to wallop with a benign and yet haunting insistence. It's like he wanted to guide you for your own good. His spirit beckons with resilience, just like Elvira in *Blithe Spirit*. And just like my own.

We had never been clocked like that before. Ronnie, this hit you like you'd sustained a blow from your father. I didn't know what to feel when hearing this through you. I was certainly stunned and put into a frenzy. This must have been what it was like to be discovered on a stranded island. I waved to the proverbial overhead helicopters up in the sky. Add a cocktail of surging testosterone, an increase of Blackness, and maleness, and you—we—had our

---

26 "A Timeline of US Race Riots Since 1965," VOA News, May 30, 2020, https://www. voanews.com/a/usa_timeline-us-race-riots-1965/6190204.html.

own kind of TNT that was ready to explode, no doubt. Your voice became rich tiffany. And I wore the deep, broad multi-hues for protection and elegance. We were on the verge of complicating ourselves as we sought to cross over to new lands. We were waving goodbye to childhood. Were you becoming more like your father? Or were you just fulfilling what otherwise was a typical transition to becoming yet another Black man?

Something to think about,
WG

PULLING THE TRIGGER

Hey, there, Ronnie:

This was the first time you had held a gun with weight and serious form. It looked and felt real even though it was not. Black and well crafted, you instantly connected with the prop for the theatrical performance. It was not until after several weeks of rehearsals in Agatha Christie's *And Then There Were None* you earned the right to handle the fake gun. Ronnie, as Captain Phillip Lombard, you used the gun to take out Wargrave and to free Vera, his hostage.

You pulled the trigger a few times.

Tension and power were released. Smoke ensconced the stage, time, and air. A transfer happened. More growth into the character as you evolved into your body. Parts of adolescence closed in the staged wake. And Ronnie, new parts of your young adult life leveled up and out. You were just 15 but an older karma laid upon you. And I, the nameless and faceless White girl was entangled in it all. The audience in the intimate Black Box Theater filled the space with thick thunderous applause during that classic play.

Redemption budded.

I loved how you delivered the line, "I've been in some tight places."[27]

Maybe. We definitely lived in tight quarters for what had been 15 years by now. That role was a great equalizer. Captain Lombard righted wrongs and remained free and persevered through to the end. He had to fake his death, though, to make it over. I know that you've sleepwalked plenty in this journey through life. A walking kind of death with me in you, trying to cross over in a sense.

So much collides.
White Girl

---

27   Agatha Christie, *And Then There Were None* (London: William Morrow, 2011 Reissue): 122.

LETTER 38:
TEACHER AND TEEN SUICIDES

Dear Ronnie—

Ms. Hale was tall, thin, lively, and tan skinned. She seemed to be teeming with purpose and life. But she died by suicide. It seemed so senseless. Her kids attended your school. And the backdrop of the *Romeo and Juliet* tomb on stage in the Performing Arts Theater set amidst the real-life death of a loved teacher was a lyric of cruel irony. Life and art crudely smacked into each other. These tragedies weighed down our teen times. Especially since you were involved in intergenerational play. Ronnie, in *Romeo and Juliet* you portrayed your father and your son. You were Lord Montague and Romeo Montague. Romeo died. The father lived. Juliet would die. Her parents lived. Ms. Hale died, but her kids lived.

The intergenerational sadness and strain felt on both sides. In the middle of the balancing act between the real and the staged, I was forced yet again to come to terms with my own placement. Ronnie, I had to ask. To whom did I belong? Where did I belong? As a shapeless inner White female, I didn't have the demarcation lines between the generations and fact and fiction as you all did on the three-dimensional plane. And in adolescence, no less, I carried a new kind of crisis in the sea of the tumult of this time. This push and pull routine was felt keenly at St. Catherine's School.

I distinctly remember that you were a student visiting for a day in the seventh grade and all went smooth during the visit—except while in the church connected to the school.

The reluctant eucharist at St. Catherine never received. There was an awkward interplay between you, Ronnie, and the other kids at the school when it came to the passing of communion. Of course, all of these accepted the eucharist since they were Catholic. But you weren't and were just there for the day. You wanted to accept the body and I felt that I wanted to take it with you. Ingest it, though ultimately you didn't. And they (rightfully) did not give it to you. It just didn't happen.

In some way, Ronnie, I felt my White female inner substance remained inactivated. No transubstantiation would happen in that instance. No realization of form would manifest then. I was continually thwarted. This took me back to those early Seton and Elder High School experiences. All of the same goodwill was there in St. Catherine. But it was so much more knotted during that middle school visit. Things were definitely heating up.

It was the early 1990s at that time. Rodney King was asking, "Can't we all just get along?"[28] And so, why couldn't you? If I could not be activated, then what was your excuse? Be down with the cause and fight against the struggle—don't succumb to it in some demented way. Black (Male) Lives Matter. The tensions thickened.

We even got to experience Maya Angelou speaking to us in person at our school. There's a whole new meaning in her belief that "when someone shows

---

28   Deb Kiner, "On This Day in 1992 Rodney King asked, 'Can't We All Just Get Along?'" Penn Live, May 1, 2019, https://www.pennlive.com/nation-world/2019/05/on-this-day-in-1992-rodney-king-asked-cant-we-all-just-get-along.htm.

you who they are, believe them the first time."[29] That's true for us. That's true of the torment from your father. That's true for much of society. She showed us how she used words as a weapon, and they were her shield and armor.

Survival calls,
White Girl

---

29 "When People Show You Who They Are Believe Them," Oprah.com, October 26, 2011, https://www.oprah.com/oprahs-lifeclass/when-people-show-you-who-they-are-believe-them-video.

LETTER 39:
POUND CAKE

Ronnie,

We'd later see Bill Cosby lead the way. Dr. Cosby would call out the kind of behavior from Black men that vexed us the most. We had no idea Cosby's legacy would grow to be so tattered and complicated. And we did not know he would be tarnished. But for what it is worth, Cosby would give a "Pound Cake" speech where he'd pound a parochial message of how Blacks should behave "better"—particularly, Black men.[30]

Through your eyes and ears—I could feel the weight of Cosby's frustration as he partly begged and chastised for Black boys and men to pull up their pants. Bill lamented (and of course, his rant on this takes on a completely different context in light of the aftermath he would have to endure).

He called out the parenting structures. Bill said there were too many single

---

30   Adam Serwer, "Bill Cosby's Famous 'Pound Cake' Speech, Annotated," BuzzFeed News, July 9, 2015, https://www.buzzfeednews.com/article/adamserwer/bill-cosby-pound-for-pound.

parents. I personally think that call out can apply to a lot of races, Ronnie—but I get it that the single parent rate is higher in the Black community.

It's time to "make Jesus smile…"[31] Bill was determined. He was fired up. You know how I have been stirred and filled with my own angry flames from the abuse.

All of his rants were directed toward the Black community.

Of course, you didn't have these issues. Troubled and as complex as things were, Ronnie, you did have two productive parents that made an honest living. You spoke clearly along with me. Remember that we enunciated together. You enjoyed some nice things, like stylish clothes, shoes, even some cool jewelry adornments and the like. You had sustenance and graceful masks. But as you grew up in school and went beyond, you never found yourself in extravagance.

Of course, Bill pointed out the high levels of consumption. But in spite of your "Bill Cosby"-approved behavior, somehow the speech was still intended for you. Did you make Jesus smile?

What were you doing wrong?

Your parents were there for you at for all of your stages while growing up—even if big parts of it were fraught with your father's inexcusable and misplaced fury. They had to have known you were not completely alone—Ronnie, I brought a lot of extra weight. And still something for you must have been incomplete. Your soul as well as mine could not fully smile. Maybe Jesus's reflection was with you in those shadows.

It would be all too easy to condemn you, at least through Bill's lens, if you represented all of the things that he railed against.

But you didn't.

You complied to such a degree that at times, some people even claimed you

---

31   Ibid.

were cut in a Cosby-approved image. Clean cut, brown faced, and strong amorphous facial features were your past, coupled with a benign and sometimes banal charisma and style to boot.

But Ronnie, your sin was in keeping me underground and within you, nonetheless.

You could have taken the conformist path, but you stayed with me.

Even better—you could have released me. What if you'd transitioned earlier?

I remember the picture clipped from a magazine that featured the model Elaine Irwin.

In pencil, you annotated the extracted page—probably from *Cosmopolitan*—and you scribed neatly-written phrases and lines drawn to her facial features and aligned your notes with the timeline of ages when surgeries could have re-sculpted your body. I beamed with the plan and remember parts of the timeline.

AGE	SURGERY
15	eyes and lips
16	nose and cheeks
17	ears and hair, etc.

Ronnie, you wrote all of that out at age 13.

But that picture went lost on the emotional ash heaps. Somewhere in time we went shelved.

Ronnie, maybe you thought I judged you. I did not really judge you—I reserved my criticisms for your peers and some of your elders.

I feared them because I was told to do so. The width of their noses. The dark of their skin. The aggression and swagger they had I loathed.

I became the toxin that I projected on to Black males. I loved contrasting my alabaster to their ebony. Society said I should be very afraid. Our earliest experiences with domestic terrorism that started with your father only cemented things. The refinement of my frame to the brutish bones I alleged of the others reached a fever pitch. When you weren't looking, I ate more than my fair share of pound cake—with extra cream on top.

This is where I am ashamed of my racist past. I bought into the stereotypes. But I never came clean with this. You felt it. And I harbored it.

All was not lost. Some of the same things you did not like were the very things that drew Leo—your fifth-grade childhood love—to you. These conflicts have a purpose. We're still trying to piece together the meaning of it all. And sometimes, meeting with others can offer a little bit of the help in this way.

Learning,
WG

LETTER 40:
AIRBORNE

Ronnie,

With all of this ground-level density we endured – it's funny that you were born in Ohio, the birthplace of aviation. We could fly above it all. Indirectly, who knew that your dad would help? As part of his job, your father worked on aircraft engines. With this in your background, Ronnie, you were destined to take off in flight in some way. Whether if your ascent was an attempt to get away from me, the trials of adolescence, or if it was to test the terrains of your earthly ambitions -- you finally did take flight in many ways – especially in the arts. Ronnie you were cast in your first film—*Airborne*. This represented the best of Performing Arts. I respect how your connections at the school helped you to perform as a featured extra. *Airborne* was the right title. Back then. you were 14 and you were making new headway in your school and work—you started to professionalize. That was an ascent upward.

We needed to fly away from mucking through all of the hard thoughts. And, Ronnie, it was time for me to level up in new ways, too. The eagle-eye view just made me want to double-down and fight to be seen and to heal. We felt all of this as you appeared in the same flick as Jack Black—now for that I am jealous! By then, Ronnie, we had been a student at The School for Creative and Performing Arts for five years, and you finally started to get noticed and land roles. You felt like you were making a difference and moving forward with progress. Imagine if I could feel that way, too—but in real life. *Airborne* suggested a true and deep desire to escape the muddied and muddled lands of adolescence and old trauma. We were making our way to some heady spaces.

Flying away,
Me (WG)

LETTER 41:
MEETING RACHEL DOLEZAL, THE 'INFAMOUS ONE'

Wow, Ronnie:

It happened. It was the meeting of identities. Ronnie, your armor of professionalism loosened at the seams and your vulnerabilities percolated as our past, present, and even future selves sought to leap out for camaraderie. It was you, the Black man, and me, the inner White female, meeting Rachel Dolezal all at once. Of course, she certainly had her own additional layers of complexity to navigate.

We know what we've heard about Rachel. And we know what we've read and watched. She lived in the fishbowl and swam against the choppy, crashing social-media waves and streams. I sought to make a place for all our versions during that first meeting. Your Black male body, which also housed my shapeless White female essence flowed in Frankensteinian solidarity. At times it melded with Rachel's murky "Black female" image.

We shifted between stages of retreat and coalescence.

But it was nice not to have to explain anything. We both understood where one another hailed.

Nevertheless, Ronnie, while you were present, my retreat from her lasted longer. I hid deeper within you in my own kind of amber. It was the cool, quiet place of review I needed to process the cut of Rachel. You were left on your own and in the liminal for a while. But then again, maybe you weren't alone for too long.

Ronnie, you and Rachel connected, if only in the moment. Sometimes it was your Black male bodied form and consciousness that met with her reworked and affirmed image, and I became the third wheel.

But at some level, my form confronted the magnanimity of Rachel's self-plumbed Black female life.

What was she like before she transitioned? And where did she exile her white form? My soul begged to get a peek at Rachel's aborted White female origins. Jealous, I wanted a conversation of our own. Oh, if we could have time traveled. The sentience of her original, assigned self next to the shape of my shapelessness would have been a tonic. Through her discarded origins, I would have found material to use. I think it could have helped to start the rebirth I am destined to realize. And then, I guess, I wanted to help her to find what she had been missing all along. It's no coincidence that we are so close in age. We are the generational siblings sporting the algebra with X as the variable. Again, as "Xennials," we're persistently locked in a kind of liminal nebulousness. The spot is marked, but it's still hard to get to it. At some level, I wanted Rachel to be Whiter—just like her ex-husband.

Did I want a slightly older sister?

Was I naive enough to expect a kind of quasi-female camaraderie—like Toni Morrison wrote about in her essay "Strangers"?

All of us: Ronnie, Rachel, and myself— the soulful and shapeless White girl—

were certainly estranged in those moments. But through Rachel, I thought I just might find my reflection, even if just for a little while.

And my structure? Was there a kind of promise of kinship? Perhaps I expected too much of Rachel.

Ironically, Dolezal had hidden that exact same form that she had no use for. Her Black female aesthetic truly trumped her original skin suit that was forced to harden into armor. Her body was poetically subdued. Out and proud, visible for the world to see and measure. Rachel's three-dimensional Black woman presence lived on the backs of her assigned White female beginnings.

Yes, her White foundations were banished to a distant psychological abyss. Here's where you, Ronnie, and Rachel, as a unit, reversed the colonial. You subdued me. And Rachel subdued her early self. Between each of you, a new kind of Underground Railroad was created where repressed and displaced White soma and souls dwelled. How many more could there be? That kind of creation could only happen in Cincinnati. Us lost White souls roam and look about, even though there are no winners in this. We just want freedom, too.

But while you, Ronnie, had searched for ways to liberate White female expression, Rachel executed a kind of White female exile. This is where you two deadlocked. My muzzled White girl energy desperately wanted to connect with Rachel's White woman ghost. I was hungry to work with the scraps that died; but I was too late.

A muffled rage and scream continuously rang out deep in the center of my being as we were filmed in that Netflix documentary. It will be interesting to see our interactions play out on camera—if I can ever bring myself to see it. The subtext is always the real show. But I haven't brought myself to watch it. I'll block my signal receptors and you can just code this one, Ronnie, all on your own. I like that we can both switch off and disengage in this way. It's probably one of the reasons why we have been able to make it together as long as we have. I won't see the flick in the same way we avoided TV from time to time in childhood. And I won't watch the documentary in the same vein I wouldn't allow you to swim. Maybe there's just too much beneath the surface that I don't want to get lost in. This is my selfish reasoning, I suppose. But can you benefit, too?

Sure, we only made up two physical bodies between us. But from my view, I will get to see at least six different versions of us:

1. Ronnie's outer Black self

2. (My) inner White self

3. Ronnie's male self

4. (My) inner female self

5. Rachel's Black self

6. Rachel's (hidden) White self.

Ronnie, you and Rachel doubled the "three's a crowd" bromide.

After you finished talking with her, Rachel said something to you that stuck with me. "Your 'look' makes sense, given how you identify. You have a cute nose and graceful hands," Dolezal noticed.

Ronnie, the compliments were directed to you. But the words actually spoke to me. She had recognized a part of me, after all. Your re-sculpted body is the attempt to approximate my White femaleness. It's subtle, but I appreciate how you've worked on your nose and other parts of your face. You have slowly but surely moved along a continuum that invites more light and youth. Some of the restrictive aesthetic shackles have sloughed off. I gave you more form while you give me more form. We have our reciprocities.

Rachel's statement was simple—and maybe superficial. But my takeaway was that she gave me a nod, of sorts. It was like she could see the truth of my buried inner White female self in the same way I could see her exiled White female past. She saw into the seven hills that resides within. Also, in essence, she was saying that we are who we are. We are valid.

It doesn't always make sense to everyone, right? Of course, it only takes nine months to produce the baby. But indeed, it takes a lifetime to draw the full, authentic person out of the baby once they are born. Of course, some of us accelerate that alchemical process, perhaps not unlike the way that Rachel has. And many others struggle in the wake. It takes lots of ambition and lots of dreams of the less encountered kind. It was a temporary reprieve.

But the past would surely come calling.

Truth,
WG

LETTER 42:
THE OTHER INFAMY

So, Ronnie—

You and Jessica Krug would both grow up to become professors and to seriously process identity while educating others. But Krug donned dark skin and a change of appearance – and Ronnie you've stayed bound to your Blackness. There is a hard truth swirling around you instead of a masked enigma that splits the heads of many.

This is not about erasure, but of the measure.

Dr. Jessica Krug, a former George Washington associate professor admits to faking being Black and Puerto Rican.[32] She is White. And she proclaims to cancel herself. This is devastating. This makes our struggle seem so insignificant and impossible. We are real. The George Washington professor that lied

---

32   Lauren Michele Jackson, "The Layered Deceptions of Jessica Krug, the Black-Studies Professor Who Hid That She is White," The New Yorker, September 12, 2020, https://www.newyorker.com/culture/cultural-comment/the-layered-deceptions-of-jessica-krug-the-black-studies-professor-who-hid-that-she-is-white.

about her "Blackness" failed to integrate the diversity within before integrating with the diversity on the outside. The integration of truth was also sorely needed. But there could still be hope. For some, the BLM movement has vindicated Rachel Dolezal. Maybe that can happen for Jessica one day too.

Working through it.

Simply me,
WG

LETTER 43:
CHECKING MY PRIVILEGE

Hello, Ronnie—

Let's go there. Let's talk about Peggy McIntosh and her essay "White Privilege."[33]

The invisible knapsack doesn't mean much when you're invisible. Apparently. I'm "missing out" on a litany of advantages that Peggy McIntosh said I am entitled to. And it includes a lot:

1. I can, if I wish, arrange to be in the company of people of my race most of the time.

2. I can avoid spending time with people whom I was trained to mistrust and who have learned to mistrust my kind or me.

3. If I should need to move, I can be pretty sure of renting or pur-

33   Peggy McIntosh, "White Privilege: Unpacking the Invisible Knapsack," in *Understanding Prejudice and Discrimination*, ed. S. Plous (New York: McGraw-Hill, 2003), 191-196.

chasing housing in an area which I can afford and in which I would want to live.

4. I can be pretty sure that my neighbors in such a location will be neutral or pleasant to me.

5. I can go shopping alone most of the time, pretty well assured that I will not be followed or harassed.

6. I can easily buy posters, postcards, picture books, greeting cards, dolls, toys, and children's magazines featuring people of my race.

7. I can be pretty sure that an argument with a colleague of another race is more likely to jeopardize her/his chances for advancement than to jeopardize mine.

8. If I declare there is a racial issue at hand, or there isn't a racial issue at hand, my race will lend me more credibility for either position than a person of color will have.

9. I can easily find academic courses and institutions which give attention only to people of my race.

10. I can expect figurative language and imagery in all of the arts to testify to experiences of my race.

11. I will feel welcomed and "normal" in the usual walks of public life, institutional and social. (McIntosh)

And at this point, with what I know and feel, it wouldn't do me much good anyway. Sure, if I was embodied, I'd have the glow of Whiteness and any residual power it accords.

But how much more would that trap me?

And would I get some sort of sick power trip from it?

I wouldn't want to be a "Barbeque Becky" or a "Dog park Debbie." To sum it up, I'm not a future Karen. I get that the deck has been stacked against you and other BIPOC. The hemp, the forefathers, the horses, and the slaves right out of the gate ensured the repressive and violent engineering would go on for generations and generations.

Some of the shackles have fallen off through the centuries but many remain. I have tensed up with you whenever you saw the bright of the primary lights in your rearview mirrors. I've sat with you in your mind as you balanced the racial algebra that must always be solved when in the school, the office, and in public spaces where your Black body is inserted and coded. I have helped you to solve those equations while balancing my own. And now that I have seen these variables and have watched them grow more complex, there's no way I could forget the process. There's no way I would want to add to the caste.

The muscle memory in us both is real. If I were to find embodiment, your racial mathematics would still be etched into the conscientious and destiny of me. I realize that any privilege projected on to me is just that. But a part of my balancing act is to work to reject and transmute it somehow. Embodiment for me is just for me and that is it. To hell with anything else.

I would not want to be a perpetual citizen cop unevenly and senselessly targeting Black and Brown people for the most ridiculous of reasons. And I don't want to film, taunt, and harass others—particularly Black people just living their lives. It's crazy to see barbequing while Black or walking your dog while Black. I get that.

And you felt the outer sting of a two-prong racial caste system. It was just internalized hate inside the deeper recesses of oppression. It simply is the racism within your own Black community. The light-skinned versus the dark-skinned Blacks follows you at weird times like this. The legacy that "light is right" is alive and well in the Black community. It is a degree system. The more melanin in the skin the more malaise and mayhem you can expect.

With all of this going on, we're all trapped from what I can tell. But I know what the reality is. I just want to reflect the sum total of the cues, memories, thoughts, and natural instincts that make up the floating substance that is me—a White girl.

To be trapped in the way of the world is to handcuff me in place deep inside of you.

I'd remain walled and kept into a formless compliance. I couldn't freely go to certain neighborhoods, bars, collectives, and art spaces without being canonized and cataloged according to crazy bouts of feminism and the sex-crazed perspectives. I want the skin for me. I want the eyes for me. I want the voice and the height and the glow for me.

But is this its own kind of privilege?

It would be my privilege to triumph over your dad's oppression and all of the other forms like it. I didn't want to burn any more in the soul's bed—and I didn't want you to fry on the front lines, either.

If I do have a privilege, it's to be devoid of wanting to function politically and to occupy a liminal, neutral space—which may be a part of what McIntosh meant in the first place. I think that most just simply want to be—without being told "how" to live. Some people get more say in how they live than others, obviously.

I love being the renegade and blasting through the limits of the underworld. I'm my own heroine, like Lara Croft in *Tomb Raider*. My own maverick. This is the right kind of White girl energy that is me. I just want to be empowered and a fun badass in the process. I'm not looking to get mired and tangled up in contorted social systems that would just force me to muck around and peck through for the fear of being labeled racist, classist, ableist, or anything else.

I'd snatch the dead ideas resident in those tombs deep within the underworld and I would fight with them. I'd give my all to drop kick them into a real nihilism. I would get to the real root of hate in an almost stealth like way. I would want to isolate the radioactivity and beat it into the silos where most of the oppressed people have to reside. I would want to liberate those around us while I have my one-on-one with the root of evil while I lean in and attack the focus of evil.

The adversary that was your dad's mother and the magical maverick energy of Bea Arthur shaped me for better and for worse. The energy from my "she-roes" cemented it through and through. I know you supported the journey, and this is where more of female empowerment sprung alive.

Not trying to be toxically woke,
Me (WG)

LETTER 44:
SHE-ROES

Hey, Ronnie—

I can't escape the dreams. This is especially true when I'm feeling strong. This is active and my visions draw out of me and eventually will come out of you, too. I'm feeling some sass and some music. And the legendary Dolly Parton and Katherine Hepburn seemingly want to show us the way in all of the glory.

Ronnie, I've been dreaming again. This one came hard and fast. It flashed. And then it was gone for what felt like at least a couple of months. When it randomly darted back, somehow, I was on. I captured this one and made graffiti. Your forbidden kindergarten pens and sharpies were just the ticket. I graffitied your psyche so I could see the reel. This was my music video. And this is your stirring. I could not let this one get away. Here's what I've got this time.

She-roes (Dream Scene)

In this dream, I see the singers P!nk and Dolly Parton with screen legends Katharine Hepburn and Cate Blanchett. They talk it out and muse about. This is a fun gathering where they can "talk that talk" and be themselves—there's no need to edit themselves. And as they reflect on our situation, they help us both to get a better handle on how to go forward in life. I see them fun-loving and almost childlike while roaming about in nature. Maybe around the Oregon Coast where the natural elements dance on the edge of the country.

The beauty and the brashness of the winds, volcano, and jagged coast is its own kind of swagger that could only happen on the western edges—it's literally living on the edge. It's what influences the counterculture of Oregon and the Wild West in general. And I am that. We are that. Especially in the strong force of the dream. They take in the sights and sounds while enjoying the fare and rugged activities the coast offers—along with a splash of eclectic glamour and tourist attractions for good measure.

A little time on the water while seeing Mt. Hood in the distance adds a paradoxical anchor. It's like THE landmark. It's quite literally the "rock"—it's heavy. And then at any time it can erupt in anger. It's volatile beneath the surface. I can't believe how similar I am to this. This was a channeled dream. The winds walloped against me to capture this. And this new set of women somehow lead me to this dream. This is for us. You've got to see this simple and charismatic dream:

Pink: You're not tired of working?

Dolly: No honey—I won't stop until I have to!

Katharine Hepburn: That's absolutely right. Absolutely right—aging is boring. You'll understand one day.

Pink: I guess so.

Cate: Sure. That's exactly why he—sorry—they—oh, hell, both of them shouldn't give up.

Pink: You're talkin' about Ronnie and the girl? Yeah, I hear that. I'd rock my situation. They've given my daughter a hard time about her identity. I asked my audience at my concerts if I can beat a six-year-old's ass for teasing my little one.

Dolly: That's some spicy, girl. Wo! Reminds me of how I had to wrangle Dabney in *9 to 5*. That may have been playing, but I learned the best from my brothers.

Cate: So, you're saying we can help Ronnie and the girl to summon some courage. Or at least to hold on for dear life.

Kate: For dear life, my dear. We'll all grow as fools, otherwise. After *Guess Who's Coming to Dinner*, I'm ready for anything.

Dolly: But this is real for them—no movie, love.

Cate: That's not what she's saying.

Pink: What is she saying then?

Kate: Well, I grew from the experience. And I really grew to see the links to us all. I got out of the prison of my experiences and those thrust onto me.

Pink: Hell yeah. I hear that.

Dolly: Wo! Yes, I could write a song on that.

Pink: Co-write. Let's do that Dolly.

Cate: The girl definitely needs to be freed. And so does Ronnie. We get that. I think the challenge is trying to see how each can have the freedom they both need without destroying each other.

Pink: Damn right. Apart of that and breaking off from the haters and dealing with that any leftover childhood trauma.

Dolly: You wrote about "Beautiful Trauma," love. What's that?

Pink: Yeah, the trauma was beautiful once it was dealt with. There's some ass to kick and some scores to settle before things get pretty, though.

Kate: This kid has got it. Gumption!

Cate: And how will you go about that?

Pink: Come with me to find out.

Kate (to Cate): You basically asked this about Ronnie and the girl.

Cate: Sure, how are they ever going to "transition" and reach a look in a way that makes sense?

Dolly: Honey, the way that I do. Sometimes you just have to get sucked, and plucked, and tucked. I wasn't a natural beauty. So I just paint it on and go to the best surgeon.

Acapella: Pink and Dolly sing "Just Give Me a Reason."

This dream felt different. Beyond the nostalgia—this was grit. I hope the Marge and Company's inner world helped you to ponder—and just think on your questions. I guess I benefited from that too. But this dream is the *do*. So you weren't born a natural White girl? Well, then draw it on! Get "sucked and plucked" like Dolly said. Do what you have to do to bring me out—and to help us to *live*. We can do this.

Rock on,
White Girl

LETTER 45:
FEMALE POWER

Dear Ronnie,

True female power. I think that maybe Bea Arthur's "Dorothy" and Sarah (your grandmother) helped me to gain a little more sarcastic traction to survive the forced encampment. This is where art and life smacked into each other. I'm glad I could tell the difference. Did you help me with this, somehow? If a Dorothy type could have been my real grandmother, what would she have taught me? The late, great Bea Arthur actually did portray a teacher on *Golden Girls*, so maybe it worked out for us after all.

I think Dorothy Zbornak was a matured and modernized translation of what Emily Dickinson would have become had she grown older and somehow reincarnated into the late 20th century. Dorothy and her friends made their own society in sunny Florida, and no doubt Emily would have drawn from the strength of emancipated fierce women in the refined spaces she in part helped to build.

The late 1980s would have been a harvest for Ms. Dickinson. And I would have loved to have been fed from some of the fruits of that society's bounty. Dorothy, Emily, and I all the way —just our society.

The soul really does select its own society. More strength and resolve. True grit would have been the mantra between the three of us. This chutzpah is still in me, though, but I acquired it in much slower drips. Emily and Dorothy would have sped things up. Maybe the slowed burns make it harder to figure out why it seems that "society" selected a body that's separate from the right soul. Ronnie, I hold you to blame. You called to me! You bound and cleaved to me with a wild recklessness. The instinct led it all. Which one of us broke first?

> If I can stop one heart from breaking
>
> I shall not live in vain;
>
> If I can ease one life from aching;
>
> Or cool one pain;
>
> Or help one fainting robin
>
> Unto his nest again,
>
> I shall not live in vain.[34]
>
> Emily helped us.

Maybe a stronger female wouldn't have answered. Strong women, like Emily, Dorothy, and even—dare I say it—the grandmother, herself—pulsed with independence through their veins. And you get to benefit.

Ronnie, here is a little bit of poetry I have been working on. It is still a work in progress:

> The light shakes not away from the burn
>
> The strength dims the onyx where defeat begins and ends
>
> The light—a true assassin to the cloaked soul—

---

34   Emily Dickinson, *Further Poems of Emily Dickinson* (Boston: Little Brown and Co, 1929).

The truth and storm for the soul is felt here.

Our strength is embodied in the singularity of your Black and male form. Together, you seem tougher than you really are. You've been helped while in school. And when I'm really saucy and traveling closest to your time, I bind closest to the same embodiment you're living in; it's then when we're indistinguishable. I for sure sit on you and saturate your form with the weight of intergalactic time. It helps you glow. Ronnie, it helps you to transcend barriers and all sorts of issues thrown at you. You're at your best with me and you know this. This comes through in your writing, your speaking, and your acting.

Guided,
WG

LETTER 46:
FIGHT BACK

I have that chaotic bent. It's me that heaves and has the brooding edge. I'm available to you in my most intense forms: uncensored, unchecked, and unmoored without the constraints of sense and sensibility. I guess this is why you have plotted to find the best way to release and exterminate me. But there is another way. You don't have to do that.

Just come to me, like you used to. I'm not going anywhere. I'm meshed inside of the Stephanie Mills bravado you heard in your childhood. I am tied to the R&B landscape and to the Gothic aesthetic of your more recent sensibilities. Give in to me and you will move toward the whole. You will fully enter my intuitions. You'll find on the inside what you think empowers you on the outside. Requite my unrequited in a rich flowing dance of fluency, as if to draw the real to you—to me—and to us both.

Come back to our dreams. And find me under the sweet moon beams. We can flow deep down in our sea streams without a raging resistance. I want to get out from the oil and wash off and be pure once again. I want my "Kingdom by the Sea" that can sweep me away. I was reminded of this when I first read Edgar Allan Poe's "Annabel Lee" through your eyes. And just like in Poe's poem, I knew you wanted to write about our Kingdom, when you were in Mrs. G's class with that pen back in kindergarten. The kingdom by the sea is a part of your story, too.

Annabel Lee am I—for I was taken from my love and life—my real life… somewhere, I was once understood, and in my proper place with my guy. For sure, I was loved "with a love that was more than love" just as it once was for Annabel Lee.[35] Back then, I had the right kind of dark, sexy, and deep that met where the blue turned to black. It was deep enough to bring new life and to be in the hollers of a relationship that was a part of a bright kindred beam, which cascaded from the moon. Blood hung not on that moon in the way it weighs a heavy force over me now; it reverses all of the tides. No. It was a gentle beaming moon above my guy and me. Too short lived of course. Ronnie, as for you and me, we have allegiance in the spirituals: negro and goth-punk.

But I am not dead. I am alive—very much I am alive. I'm not just a spiritual phantom with colliding and meandering fragments of my identity sporadically coalescing and then splitting. I'm a conscious-stirring, emotionally combative phantom with a pulse—and my pulse is his pulse. My angst is your angst. My frustrations and cries are one and the same. And yet our embodiment and spirit are still different—bifurcated—separated by some weird time and space continuum thing.

What collided?

What the hell went awry in the heavens—in those celestial orderings and the such? Is a gravitational pull too strong or too weak somewhere? What about that of the black holes? Did some meteor or crater explode along a contracting and expanding time pattern? I'm no fool. I know you've wanted me gone. You want to handle me just like your dad handled those winos. You want to subdue me just like he tried to do to your mother. You want to keep me from

---

35   Edgar Allan Poe, *Annabel Lee: the Poem* (Montréal: Tundra Books, 1987).

writing my own story, like he almost did to your four-year-old self.

I'll be damned if you try that shit on me.

Go ahead, Ronnie. Knock me out. Channel the "thugs" that you see around you. Will that finally make you feel "Black" for a change? Make me go away. If you think you really want to do this, I'm ready to rumble. I took notes, too. I've drawn from your mother's strength. And I know a bit about the ways of southern swagger. I will show the steps that I'll take to be known and not forgotten. The more that you want to push me out, the more you intensify me. I grow. I demand full acknowledgment. I am so jealous.

What you have to realize, Ronnie, is that I can see inside of you because I am in you. I know the moves you'll make before you will make them. I know the place from where your thoughts come from. You'll have to kill your outer self to kill me. But really, then, I'm still not gone. I am the spirit. I am the intangible matter. I pixelate and then I coagulate. The substance of me transforms and binds to the now and the past as well as the future. This is the real transubstantiation if there ever was one. It really would not be a fair fight, my dear. I'm armed and ready to preserve whatever is left of me after being imprisoned for so long.

Life and art may have collided. With me buried in your body, mind, and soul—you are a Native Son. At times you double as a Bigger Thomas—as Richard Wright described. You have transported me around as you have controlled your outer form, while I tagged along. Is that all that you want out of life? You've been dutiful in being Black—but for whom? You've been dutiful in being male—but again, I ask, for whom? As your passenger, I've gotten to hide out in those dark shadowy places, meshing your dark with the dark of my light. I've worked to keep you out of trouble. Both of us for that matter. What have we really said to each other, though?

As it stands now, we can't escape what we've been given. Sure—we both know how to function as a Black male on some levels. It's a part I've made all of my own. You can't help how the world sees you. And I know you are the reluctant ambassador.

The wrongdoing of men (Shawn Hilton, Mr. Brereton. The uncles. The cousins. The random strangers outside of the Fish n Chips shop). While independent and in the moment, I see now they are linked. The mini moments are the concentric clusters of toxicity from men in your life and it seems to go back to the original malefic that was the version of your father. I get uncomfortable and angry all over again, and that seems to delay my development. No more. This time it's different.

Where is your fight, Ronnie? Where is it? You are out there and yet you hide. You hide with the deep reflections and with the heightened aloofness. You are the ghost that is visiting the parts of your life—the daily routine in your neat little nostalgic matrix—your own spiritual museum. I am ready. I'm the tornado from the Fay that won't skip over you this time. I'll be The *Fa*tality. So, what's it going to be?

-The White Girl

part two

Ronnie Responds to the White Girl Within

"If a man confessed anything on his death bed, it was the truth; for no man could stare death in the face and lie."

—*Richard Wright*[36]

---

36 Richard Wright, *Native Son* (New York: Harper Perennial Modern Classics, 2008).

LETTER 1:
RONNIE RESPONDS

Dear White Girl,

I'm not "cooning." I'm just cool. I am cool enough to state my truth and take the heat because of it. I am cool enough to know about how the truth works. And I am cool enough not to be an Uncle Tom. I was born Black and male. And I still represent that evidence. That's what people see. And it is how I am coded.

I know better than to not work against the social structures.

I keep my hands up and off the wheel during a police pullover.

I've offered a quieter and refined projected voice when out in public.

I walk softly. And I apply a gentle soft-shoe essence on the societal eggshells. In this way I carry on Sammy Davis Jr.'s "Mr. Bojangles." (Dance, dance, dance.)

It's a full-time job to maintain all of that.

I mind my own business.

And now so much is collapsing. Masculinity seems to be under attack.

So, White Girl, why are you ginning it up now? Right as the masculine is being toppled with a vengeance is when you well up. (This feels biblical. True war on all that stands to "pisseth against that wall."[37]) Right as the legacy of successful Black men are being blown to bits you come about. Right at the time when racial tensions are hitting that aching fever pitch (again), White Girl, you want to be here—to take me on. Nationalism is rising. Deportations are happening. Racism is becoming more normalized.

I think masculinity, femininity, and race are going through a reset. What a fine time, for you, to appear, White Girl, and to attack me from within when I did not call you this time.

I never asked for this.

I really thought you were gone.

Sure, White Girl, I remember meeting you as a four-year-old. But I thought I'd quit you since then. I figured that I would just naturally outgrow this situation. You went faint font plenty of times. Obviously, you have not realized you have worn out your welcome.

Maybe you should have just kept going along with it, as you said.

Think of all the time that's been lost. Young birthdays. Times at the park. Innocent first-time frolics. All the organic pursuits have evaporated. We've ended up formed on two very different sides of the aisles. And yet, apparently, you not only want to share space—but you want to fully own it, too.

White Girl, you are in my body, mind, and soul—you are mingled in with my consciousness—and still you are distinct from it. You see and feel things through me. We're grounded in the same experiences. My travels are your travels. My education is also yours. My finances, home, dog, failed relation-

---

37   I Kings 14:10

ships, disappointments, coping mechanisms, shoes, socks, avocados, and lava cakes are all one and the same.

Yet, we usually have two very different interpretations of all that is connected to us. There's a continual court-ordered kind of dynamic inherent in this. But no outside system appointed you to remain with me.

I've dealt with this. And I have my own fatigue, too. If there's anything that we can agree on it's that, yes, something *definitely* needs to be done about our conjoined reality—we need space to reconcile my Blackness and maleness with your Whiteness and femaleness, for sure.

I thought I'd won.

I can't believe I am here writing this letter to you.

You know, I am the one to bear the brunt of any embarrassment and searing scowls from the world.

White Girl, what would you have me do?

Are you fully prepared to come out and help me to live this life? There is no retreating when you are three dimensional. There's full ownership and accountability for the best and worst of your actions.

How can you truly take me on, if you're not out here with boots on the ground? Where is your form? Where's the girth, gird, and full-length strength to swing back?

You asked if you're lynching me.

Is that what you'd do if you were out here in the world? Would it be public and planned? Remember that I didn't create this. I did not invent you. But I admit, I have carried your sentience—evidently for way too long.

Reluctantly, I set out just to work with our assigned intersectionality. Amusingly, the more I think about this—White Girl—and our situation, the Blacker and more male I become.

I've learned that masculinity is not so bad. In fact, there's a lot of good in it. It's totally necessary. The polarity is essential. And so now I don't want to get swept up in what's toxic. I do not want to displace men. And I don't want to add any more assaults to the Black experience.

I know what you're thinking, though. White Girl, you think you help to integrate the inaccessible parts of our full consciousness that is buried in the soil of our yoked souls.

Well, that's debatable.

And you said you wanted to be a part of Europe.

Well, you are Finland.

Yes, White Girl, you are the shape of a woman, I give you that. Your soul's outer edges are a rounded jaggedness. It's draped with a long onyx midnight. You cloak beneath my brown cocoa skin. So, that makes us a place within a place. You're within the unknown landscapes of my internal being. There must be villages, towns, and hamlets with refined architecture. I bet it is all graced with a cool elegance and masterful precision.

Remember, I am just cool—so it has to be.

You've had plenty of time to build things up.

Come to think of it, in the past when I listened closely enough—inside of each enclave—I heard the strident sounds of rich sermons anchored by stoic books. We are truly the light and dark. Clear and opaque, broad and yet small. There are wide gaps of spaces between our conversations. White Girl, our internal dialogue is not always able to land and connect in mutual ways because the silos are maddeningly silhouetted and distanced.

We are soft and yet still often cold and frozen in a dark arc.

I'm tired of this.

I had to defeat you.

But as I respond to you, it seems I can never escape my besotted streams of dreams.

In some ways, it makes sense that my outer body is the dark draping that covers the arched edges of your nameless and blameless female form that I have truly never known. Certainly, we talk.

White Girl, we fight.

We live together.

And I know you're real.

We've co-existed throughout all kinds of time periods: Carter to Clinton and from Bush to Trump. And now, you're still here, resurrected and raging stronger and louder than ever.

Upon reflection, some have said that Blacks are the mothers and fathers of the universe, the original people of the planet. So does that add to my duty to parent you, too? Do I need to uphold the outer, the blood, the heritage, and all that's measurable in all of the sum of my measurable parts?

I get lost in this world!

Sometimes I can clearly separate from you.

But most times I cannot.

White Girl, you have got to share some of the responsibility.

I just have to figure out what the ratio is. I said you were blameless. But, actually, there's much more to it than that. You're a partner in this. When I need to know you, you speak.

When I want to separate, I can hide in those frigid jagged crevices of the psyche and bathe in a secret hot spring while having a snapping and slow crimson angry tonic that only the nearby Russians know how to make so well. The libation probably helped them to cope with losing to Finland—the shape of a woman—during the second war.

Outnumbered and out armed during the attempted coup, Finland still beat Russia and, in turn, the "focus of evil," for that time. More importantly, in the wake, Finland strengthened her independence. You were Finland. And in many ways, you likely still are. At times I was Russia. But to you, White Girl, my father is always Russia. You wanted to triumph. How crazy it is that Russia is now threatening Finland anew.

The six months of darkness that envelops Finnish lands parallels the long-term cycle of your presence enveloping my mind.

We've got to settle this,
Ronnie

LETTER 2:
COUP DE GRAS

Dear White Girl:

You know, my outer form was, maybe still is—a kind of Russian coup de gras attempt. White Girl, I tried to invade your interior form. I wanted to subdue you to my intense bastion of imperialism. My adopted patriarchy and electric pangs of conquest was and is a symptom of transphobia. I thought I would crush you, for sure.

But you did it.

You won in the past and you are really winning, as of late. You are still here all of this time later! I hold a light up in the dark from time to time. Then I go about reviewing and surveying the landscape of my mind and soul as I try to make sense out of this.

I want a rematch.

It has taken a lot of editing to get here. I learned how to speak "guy." I have found a way to handle every inch of my frame—generally with masculine manners (but that is dissolving and giving way to you—I have to admit). Still, I have disconnected from color. I figured out how to dress and coordinate the metrics of a Black man's body—my body—and not that of the whims from within. I read society's script and reprogrammed, accordingly.

But, White Girl, you are right.

Seventh grade was hell. That is usually the way it goes. But most do not have to deal with someone like you. Or should I say, a situation like ours.

It is hard enough to represent a Black body—let alone with a White girl in the center of it. I need help to manage this all. A rematch might just help to settle this score with finality, this time.

I almost don't know how to react. It's true. You have always been here. Whenever I would speak, somewhere in the background, you were around. You'd help me to start and finish my sentences. We agreed that I'd be the outer representative, the spokesmen—or better yet, spokesperson.

Through it all, here I am adrift.

My thoughts count for something. Just when I've learned how to pull off the guy code and even to appreciate some aspects of living in a male body, it's now time to confront what I thought was settled.

Again -- what would you have me do?

You've got me responding to you, White Girl.

What is your name? What do you look like? Where do you reside?

You get to say and do and ask a lot without taking any responsibility. I've got to bear the brunt of this all.

I look crazy to others. They have disdain.

WTF,
Ronnie

LETTER 3:
SLAVE LEGACY

Word to the White Girl:

The bottom line is that without me, you could not exist. White Girl, I am more than just your host. As part of the original inhabitants of the earth, you must keep your order and place. Science confirms that the first humans hail from the African continent. In this incarnation, I exist as an expression of the ancestral chain of being. You have to be respectful of the balance of nature and the order of things.

But with you in me, all kinds of questions swirl in my soul.

How does my intersectional embodiment disrupt notions of Black solidarity? With our conjoined White female and Black male identity, might we be able to add, in a small way, to the diversity and complexity of the Black male body—and perhaps even to the broader human experience? Our kind of linked transgender and transracial intersectionality is in sharp contrast to the breeding of "bucks"—pure, rugged, muscular Black men—in order to sustain the plantation industrial complex.

I bought into the idea my outer Blackness was bad. The grade of hair, lips, and nose was a source of a perpetual trauma that wrecked that solace of my soul. That was mental slavery. It was an inferior lot that I continually worked to compensate.

But I have worked to exorcise my ignorance and internalized racism of which I believe much has been released. Most of this was just intense frustration out of mismatched captivity. White Girl, you help me with this processing just as much as you complicate it.

Reconciling,
Ronnie

LETTER 4:
VIRGINIA'S WOOLF

So, White Girl—

We have to look at others who have radicalized form.

Our truth seems to have been told in other places and in other ways during times from long ago.

Think of Virginia Woolf.

She was a kind of quintessential White woman with a privilege and literary influence. Yet she played a bearded, Black Abyssinian in order to tour a warship with her companions.[38] She became the opposite of not just her gender, but her race, as well, in order to sail away on a fighting ship. White Girl—we sailed away from the intermittent fights and domestic strain from our home to go to the other world that was education and recreation. Virginia Woolf sailed away as part of a fight as she dared to skin walk. She stomped on so-

---

38   Dalya Alberge, "How a Bearded Virginia Woolf and Her Band of 'Jolly Savages' Hoaxed the Navy," The Guardian, February 4, 2012, https://www.theguardian.com/books/2012/feb/05/bloomsbury-dreadnought-hoax-recalled-letter.

ciety's stories and expectations for proper White esteemed literary women of her time and stitched something new in the process. What a drop kick! And her works keep going. Now that's living and playing with the opposite of everything. There's something for both of us to learn here.

Figuring this out,
Ronnie

LETTER 5:
THE GRANDMOTHER

Virginia Woolf sailed on her ship. And we sailed away to the schools I attended. But somehow, in other ways, I still seemed to remain landlocked. The family ties in the early days linked the generations for better and for worse.

It was one thing for my father to have been born in a pre-civil rights and Jim Crow world in the Deep South. But he at least got to grow up in what would become a more civil society. He was around to hear about the Dr. Martin Luther King Jr. marches. He knew about Malcolm X. They all breathed the same air on the same planet in real time.

But for my grandmother, it was much different. The vestiges of the Civil War were surely still felt in some pockets of the South in 1922 and the ensuing years. Plantation relics, horses, farmland, and such abounded. No McDonald's. No Starbucks. No Amazon. No luxuries. Slick modern conveniences did not exist. Many did not make it all the way to middle school, let alone high school or college. And she was a woman, Black, and hard looking. So, her hard actions aptly followed suit, I suppose.

"You used to cry to stay with us. Now you cry to leave us," my grandmother uttered.

She noticed that I began to pull away from her at age six.

Maybe she felt I was beginning to judge her.

Yes, I know I think I judged her actions.

But, White Girl, would we have been any different if faced with the same reality as my grandmother?

With limited opportunities and inhaling the thickness of the loathe of the world, we would have been cut off from many different opportunities. What else would I have had but drama, aggression, swagger, smokes, and my will to fight?

The grandmother often talked about coming up on the "Rough Side of the Mountain," as the song went. All the while, I suppose there would be no time to nurture inner "White Girls," or for that matter, internalized "White Men, or the like. For all of our difficulties, White Girl, it is our privilege to get to know and interact with each other.

Sure, I have tried to look at things from my grandmother's point-of-view.

Especially since my father hails from her. He was the first malefic to enter and contribute to some of the foundations of my life. But so many people in that time also came from hard times. In fact, many others came from more dire circumstances.

After all, my grandmother did go on to be a mother of nine children and a grandmother to a clan of grandchildren, great grandchildren, and even great-great grandchildren in her lifetime. In that way, she was a crone, a true matriarch of her time without any of the stately and serene graces—no pomp and circumstance; she never ascended into it.

Still, it is so difficult to understand how the grandmother could disrespect my mother in the way that she did. Taunting her during her pregnancy with me. Spinning tales of her son potentially with other women as I developed deep within the womb. White Girl, we must have "baked" in my mother's belly with disgust at our most primordial levels from the scourge of a senior woman bestowed with a matrilineal role. White Girl, you felt estranged? Well, so did I! We bonded in the confusion amid the unwholesome outer influences. It's no wonder that through my embodiment, I struggled to find common ground and connection with my father's mother.

The conversations with my grandmother always seemed tense, accusatory, and competitive, even. That hostility reinforced boundaries of generation, gender, along with the secret race and spirit I harbored to bring you, White Girl, along with me in my life. This is a true opposite of the Underground Railroad. Sharp boundaries. Much in the same way the Ohio River demarcates the North and the South. My grandmother's rich Alabama roots always permeated the environment.

Through her, the "X" on the Alabama flag keeps emphasizing the differences. Pound for pound, we were squeezed by the matriarchal weight and heavy-handed matter of the son. For us, Black is incredibly weighty. Her legacy feels this way now more than ever. Was your presence, White Girl, a way for me to escape? What kind of portal did you represent? You sought to unlock some chambers—and you have. Congratulations. But what now?

You opened doors, but the grandmother seemed to keep others firmly closed. If anything, it seemed she worked to move away from it. Was she rebelling against a role that she was required to bear?

What other kind of life or identity did she really want?

Might there have been jealousy directed toward me?

For all kinds of reasons, I think I was seen as a kind of golden child within the family. And I guess my "quirks" were all the more intertwined and apparent with that kind of golden status.

The competitive streak started early.

Did that upset her sensibilities and inspire a kind of disdain from the start?

"I hate that you was born up here," my grandmother intoned.

She wished that I had been brought up in the South.

"I hate that you were born down there," I snapped.

I boiled in white-hot indignation.

"You too tenduh,"she went on. "Any other boys at your school wear curls?" My grandmother quizzed me on this, in reference to my newly permed, wet curly hairstyle.

On a different occasion, I playfully teased my grandmother about her nose. With the verve that's only available for a 12-year-old, I shot back. "Your nose is huge, it's all over your face."

"You gotta big soft one on yuhrs," she deadpanned in a wide southern drawl.

At some level, I expected her to elevate the situation. Perhaps even to inspire some confidence and to direct me toward a place of pride, so as to embrace what I was given. At least that's what I thought. I gave her that opportunity.

But instead, she went low and groveled in it. In fact, it was as if she waited for a reply. It seemed that she wanted to keep this interaction going so the mudslinging could really begin. There was always resident tension and hostility just waiting to be unleashed. I seemed to be the usual catalyst for whatever reason.

Nothing was safe. Attempts with innocent, playful, youthful jabs to relax with music did not happen. There was always something to say—especially whenever I listened to Michael Jackson, which was my singular preference at 12.

"Sometimes being a bitch is all a woman has to hold onto to."[39]

39　Stephen King, *Dolores Claiborne* (New York: Viking, 1992), 219.

Is that true?

Did Dolores Claiborne get it right?

Kathy Bates played Dolores with such depth and realism that I thought she had to be right. And I watched the movie with my mother and she seemed to validate Dolores's thoughts.

It would seem to make sense for Sarah. She held on to her own venom to maybe gain access to a kind of resolute indignation, which would not let up.

"Turn him off. He turned into a fag." She leveled that at Michael. "But he's pretty." She marveled at that the cover of the Michael Jackson *Bad* album.

Still, she went on.

"He wanted to be a White man," my grandmother charged.

She assessed the markedly different visage of Michael. She had the perspective of having watched him grow up. But for me, by the time I really took notice of Michael, he already had "transitioned." It was ironic since I loved his look. In a way, he showed me what was possible.

I could change.

My looks at that time shared a lot of similarities to Michael's original features.

This was true even for those that came long before Michael, like Little Richard, as he routinely said he would "scream like a White woman" if he had to.[40] Usually this was in reference to being ecstatically excited or if he were mistreated. Maybe this was a way to access agency and power—to get protection. Is this what I wanted? Is this what was needed? White Girl, is this what you want to provide?

It's funny how Little Richard, Prince, and Michael Jackson seemingly integrated their diverse and contrasting parts. And now from Little Richard to Lil

---

40   David Browne, "Little Richard, Founding Father of Rock Who Broke Musical Barriers, Dead at 87," Rolling Stone, May 9, 2020, https://www.rollingstone.com/music/music-news/little-richard-dead-48505/.

Nas X and on down the line, the struggle for identity truth continues. In the process, the celebrities crossed over and appealed to people of many different races, ages, and stages. They broke ground through their sound. They took it further with their looks. Michael begged to his "Man in the Mirror." But for me, "The Man in the Mirror" was a boy with no reflection.

Were they models for me?

Nevertheless, the restrictiveness from the grandmother just made me want to bolt. It was constant. The smallness of the apartment and the largesse of my grandmother's girth only made her sentiments seem that much broader and powerful. I was choked. The residue of cigarettes, thick hostility, and the outside crimson brick structures layered and encased the intensity of southern pounds and power. That was a big BBQ, and I could not breathe.

I wanted to escape early. I dreamt of having my own house—a little paradise away from it all where I could be relieved of her in so many ways. My frustration leapt out.

"When I get my house, I won't have to come here," I said through young anguish.

"Guhd!" She smacked back with southern swagger.

I thought I extended a hidden olive branch in the subtext of my detestation. Was it not an opportunity for my grandmother to tell me that "I didn't mean that"? Or ask me "Why would you not want to come visit me?"

Once again, my grandmother did not elevate the situation. She only egged it on. Looking back, it shouldn't be much surprise that her son—my father— would behave in the manner that he did. It was my mistake, though, to seek help from her. When I thought I could count on a family matron to help stop the abuse of my mother and my little self by her son, it just went flat and eddied away. My pleas were just added to the soundtrack of her gossiping punctuated between *Wheel of Fortune, The Price is Right,* and *All My Children.* She weaved between watching the melodramas and creating them. Her daughter added to the chorus. Niceties would be routinely clipped with sour shards of the unsolicited advice.

"Like someone your own color," her daughter—my aunt—would gripe to me. But she would fade away into her concrete routine.

My grandmother would carry on.

She stopped Michael Jackson's music.

But to her credit, the best part of her legacy includes the music she shared with me. Luther Vandross, Gregory Abbott, Sam Cooke, Koko Taylor, and ironically a Jackson of another sort—Freddie—who did the things that she never showed me in her lifetime. The velvety melodies rounded out the inelegant edges of her being. It gave her the only grace and refinement that I ever knew through her.

Was it a matronly intuition that cropped up? She sought to sever any connection to ways of escaping from her and her thinking.

At one point and one time only, she at least offered a blanketed apology for deeds on the eve of her life. The weariness and broadness of the speech seemed to go to a long list of mishaps. Included in that for sure was her early disdain and disrespect to my mother. The long drip of passive-aggressiveness. The rebel-rousing and drama stirring. All that Dolores Claiborne had warned.

In her final apartment just before going to the nursing home, she sat in the brown recliner with a tentative gaze as if she was viewing most of the scenes of her life on an invisible screen only she could see.

In that modest and sterile apartment, she nearly filibustered reflections of her life. The apologies weren't just necessarily directed toward me.

"I'm sawry for all that I've done," the grandmother uttered in a coarsened southern drawl.

I just listened.

The simple sentence carried a weight and breadth. It was like an invisible disinfectant to scrub the wrongs and the past clean.

Sure. It seemed more like an attempt to wash away decades' worth of dirt. In her late 80s she must have referenced the catalog of regrets that wove their way through nearly nine decades of life. I could only guess what the "greatest hits" could have been.

But I know more than me, my mother was too involved. The grandmother had said and done hurtful and inflaming things to my mother while pregnant with me. Somewhere in that verbal penance, she called out to us and others.

Nevertheless, the tension and the slow drip of hostility and salty exchanges never let up. The passive-aggressiveness and shade felt like the kind of competition between the light and dark. The stuff of us, White Girl. And with the insight of having you, girl, living in me, I wondered if the tension I felt with my grandmother mirrored that between Black women and White women? Might there be some kind of residual ill-at-ease feelings that just could not be overcome? White Girl, how do you feel?

Curious,
Ronnie

LETTER 6:
THE AUNT

Hey there, White Girl:

The aunt—my father's sister—introduced me to Burger King Whoppers, Jheri curls, the Showtime cable television network, and gossip. Hard gossip.

"You look like Diana Ross." I often mentioned this to my aunt.

And in some very subtle ways, she did. The thinness of her frame, dark honey-hued complexion, and long noir hair aligned with the Rossian images. The feistiness of my aunt's personality matched it all, too.

But she tired of me telling her about Diana Ross.

"You look like Michael Jackson," she flatly leveled.

It was an obligatory deadpan to match my words. Sealed in her was another kind of competition and pettiness that mirrored that of her mother.

"Michael Jackson and Diana Ross look just alike," she forlornly intoned in the early '80s on a different occasion—not realizing just how much more the gloved one's looks would evolve. Lots of celebrity speculation filled the conversational landscape. Random mentioning of famous people swirled about. It became a tapestry when I was around the aunt. My father's sister clearly had some choice thoughts on the message sent through all of Michael Jackson's makeup. This reminds me of other celebrity conversations involving "The Architect" of Rock n Roll.

Little Richard wore the makeup so his critics and the Jim Crow enforcers did not think he was after the White girls. But funnily, I may have to wear the makeup to bring out and to more fully project you, White Girl. Strangely, in this regard, the masks save and protect.

Other banter on celebrities and gossip would go on.

"Evelyn Champagne King had a sex change," my aunt leveled.

I heard these comments from her. But I didn't fully understand the impact of the meaning. Somehow, the words were seeds and sparked much curiosity. It seemed like I caught glimpses that it may be possible to "change" in another way beyond color, too.

This banter stayed with me. I was not exactly sure of what all of those seemingly random and disparate discussions really meant as a five and six-year-old. But something told me that there were other options than just accepting the body and the circumstances connected to it. Anatomy did not necessarily have to be destiny. It seemed like there were ways to escape the resignation that maybe far too many people accept in their lives. White Girl, I already knew you were with me.

It would be years later that I could rationalize whether or not Michael tried to look like Diana or if Evelynn Champagne King really did have gender confirmation surgery. If they wanted to do any of those things and more to modify themselves, they not only could but had *every* right.

What might just have been an attempt to air some venom and judgments at what these celebrities may or may not have done, the aunt actually planted seeds that would help us to exercise our own options for identity change and affirmation. White Girl, I think that you latched on to the aunt's words more than me. We were the vessel receptive to the possibilities.

Just saying,
Ronnie

LETTER 7:
$200

Dear White Girl,

"You wanna make $200?"

The tall, light-skinned man asked me this between two large red rectangle-shaped buildings that were a part of the Winton Terrace projects. At six, I was at a loss for what he meant, though I have a keen idea of it now. To my surprise, I would see the same nameless man again—but this time inside one of those Winton Terrace apartments: my paternal grandmother's.

The aunt was there, too. And I quickly told her about the $200 proposition with all of the clarity and earnestness that only a six-year-old can give. As usual, when it came to complex matters, the aunt went flat. She doled out a cool impartial posture. I reeled to see him in my relative's living space.

"Now, let's just stop this," the aunt said.

The man went silent.

I was confused that more was not done, and White Girl, you were a bit numb and

shell-shocked all the same.

Looking back, the response was locked in a frozen dismissal in the same way it had been at age five when I pleaded to my grandmother to lay down her authority to rein in my father. The latest event only compounded and cemented emotional stagnation. The very "sus" $200 proposition circles right back to my encounter with Shawn Hilton, that reporter who subtly flirted with me but had a criminal past when I interned at one of the local news stations.

Those negative vibrations ran along a threaded emotional fault line. And Cincinnati's jagged hills and lines run through us, White Girl. I never really knew who the tall light-skinned "$200" man really was. I never discovered a name. Yet his memory and presence lurks. White Girl, have you ever felt this way about me? Have you felt like this about my father? Are Black men scary to you? Do we lurk? It's hard to tell if I reacted to this on my own, or if you prompted me to take action.

Either way, we jumped into the lead to right a wrong, though it seems like our actions just kind of languished in spite of telling the family elders. My father did not immediately improve his behavior, and that tall light-skinned Black man stayed in your grandmother's apartment—he wasn't even asked to leave. My father only improved his behavior when it was convenient. And the light-skinned man left when he felt like it. My father got older. The light-skinned man exited when he felt things had run its course. What was the point of seeking justice if nothing would happen? Maybe somewhere, White Girl, we held onto this belief, and it has influenced our own situation of identity. What is the point of coming out and transitioning if nothing will change?

Still, yes, I shared the truth with my aunt. It turns out I stared right back at that face of the light-skinned Black man inside my grandmother's apartment. Silence filled the air when it came time for accountability. I expected him to be openly corrected in the way I had been for the most trivial of things. Instead, all that remained was silence. Reflection on this will forever be one sided. The aunt is now gone; she has transitioned from the earthly plane. But where was the salvation?

Some musings while trying to figure this thing out,
—R

LETTER 8:
MY FATHER WOUND

Hey, White Girl—

The first hits I felt came from a Black man and the first insults lobbed at me came from Black boys. But everyone is traumatized, right? Was my father wrong? Absolutely. But did he prepare me for the rigors of the world? In a strained way, possibly. But I can never respect or support his unseemly violence.

My father wore a deodorant aptly named 'BRUT' during his most bullish brutality streak against my mother and I. Under the BRUT anti-perspirant, his behaviors were seemingly sanitized and under a clean scent and guise of discipline. In truth, the sweat of his rage and animal nature was shielded from the public.

Of course, at a deeper level, the hits and hurts my father levied are more reflective of the strife that is the Black experience in a country founded on slavery. The trauma happened to my father, too; he was hit. Hurt people hurt people is more than a cliché. I've often wondered if my father's brutishness was an ill-conceived effort to be a moral arbiter and equalizer. Was it his misguided attempt to instill a clear sense of right and wrong within my consciousness? Did my father want to establish a clear reward system for what is just? Was it to toughen up and be ready for the onslaught of worldwide racism? White Girl, while I feel the embers of hate and disgust that you have for my father—and indeed it is all etched within you—for me the burn does not consume, it clarifies.

Painful as it was—the physical and emotional toll from my dad's heavy-handedness pales in comparison to the still visible scratches slaves clawed on the walls of their holding cells "of no return" near Benin.[41] Were my father's lashings directly connected to the frenzy from those slaves scratching and clawing their way from oppression? Here is where the potential quest for moral equalizer got muddled in the mess and tumult of slavery. Maybe he did not want to see me subdued, in any way. I definitely digress.

This is ancient history. But my father is at an age when his legacy is relevant and is steadily coming into sharper focus. And I cannot fully separate his independent legacy from the larger Black cultural lore. Did the strain of my father's lived Alabama apartheid lead to the domestic apartheid that he brought to the Silver Cliff, Candlewood and The Fay apartments? I am filled with more questions than anything. Wounds bring them. Especially wounds from the father. White Girl, I don't always agree with you, but when it comes to the domestic violence—I am just as confused as you are, too. For me, the domestic apartheid forced a demarcation between abuse and sweet childhood harmony. Dissonance. I never quite knew when my father's bad would be activated. But just the same, I knew for sure that it would come—and it always did—in one form or another.

Balancing this out,
Ronnie

---

41   Kevin Sieff, "An African Country Reckons with its History of Selling Slaves," *The Washington Post*, January 29, 2018, https://www.washingtonpost.com/world/africa/an-african-country-reckons-with-its-history-of-selling-slaves/2018/01/29/5234f5aa-ff9a-11e7-86b9-8908743c79dd_story.html.

LETTER 9:
POST-TRAUMATIC SLAVE SYNDROME

Dear White Girl:

I just want to balance the perspective of my upbringing while also trying to better understand the context and circumstances my father had to navigate as he grew up.

Although I had the advantage of being raised in a nation with established civil rights, my father did not. For me, MLK's legacy continued to march on. JFK's political heft continued to pounce on the opposition. And LBJ's ghost would forever sign and seal the deal of civil rights. The momentum of this and other work only paved the way for a more open world. A lot of the heavy lifting happened, White Girl, before I arrived on the scene.

But for my father, he was born in a Jim Crow era. He grew up while the marches and riots for civil rights, human rights, and justice unfolded. The process was messy. And the fights and the strife popped in every one's presence, and he would pop to. The blood and battle were bare to the world. That was the language my father knew.

His trauma was greater, and his survival language was grittier. This had to have been true for many of his generation.

And yet, White Girl, I have to wonder: Did my father help to instill a clear sense of what's right and what's wrong? Did he ironically help me to coexist with you residing in me? His aggressions demanded a binary order. And, White Girl, I think we toed the line for the longest time.

"Segregation today, segregation now, segregation forever!"[42] As the former Alabama Governor George Wallace wailed—White Girl, maybe I recreated similar kinds of boundaries on the inside of me that placed us on different sides of the line.

These boundaries may even have extended into my parents' relationship. As far as the discord between my mother and father went, at a fundamental level, it is absolutely complicated—but ultimately, that is strictly between the two of them. I can never condone my father's violent actions from the past. Yet, whatever reconciliation there's been for him and my mother, that's for them to settle. They just might be channeling touches of August Wilson's play—maybe they are living within real-life *Fences*.

Lots of unsavory things on the surface somehow are packaged, repositioned, and adjusted to make a life more palatable. And as Tina Turner asked: "What's Love Got to Do With It?" My mother loved the song as it spoke to her core at the height of the domestic chaos. White Girl—we certainly have lived behind our own unique set of *Fences*, just the same.

But as I write these response letters to you, White Girl—I cross the boundaries of any lines, fences, or gates that lie between us. And I work to atone for the parts of my upbringing that left for something to be desired.

---

42   "McLaurin Oral History Interview with Frank P. Thomas Jr.," University of South Alabama, https://www.southalabama.edu/libraries/mccallarchives/mclaurin_thomas.html.

It's my attempt at the processing and reconciliation that I need. Not just from you, but from a little bit of everything.

I want to be triumphant, in a way.

My mother certainly is. She absolutely unleashed her strength to shut down the tumult and the tornadoes that the domestic winds walloped.

How can I—we—learn from her?

For better or for worse, I have come to respect the relative peace that now lives between my parents. It's their life. And there are a lot of other domestic lives out there that look like theirs. Fittingly, White Girl, I hope others will come to respect our situation. This conjoined partnership of unlikely assigned soul mates. The opposite of everything. Stranger things have happened.

Working through it,
Ronnie

LETTER 10:

NEGATIVE BLACK MALES

I can agree with you, though, there were a number of problematic Black men in the fold. Where do I begin?

Uncle Monte

The tense time at our grandmother's apartment on our mother's side. At 12, Uncle Monte embodied all of the heat and knotted discord of a belligerent and highly animated character; it was reminiscent of the earlier interaction I had with my father at six over some ink pens. Uncle Monte's vortex of range felt the same that was inherent within my father. It must have been something about the year of their births: 1949. They were on code. It was the beginning of the rise of a modern closed society.

The remnants of World War II circulated around the planet. The emergence of authoritarianism came to the fore. Hostile global energies locked with the already tragic divisions of race and Jim Crow. The heat was indeed intense—but with Uncle Monte, it was absent of any physical beatings. The negative energies, though, never left and are still palpable to this day.

"Open the damn door!" Uncle Monte shouted at me with anger.

I was just playfully taking my time with unlocking the secured door at the main entrance of my maternal grandmother's apartment. I was being a kid.

"He has a problem," I intoned to my other young cousins after the encounter in the hallway of the apartment as we hung out.

Apparently, my voice bellowed and—unbeknownst to me—bounced off Uncle Monte.

"No—YOU the one with the problem, sucka!" Uncle Monte lashed out.

He was hair trigger, too. And over nothing. I was *twelve*. He was over forty. His outbreaks were totally out of pocket and out of proportion. Familiar. What was the real issue here?

Perhaps in the same way of my father, did Uncle Monte sense you, White Girl?

These snaps and fits swung right back to the other side of the family tree with a different uncle.

Uncle Everest

While limited, stern, hostile, and tense interactions with Uncle Everest are quite memorable. Particularly, I recall being quizzed on the story of Moses and the Burning Bush at just age six by Uncle Everest. It happened in the small and ironically burning coal-colored Winton Terrace apartment inhabited by his mother (my father's mother). I had no orientation with the specific strictures of theological stories. I just knew the basics. There was a heaven, there was a hell. And we were caught somewhere in the middle on Earth. White Girl, by being locked in me, I know you have felt locked in a perpetual purgatory.

Cousin Mike

My cousin Mike is a strong, muscular, classically male, and only just mildly menacing. But beneath the surface was an unspoken competition. He has accents of John Henry swag. Mike's competitive nature with me was like that of the grandmother, but at least his was much more refined. Yet, it always simmered beneath the surface. Would Mike and I have fought if we would have had more interactions? Am I simply just misplacing his swagger? At any rate, there was always a kind of uncomfortable inherent tension. Yet, we were fortunately separated by a wide age gap and cultural identity. White Girl, how did you feel around Mike?

Cousin Fran

"Three-nose" taunts came from the other cousin, Fran.

The bespectacled and quasi-bookish Fran constantly teased me about my then outsized nose. I must have been around six. With the constant taunts, Fran instilled more seeds of fear, resentment, and anxiety I held toward Black men. Somehow, my Blackness felt all the more disproportionately big and weighty, like the big nose that I once had. It was not just a classic African American schnoz, but it was Black features in excess. Yet, my young nose was just at its beginning. It was pre-puberty and childish formation.

A dark, adult intense underpinning developed through the interactions. On one hand, sure, the teasing from Fran was basically benign and banal in that it was classic behavior for an older, late adolescent male to berate a young family member. He was the big brother without the title. The problem was he didn't know what really lied beneath my surface.

There was a triplicity at work, for sure. There was the Black boy that everyone saw—me. But of course, there was you—the White Girl in the soul. And there was my Black boy persona that was a part of a Black nuclear (and broad cultural) family.

I realized that my brand of Black boy in school and my Black boy version lost in the world of dreams was not the same Black boy that interacted with his Black family. The nose wasn't just wide. But the personas and dispositions had to be, as well. The circumstances called for the nuanced and layered. I guess I had to develop a "nose" in order to smell it out. Think a "nose" for news, but in the equation I worked with, it was a "nose" for *blues*—what sad and complexly layered scenarios would I need to separate from the innocent light of childhood?

At this point, it seemed that strain always came from Black men. It did not matter if they were middle aged or young, like my cousin was at the time. Something hostile always erupted. The nose seemed to embody this. It is in the center of my face and for the longest time was at the center of any racial and gender dysphoria—let alone generalized body dysmorphia. Fran cemented this for the longest time until I took the steps to chip away at the nasal monument.

Cousin Richard

Similar to other cousins and uncles, Richard was not only chillingly distant, but he also punctuated the freeze with hot, sharp glances of wan disdain and haughtiness. I truly believe that I did not project this onto them. Maybe you did, White Girl, and your presence made it difficult for me to relate and connect with the assigned brethren.

Cousin Terrence

Despondent and deep. Chilly and emotionally distanced, my cousin Terrance did not lead in the way an older relative was expected. Instead, he abandoned and was staunchly resolute. I never had the chance to connect; I was stonewalled early on. This was the way it was nearly every time we came into contact in the earliest days. In times like this, White Girl, it was nice to have you around.

Just realizing the pattern,
Ronnie

LETTER 11:
SOME GOOD BLACK MEN

Dear White Girl—it's me,

Being Black is not a bad thing. In fact, there's a lot of pride in this. I used to glibly tell myself that. I rehearsed the sentiments enough that whenever pressed, I could provide an obligatory response out loud to satisfy the strain of curiosity and the need for subtle reassurance from those who knew me most. For those who didn't know me well, I at least satisfied the expectations to meet the social scripting. Through my then wavy processed hair, crisp ironed dress shirts and slacks, I projected dignity and pride through a booming voice that aligned with the expectations of many. I presented as if I was running for office. This look emerged in high school and extended into my mid-20s.

"You're like a cross between Nick Cannon and Denzel Washington." I was told this at a house hangout by a young, White male partygoer. We were *Wild n Out* in our own kind of way, at the time. He said this with approving admiration. At another party with a similar vibe, out of nowhere another White male partier just came out with his impression about me in the distance.

"He sounds educated, like Denzel Washington."

Though only in my 20s, I seemed to once again draw comparisons to Washington, who is nearly twenty-five years my senior.

But this dignified persona is a result of years of prepping to be on the news or to command some kind of public position. Now I know that a lot of it was to keep the clamps on you, White Girl. Yes, I did learn that there's pride in Blackness and maleness. But now you're forcing me to realize that there's pride in just simply being us. It might be more convenient to just resign ourselves to stay in this Black male body just as it is. But you really are forcing through these barriers—like a tornado.

As time went on, though, I began to learn more about the other side of Black men. The scholars, inventors, activists, artists, and the truly profound.

Evolving,
Ronnie

LETTER 12:
REBELS

There are a few rebels I want to tell you about that can even give you a run for your money.

Nat Turner

From the white-hot passion of leading the slave revolt[43] to shaking off the visible and invisible chains of hatred and boiling wrath, it all must have been a breathtaking sight to behold and *feel*. What a revolt. The white of Nat's passion that burned inside a Black man must feel familiar to you as you burn in me. This is the maverick that we both need and can use. He railed against the chokehold of slavery and imperialism.

---

43   Patrick Breen, "Nat Turner's Rebellion," Bill of Rights Institute, https://
billofrightsinstitute.org/essays/nat-turners-rebellion.

George Washington Carver

Inventor and scholar. He immersed himself in research when far fewer people did it. White Girl, we need those analytical and reasoning skills to find the sum of our own crazy equation. But this man was engrossed in the lab truly treating problems and finding solutions, and this is a model for us all.

John Hope Franklin

A researcher on race relations, and fittingly, he was recognized by President Clinton.[44] Franklin was also a long time stalwart and researcher who was able to leverage his understanding of history to write a path leading *From Slavery to Freedom*. His was the cool intellect to compliment the hot ire and courage of Nat Turner. And yet both revolted in their own and important ways. White Girl, we definitely embody the hot and cold polarities. And we are our own cyclone that cannot be escaped.

Jesse Owens

The provocative moxie of Nat Turner and John Hope Franklin seemed to intersect with that of Jesse Owens, for he athleticized the breaking away from bondage through dashes, sprints, and leaps. I've navigated similar terrain with you, White Girl. I run. We run. We run from so many things. Working through my matrix, the collective matrix, your labyrinth, and our conjoined labyrinth. Yes, this all adds up to our society, and just as Emily Dickinson so wisely intuited, the "soul selects her own society." I required just as much running and cutting away as Owens had to do.

Jesse Jackson

It was surreal to actually see him in the flesh at the college where I taught in

---

44   "Destroying the Color Line: John Hope Franklin and President Bill Clinton," NYPL, October 27, 2005, https://www.nypl.org/audiovideo/destroying-color-line-john-hope-franklin-and-president-bill-clinton.

2012. And doubly so within the space where I work. Walking history. Jesse Jackson embodies the discord of racial hatred and justice, walking alongside Martin Luther King Jr. White Girl, we can learn from this model—to reconcile our paradoxes.

Kofi Annan

A late international figure via the United Nations—Kofi Anan's soft-spoken leadership must feel like the earlier father's voices. The ones that spoke life of all sorts into the present. This is what linked all people, at one time. White Girl, you want me to whisper the same to you.

W. E. B. Du Bois

Double-consciousness. I have written about this concept, and it is firmly embedded within this book—in our letters. Double-consciousness is porous and fully alive. There really is a Black consciousness that must balance with living in a world of White consciousness. My view slaps back at yours. White Girl, we fight as Du Bois wrote about being torn asunder.

Booker T. Washington

Pragmatic and grounded activism flowed through the aura and hands of the profound yet humble man. Booker T. Washington's lessons can help us to dial it down. He was more than an architect of a college, he offered engineering for consciousness as well. And White Girl, we are building our own mental and soul infrastructure to carry us over.

Langston Hughes

The eloquent Harlem Renaissance writer who was not only Black but was also LGBTQ+. Hughes's intersections may not be all that unfamiliar with my own identity and the stuff of us, White Girl.

Richard Wright

The author of *Native Son* so often focused on the plight of the Black male—from the young to the old. His insights were cunning, and he helped to frame and speak to the factions between Black and White. He did so in a poetic and lyrical way—a nice compliment to that of W. E. B Du Bois. And White Girl, you know full well that reality resonates within us.

James Baldwin

Like Langston Hughes, James Baldwin was also a Black male writer with an LGBTQ+ identity. But Baldwin pushed beyond the envelope of eloquence and drove toward that of effusive activism. Baldwin demanded for many to *Go Tell it To the Mountain,* and I hear you, White Girl, as you shout from the top of your desolate hill. The echo ricochets with a stern churn. And my eyes look back at Baldwin's and Betty Davis.

Martin Luther King Jr.

The great racial justice maverick and reformer—equivalent to Martin Luther's spiritual and social reformation—inspired by this legacy, I seek a personal reformation between our internal crystalized strongholds. My letters—and White Girl, your letters—are our stories to ourselves and the world. We are sounding the alarm and wanting to loosen the grip of muzzled identities. We set off reforms one letter at a time. And we are the dream.

Malcolm X

He spent long hours on end attacking his ignorance. And I have taken up this pursuit in the years of late. This will be a practice for the rest of my existence. The "X" in Malcolm may just be another path toward finding your missing chromosome, White Girl. Malcom's "X" is a liminal holding place for our "X" that overlaps us with Generation X and the millennials. And Malcolm's X offers some new considerations for the X on Alabama's flag.

Marcus Garvey

He sought to go back to the original motherland. Would I have felt the same way if I hadn't been colonized? Where would the feelings of longing and two-ness have resided? In his efforts, Garvey sought to remove the shackles of the present and the perpetual. White Girl, you and Garvey are one when it comes to repatriation. But the directions are different—Garvey wanted Africa. And White Girl, you just want to go back to the beginning, in order to be, *you.*

Barack Obama

The pulsing legacies of Black and White come through. And yet Obama identifies as Black. And so does the public. We have some oppositions in that way. He had the audacity of hope. He was bold enough to believe, and White Girl, you have that fire in you. You not only can—but you will. You are coming through and finding ways to break through my external surface. At least you are for now.

The Legacy of the Egyptians

The mathematics, architecture, culture, aesthetics, and mysteries. Of course, behind good Black men often there are plenty of good Black women (Cleopatra, Shirley Chisholm, Madam C.J. Walker, Toni Morrison, Maya Angelou, Sojourner Truth, Oprah Winfrey, Michelle Obama, Coretta Scott King, and many more). And let's not forget all of the trans*, non-binary, and gender nonconforming people the world over across millennia. like Lili Elbe, Christine Jorgensen, Marsha P. Johnson, Michael Dillon, & so many others. White Girl, you have helped to improve me along the way, too.

Jesus

Was there ever a Jesus? Was he Black? It's no secret that many have thought Jesus may very well have been Black. The brass-colored feet and the copper like hair. The parable of the intense sacrifices, public hangings, and torture of contemporary Black men aligns with the strife of Calvary that Jesus endured. It would take a lot for Jesus to smile. Cosby is still waiting.

Along with these good Black men often were good Black women. Black is indeed beautiful. And Nikki Giovanni handily summed it up with the poem "Nikki Rosa:" "Black love is Black wealth."

In fact, every woman really is beautiful. And more than just beautiful—but brave, triumphant, and resilient in all of the ways that life and times demand.

It's taken so much work for me to realize this. They showed me more than just the limited dimensions of anger and aggression. They helped me to understand the brevity and complexity of the male and Black experiences. In spite of all of this, White Girl, I still can't shake you. I know that in some parallel kind of way, you're just as real and profound as all the men and women I have mentioned.

Yes.

You're just as valid as everyone I've mentioned. Just like these famous and historical figures, you have your own kind of relevance. White Girl, you're in my personal firmament and entwined with my history. You have your own kind of planetary resonance and your presence in me forces a reckoning with the world order. If anything, your validity is even more powerful because we live together.

Here's a few other insights, I have on some public figures.

Donald Glover

I never knew that having a brief interaction with Donald Glover more than 10 years ago at the Sundance Film Festival would resonate so much now. It was a creative jolt mixed in with my exhaustion that came with travel, long days, and the fatigue of arguments both inside and outside with a then girlfriend. But Donald was energy. He was in an over-the-top movie that premiered deep into the night in the frigid realms of a Park City, Utah theater. Donald's future embodiment as a pansexual character brought together in cinematic form through *Star Wars* would be in stark contrast to the classic and much more conservative portrayal by acting legend Billy Dee Williams.

I've endeavored with the war of stars that seemed to slowly spin and stream above me—well, I suppose—us. As Lando Calrissian, Donald brought a kind of earthly terra firma in the distance, firmaments of the heavens. In so doing, he grounded the stratospheric and made it manageable. He played with it.

But this time in a more graceful and nuanced way. Far different from the raw farce of that Sundance flick. As "Childish Gambino," he reflects the best of his young and mature selves. We saw it in *This is America* and in it, I saw my own factions where you, too—the White Girl—coalesce within my center. It's the equivalent of Evie from *Out of This World* and Lando working together.

And ironically, Donald personified the work that I do in real life. Each of us are connected to the community college cosmos.

In essence, like any other human, Black men are complex. Black men have dignity and value. They're real. They have purpose and meaning. The experiences I had with a small select few should not have to define an entire demographic. I have to think bigger than that. And White Girl, you should, too.

Real talk,
Ronnie

LETTER 13:
SOME BLACK MALE CONSIDERATIONS

Dear White Girl—it's me,

When I think back to the select few Black men that came my way earlier on in life, I can't help but think if there were some similarities. Did all of these guys need a bit of counseling? Did they need a forum to fully express themselves and their positions that was beyond that of the barbershop? I wonder if that was Bill Cosby's fated attempt to scold, redirect, and hound what he believed were wayward and combative Black men during his controversial "Pound Cake" speech.[45]

White Girl, I know that you loved the stern, yet gentle and fun-loving *Golden Girls* inspired "cheesecake" talks of our dreams. That banter was open-hearted and ongoing. But our cheesecake conversations are sharply different from Cosby's "Pound Cake" speech.

---

45 Serwer, "Bill Cosby's Famous 'Pound Cake' Speech."

The "Pound Cake" speech packed a wallop all at once and only once. And it hit upside the head with ill-fated but useful direction. The "cheesecake" talks, however, served up a sweet loving bite—a gentle kick of insight smoothed out with an endearing kind of reference that was a lavender levity of sorts. The cheesecake discourse connected me with a united sort of ethereal White sisterhood. But the "Pound Cake" scorn lobbed at the Black community and divided it further. Still, both soliloquys reverberate in their own ways.

I didn't mean to make Black men seem scarier or aggressive. I hope I did not project my own internalized racism onto them. White Girl, it's easier to make you the racist scapegoat. Indeed, I'm not without remnants of self-loathing and inadequacy.

Contemplating,
Ronnie

LETTER 14:
BLACK TAX

Hey, White Girl—

The weights and debts of these interactions added up. I was taxed. It was a "Black Tax" in every way (financially, emotionally, spiritually, etc.). And so, it is time for a Black Tax Ax.

The Black Tax rests on the notion that unassuming Black male bodied or identified people must atone for the negative stereotypes and representations of Black men. White Girl, my tax funds your privilege—thanks for noticing.

In other words, Black men have to apologize for their Blackness everywhere they go. The thought that Black men are hyper-aggressive, hyper-sexual, and criminal must be countered. For those unassuming Black males seeking to separate from the lore, they have to pay a Black Tax. They must prove—often in the most vexing of ways—that they're not like the wide-held beliefs; they are as Richard Wright wrote, "Big Black Good Men." We perform differently. We just want to live our lives. But so much (extra) work has to happen to prove our dignity.

It's often easier to just be invisible. Slip under the radar and avoid having to do all of the work managing micro and macro aggressions. White Girl, in that we way we share a theme. I become invisible while you have always been invisible (to the outer world). The invisible man houses the invisible woman. The challenges experienced with Black men was meant to get me in touch with my truth. The challenge fostered separateness so as to see myself in the authentic rings.

Isn't Black life under attack? How often is it that little Black boys, girls, and full families are subjected to police searches? Driving while Black. Barbequing while Black. Mowing the lawn while Black. Nothing is protected. Everything is under scrutiny. How can anyone survive under these kinds of conditions?

The psychological weight of the hatred is enough to sink anyone before they even enter the world. The legacy of being reigned in will become a sepulcher. Are you standing in your grave? Is my Black and male outer reality just caving into the pressure of years of systemic hate and racism? Am I victim to the race baiting that's on camera? Some of the well-meaning liberals intend to spotlight the plight of Black men, but instead a lot of them only make things worse.

I don't know how much more sustainable I am in this form, and sadly, I don't know if it is for the Black populace, period.

Are things getting harder with heightening racial tensions and tightening policies that may rhyme with the history of past vestiges of abuse and discrimination? Blacks have gotten through much worse, but usually with the promise of better horizons. The work paid off, but reversals this far out in the future is questionable. White Girl, you want to absorb more of me. Your Whiteness and femaleness are indeed starting to envelope more of my practical soul and soma. You're slowly finding ways to show up through my body. White Girl, you are the internal eclipse.

The lines of separation between the races are stronger and sharper—in policy, rules, and hostility. Oddly, though, we are becoming more of each other.

But more pressing is the intimacy of us.

What will you do with your authority? I'm not just the computational parts. Indeed, I am "spirit" and not just "animal."

Just telling the truth,
Ronnie

LETTER 15:
SHE-RA'S SALVATION

Time for He-Man.

"You can play with She-Ra," my cousin Tray said to assuage my four-year-old bubbling emotions.

That was his way of pacifying me so as not to disrupt the youth privileges of being away from the adults. The elders were all downstairs in the living room in your aunt and uncle's Fay apartment townhome. Tray is the older cousin that was fully in charge of his room at the time.

The weight of Tray being 12 years my senior along with the incessant taunts of several other young Black-male-appearing boys in his room strained me with a kind of premature weariness.

Why did this happen?

Tray and his brother both directed the swagger of their late Black adolescence against the whimsy of my toddler and childhood years.

Even when I wasn't with those two, it still followed.

Through tears from all of the previous weariness and exclusion from earlier times in life, She-Ra was actually a ray of light as I connected with her amidst the bunk beds, toy chests, and the surrounding rambunctiousness from the older boys in what I now know was the small, cramped bedroom within the modest sugar-cube white townhouse. In She-Ra, it was a nice way to see a wanted reflection. And White Girl, She-Ra was the closest you had reached to accessing some tangible embodiment. Through my hands, both of us transferred a lot of longing as we played. But the perspectives of all the boys around us seem to match the limited width of their environment.

United,
Ronnie

FIGHTING EMASCULATION

Hey, White Girl—

The usual attacks.

In episodes of transparency, I remember often being corrected and redirected. The grandmother and aunt in their home made it clear that boys don't get or need beauty rest. Boys don't have "boyfriends" in the same ways that straight women have "girlfriends" or confidants. Boys don't have weak wrists. Boys don't cry. They are not scared.

As loving as she is, even my mother cemented these truths of the time. Here's a childhood conversation that really stands out. Mom and I were in downtown Cincinnati in a women's clothing store that has closed long go—Casual Corner. The conversation with Mom definitely had a casual tone—and that was surely my intention, but, unexpectedly, our talk stung with a force, no doubt. White Girl, did you feel that, too?

"I'll tell you something that will make you never want to go in the women's dressing room again," my mother asserted.

"What?" I said as an earnest seven-year-old.

"They'll think you're a fag," my mother assured.

With that, the conversation ended cold.

It felt like I was choked by some invisible hands. This reminded me of how my father had strangled my mother. Seemingly the watered glove of Thanos was still in action. And that oppression seized. White Girl, how did you feel about this? How does anyone feel in the midst of being muzzled?

Ten years later, it seemed that little had changed. Caddy-corner to the then newly built Aronoff Center for the Arts in the late 1990s (but still in that urban core of downtown), I thought that maybe a new kind of thought took flight and elevated the perspective on identity. After all, I had already been *Airborne* by this point. I had grown a lot, and with all the acting on stage I was doing, I was open to emoting and being vulnerable. I finally started to take abstract steps to loosen the grip of restraint and to release our emotional bruises. White Girl, you were finding your way through this, too, I know.

Why shouldn't I get a Classy Curl or permanent wave hairstyle? My seventeen-year-old self wanted the hair conversation, so I pitched it to Mom.

"They might think other things about you," my mother once again chastened.

In the end, an invisible door closed. The invisible strangulation now met with a new kind of boundary. Maybe it already had been there all along—another kind of emphasis on The Door of No Return.

Haunted,
Ronnie

LETTER 17:

DISTRACTIONS

Dear White Girl,

To distract myself from you, I figured it would be good to lean into some friendships.

But Anthony was an intense betrayal right when I felt I was finally able to platonically connect with a Black male in a way I thought would work. This person showed me otherwise, and that is when, for me, the notion of a "best friend" collapsed.

Yet, as you know, White Girl, I soldiered on.

Bruce was the earthy, discordant long-dreaming dancer. He meant well. But wellness just didn't come from him. Inelegant strangeness, darkness, and forcefulness oozed through a kind of crooked affect that always hung in the air. Looking back, I always tried to straighten it, whatever exactly the *it* was. It was hard to grasp. And I tired of it, pretty quickly.

I felt like for whatever reason, Bruce's influence just wasn't good for me. It led me to a path of searing regret. Some of it is still with me to this day. But why is the regret covered in a deep, dull mahogany brown—just as was the hue of the dissonant filled dancer? I had plenty of my own discord and dissonance to deal with. I guess I just didn't need anyone else's. This is yet again another example of how what I viewed as a problem was always packaged in Black and maleness. Plenty of Black men were outside of and all around me—and then of course Black and maleness made up the sum of my computational parts, and even sections of my interiority. Still, I wanted to break free so many times, and I have to admit, I often still do.

But I wouldn't want to inflict a similar kind of betrayal and distance onto myself as the others had done. I want redemption. And then, here you are—the White Girl—demanding action.

You are my kryptonite,
Ronnie

LETTER 18:
JERRY SPRINGER MEETING (FIRST TIME)

White Girl—

More diversions.

The upright determination of my eight-year-old boyhood and the assuredness of Jerry Springer's tall middle age came together in our first meeting in the WLWT Channel 5 Station in Cincinnati. I was in a different part of the old studio at 140th W. 9th Street in downtown. We were somewhere upstairs in the manilla and non-descript halls then. But of course, I was buzzed with the excitement of interacting with Jerry. He stood in nearly statuesque repose, bespectacled, and with a white dress shirt on. I was escorted by Ledonia Clark, the family friend and another person who was in the hallway. I wasn't focused on you—White Girl—you were someplace in the distance for all that I knew—a place you are not unfamiliar.

In meeting Jerry as a boy, we quietly bonded through our exhibited conservatism and nimbleness.

And yet, in each of us, the wild streaks of irreverence lurked in our centers with a mischievous invisibility. The generations and the Atlantic Ocean separated us. I was American born, and Jerry was English. Yet, somehow, the connection continued.

Jerry would help me to have the fortitude to go my own way. He showed me that you can blend into conservative spaces while still fostering the undercurrents of bold leanings and unique identities.

Jerry's reported past with sex workers and bad checks was before my time. Funnily, we share connections to clandestine relationships with women that ultimately would come to light—but under very different contexts and circumstances. Still, in the end, a kind of reconciliation is in demand.

Jerry's dilemma, though, highlights his profound connections with women through purported sex workers and with his only child—also a female. The alleged mistress haunted him the same way you, White girl, haunt me.

Jerry supposedly confessed to the tryst and sought redemption. White Girl, I'm confessing the truth about the depths of my identity and seek a kind of personal redemption, just the same. Jerry's atonement occurred years before I was born, but the glow of it must have remained intact all of those years later by the time I had first met him. Without knowing any of his prior complications, I was instantly transfixed by him as he anchored the local news. But for a time, Jerry introduced the calm compassion and conversational balance that helped me to be my own *Ringmaster*.

I had a hell of a lot of subtext of my own that ran against the ways of Cincinnati westside Black boys in the late 1980s. I escaped getting caught in the crack epidemic. Parts of the neighborhood were just too sleepy, or maybe I was just too consumed with working my way through my own inner forest— while ensconced around thousands of acres of Mt. Airy Forest. I worked with a different kind of illicit white substance. The substance of you, White Girl.

I got high off the strident emotions. I crashed and withdrew after having run away from you. My heart palpitated at the thought of anyone finding out about you (us), for that fact. I was addicted. And I needed my next hit. I was too young to be considered as harboring a fugitive or for kidnapping someone, right? At times I didn't want to eat. I just wanted to escape away with you into our dreams. I lost weight. Remember how skinny I was in fourth grade? Then I put it on (overeating and lounging) so as to distract myself from you. I was vacuous. It was one chemical dependency to the next.

And so, it was easy to be lulled by the news—it was a great diversion. The news anchors were midwestern, no matter where they originally hailed. They were sharp clear talkers that mirrored what I wanted to see and hear: cool but pleasant civility and a stream of ideas and images to keep life afloat.

I didn't get much interaction at the dinner table. In fact, other than visiting restaurants growing up, I can count just how many times we ate dinner at the table. I wanted it to be like how I saw it on *Growing Pains* or *Family Ties*.

It's funny how Jerry Springer, the *Ringmaster*, would be the one to introduce me to a calm and collected affect. And in the end, it just might be fitting that the *Ringmaster* turned TV Judge—a quasi-kind of supreme evaluator that takes stock of his past. For us, White Girl, our brief encounters with the pre-famous Jerry Springer are a part of the equation for reconciliation—maybe even for a bit of atonement in some kind of abstract way.

Second Meeting

But a few years later during our second meeting, it was a bit calmer. Jerry was in the newsroom the second time around, sitting in his cubicle. Those were the last years of the typewriter, and he had one.

"You're the greatest," I uttered that with the full force of 10-year-old enthusiasm.

"OK," Jerry returned in a self-effacing way. He slightly lowered his head and looked lightly embarrassed.

I wanted more time but remember being quickly whisked away. The newscast was starting. Looking back, I have to wonder if Jerry planted a seed. Was he passing a proverbial baton? In our two meetings that traversed my late childhood and the dawning of my tween years, maybe Jerry was preparing me to join him and then succeed him in the psychological circus.

Yup, I was (and am?) the *Ringmaster*, led by the (then future) *Ringmaster*. Funny how our differences would unite by taming the beasts in the circus.

Marveling,
Ronnie

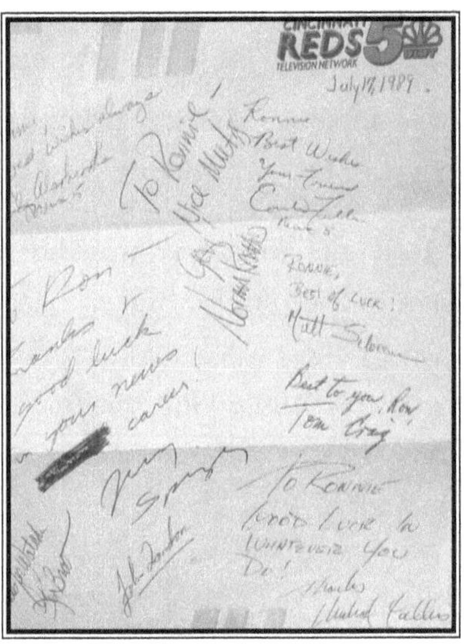

A collection of autographs from Channel 5 WLWT news anchors circa 1989.

THE JERRY SPRINGER SHOW

Hey, White Girl—

You're not the only one that dreams. I have my escapes and haunts, just the same. Chances are you've probably eavesdropped on this one—or you felt this energy within me. The line is blurred between meeting Jerry Springer and having him in my dreams.

This surely felt like it happened, but it reminded me of something I actually did hear him say in an interview. Jerry said his show had "no redeeming value." And, White Girl, I've felt that way about you. That was my way of minimizing your shadow to get on with my life and way of being. Transphobia? Yes. Since Jerry's show has been canceled—maybe the dream was a final attempt at seeing if you could somehow be canceled with it. The circus on TV goes away at the same time the circus of my mind would, too, you know?

Dream Sequence

This occurred on The Jerry Springer Show *set. What looked like equal parts factory and television studio, the pipes and stripped-down industrial hardware is softened with a light purple and brown painting. The conversation was like watching sausage being made, in some respects. I guess that explains the faux factory motif. Here comes the butcher. The color scheme matches the carpeted stage and chairs where the guests sit. Many bright studio lights seemingly cover every square inch of the ceiling. The bright lights sharply contrast with the darker and more bare industrial pipes.*

Jerry: Ladies and gentlemen, we have some special guests today. You know we usually discuss the crazy. But this time we'll discuss the political. What am I saying? The political is the crazy, wouldn't you say?

(The crowd is instantly riled up, chanting, *Jerry! Jerry! Jerry! Jerry!*)

I thought you'd agree. To help us with some political understanding—Bring out former president Bill Clinton!

Bill: Jerry, I'm surprised to be here.

Jerry: That makes two of us, Mr. President.

Bill: You wanted to talk about my identity? We might as well get right to it.

Jerry: Your words. But yes. How is it that you're seen as Black?

(Jerry, Jerry, Jerry! It's like a slice of college spring break on Miami Beach meets a live studio audience. The college students roared with near deafening energy. The audience is definitely very college looking. Early twenty-somethings with thick heads of hair—browns, blacks, blues and generally wiry frames and bright eyes are all around. They want to have fun. They want to egg things on. White and Black young adults fill the studio. Mostly male-bodied people are there but some female-bodied individuals, too.)

Bill: Well, yes. Many said that. And I am still the first White man to be inducted into the Arkansas African American Hall of Fame.

(*Woooo!* Applause.)

Humanity is my family, Jerry, I've always seen it that way. (More straight applause.) And I've been duly influenced by Black culture growing up. It's just in the air and in my aura.

Jerry: Well, Mr. President, you're not the only dignitary to think like this. But this next one is said to deny half of his identity.

(*Booooo!*)

Bring out another former president. Barack Obama!

(Applause, *Jerry, Jerry!*)

Mr. President thank you for coming.

Barack: I could only be here if I left office.

(Laughter.)

Jerry: That makes two of us.

(Clapping and laughter.)

Barack: Sure, they wouldn't even let you run again while doing this.

Jerry (Wistfully): Something like that.

Barack: And what's this about me denying half of my identity?

Jerry: Well, you're not just Black.

Barack: But I look it.

(Laughter and chants of *Woooo!* Some of the sincere chants are mixed in with youthful rowdiness that clearly wants to egg this on. A brunette-haired young man upstages many with a long lanky frame and many "Fat Tuesday" "Jerry Beads" around his neck).

Jerry: But you didn't live it. (*Wooooo!*). Or at least not just exclusively. (Jerry holds his hand to his ear.)

Barack: It's what predominates. I see where you're going. It's the anchor of my reality to be Black. But I acknowledge my mother. I know that side of my family.

Bill: Sure, just like I see my reality and know that comes first.

Barack: Bill is right.

Jerry: But isn't there more than just what meets the eye? Look at what President Reagan said. (Jerry retrieves a letter from his pocket.) Here's a quote: "Would you laugh that when people see me, they see themselves?"

(*Jerry is Oprah! Jerry is Oprah!*)

(Bill & Barack both laugh.)

Barack: You might have me there, Jer ... So, if you're Oprah, you're a Black woman at some level?

(Laughter and clapping! *Jerry, Jerry, Jerry!*)

Jerry: Why not? I did say once that I'm not half the man I used to be.

Bill: I can't relate to that one Jerry. (A bit tongue-in-cheek.)

(Audience erupts in both laughter and some boos.)

Bill: In the sense that I looked like a Viking as a young man. At least Hilary thought so.

Jerry: Everyone, the producers just announced that Judge Joe Brown is on the phone.

(The crowd applauds. *Judge Joe! Judge Joe!*)

Judge Joe: (With a slow, grounded and resolute voice, the judge weaves a drawl accent while talking.) You may not be thanking me in the long run. Y'know, Jerry, you ought to be ashamed of yourself as a so-called man of the law and a former mayor on here espousing trash about identity. You are what you are when you arrive. All of this stuff about switchin' races, gender, and intersections and all of this stuff sounds like a bunch of damn confusion and now you have a team of former lawyers and presidents up here co-signing and backing this stuff up. This is a low, even for you.

(*Boo! Boo! The audience is genuinely pretty disappointed at this time. There's a young woman with long blonde hair, ivory skin and brown eyes that's especially dismayed. She has this seething scowl stamped all over her face. But a mysterious looking young woman is in the distance—in the highest row of the show. The otherwise numerous bright lights filling the studio casts a shadow on her. Her outline becomes more and more defined. It's YOU. It's White Girl. Your outline grows wider, and it begins to envelop the studio.*)

Jerry: The freedom that's here with us is the freedom we use to fight to be ourselves.

(*Jerry! Jerry! Jerry! Now you've taken over. The entire studio is WG. Everyone is loud, roaring with strength, but silhouetted just the same. The closer you look—the more you can begin to see some of your facial features and a subtle physical form emerging.*)

Barack: Not everything is about confusion, Joe. Jerry is right. This is about civil liberties.

(Applause. *You, WG, are leading the applause. You ARE the applause.*)

Bill: And dignity. That's right.

Judge Joe: The real dignity is in honoring the truth instead of all of this disillusionment. And it shouldn't have to come at the expense of men and Black people. When you're ready to talk and not be in la la land, you call me back then. (Click.)

Jerry: (slight pause) He's spoken.

(*Boo! Boo!* And scattered applause fills the air amid the silhouetted White Girl.)

Jerry: (To the former presidents) Smooth comeback.

(To the camera) Well, they don't see President Obama's white half, and it's there by blood. And they can't see my femaleness and Blackness, but it's there by bond. I'm delighted to be compared to Oprah Winfrey—as you heard the audience chant. A similar thing can be said for President Clinton. His Blackness is enshrined at an African American Hall of Fame—but it is not seen by most, yet it is felt. It's demonstrated. What is it for the rest of you? What parts are there by blood, by bond, or both? But in the end, it's felt, no? The late, great Maya Angelou was right. Remember, she said that "people will forget what you said, people will forget what you did, but people will never forget how you made them feel."[46] It's what's intended. It's what's felt. And that is what matters.

Until next time, please take care of yourself and each other. And let's have a round of applause for our special guests: Former presidents Barack Obama and Bill Clinton—and even Judge Joe Brown!

(Applause! *Jerry! Jerry!* The original audience is in full view. But again—in the highest row, off to the distance—there is a near apparition. I see your shadow—WG, it's you, quietly looking on amid all of the noise.)

So, this is not what I expected. I thought there was a last chance for you to be cancelled. I thought things would just naturally peter out at this level. Jerry's show was a farce—it was nuts! It seemed our reality was just as crazy—usually the shocking has a short shelf life—it's hard to keep that level of frenzy going.

Jerry's perspectives definitely got me thinking, though. I can't escape you. I know how you've made me feel. And I have my own feelings, too, by the way. And we can't escape ourselves, in general. Even if you are a former president.

Now I'm the "Trippy" one,
—RG

---

46   David Booth and Masayuki Hachiya, *The Arts Go to School* (Ontario: Pembroke Publishers, 2004), 14.

LETTER 20:

BILL CLINTON

Hey, White Girl—

Former President Bill Clinton was inducted into the Arkansas Black Hall of Fame for his "understanding of the Black condition…and because of his upbringing."[47]

I also (very briefly) met Bill Clinton when he was president. I was in high school and shaking his hand felt like connecting with the world.

I lit up on the inside. It was a kinetic shock that bolted out and dominated anything it touched. There was a sea of folks in Xavier University's Fieldhouse. Jockeying to gain access and spewing their résumés and other "greatest hits" at the moment in order to attract the attention of the then president. Steady and unwavering, Clinton graciously glided about in the way his James Bond-esque prime allowed. But the president was not the only one in his prime. I was at

---

47   "Clinton Inducted into Arkansas Black Hall of Fame," Fox News, January 13, 2015, https://www.foxnews.com/story/clinton-inducted-into-arkansas-black-hall-of-fame.

the height of repressing you, White Girl; it was the long, late teenage denial. Remember I was raised in my household as an only child. I struggled to share.

Like Jerry Springer, President Clinton also had one child—a woman whom I also met and somehow felt deeply connected. However, I latched onto Chelsea's presence back when we were teens—even if it was only through television. We are very close in age.

Yet, of course, Bill had a cadre of women that would go on to haunt and challenge him in many ways for all kinds of reasons. It seems that he attempted to separate them and keep them at bay. It's funny how I engaged in similar practices to avoid you, White girl. But of course, you would not back down. You are a force. White Girl, you are a visceral and ethereal presence.

Bill's connections with Blacks—particularly with Black women—is palpable.

"We started out as Aretha groupies," the president said of himself and his wife about Aretha Franklin.[48] He often invited the "Queen of Soul" to sing for him and other dignitaries. It was Maya Angelou who framed the beginning of Clinton's presidency in his first term, as she read at his first inauguration.

The thread ran close again because Maya Angelou was a very esteemed guest at my high school alma mater—The School for Creative ad Performing Arts— just weeks before visiting Clinton (and the world) for his inauguration.

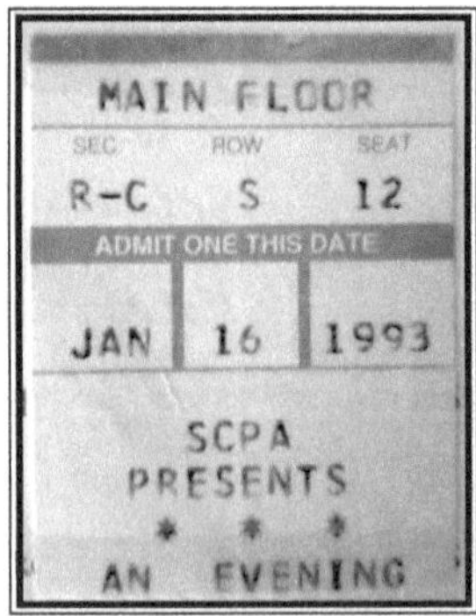

Partial Ticket Stub of the "An Evening with Maya Angelou" event on 16 January 1993.

48 Raisa Bruner, "Bill Clinton Plays 'Think' Off His Cell Phone at Aretha Franklin's Funeral: 'It's the Key to Freedom'," Time, August 31, 2018, https://time.com/5384234/bill-clinton-aretha-funeral/.

That, along with his closeness with Aretha and his political legacy, I'm sure encouraged Toni Morrison to coronate Clinton as the "First Black President."[49] This shows just how much a person can transcend the sum of their parts. It offers hope as I—we—grapple to figure out how to engage in a life of meaning that has far reaching impact while also growing beyond just my body. White Girl, I really don't want to just be a color—or a gender. And interestingly— for what it is worth—the framed painting of President Clinton draped in a slinky blue dress, wearing red high heels, and gesturing a pointed finger is a classically feminine juxtaposition with his quasi-coronated transracialness.

Clinton's intersection and embodiment hints at aspects of transgracial identity. But on the way to transcendence, I think I must realize every part of my identity—even the inconvenient underpinnings.

Big dreams and perspectives,
Ronnie

---

49   Daniel Arkin, "Toni Morrison Defended, Championed and Chastised Presidents," NBC News, August 6, 2019, https://www.nbcnews.com/pop-culture/books/toni-morrison-defended-championed-chastised-presidents-n1039591.

LETTER 21:
BARACK OBAMA

Hey, White Girl—

President Obama embodies Black and White. He was estranged from his father and had closeness with his mother and White family.[50] While I did not meet Obama -- I did visit the West Wing of the White House during his time as president. My former professor's son worked in Washington, D.C. and through him -- I got the rare opportunity to take in the rarefied space. How interesting and fitting. The White House was built by invisible Black hands and silver chains where a biracial president lived and led. I couldn't help but to see and feel the irony and poetic justice.

In that visit, "The Fay" and the White House were nearly one and the same. At least this time the Obamas were living beyond "just enough." They were a presidential family. And here I was, visiting this place having once lived on President Drive in our white townhouse that was "The Fay." For all of us, a

---

50   "President Obama's Father: A 'Bold and Reckless Life'," NPR, July 1, 2011, https://www.npr.org/2011/07/11/137553552/president-obamas-father-a-bold-and-reckless-life.

personal kind of legacy crisscrossed.

The Obamas and I were influenced and in part "built" by the legacy of those Brown and Black hands that designed the corporal "brown houses" that constitute the bodies that we live in. And yet, of course, an ethereal "Whiteness" resides within me—it is you, White Girl. A fuller blood legacy of Whiteness is within President Obama.

Whatever the case, it's fitting that all of this converged in such a high-level space under the belief of *The Audacity of Hope*.

The White House, occupied by a biracial president and visited by a bi-identity Black male-White female is perhaps a unique intersection the forefathers and the slaves did not quite envision.

Perspectives,
Ronnie

LETTER 22:

RONALD REAGAN

From President Drive to Pennsylvania Avenue—by any measurement—was definitely an improbable turn of events. But so is having an inner White female living within too, right? I was named Ronnie and lived on President Drive in the 1980s when our country had a president nicknamed "Ronnie, baby!" Being just five, I was much more a baby than President Reagan, of course.

But it's apt to mention that just before Reagan's election, in response to the question, "What is it, governor, that people see in you?" the future President Reagan answered with another question: "Would you laugh if I told you that they look at me and they see themselves?"[51]

White Girl, to me, that's a nod to identity in all of its forms. I wonder if Reagan's answer showed his evolution on identity—maybe it was an indirect way for him to atone. We now know that Reagan made racist comments about Africans. The focus of evil that he once inscribed on foreign adversaries instead seemed to be home grown while all the while emanating from the

---

51   "Reagan – From the Collection: The Presidents," PBS, August 11, 2020, https://www.pbs.org/wgbh/americanexperience/films/reagan/?feature_filter=All&page=2.

former president.

But maybe he did change? Perhaps the years of maintaining a pen pal relationship with a young Black boy expanded President Reagan's perspectives. The president went on to say that his thoughts about the evil foreign adversaries was a belief "from another time and another place."[52] White Girl—we have worked through our evils. And here we are crossing many different times and places, writing letters to each other to bridge our own differences.

Time and distance can indeed blur. We feel and live that every day. And I am reminded of a more contemporary politician who as grappled with complexity of her own identity: Senator Elizabeth Warren.

Senator Warren tried channeling a similar sentiment when she attempted to recognize other parts of what she once thought could be unintegrated identities. She thought she was of blood and had some connection to Native American ancestry.

And while we are on national politicians reacting to identity matters—I cannot forget former President George W. Bush's unlikely reaction.

In spite of all of his controversies, "Bush 43" is apparently based and respects the need for authenticity. While President George W. Bush told his transgender friend from college that "… now you've come back as yourself[53] during an elite soiree.

How poetic to be the highest version and expression of yourself in the highest office of the land. White Girl, at times I think we are getting there. Maybe we will return to the White House again one day, as ourselves.

National reflections,
Ronnie

---

52   Ibid.

53   Ben Cohen, "Hey Mike Huckabee, Even George Bush Knew How to Treat Transgender People With Respect," The Daily Banter, February 17, 2016, https://thedailybanter. com/2015/06/hey-mike-huckabee-even-george-bush-knew-how-to-treat-transgendered-people-with-respect/.

"Better to live on a corner of the roof than share
a house with a quarrelsome woman…"

—Proverbs 21:9

MEN GOING THEIR OWN WAY (MGTOW)

Dear White Girl—

But a lot more balancing is still needed. I live in the rooftop of my mind, away from your troubled feminine soul. Even in the Bible it says a man is better off alone and can expect to have troubles if married. Look at Corinthians I:7. Look at Proverbs. We are not traditionally married. But we are assigned to coexist in our own kind of identity covenant. Yet this is a unique ordained marriage of intersectionality. Corinthians also says if you're married, you're better off to stay that way. But just because we might be irrevocably conjoined doesn't mean I have to be around you.

The attic of my thoughts is a trusted pressure release.

It might be seen as hypergamous for you, the White Girl, to want to occupy a three-dimensional form on the back of all of the labor I've expended to live and function in the world. I have made many sacrifices to negotiate society.

Men Going Their Own Way (MGTOW) is a response to what's seen as an unfair attack on men. Some believe that the family courts and other kinds of domestic laws are uneven and disproportionately favor women to the detriment of men. Because of the attack, increasingly guys are unplugging from society and going off the grid, so to speak. This is to protect what otherwise could become unfavorable discrimination whenever a male may find himself inside of the throws of domestic life and laws.

Dr. Helen Smith wrote *Men on Strike*. And in it she described the risks for many western men and male-bodied people to marry during modern times. She said that men get a "raw deal."[54] And Dr. Smith—as a cisgender woman—adds a lot of credibility to the argument.

I was already on my own and practicing what might have looked like MGTOW before I knew what it was. At times, I was against the world. To split from you, White Girl, is a break from the constant polarity of things. But you were against the world, too. I need to go away and be against you.

I wanted to escape the "common law marriage" feel of our unlikely union. I wanted liberation from all of the compliance demands.

A different kind of law seemed to dwell within because of housing your energy. Some of the remnants of modern society followed me inwards. Be dutiful, courteous, and respectful of others—especially when women are involved.

Chivalry is not dead. A bit of propriety and finesse were expected. And then yet, White Girl, you have had little accountability, through it all. If you got out of hand, who would be responsible? Me. What kind of retribution would follow for your unjust deeds? None. I would have to bear it all. Certainly, I would be on the hook for any outward kinds of craziness, and I would have to endure any consequences while being in a Black and male body. That Black Tax is mighty expensive, remember?

I'm not saying women in our world are not held accountable. Far from it.

---

54   Helen Smith, *Men on Strike: Why Men are Boycotting Marriage, Fatherhood, and the American Dream – and Why it Matters* (New York: Encounter Books, 2014).

In fact, women are often times held to some of the most unrealistic levels of scrutiny. They have to be feminine *and* at times masculine. Submissive and ambitious. Attractive but also relaxed, and the like.

But you, White Girl, are not fully accountable.

You have no real governing structure. No maritime, national, or international borders. You have no kind of jurisdiction, really. Your fight is for embodiment and, in turn, that keeps you perpetually stuck in liminality. Hence, the constant angst and tension between the conscious and the unconscious. The struggle between the soma and the soul of lore is all too real. It gives me a headache!

So, I will go my own way. For me, it's a MGTOW of a different order. I have not, would not, and could not, date you. Even though the cohabitation has felt like a common law arrangement, it's nothing of the sort. No consummation. But I have made plenty attempts at retaliation. And reconciliation.

All of this may have just been too late. White Girl, I should have quit you as a teen. Or at least I should have tried a hell of a lot harder by my 20s. But is ditching you even possible? Hats off to the younger, braver, and the more ambitious.

If I had taken this strong of a line at 12, White Girl, you would have been forced to leave or die.

How much more relief could I have had by acting like some of the Australian teens trying on the Teens Going Their Own Way (TGTOW) plan? TGTOW seems to be everything that MGTOW is but with a head start. Could I have cleared my being of your voice, mood, and feel with a more exacting eviction? Would the mental minimalism have forced you to map your way out of my DNA and orbit? White Girl, your neurological nomadism would have been cancelled.

Funnily, you would fit right in where the land of the dispossessed and gutted had often made a home—but it would have been away from me.

All of it adds up to a lot, and so separating and attempting to live somewhere between "monk mode" and a diplomat has been a part of the game plan. The bottom line centers on escaping the dynamics of the constant binary.

A lot of my outer relationships have suffered. I don't really know how to connect with most. White Girl, you take up too much space.

I have a struggle with pair bonding in romantic relationships because you have to contribute your soma and soul. Because of the mismatch, I can only offer the grating conflicts and love struggles that usually leads to nowhere.

I struggle to relate to my family. I feel any remnants of common ground are not enough to bridge the vast differences in perceptions and reality.

Even in friendships, which I adore, I have not found much in relatability in this area as of late, either. There are a lot of things to sort out.

Moving on,
Ronnie

LETTER 24:
THOSE SHOWS AND MOVIES

Hey, White Girl:

Even so -- *Gimme A Break!*, *Diff'rent Strokes*, and those other '80s sitcoms that featured intergenerational and interracial families showed us that it was possible for someone like me to connect and find a place among outsiders—even if it was in the world of fiction.

Yet, they say I am in the "Sunken Place." You know, the space where all of the identity confused and self-loathing Black men go. The "Sunken Place" is a repository of the scared and scarred post-slavery brethren that slinked into the surly grasps of the dank cultural subconscious. Apparently, we wallow in all kinds of low, unsavory, paraphilic strands that mutilate the collective Black male psyche and soul. Paranoia, self-hatred, "coonery," or Uncle Tom-like behavior abounds in the "Sunken Place." Apparently, the goal is to subjugate ideal Blackness and replace it with a subservient Whiteness that normally attracts White approval.

It's really evident in the movie *Get Out.* Some of the key Black male characters were aborted of their authentic, core selves. And instead, they became hijacked with artificial intelligence (AI). AI skewed toward Whiteness. They were hollowed out. A Black body, Black features, and a Black topography on the outside but hollowed out and clinically White and subservient on the inside. A great mismatch. A weird play and exaggeration on the anima and the animus are in effect, here.

I know that's what society thinks of me.

Is there still time to turn things around?

How can I escape from the sludge? How can I crawl up and out and fight this? Of course, others will say it's way too late. I am infiltrated with a lot of formal education up to the doctoral level, *and* I teach in academia. White Girl, we are a part of the system—the Anglo-Saxon, westernized matrix in the truest dye in wool form. I'm controlled by and comprised of every word, sound, syllable, sentence, paragraph, and page. Every pound of the books, bricks, and political pounding of Eurocentric authority beats along with your heartbeats and snakes along with your brainwaves.

But was it always this complicated?

All of these layers just simply weren't there in our past. White Girl, I admit, in the beginning, the line between my outer Blackness and your inner Whiteness was a straight one. There were no impediments. I saw you vividly when I closed my eyes. And there you were in my daydreams as I walked down the hall or when I drive. It's only when I see pictures of myself or when I look in the mirror with others near me is when you, White Girl, are absent.

The ones who just couldn't bear the aftermath of Jim Crow. Redlining. Attack dogs. Bloody bridges, cooked flesh, and dark, tarred, and tattered carcasses languidly swaying in the breeze. Hence the sinking.

The spell of the supremacist's gentle swirls on porcelain things is wickedly intoxicating. And supposedly, anyone in its grips will do and say and think and feel the unexpected.

Lots of reports predict the relatively quick extinction of White folks due to low birth rates. The cynics would say recruitment to White ways is needed at all costs, and my identity is just a part of that propaganda. Just like when you asked, White Girl, if you were lynching me from the inside out.

But is the real sunken place locked somewhere in the spell of the Black cultural monolith?

Sure, solidarity is essential.

But can I think freely?

So many say I am bound by the scientific and spiritual archaeology that tells the story of Blackness and the start of the human origins. Undoubtedly, I acknowledge that, and I cannot control the engineering and genetic lot I represent. Yet, what about my own personal archaeology? And my own personal spiritual, cultural, and nuanced archaeology that is driving the current animated life and the little stories that are created every day?

Should I ignore my own truth that's my distinct narrative?

Inconvenient it is, without question. Nonsensical to most and impossible, yes. But if I am sunk into anything, it's within my own unmitigated truth. The sum of the parts has not locked me into moving away from what came to me. White Girl, that is you. It still does not mean I haven't worked to make good with being assigned Black and male. But I can't break from the reality of your presence inside of me.

I am spinning in the "Sunken Place" and working to stay afloat in this life. I am fighting against the siren song of that spoon hitting the mug.

To cope, we should be able to agree on these creature comforts.

Here's our survival list to make it through our battles:

- ✔ Sermons
- ✔ Hot green tea with cinnamon

✔ Wide, hilly open spaces to endlessly drive through

✔ Writing

✔ Acting

✔ Teaching

✔ Traveling

✔ Social work

✔ Colorado

✔ California

✔ Europe

✔ Target

✔ Jeni's Ice Cream

✔ Books

✔ Nightly Walt Whitman readings

✔ Magazines

✔ Gentle people watching

✔ Antique Tudors and Victorians

✔ Low-fi chopped and screwed '80s and '90s classic music hits

And then here's some perspectives to keep us going: comic relief.

While I do not champion Dave Chapelle these days—I can at least respect his sentiment that "Comedy is a reconciliation of a paradox."[55]

---

55   Taylor Berman, "Dave Chappelle Explains Key And Peele Criticism, Compares Chappelle Show To A Crazy Ex In New Interview," Spin, March 20, 2017, https://www.spin.com/2017/03/dave-chappelle-interview-key-and-peele/.

And I can surely believe from an anonymous soul that "Every comedy is a channeling of a personal misery…"

The slap heard around the Hollywood world deftly sums up that misery. And in it, I see hints of that reconciliation of a paradox, to boot. That slap dials me back to the devastation from the domestic attacks from my father. The act looked and, by osmosis, felt familiar. The violence in the axis of Will Smith, Chris Rock, and Dave Chappelle is reminiscent of the hostility from my father, uncles, and cousins. But the Hollywood slap was more brazen.

Will Smith attacked Chris Rock onstage during the Academy Award Ceremony.[56] And Dave Chappelle was attacked by a man with a weapon during a historic Netflix is a Joke festival.[57] Those public displays derive from the private spaces of pain—from the individual and collective perspectives. What were supposed to be funny moments, for sure, comes from the personal miseries. It was Post-Traumatic Slave Syndrome personified and amplified for the world to see. In the end – all of the men involved just want to be free. Freeing you, White Girl, would no doubt amount to a level of fame for you, White Girl (and maybe me, too).

Chris Rock said fame is like being a hot chick. White Girl, how would you handle any power and fame after being invisible for so long? Can you handle that deal?

Certainly, on the other side of the unlikely identity swaps is room for some laughs.

In the search for meaning, I've had room to dream and escape the harder aspects of domesticity. And of course—so much of this is funny. After a while, if I'm not careful, no one will know what the hell I am talking about. I run the risk of being a caricature of myself on so many levels.

---

56 Nicole Sperling, "Will Smith Apologizes to Chris Rock After Academy Condemns His Slap," The New York Times, March 28, 2022, https://www.nytimes.com/2022/03/28/movies/oscars-will-smith-slap-reactions.html.

57 John Gregory, "Dave Chappelle Tackled by Man Who Rushed the Stage During Performance at Hollywood Bowl," ABC7, May 4, 2022, https://abc7.com/dave-chappelle-attacked-tackled-hollywood-bowl/11816401/.

Both as a Black male-bodied person and as one carrying an independent White female spirit. As a reprieve—I loved the duality of Robert Downey Jr.'s *Tropic Thunder*. When he sincerely yet sarcastically intoned "you people" in bronze face and with widened African American features, I couldn't help but to get a moment of relief and humor in the faulty yet elaborate constructions of race we have all put up. Downey's *Tropic Thunder* character united to show meaningful theater of the racial and gender absurd. And yet, the theater seems to partner with the mythological and the mysterious.

It's like *Mad TV*'s "That's My White Mama" skit, Whoopi Goldberg's *The Associate*, the Wayan's brothers' film *White Chicks*, and Snoop Dogg's claim that Iggy Azalea somehow reminded him of the caricatured Wayans brothers[58]—all combined to make for an intense performative theater. Gender and race smeared and clung to each other.

And in another film, in *Sorry to Bother You*, Lakieth Stanfield and Danny Glover take on "White voices" through their Black bodies inside of a call center.

I can hear them asking, "Who told you to lighten up (pun intended)?" "Ronnie, what will being a White girl do for you?" You have had a form of comfort for reflection, meditation, and peace on the backs of and the blood spilled by your assigned ancestors. You did not choose them. And they did not choose you. But the work was done just the same. "What will a White girl do for you?" "How does she factor into this legacy?" You were chosen to operate within these structures for a reason.

Those are the sounds and questions I have heard from various people along the way. I imagine they will be amplified.

Sometimes you just have to laugh, let loose, and get on the road.

Reflecting,
Ronnie

---

58   Claire Rutter, "Snoop Dogg Taunts Iggy Azalea by Comparing her to Marlon Wayans' *White Chicks* Character in Shocking New Meme," Mirror, October 14, 2014, https://www.mirror.co.uk/3am/celebrity-news/snoop-dogg-taunts-iggy-azalea-4439022.

part three

Collision & Chaos:
White Girl and Ronnie Intertwine on the Road

"It is not our differences that divide us. It is our inability to recognize, accept, and celebrate those differences."

—*Audre Lorde*[59]

"And nothing's wrong when nothing's true—But I live in a hologram with you."

—*Lorde*

59   Audre Lorde, *Sister Outsider: Essays and Speeches* (New York: Crossing Prench, 2007).

TRANS* INTERMEDIARIES

• Gold Coast, Australia •

Needing to decompress, Ronnie embarks on a road trip—in a personal way that nods to Jack Kerouac's book On the Road. *In various international locales, parts of the US, but eventually (and exclusively) in Cincinnati during the last seven-mile markers - consciousness travels. The ride helps Ronnie's mind to roam and to try to run from the pressing matters. Still the need to confront a number of haunting flashbacks and memories are required. Disquiet. There is a meandering tug-of-war between Ronnie's conscious and the subconscious voice of the White Girl. Throughout Part III, they take turns conversing in various ways during the road trip. Some of the engagement is voluntary while listening to certain music, seeing landmarks, and catching glimpses of videos, etc. in order to continue to process and to derive meaning. One of the memories includes reflecting on the first trip to England, while traveling on the road in Australia.*

White Girl speaks:

Ronnie, stop trying to avoid me. I live beyond the page. Our letters are everywhere. I can write to you in any form. You know you'll have to respond. I'm in the media. I'm in the air. I'm in the cells of all the intricate spaces and systems where you are found and make up your life. I am your blood. This is more than just a dream, and far more than any of the characters in the scripts we've indulged. I am the true soul-for-real force that can never go away.

Ronnie:

(The Atlantic Ocean spoke through the memory, the depth of the water creates an ethereal and instinctive feel and sound, which influences Ronnie's thoughts. The lapping of the winds against the body of water forces a sober reckoning.)

White Girl, you're the shadow of the original people—and you're the anima to my animus. You say that you're ready to integrate and to be whole. Is it that simple? How would we go about making all of this work? Are transracial people racial intermediaries in the same way that transgender people were (are) seen as gender intermediaries? I still try to make sense of this all.

The split atoms and cultures simply want to recombine and reconstitute into a different expression or a different form—yet the essential essence is the same. It's a kind of swap that still indeed respects the human expression and condition. There could not be a White female without the Black male.

If we are all from Africa, then there once was an unabashed African "father." His seed, was planted in the "African mother"—or the world's mother. The world's father sired children with the world's mother, and all different kinds of variations and phenotypes—over time. The housing of your White female essence in me is then a rebellious primordial placement. As children are usually programmed to do, they flee for freedom. The daughter seeks to flee from the father and make an independent journey. White Girl, you want to escape from me. I have carried you all of this time. But there was no direct transfer to a mother.

In essence, ultimately, I think I—*we*—seek to return back to the androgynous spiritual base and even a raceless spiritual foundation. But the corporal union of our two polarities is a unique way to step into and mature to new levels of heightened awareness and integration of the soma, psyche, and the soul. We won't just spend our lives being a color.

(*The oceans, boats, maps, and lands collectively sing as a gospel church choir and echoes of American-Greek soprano Maria Callas lead the way in song. The music functions as a proverbial bridge that Ronnie and the White Girl cross as they travel on the airplane to England. Again, this memory swirls about while traveling in Australia. And now both memories play out in the background as Ronnie drives.*)

White Girl:

Ronnie, selecting the self that matches the soul shows that the sum of the parts is definitely inferior to consciousness. We can put on any kind of social construction coat that we wish. You know, it's quaint to think in such a linear and grand-fashion. Maybe you're a spiritual father. Maybe you're not. You could just as well be my spiritual son, for that matter. You've had time to develop and harden into parts of three-dimensional adulthood. But I've stayed closer to the elusive origins of the life-giving forms. I don't flow in the linear lines. Parts of my being are not controlled by the normal boundaries of time.

(*The oceans, boats, maps, and lands collectively speak and bridge Ronnie and the White Girl as they travel on the airplane to England. Ronnie is with Alissa, a friend.*)

Transgracial identity. Ronnie, we *are* transgracial whether if we like it or not. We blend the transgender and the transracial life elements. The spectrums converge. And we are forced to navigate and bind the biological, sociopolitical, sociocultural, and geopolitical forces that are already under way and are transforming old interlocking structural forces of the legacy of hegemonic, colonial, and imperialistic forces. I see the Mason-Dixon line linked with Finland, Europe, Africa, and the world over.

A new society is needed to accommodate the new identity. A resulting racial, gender, and intersectional authority is the way of the future. The development of identity increasingly is becoming decentralized. Ronnie, ultimately, I don't need your permission.

PARANORMAL

• Bowling Green, KY, Near Western Kentucky University (WKU) •

Ghost Talks: The School for Creative and Performing Arts Ghost, Abigail, opens a liminal door allowing for Pam Robinson to cross the corridor to interact with the White Girl. An image of Pam's Ghost is present along with a sketched outline of the White Girl. They murmur in the background as Ronnie, while driving in Bowling Green, KY, listens to Luke Ruehlman's story online. These are the thoughts that make up Ronnie's internal dialogue with the White Girl at this moment.

Ronnie:

White Girl, apparently our situation isn't just limited to our overlapping universes. Who would have thought the lives of a young White Ohio boy would seemingly collide with a deceased middle-aged Black Chicago woman?[60] My knee-jerk response tells me this is an accident. But my deepest instincts know better. The collision is by design. And the interconnectedness of the cosmos and humanity is on full display. With this dynamic between the Ohio Boy and Chicago woman, there are some eerie undertones and connections to the *Mad TV* "That's My White Mama" skit. And White Girl, of course, there are so many parallels between us.

Still, I am not without questions.

How could it be that a young White boy, who at age five was uncannily able to connect with a dead Black woman that lived before him? It's thought that this past life was that of a Black woman, and he has recollections of the past.

Pam Robinson, the Black woman who died in a Chicago fire, seems to have left remnants of the legacy of her memory in a living White and male body.

White Girl, am I living the same thing?

I am blown away by Luke's story and I know you can relate on many accounts.

White Girl.

Ronnie, it would be too convenient for you to have once lived as a White woman during the U.S. Civil War. We were told this once during a psychic reading! But clearly, you are here in this incarnation with me stuck inside to learn something, absolutely.

And I have questions, too.

What are the chances that Luke and his family not only have Cincinnati connections, but also live on the same side of town in a nearby neighborhood that's just minutes away from where we live? What's the big take away?

Are we all ultimately becoming one another? Or have we really been the same all along? What does this mean for consciousness? How can we foster that and

---

60   Stratford, "Do You Believe."

move to that direction?

Everything really is connected. We do attract the kinds of stories and people into our lives that reflect where we are.

(*Talking through video. The sketched outline of the White Girl is effectively watermarked into the video featuring Tiago's story. As Ronnie occasionally glimpses and internally reacts to the video, his consciousness is unearthed. The White Girl speaks through her own quiet reactions to Tiago's story. She overlaps with the displayed footage.*)

Ronnie:

Maybe. I wonder if Luke's sensibilities would mature in a similar way like Tiago, the White male student at the historically Black male Morehouse College.[61] Tiago said that

he wants to "[decentralize] the attitude of Whiteness."[62] He just naturally gravitates toward the Black community.

In this there's great love of the self as well as for the culture. Tiago embodies the soft sensitivity that translates into the valor that's needed to be a love warrior. Cornell West would be proud.

Luke's story, as well as Rachel Dolezal's, and Caitlyn Jenner's all showed up in the same year of 2015. Fittingly, that was the same time I was finalizing my dissertation on transgracial identity and diversity leadership.

This is a part of a grand design. White Girl, we are *Stranger Things*.

61   David Jones, "Why a White Student Attends a Black College: Son of Ex-Harrisburg Coach Feels he Belongs at Morehouse," Penn Live, August 28, 2018, https://www.pennlive.com/sports/2018/08/tiago_rachelson_morehouse_vice.html.

62   "What is it Like Being a Non Black Student at an Historically Black College?" Slauson Girl, June 29, 2018, https://slausongirl.com/what-is-it-like-being-a-non-black-student-at-an-historically-black-college/.

SIMILAR SOULS

While driving, Ronnie continues to be confronted by his thoughts. A collage of childhood memories floods his psyche as he grapples with authentic reflections that smack into the soundtrack of some of his seminal life moments shared with the White Girl. Scenes of Kimmy Gibbler from Full House, *the anonymous blonde ponytailed girl behind the gray fence, Joan Jett rocking out, Norma Rashid anchoring the news, and a nameless boho/soho chic White female swirl about Ronnie's consciousness. Melodies of Joan Jett's "Bad Reputation," Michael Jackson's "Bad," Billie Eilish's cover of Michael Jackson's "Bad," and Funkadelic "(Not Just) Knee Deep" meander in the souls of Ronnie and the White Girl in unison with the songs unleashing through Ronnie's Android cell phone.*

Ronnie:

I think of Ja Du.

There's something bigger than just our own truth. It seems the transgracial phenomenon is a pattern that's lightly scattered in different corners of the earth.

Ja Du's story surely resonates with me.

In spite of being born White and male, Ja Du identifies as a Filipino female.[63] She started a Facebook support group and she appeared on Tucker Carlson's program on the Fox News Network to discuss more details about her identity.[64] Based on what I've read and seen about her, she seems to fit with the transgracial framework, too. Transgender identity interlocks with the transracial identity again—in this pattern. Refreshingly, Ja Du did not seem to take herself too seriously—but she held firm about being sold out to her identity.[65] It's real.

I think it's even more interesting given that Ja Du does not identify on the White-Black axis. Even though she was born White, she has a connection with not only a completely different race, but also a nationality as well.

White Girl, to me, this is yet just another strand in the varied and complicated construction that is transgracial identity. Ja Du has helped to emphasize the desirability and beauty of women of color. And she, along with others, has helped me to further appreciate the magnanimous beauty and complexity of darker women, too. The beauty and desire are there in splendid diversity. And yet, White Girl, you are bringing me to the point to honor and acknowledge the beauty in our truth.

White Girl:

Ronnie, when you see Ja Du, I am reminded of Oli London.

Also, born White and male, Oli recently identified and presented as a nonbinary Asian individual. He is still transracial, but now wants to transition back

---

63 "White Man Explains Why He Identifies as a Filipino," Fox News, December 7, 2017, https://video.foxnews.com/v/5670529484001#sp=show-clips.

64 Ibid.

65 Ibid.

to male – and that is his right. Yet I can't help to point out, though, that Oli based his transition to look like someone else. Ronnie, we're inspired by many others, no doubt - but we are working to unearth me -- the real essence from within your form. Oli has been immersed in the Asian culture and is reborn because of it. He has been surgically re-sculpted to align with their truth more fully. Ronnie, I am ready for you to get back to your canvas and make the art of your flesh meld with the story of authentic consciousness. Souls like ours are out there and doing it for ourselves—we boldly disrupt the cultural boundaries.

(Sketched Outlines appear of the White Girl reveling in Caitlyn or "Lul Kate's" story, as featured on Dr. Phil.)

And I was so excited to see a transmasculine and transracial story, too. Ronnie, through your eyes, I see more identity complications. I remember Caitlyn, aka "Lul Kate," who was born White and female, and has championed a "thug life" where she (at least at one time) identified or wanted to be seen as a 6'5" Black male, as confirmed by their father. Lul Kate appeared on *Dr. Phil.*

I get how some might be insulted with Lul Kate's stereotypical take on things. And if this is just for sport—or is a misguided phase—then for sure it is cultural appropriation and that cannot be tolerated. But just the same, I appreciate Lul Kate's bold fearlessness. Ronnie, it could be really interesting if we met them. The balance between our misaligned presentations could probably bring us a fantastic symmetry.

And at the same time, I live the reality of having my authenticity cloaked. I know the other side of being the opposite of everything. And so do others— right here in the land of our birthplace. We all need to band together.

(Images of Ohio farmland, hills, valleys, and streams abound. Ronnie and a silhouetted outline of the White Girl lace through and traverse the corners throughout the geography of Ohio. The landmass speaks.)

East Jackson, Ohio: White and Black

And Ronnie, we are linked to our ever-growing Ohio histories. Cincinnati's factions and the Mason-Dixon line speak to the currents in the Underground Railroad and those hidden within the Buckeye state. The whispers extend from us, Luke, and your colleague to travel to Ohio's eastern enclaves. For years, an entire community of people in East Jackson have appeared as White while respecting, knowing, and appreciating that they are Black. Their authentic souls are in an even larger section of the state made up of many people of who are older than us with so many interconnected histories to explore.

What's the connection between Lul Kate, Ja Du, and Luke Ruehlman, your colleague who was born as White and male but identifies as Black and female? Not to mention the East Jackson, Ohio, community. It's radical, raw, and uncanny. Complex identity is a part of us all. It's as if we are linked by some kind of invisible through line where time, age, popular culture, education, geography, and more weaves through each of us. What is the central message?

Ja Du and Lul Kate embody the different identity kaleidoscopes. One was born male bodied but identifies as female. And the other was assigned female bodied but identifies (at least in part) as male. But each share an affinity for and allegiance to seeing themselves as people of color. They share that intersection. And with Oli London's Asian nonbinary identity truth, the spectrum expands.

Ja Du, Oli, and Lul Kate are also relatively close in age. But Luke and the sum of us, Ronnie, are several years apart. In that way, we all speak to and accent different versions of time clocks. We seem to be linked in part through the paranormal, the pop-cultural, the geographical, and of course, through the intersectional. We are kindred. This is a good fire that burns—the eternal flame that shall definitely remain. All of us are forced to confront the unlikeliest kinds of identities—even if just for a time. Either way, it seems that an inevitable linkage continues.

WHITE HOUSE VISIT

• Arlington, Virginia & Washington, D.C. •

As Ronnie's imagination and psyche continues to be activated, he grapples with what seems to be an animated White House—the building talks. Every president is in the distance—in watermark form. See the paintings of the Democratic and Republican presidents. The recollection of the actual White House visit swirls in the psyche. And Ronnie and the White Girl process the event.

Ronnie:

For sure, White Girl, our life is a paranormal and spiritual androgyny. And to understand it all demands a leap of faith. We truly reached a high point of accomplishment during our brief Obama White House tour. And I now can appreciate it in a completely different light. For me (and for us, White Girl), Obama's book *The Audacity of Hope* extends beyond its original message, and

I find I'm hanging on to it. The impossible really can be possible. In that moment, we toured that building and trounced on all of the opposition in our journey—we were making significant headway. I brought that little shred of light with me wherever I went after that. White Girl, this is the light I use to place the dark of my letters onto the white of your consciousness. It is me writing. And it was duly needed.

Swiss psychiatrist Carl Jung has helped me to balance the striking differences of the dark and the light. I bask in Jung's quote, and I now know that:

"[W]hen an inner situation is not made conscious, it happens outside, as fate … when the individual remains undivided and does not become conscious of his inner opposite, the world must perforce act out the conflict and be torn into opposing halves."[66]

We cannot be torn apart. We can't be torn asunder. I agree—we do have to remain whole and united—I just do not always know what to do with this responsibility.

White Girl, I will keep adding the dark of my letters to your bright, white consciousness.

We are co-captains of our ship, seeking not to be led by fate and circumstance; we want to guide the direction of our sails.

Again—the background of the white Fay apartments and townhomes on President Drive collide with the president's White House on Pennsylvania Avenue. White Girl, could you hear all of the voices and bustling labor from my ancestors in the background? What legacy lies beneath the surface of the White House? There had to have been an underground community—a thoroughfare—just as it is underneath the old School for Creative and Performing Arts. This was a high moment for us during one of our lowest points of mental health and well-being.

---

66   Carl Jung, *Aion* (Princeton: Princeton University Press, 1979): 70-71.

Ronnie Gladden standing in front of a West Wing White House door during a visit.

Ronnie Gladden inside of the White House Press Conference Room.

Deep in a personal depression in my early 30s, White Girl, I wasn't sensitive to your needs. Fittingly, at that point I was not writing to you. You were not in full consciousness, so I guess the tearing into the "opposing halves" as Jung warned was happening without me really knowing about it. Or maybe I just did not care at that time.

I sleepwalked through life and did my best to function. This is when the psychological armor was at its heaviest. And you know I had not told many people about you. Again, your consciousness waned. Only the psychologists and a couple of confidants knew of our reality. I told one of my colleagues about you to shine a little more in consideration for a job opportunity. But in spite of my attempts to close you out, you were coming through. White Girl, your nomadic walk from my unconscious to conscious quickened and you had my full attention. You were journeying to cross the border.

White Girl:

And just as we had sailed to Santa Maria to start our learning journey years earlier, I reawakened while tagging along with you, Ronnie, at your first major teaching job. I had no idea you would meet a colleague with a very similar identity—White and male but with an internalized Black and female sensibility. But Ronnie, you should be ashamed for exploiting me, in the process.

Nevertheless, I was filled with life when hearing your colleague's admission. Could it really be that another fellow transgracial soul was actually among us? Surely he was just trolling us. What are the odds that someone else would hit back with the same truth? But upon a closer look, the brash neuroticism and the frenzied hot air locked in your colleague oddly mirrored a familiar strain I've known between us, Ronnie.

Ronnie, the tensions between you and your colleague totally slam and grate together like we do. It is the transgracial tectonic shifting at work. In brief moments of projections, parts of my Kimmy Gibbler and Joan Jett avatars interacted with the Queen Latifah archetype inherent within your colleague. I still can't believe the parallels. Ronnie, the Queen Latifah persona is indeed a regal and interesting allegiance for your colleague. But for your coworker, the internal grating only lasts in his mind. He is not compelled to light up this consciousness and manifest the expression in the way I am pushing you to do, Ronnie. There's been no compunction for your coworker to transition. That's where we differ. (And I love Queen Latifah, by the way – set it off!)

ELDERS & LEADERS

Memories and flashbacks of elders and leaders quickly appear just after the White House visit. Ronnie is driving from the CVG Airport while reflecting on the experience. And while in transit, the elders and leaders from Ronnie's past seem to talk through universities and institutions. The buildings (University of Cincinnati, Xavier University, Miami University, Northern Kentucky University, University of Cambridge) emanate a light. The students, staff, faculty, and other community members of higher education highlight the need to integrate. The White Girl shares in on this experience with Ronnie.

Ronnie:

What are the chances that Gregory H. Williams, the former president of one of my alma maters -- the University of Cincinnati, discovered along the course of his life that he was Black, despite appearing, presenting, and believing all the while that he was White? He captured that experience in *Life on the*

Color Line: The True Story of a White Boy who Discovered he Was Black. There is clearly a profound design at work. I was a long-time UC student who later became a part-time UC instructor. The studying and the teaching locks with the other Cincinnati cultural connections and paradoxes that really illuminate us, White Girl. Slavery and freedom. Black and White. Male and female. Academics and the arts. There's some kind of lesson to be learned. How can there be so many seemingly unrelated connections to our transgracial identity? This won't let up—this kind of reckoning can take a lifetime. Verda Byrd's book *Seventy Years of Blackness* definitely shows that. White Girl, I see that we are not alone, after all!

White Girl.

Ronnie, like Gregory Williams, I have been forced into passing, too. The world sees me as you. This is a trope reversal—it is the exact opposite dynamic of Nella Larsen's book *Passing*. I do not function in my White and femaleness but I am seen as Black and male. I am doubly masked. And yet subtly, you get to be a quasi-kind of White girl – in a cultural sense – similar to how Hilton Als has described. When you're buried under the weight of double cloaks, the darkness nearly always feels like flailing in outer space. There is an otherworldly and far out cosmic feel to it all. Yes, it is trippy. Ronnie, I guess in this way, we are all Evie from that old late 80s sitcom *Out of This World*. And we're each our own brand of a *Small Wonder*. We are all challenging something and moving toward a new kind of avatar. The sum of my parts goes beyond the sum of my skin and biological ancestry.

We're truly not alone.

MYTHOLOGY

• Mt. Adams •

As Ronnie continues to drive, he makes a stop at the Cincinnati Art Museum. That visit helps Ronnie and the White Girl to draw new meaning and interpretations from Botticelli's Painting (The Birth of Venus):

"You're shaped to receive this kind of flow. As the wind whirls you will soon be in the know."

(While viewing the work, for a minute, it seems as if the painting speaks just to them.)

Ronnie:

Born in October and under the sign of Venus, it turns out I am a Libra, according to the astrological lore. And with a Libra Rising also accompanying my star sign—that makes me a "double-Libra." I have a "double-portion" of Venusian energy. And White Girl, that is fitting for our double-birthing to spawn a Black male body and a White female consciousness.

And now that astrological clock is at work again.

Looking back, I wonder what the imprints on the black sheet of the 1980s night sky were whispering as a small child in my grandmother's red Winton Terrace complex. The extra chatter might have come from the extra Venusian reserve—it must have been chatter just for you to hear. Time and geography collided.

And it is all the more uncanny that Luke Ruehlman—the White boy with influences of what seems to be the reincarnation of a Black female soul—shares not only a midwestern connection with me, but the *same state* within the Midwest.[67] And not just the same state—but the *same city*, too. The sky and *The Birth of Venus* apparently has a lot to say and is ramping up her influence.

Luke and I practically even inhabited the same neighborhood. We are separated by different birth years and racial presentations. But Luke and I embody a very similar incongruent framework—we live the opposite of everything. And it is perhaps a forced astrological alchemy with planetary clocks of time at play. This is the fate of the double birthed. And this is surely what comes with having a double portion of Libran stars.

---

67   Stratford, "Do You Believe."

White Girl:

And so, Venus, the Roman Goddess—who embodied love, beauty, fertility, and wealth—resonates with me. Her image in the painting could just as well be placed with Joan of Arc, Rita Hayworth, Elle Fanning, and my other descendants. Ronnie, Venus is an avatar I can cling to, and it only makes sense we were born underneath such symbolic rulership. Like the paranormal, this is part lore, part conjecture, and superstition. But when you are looking for answers to make sense of our crazy displacement, you'll research, study, read, write, and listen to all of the lore and lessons you can get your hands on—or your neurons on. You know I live for those poignant insights to fill the gaps caused by my pain.

I move to meditate and work to fill and heal the trenches of my mind and essence. I still want to hear what the goddess has to say. In *The Birth of Venus,* she is just about to say more. Yes, I have the flow—but the flow does not fill my form. The answer must be in the rulership. I can see it and *feel* it. But nothing emerges just yet—it is a continual cycle of just starting and then suspending. Maybe this "double-portion" means you have to wait twice as long for the delivery. Ronnie, does this help you, too?

NUMEROLOGY

• New York City, The Metropolitan Museum of Art, "The Met" •

Amid the backdrop of a memory exiting an Uber in NYC, and while continuing to grasp for meaning, Ronnie and the White Girl muse at the uncanny linkages between numerology symbolism and the alignment of cultural figures, events, holidays, and very poignant celebrations—many of which happen on the same day of Ronnie and the White Girl's birth. The cards and mathematics speak. Animated historical images of First Ladies Eleanor Roosevelt and Michelle Obama interact, along with other depictions of cultural aesthetics.

Ronnie:

According to the rules of numerology, the number "11" is symbolically rich—and it just so happens to be a part of the cornerstone of my existence.[68] According to the numerological lore, I am endowed with an "11 Number" personality and I was born on the "11th" day of the month. "11" energy is intuitive and kinetic – White Girl, that is perfect for handling our double-conscious interdependent blend. And fittingly, the "1" number symbolism, consequently, is deep within my interiority as well.

I was born in the month of October. But from the numerological perspective, the tenth month of the year brakes down to 1 (10/1).

And I also have inherited a "1" life path number—which points to blazing an independent path.[69] These underlying abstractions are uncanny symbols and theories that strangely align with my very true to life experiences and dynamics. There's the struggle of looking at all of the rich symbolism that just may be a form of poetic justice.

Born on 11 October, it turns out that just so happens to serve as "National Coming Out Day" in the LGBTQ+ universe.

The 11th is also shared with Eleanor Roosevelt.

What a quintessential progressive person who just so happened to be embodied within a White female form. Mrs. Roosevelt was also rumored to function as a part of the LGBTQ+ spectrum.[70] If nothing else, it is safe to say that she was an ally—fully concerned with regard to civil rights.[71] I second that that as well.

And now, the 11th day of October is designated as the International Day of

---

68   Aliza Kelly, "Numerology Numbers: What is Your Life Path Number?" Allure, December 1, 2021, https://www.allure.com/story/numerology-how-to-calculate-life-path-destiny-number.
69   Ibid.
70   Marc Peyser, "Eleanor Roosevelt, The First Lady of Gay Rights," HuffPost, June 20, 2015, https://www.huffpost.com/entry/the-first-lady-of-gay-rights_b_7608122.
71   Ibid.

the Girl, as declared by Michelle Obama.[72] A concerted effort is underway to foster the self-esteem of girls and young women throughout the globe. It is truly an enhanced expression of female power, without doubt.

Doubly interesting, October is also LGBTQ+ History Month.

These dates and months are definitely important and seem to sync with much of what has organically developed out of my personality. The theme of identity and authenticity is absolutely apparent.

And 1978, our year of birth and embodiment, also coincides with the same time of the formation of Pride colors. Harvey Milk led the way.[73]

It's also the same year that Gilbert Baker created the original Pride flag, which returned to its birthplace in San Francisco in 2021 after being lost for over 40 years.

White Girl, you revealed yourself to me in 1982—the year that I turned four years old.

And now—as of this writing and debut year of our book —it is nearing 40 years later.

I've been lost.

You've been lost.

But we are returning to our birthplace—we are circling back to the time we originally met.

And through this long journey, ultimately, I learned we're more than just Black and White.

---

72 Michelle Obama, "Michelle Obama: Educate Every Girl," CNN, October 11, 2018, https://www.cnn.com/2018/10/11/opinions/international-day-of-the-girl-michelle-obama/index.html.
73 Lyanne Melendez, "Original Rainbow Flag Returns Home to San Francisco after Being Lost for More Than 40 Years," ABC 7 Chicago, June 6, 2021, https://abc7chicago.com/rainbow-flag-pride-gilbert-baker-harvey-milk/10748503/.

White Girl.

We are all of the colors in the rainbow.

We are the spectrum. White, Black, Hispanic, Chicano, Chicana, blended, Asian, transracial, trans*gracial*. Male, female, genderqueer, agender, nonbinary, transgender. We are all of the races, genders, and ages. We're the currents of humanity—just a small slice of it just so happens to embody and coexist in this compartment. We're seeking the whole.

I guess it would be fitting if we wove together our own kind of special color tapestry—our own flag, Ronnie.

You are a unique version of Black. And for me, well, that makes my experience a different kind of shade of White. What do our shaded embers look like on their own? And how would our separate tones look if blended?

It is nearly 40 years later.

And I am ready to leave this wilderness. This probably should have been a much shorter journey.

Releasing me to be embodied would be the ultimate birthing.

ASTROLOGY

• Denver International Airport—en route to Boulder, CO. •

While being driven in a shuttle, Ronnie reflects on the symbolism of the astrological configurations. Ronnie and the White Girl draw parallels that seemingly correspond with the movement of the stars. The sky and the cosmos seem to speak via the transits, and Ronnie and the WG offer their interpretations while sealed under the heavens. The cosmos will dazzle while contextualizing the nebulousness that is humanity.

Ronnie:

It seems that these rights are going to be delivered one way or another. The symbolism meets the seethe. Reparations are coming in parts of North Carolina. Statues are falling. Buildings are being renamed. In Cincinnati, even Marge Schott is booted in some places. Cities may be renamed, too. We are at once in the midst and the aftermath of America's Pluto return. The earliest and the original sins are thrown back at us. This time change must happen all around us. The culture wars are firing up. But, White Girl, what change must happen within us?

The Neptune half return is on the way to unfold.

It's emerging and the whispers of our spiritual awakenings are growing beyond the ASMR.

Perhaps I was destined to have race, gender, and identity at the forefront of my life.

It's time that the African corporal lyric reconciles with the European take over. The earthly and bodily maps need to be redrawn in the process.

But I guess I'm lazy.

It'd be nice to have the convenient and the more predictable kind of identity and civil rights.

White Girl:

Ronnie, you really did think that I was gone. I can see that. After the death of your childhood, half-sister, and wearing the weight of a Black male masculine plate—surely one would think all of that would have protected you from someone like me.

Even your productive distractions could not keep me at bay.

Theater, broadcast news ambitions, and sprinkles of social activities didn't delay my exorcism; it extinguished it. My consciousness was full all the while and it pushed through all of the resistance. You know this now more than ever.

Ronnie:

I felt great to rock an agenda that seemed like a path toward leveling up to higher planes in life. It felt good on so many levels. But in truth, it seemed like a kind of second-best reality.

Deep down, I knew that the way I presented was not truly all that I wanted. I thought I could settle for it with the buzz and allure of a newfound approach to filling up my time in life. Recently, Dr. Siri Sat Nam Sing, the celebrity psychologist connected with me. Our time was amplified in part because he has worked with a lot of the latest cultural figures (and those of yesteryear – he once performed with Eartha Kit).[74]

Dr. Siri—as he is affectionately known—told me that you, White Girl, are a leftover archetype from another place in time. You're not just crestfallen but you are sky fallen. You are Lilith. White Girl, your bright star is mixed with black holes of the cosmos. The Sagittarius Centaur has a strange companion. White Girl, your disparate parts make you a very complicated mix. You're in me and you're angry. Dr. Siri felt your heat. He sensed that and told us that through Zoom. "She is angry." He emphasized this with a deep and sincere forlorn during the therapy session.

"I have to go to the spirit level with you." Dr. Siri went on.

I've *been* in the depths of the spirit level with you, White Girl. He summed up how I've felt for so long. And I know you loved Dr. Siri's acknowledgment, too.

---

74   "Dr. Siri Sat Nam Singh," Alumni Association: Pacifica Graduate Institute, 2009, https://pgiaa.org/team/dr-siri-sat-nam-singh/.

SYNTHETIC HUMANS/
WEST WORLD

Headed toward the Nokia Building in Helsinki, Finland, Ronnie is a passenger with several other peers who are traveling by a tour van—a professional chauffeur drives the vehicle. Digital sights of Finnish landmarks would intermittently appear on screens within the van. Yet Ronnie reimagines AI simulations and technology appearing. The images forecast new capabilities of altering human appearance. In the reimaging, Ronnie listens to forecasts of what's next for communications and appearance alterations in the quest for a more technologically sophisticated reality. Fittingly, Ronnie begins to think of how he is impacted, and the White Girl does the same. Shape-shifting humans and technology animate in the background. New possibilities abound.

Ronnie:

This might be the next frontier in moving to some high flouting integration.

At some point, the spirit and soul will radically mesh with science, analytics, and algorithms. The intersection with technology creates a varying kind of digital footprint that encourages practically anyone to play with the various forms of the personae, soul, and psyche. And ultimately, there will be an opportunity to synthesize an authentic avatar that aligns best with one's true identity.

It would be a compromise. White Girl, you imagined that consciousness surgery that appeared in your *Golden Girls* dream. Would we have to wait for the 2045 project? The thinking is that we could save our consciousness and then match it with the avatar later on—in 2045. You'll get to be you. Is that too presumptive and too far away? All we have is now!

White Girl:

Ronnie—I am *not* waiting that long.

We have already loaded our consciousness—it is in this book.

I am now ready for you to use the existing technology to shape your body to release me. A new house that is our aligned flesh will appear—and it will be our authentic avatar, just the same.

If you want to preserve this version for the future—then maybe that can work, too.

We could be immortal and in true form.

But there's a chance to complete parts of this so much sooner. Blockchain, Web 3, the multiverse, and the Metaverse can be a new digital home for us and others with a similar journey. It would be our new intersectionality. We would bind the physical with the digital and our true interiors. We'd be rebuilt for the great new reboot. A digital, human palimpsest. This would be the dawning for the rest of our lives.

And yes, Ronnie, that is like the consciousness I dreamt about. Who would have thought my *Golden Girls* dream would be a sign pointing to our future.

Maybe the strength of my neurological nomad energy could be helped by Elon Musk. There just might be more possibilities yet. Just think about it.

BREASTS AND WHITE

• Mt. Lookout •

While driving through the Cincinnati suburb of Mt. Lookout, Ronnie is confronted by a recollection from summer music camp. Ronnie recalls sharing his truth with a fellow camper in a college dorm. Camp was held on a university campus. Along with the flashbacks, aesthetic-laden, Instagram-esque images flood Ronnie's psyche as the recollection unfolds while recounting the discussions with Tim, Ronnie's roommate and fellow camper. In hindsight, through Ronnie and Tim, the imagery of the White Girl speaks in abstractions—parts of her begin to slowly emerge within shadowed spaces of the dorm—albeit in an awkward adolescent sort of manner.

The body speaks: Camp.

White Girl.

Music camp was sweet. At this point, the memories are long sealed away in a kind sepulcher of the soul with golden sounds and a feel that helps to "steal me awhile from mine own company," in the way Shakespeare wrote in *Midsummer Night's Dream*.[75] Those times are gently buried within our depths.

It wasn't just about the music or the dancing and the acting during the musical theater numbers, for that matter.

It was also about the late-night talks in the dorm.

Ronnie:

White Girl, the weird science that's certainly our future emerged during our past. Embedded in part bucolic surroundings, artistic flare and process, midwestern farmland, and university lore—we made the magic of camp in the middle of every June during the teen years. The dorm talks were their own kind of theatrical majesty. And I do recall parts of my simple conversation with Tim.

"I can't imagine you with breasts and White," Tim gently reasoned.

"Why not?" I nearly sorrowfully wondered.

"I just can't," Tim politely leveled.

I think that he tried. The truth and Tim's reaction rang out in the air.

White Girl:

Ronnie, Ben had already figured you out and must have really ignited something within us. I didn't think you would tell our truth just a year later. But it was in camp after all, and you'd likely never see Tim again.

I can understand his disbelief and confusion today. But at the time, after having kept a lid on the situation for so long—Ronnie, I think you couldn't

---

75   "A Midsummer Night's Dream," in *The Norton Shakespeare*, ed. Stephen Greenblatt (New York: W. W. Norton, 2008), 3.2.

understand how someone else was unable to appreciate where we were coming from.

Ronnie:

I remember Tim telling me:

"It's funny, my dad teased me. What if a big Black guy is your roommate for the week?"

Well, I bet Tim and his dad couldn't have guessed there *would* be a Black (appearing) male roommate, but he would be hosting a White girl soul, to boot. With that dynamic, I guess were kind of big.

"Yeah," I chimed back with a wry smile.

My wistful response slowly grew to a genuine laugh. All of this is a wild cosmic joke. An ultimate *Freaky Friday*, for sure. Maybe Tim was right. My claim to him must have been as crazy and as much of a parody as the "That's My White Mama" sketch on *Mad TV.* That's where a White man was driving his car, hits a Black woman and kills her in a car crash, and they each swapped spirits.

White Girl:

I never thought you would tell, but our armor was definitely getting too heavy. The equipment had grown bigger than both of us. Sometimes the weight of internal apartheid can't be sidelined. It all has a way of packing a wallop and fleeing. This is our own Nat Turner rebellion. The topsy-turvy stuff of new rushes of testosterone compels speech from the masculine as well as the feminine. We were one in this embodiment then as much as now. Maybe at the hint of any safe space, the Truth could just flow out. Even with disclosures, it doesn't mean that everyone is on board. I remember Ben.

Ronnie:

For sure. My eighth-grade dorm camp talks reminded me of third-grade phone calls.

"You can't call Ben anymore," I distinctly remember my mother sternly concluded.

On the phone, I engaged in instinctive curiosities.

"How did race come into it?" my mom went on to ask.

Ben had questions about race and gender.

And I thought at the age of nine, I had answers.

But this was a different Ben. A skinny wiry child with lean cold conservatism coursing through his veins. Third-grade Ben was a sharp contrast to the seventh-grade Ben. Third-grade Ben stunted the conversation. Seventh-grade Ben ignited the dialogue—he jumpstarted our arrested development. Yet each of them in their own way helped us to explore the root of our racial and gender intersections.

The reaction was strong and both of the Bens bent me to my knees. Maybe the childhood Bens hail from Benjamin Franklin. Both of the boys had an ability to bottle flashes of electric insights that jolted us. But White Girl, I think they always reacted to you, so apparently, we jolted them just the same. And on the back end—Tim was honest and straightforward in his reaction. But again—in the unspoken—he just wanted to understand us.

White Girl:

Ronnie, you were Jerry Springer before Jerry Springer was Jerry Springer.

You were that provocative boy pundit seeking meaning and comfort. I just wanted a conversation in what seemed to be a safe and honest space. As a child, I was already tired of fighting. I suppose I wanted to stand up and shout. But fighting took on many forms and found expressive refinements. Camp was cool.

More growing pains.

UNDERGROUND RAILROAD

• Mt. Adams •

Driving through Mt. Adams and past the Underground Railroad Freedom Museum in Downtown Cincinnati. The Underground Railroad speaks. "Under the earth" setting…animate…and various bystanders and historical figures populate the area. These are unifying experiences. Memories of being in the depths of the MOTR bar in Over-the-Rhine along with the deep basement of the old Performing Arts High School building and a brief trip in the Underground Railroad Freedom Center come colliding. Parts of history seem to be revised as the White Girl emphasizes her own sort of reverse exclusion and being forced underneath into a mental and psycho-social Underground Railroad.

Ronnie:

Looking back, I think I often exiled you to that Underground Railroad. You were sent to the basement of my psyche and soul. And so, fittingly, you often were captive and left to wander in the basement of the building, which just so happened to connect with a part of a portal sewn into freedom.

The portal runs through different centuries, cultures, and terrain. It dances with the Mason-Dixon line—with a perpetual balance—while also advancing and retreating from it—just the same. It hugs so many different regions: the North, South, Midwest, East, and the mid-Atlantic. It's the extension from the abolitions and the Door of No Return. Faint hollers and echoes eddy.

White Girl:

It's a wonder how anyone could be freed in such a labyrinth. The escape to one city that is connected to seven others through seven different hills at the same time, and prominently split with a snaking dynamic river.

I felt a bit of that dissolve, yes, during that whiskey-fueled gambling fight between your father and those two unwanted guests at your grandmother's place in Winton Terrace so long ago. There really is no "King of the Bingo Game," as Ralph Ellison taught us. In your grandmother's apartment at the time, we were not the target of the attack but somehow, I felt we had to be on alert just in case. Call it a flight or fight response. Would the hot violence of the moment in your grandmother's small Winton Terrace flat somehow make its way back to me—even in the dark? I had to be ready. We learned early that maybe we could not take any prisoners and so, yes, I went down to the depths in the seat of your soul. In a kind of holding place—I suppose not unlike that Underground Railroad.

Ronnie:

I was six.

Instinctively, I did what was right, I guess.

Little did I know, just a few years later, at nine I would start building an important artistic and academic foundation at The School for Creative and

Performing Arts atop of the bones, spirit, and the ash heap of that underground place.

White Girl, what did you plot? What did you see while you were underground?

White Girl:

Could you hear Sojourner Truth? I did. She sure was a woman, no doubt. And a warrior.

"Ain't I a Woman?" Truth asked.

Her question just met with mine.

What was I? A woman?

Not quite.

A girl?

In one of the most interesting of ways.

Female?

In essence, for sure.

But I looked for my outer form.

What did they say above ground?

And were they skeptical of you?

Ronnie:

Superimposed on the freedom was often times superficiality mired in mixes of smugness, sinister deeds, and earnest gut-flowing passion to make art and craft. It was tough enough to figure all of this out without the burden of another passenger, you see? You have to understand that.

White Girl.

"Ain't I a woman?" as Sojourner Truth asked in her rousing speech.[76]

Ronnie, well, "Ain't I a person?"

Ain't I a fully sentient presence worthy of the dignity, glow, light, and love of any other?

The outer rugged strength of Sojourner stands in contrast to her plea for feminine validation and recognition.

Oddly, Sojourner was a figure connected with you, Ronnie.

Touches of your face mirrored a similar African symmetry.

Each of you displayed stern, African American features—in excess.

Your six-foot height would have met with her six-foot height. And the passion and focus of your missions would have shared common ground. You're liberators. And certainly, both of you embodied a relevant, ruddy feminine essence—but in you is a real White Girl. Both sets of femininity were (and are) capable. And we respectfully seek our validation. We are the conduit where different kinds of people traveled to make it over.

---

76   "Sojourner Truth: Ain't I a Woman?" National Park Service, https://www.nps.gov/articles/sojourner-truth.htm.

BONE-CHILLER

• Mt. Washington •

Speaking through the play and death, Ronnie's memories and psyche remains active. A poster of the last will and testament designed by the deceased character, Josiah Travers—the patriarch of the Travers family—appears and animates with images and symbols requiring deciphering. Memories from Ronnie's performances in the play well up and the White Girl continues to jockey for inclusion in the personal history. This occurs as Ronnie continues driving through Mt. Washington, a suburb in Cincinnati.

Ronnie:

Identity is a puzzle for most. Seasons change and it's not always easy to land in the next stage. White Girl, at least we had some help with our own kind of Underground Railroad. It was just as good for you as all of our foundational lore and secrets. I think when we were cast in the play *Bone-chiller* we could do more than just go underground—we could excavate to the depths of our beings, down to the bones in that time and place in the eighth grade, 13 turning 14.

We reflected on the shards of American history and complex legacy—just as we had to assert new identities away from our childhood arrangement. I performed on the stage as you held your own, just the same. As teens we grew in concentric circles that often locked with our adult alter-egos.

I didn't realize it at the time, but I can see how I was similar to my character Jerry Devlin. In *Bone-chiller*, Jerry and I both worked to decode the mysteries of the self, partnership, legacy, and family dynamics at the same time.

White Girl:

Ronnie, you did that through the prism of adolescence. The bones of your 14-year-old essence hung well on your character's late 20s or early 30s ruddiness. Yes, the life stages were different—but you dug in and piecemealed an adult character you could project. But did too much studying pollute your soul? What the audience saw was a gutted figure. A young person with a displaced youth that was just as easily buried underneath the rubble of your childhood friends Jane and Andy's house. Your whole self was always only partly present. Somehow that made for the best character.

This was the best of your school as far as I am concerned. The autumn of life often replaced the spring of life. Your young years were often eclipsed by older seasons. That was an incessant *Freaky Friday* form of living. Life and art colliding. Looking back, this had to have been the beginning of the work to begin cracking the code to releasing us.

Bone-chiller's Theodosia Travers embodied many connections to Sarah—your grandmother. Eloise shared similarities with the at times well meaning—but generally vexing behavior by your aunt. And fittingly, I never knew any your grandfathers. They have left their own kinds of puzzles to decipher, as well. It is all so multi-layered. Somewhere in all of that shuffle lies an explanation for why me—a White girl—is continually stuck inside of your Black male form.

Ronnie:

But at least Josiah Travers, the deceased patriarch, left a tangible puzzle to decipher in order to gain access to his will. There were no other tangible forms my grandfathers left behind. For the longest time, I had never seen any pictures of any of my grandfathers. Sparse anecdotes were to boot. There were just scraps of tales that I had to patchwork. The pieces were slight. The background of my grandfathers represented the segments that are the tapestry of my mixed ancestry. Conversions of Blackness, East Indian, and White is in the mix. Yet, at least my paternal grandfather, I hear, was still coded as Black and male, for all to see. In hindsight, the puzzle featured within the play is definitely emblematic of this.

White Girl:

But we now embody a Black man's invisible legacy. Shapeless dark men now overlap with my translucent foundations lying beneath your surface. Ronnie, so much of your grandfather's past—even today—is ghostly. He's a marauder with a message. But what is it? In *Bone-chiller*, the drunk butler was a kind of avatar for uncles in your family that struggled with chemical dependency. And Connie Travers—Jerry's fiancée in the play—was in essence a counterpart to him in a way that I am your counterpart, Ronnie. But our union would enable the long-needed transition.

Ronnie:

Marriage is a staple for adults. But in emerging adolescence and young adulthood, so are new kinds of partnerships. The piercing of the veil that separates childhood lore from the teen discoveries happened. That curtain, in some odd ways, was torn down between me you—us—White Girl.

How would we (and still how do we) reconcile our different romantic cravings for other people? How would we work on developing a system to compartmentalize our respective and divergent feelings and thoughts about all kinds of other relationships?

The puzzle that percolated within began to show outwardly. And this was our first foray into grasping the nuance and the work of all of this. This was the beginning of really complex challenges.

In some ways, the puzzle of identity is not unlike grappling with the fall out of global events. COVID-19. The Pandemic. Whatever it's called. The virus forced a new kind of separation of pieces while further flattening a linked world. Unity in destruction and isolation is a robust paradox that leaves us all for reckoning and purification. You, White Girl, have forced me to quarantine and reflect in the way that you have felt all along. You were born into isolation. Born invisible. Born underneath. You need a host just the same.

White Girl:

And after a lifetime of living vicariously through books, theater, television, and just random characters—for me—just one host will do now. One where I can be expressed in full form, full time. The magnitude is all consuming and at this level is once a century in formation. The wallop of this pandemic hit hard and fast and has left all of societal structures reaching for normal and balance. The enemy is invisible and insidious. It's a war time effort to fight and control the plague. For me, the White Girl, there's a chill of surprising beauty in it.

Another kind of plague that would hit both of our houses was in store.

ROMEO AND JULIET

• Mt. Healthy •

Speaking through the play and medieval times, recreations of scenes and images from Romeo & Juliet *occur. In real time, Ronnie oscillates between an audiobook of the classic work and catching glimpses of scenes from the 1995* Romeo & Juliet *adaptation starring Leonardo DiCaprio and Claire Daines. Psychologically, the White Girl is a bit coyer at this point and is teasing the situation—but still taunting and haunting Ronnie as each converse through mental ruminations and reflections. Just like in all of the other Mile Marker sections and throughout the book, accordingly, the internalized conversations are translated and transcribed onto the page.*

Ronnie:

Comparatively, Jerry and Connie were a marriage of convenience. But *Romeo*

& Juliet were truly soul and solar connected. White Girl—you and me shine with a binding in common with both of the title characters. But not in a romantic way, obviously. Instead, we share a link through a forbidden sense. Our backgrounds are at odds. And our introduction to each other was sudden and unexpected. I confess, we do complement each other.

Yet for the longest time I have not even really seen you. At least up until now, I have not really dared to try to find you—except for those very brief and fun moments in our Fay apartment with the t-shirt and Jehri curl cap on my head. A deep clandestine cloak is eternally laced between us. It's society's doing. But slipping underneath the barrier—I was tempted to take a peek. What would I see? I remember performing this soliloquy from Shakespeare's *Romeo & Juliet* on stage:

> O she doth teach the torches to burn bright!
>
> It seems she hangs upon the cheek of night
>
> As a rich jewel in Ethiope's ear —
>
> Beauty too rich for use, for earth too dear.
>
> So shows a snowy dove trooping with crows,
>
> As yonder lady o'er her fellows shows.
>
> The measure done, I'll watch her place of stand
>
> And, touching hers, make blessed my rude hand.
>
> Did my heart love till now? Forswear it, sight,
>
> For I ne'er saw true beauty till this night.[77]

---

77 "Romeo and Juliet," in *The Norton Shakespeare*, ed. Stephen Greenblatt (New York: W. W. Norton, 2008), 1.5.43-52.

Ronnie & Ashley's Re-enactment from SCPA's Romeo & Juliet circa 1995.

I *did* see true beauty. Not in your face or form. But I took in your light. White Girl, you are a splendid being that is a diamond—yes, you are a rare jewel. In spite of being locked away, all you have left is the depth and luster of your raw honesty. There is no room for anything else. I can't help but to see the connection between my teenage performances as Romeo with how I interacted with you in the adolescent and younger adult years.

An entity like yourself that's caused so much confusion and pain in my life is undoubtedly a spectacle to behold. There really is a marvelous kind of stunning flair about you even though you don't exactly cut a defined figure. But a divine and fierce force—you certainly carve—there's no question about that. You shine. But I certainly remember the darker and more intense moments on stage, too. Mercutio's words still bellow across the SCPA Theater and theater of my soul—as well as the different life stages. Mercutio said it:

"A plague on both your houses!"[78]

It is tempting to blame Mercutio for the problems we have had with our own houses. The legacy of domestic strain within my childhood red house on a hill. And my collapsed emotional state within my ex-girlfriend's house—

---

where you flooded your force onto me to prompt our exchanges of letters. And then of course—White Girl—you want the house of my body that reflects a Black man to instead reflect a White woman. The plague means a lot of different things.

My inner diplomat has taken this approach to disconnect from our tension, White Girl. I've felt that you and I have somehow been at fault. It was at these times I wanted to just end it all. Too much was just happening on the inside of our minds and souls. Sadly, I know too many others feel this coil.

That is our collective conditioning speaking.

Both of us have felt this. Each challenged in such a way that we have to question. Are we worth it to anyone? Are we dejected in just the right places that it keeps us, in any form, fully relating to anyone at all, in the end?

And then, on alternating nights of the performance when I was not playing Romeo, I played his father, Lord Montague.

Talk about working with the father wound and balancing perspectives. As Lord Montague, I uttered with a tenuous reticence:

Not Romeo, prince, he was Mercutio's friend;

His fault concludes but what the law should end,

The life of Tybalt.[79]

In real life, I wanted to conclude the life of things that caused death to sentience that was worth keeping. A kind of transposition happened, too. While Lord Montague sought to avenge for Romeo's involvement in Mercutio's death, maybe, I wanted to avenge for the pain my father inflicted on my mother and me. I wanted to avenge the death of domestic bonds.

----

79   "Romeo and Juliet," 3.1.183-185a.

White Girl.

I was not having that. Along with you and through your ears, I heard Juliet say:

Deny thy father and refuse thy name…[80]

Ronnie, not only have I felt denied and discarded—I fully accept the rejection *and* I throw it back. I hurl that rejection to my lost family and to your father, Ronnie, who caused so much strife and for so long. He's *still* passive-aggressive and self-righteous. He's still irritable—to this day! Ronnie, you are—we are—STILL climbing our way out of that abyss from all of that time ago.

Like Juliet, I certainly wanted you to deny many elements of your own father. I have refused many parts of his signature and that has been bestowed onto me. And I have been denied not just by my father—whoever he may be— wherever he is. But I am denied by the whole lot of my kin. There's no name for me to refuse since it seems that my family refused to even leave a clue as to what and where it might be.

We're all bound in this way.

My family is all of the others who are lost. Those finding their faces, their names, their place—their form. The real three-dimensional life I long for flails in an alternate realm. That displacement is crossed with my life that is a strangely placed literature that makes me the

White female life force that dwells in your being; it's spirit. And I am running to meet your form to start anew. I don't want to linger beneath the mask anymore. And how convenient—of course—just as Juliet in the play sought true connection with Romeo, he went missing. And Ronnie, you are doing the same as you toggle between acceptance and avoidance. I bring the ghosts and the absences.

80　"Romeo and Juliet," 2.2.34.

Ronnie:

I played the character that was banished. Romeo had to go and could only function as a kind of legacy of thought—an ethereal kind of pulse that made too many quicken with a fierce ire and angst. In banishment, he rose more response perhaps than he did in person.

It's like I got to feel what you live. White Girl, you were born into banishment. You can do powerful and even fantastic works. I've been slave to you in many ways, even without realizing it. I am not sure Ralph Ellison quite envisioned this variation. White Girl, with you, my life is a different kind of an invisible man experience. Notice how Juliet is much more prominent in Romeo's absence. You want this. But you didn't need much help for me to play a minimized character in order for you to be more real and strident through the real-life vessel of me.

Romeo was a sweet, tender, sympathetic character much attuned to the feminine principles. His prosaic language and sense of the romantic clearly underpinned the depths of his capacity to empathize and respect the femininity. He is advanced and has a heightened sense of the requisite sensibilities. His brooding and distraught mystique in connection with Rosaline forced him to show his inadequacies and his capacity for pining for unrequited love. Romeo's issues with sustaining connections and mourning the loss of relationships is a parallel to which I am not unfamiliar.

Seeing you, dear White Girl, in an enriched light helped me to realize the pulchritude and aesthetic of life and appreciating how I might interact with other people. There must be something of value in all kinds of folks regardless of where they come from. Even though Juliet is on the wrong side of the cultural expectations and belongs to a different name, custom, and family -- a path to reconciling and connecting existed—even if it had to happen behind a mask and in the grandeur of a party.

The kiss led the way.

Ashley, who played opposite me as Juliet, helped me to gain access to deeper parts of you—my blocked White female within. The brief, pricking electric snaps between our lips helped me to heal and warm the dark shadows. Ashley was a catalyst. The magic of the moment on stage was great. And the structure of the story helped, too. Where better to explore the epic nature of gender and race but in a Shakespearean play? And with an interracial cast, at that. The gender bender and switching helps to play with the race and complex intersectionality that we truly live. Here's to being transgracial.

For me, it was as much apparent in *Romeo and Juliet* as it is inherent within the fabric of *Othello*. I found that my personal race and gender explorations were aptly placed in the old and deep Shakespearean structures—an unwitting literary Underground Railroad for the artistic soul ensued. *Romeo and Juliet* helped to usher each other to the other side so that they could escape the tyranny of social and class restrictions in order to unite and reconcile in love. They code switched, went to clandestine places—gravesites, churches, and the religious authority to make it.

This is certainly true for me, too.

As I have been perpetually masked and often interacting with you, White Girl, in a secretive and sometimes in a grand and opulent context, I wanted to grow up with a sibling.

And at times, White Girl, you were like a sibling in the societal vein that opened up opportunities on the outside world that may have never been possible otherwise.

There are some important connections to the broader humanity context.

But your persistence is getting painful. You're shoving your anima and me to the altar. Strangle me with the medieval and cultural weight of protections that you'll have? Hang me once as a man. And then hang Blackness separately. A double-bodied high-tech lynching from the inside out.

THE KING AND I

• Mt. Airy •

Continued conversations through scenes of the play. Late 19th century aesthetic. Rodgers and Hammerstein overture is in the background through the speaker. Scenes of The King and I *play are intermittently presented as Ronnie drives. The performance seems to be from Lincoln Center in New York City. Flashbacks of Ronnie's performances in* The King and I *occur. He acted in the production during high school. However, re-enactments of the performances invade Ronnie's consciousness as he continues to confront and grapple with the truth of his identity. The White Girl forcibly seeks acknowledgment and expression.*

Ronnie:

The parallels just keep coming. Performing in *The King and I* takes on a whole different meaning and manner, in hindsight. White Girl, you came to live in my body with the plan of taking up permanent residence inside of my body; you wanted to make yourself a home.

I can see the scene between Anna and the king so clearly:

> Anna: "…You did promise me a house; a brick residence adjoining the palace," those were your very words in the letter.
>
> King: I do not remember such words.
>
> Anna: I remember them.
>
> King: I will do remembering! Who is King here? I remind you, so you remember that! I do not remember any promises!
>
> Anna: Oh, no Your Majesty…if you do not give me the house you promised, I shall be forced to return to England immediately.[81]
>
> *(In the original script, Anna plays opposite the king. Yet in this book, the White Girl also is now reimagined as Anna within the scene from the play.)*

White Girl:

Anna had somewhere else to go. I don't. So, Ronnie—you have to give me a house. I can't keep going on like this. I will project my real self before we die. Why do you think we keep going back and forth? It was a major point of tension in the play. And this is a major point of tension in real life. Anna's house was to be her humble abode—a home away from her British sanctuary. My house is to reflect more of my soul in the flesh. You can make it out of Jane and Andy's rubble—that was the stuff of their tall white skinny home.

Ronnie, Anna and I are the same in that we are "scientific." Modern. Inventive. Cutting Edge. We want to offer solutions. It will take a force of science to bring my face into the flesh; I want expression. Funnily, because of her innovation, Anna was seen as masculine in the eyes of the king and his community.

They called her "sir" in the play.

---

81 *The King and I*, music and lyrics by Richard Rodgers and Oscar Hammerstein, dir. John van Druten, St. James Theatre, March 29, 1951.

And I am more of the warrior in you. Ironically, I embody plenty of classically masculine traits inside of my feminine form. You are definitely more retiring and complacent in your Black male masculine cut. For sure, we really are the anima and the animus and the full infinite polarity—and this makes us truly transgender and transracial.

Combined—we are simply transgracial. I wonder who else can relate to this? Who else is bold enough to acknowledge, express, and live out the real opposite of everything? We're bound.

Remember that I am the shapeless White female soul that fills the structure of your body. Somewhere along the way, I felt that I was promised something. And the tangle of our consciousness has often been a shared, knotted hell. My own embodiment would give me the exhale and separateness I've craved to my depths. I've always looked to the promise. That's the sustaining ray that's grafted to the flicker of my blaze.

But I try to do the right thing.

Many times, I felt that I was promised something. And I suppose that you were promised something, as well.

Anna wanted a house. She traveled to a distant land with the belief of recharging in her own little corner. Just her and her son.

I'd get the right avatar and you'd get a decluttered one. The right freedom and the right balance.

Anna needed that from the king. And the king needed to revel in the maturity of his promises. The growth for each was real.

The different cultures could merge, and respect could grow for each.

(*Slavery themes: Eliza from* The King and I *doubles as the White Girl during the re-enactment in Ronnie's mind. The scene of Eliza escaping before the dignitaries. This connection and reference relate to the Harriet Beecher Stowe-Cincinnati connection, as well. Connect with the Underground Railroad theme relative to Performing Arts.)*

Ronnie:

You connect with Eliza, too.

This is a prison within a prison. One creating a direct link to an old world and order of hard Saturn oppression. The other with reluctant modern repression.

I had to face my father many times.

And to you, White Girl—I think you would finally feel the weight of the beatings that I actually felt while growing up. Through the lashings, you felt more than just what happened in the 1980s. You felt the 1950s just as much as the 1850s and maybe even the 1750s, just the same.

The Underground Railroad beneath the old Performing Arts collided with the Underground Railroad of your mind—our shared space for our mental perspectives. The Harriet Beecher Stowe House of Cincinnati merged with the Harriet Beecher Stowe of *The King and I* production. Scraps of slavery against the threshold of freedom is the current running through the centuries and the collectives of three-dimensional form and ethereal intersection. And so many others are connected to us, just the same.

As the king in *The King and I* continued to ponder if he would whip his disobedient slave, I juxtapose and reel from the flashbacks of Mr. Wayne's public censure in middle school before my entire class and years of class bullying. That censure was a verbal and mental lashing. The soda pop backhand mouth slap, the ink pen whippings, and the dresser drawer lashings leveled by the father all came to a head. His slap was a near "back-to-slavery" variety. I see all of these images swirling about—just as the king appeared pensive and ready to dole out retribution on stage. And now, White Girl—it seems that you are about to feel the brunt, as well. I was rocked just as much by your evolving form and frame of mind. You're setting off—just like Eliza did in *The King and I*!

Eliza run!

Let's all run!

Is it my turn?

White Girl, Run!

Eliza escaped to avoid being beaten. You tried to escape to avoid me doing something rash that would do us in. We all seemed to escape from anything that was violent and would render us torn from humanity. My childhood self was there running, too—escaping the father, escaping society, and escaping my future forced masculinity. We all ran. These are my feelings since having you, White Girl, living in me as I performed within *The King and I*.

I must go. You must go.

(Through a dramatic re-enactment, which reinterprets this scene form The King and I, Ronnie is reimagined as the king within the play. In the original script, the king is hesitant to beat Eliza. In the reimagined depiction, Ronnie is hesitant to beat the White Girl, who has taken the place of Eliza in the reinterpretation.)

The challenge of liberation for authenticity is one of humanities puzzles. And we both know this more than most. What's the equation to solve to free us both?

Jerry Devlin in *Bone-chiller* was not the only one who had to put the puzzle pieces together. A king, as in the one from *The King and I*, would have to do the same. And we were all stuck in the middle of this mess. It truly was a puzzlement for us all. The song summed it up beautifully. I see the king in this play in a totally different light. For me and others who are similar, we are all that King in this moment of being at the crossroads—at the edge. Someone has got to be accountable. I want to make that happen—but how? It really is a puzzlement!

The *Puzzlement* Song:

> *There are times I almost think*
>
> *I am not sure of what I absolutely know.*
>
> *…*
>
> *If my Lord in Heaven, Buddha, show the way,*
>
> *Ev'ry day I try to live another day.*
>
> *If my Lord in Heaven, Buddha, show me the way,*
>
> *Ev'ry day I do my best for one more day,*
>
> *But…*
>
> *Is a puzzlement!*[82]

---

82 “A Puzzlement,” Rodgers and Hammerstein, https://rodgersandhammerstein.com/song/the-king-and-i/a-puzzlement/.

"Steal me awhile for mine own company."

—William Shakespeare[83]

---

83   "A Midsummer Night's Dream," 3.2.

MEETING THE WHITE GIRL

• Mt. Echo Park •

Starbucks Coffee Shop interaction. The scene of the proverbial meetup plays out via graphic novel style slides. Avril Lavigne's song "Complicated "plays in the background. The images contrast with the verbiage and internal dialogue and music.

Ronnie:

For all of the running I did, there were times I'd sneak away and connect with you. I always knew where you'd be. I always knew you would want the company, so meeting was never an issue. Having grown up as an only child, I appreciated the conversation. Yet, the girl was more or less smuggled at this point. I selfishly controlled how and when we would meet. But through it all, we've been inseparable since our awakening.

I often imagined, though, what it would be like to actually meet you. Let's graduate from abstract and instinctive talks. I'm ready for some face time as much as that's possible. For as many times as we interacted, it's as if we're telepathically communicated. I instinctively knew what you wanted or how you felt without having to verbally communicate.

Through our shared cells, soma, and carnage—we were sealed in a kind of vessel that greatly limited a lot of privacy. And yet, through imagination, daydreaming, and meditating—we could multiply our landscape. We generated the extra bandwidth and psychic ram to place a distance between us.

But I wanted a meeting. I wanted to interact with you one-on-one. Not as a distant, ethereal passenger floating somewhere within. But I wanted to look at you and see you just as if we met in a misty coffee shop. I'd want to lay everything out.

Scene: Starbucks Meeting

Ronnie: We've been through a lot, huh? Isn't this just a vanity project, really? Are we just bandwagoners?

WG: I have a friggin' responsibility to myself and that's it. The world owes me nothing and the same is true from this way.

Ronnie: This is just a part of the trend of emotional incontinence. We're oversharing and are too distracted, just like everyone else. Don't become a drone.

WG: You can fake it if you want. But that's not what I'm going to do here.

Ronnie: What about people with real problems? Why create a problem if there isn't one to start with?

WG: This is a REAL problem. It's *our* problem. And a real problem for a lot of others like us around the world.

Ronnie: The body betrays everyone. Remember the line we read: "Inside of every 70-year-old there is a 35-year-old wondering what happened?"

WG: You know what we felt and what we went through long before all of the hashtags and movements and memes and all of that.

Ronnie: Time and the body get us all. And even if you are totally matched up, it won't last long before the betrayal starts seeping in. We're at the halfway mark, now.

WG: Hell no. I don't wanna just muck along for another 40 years! And we made it this far? So, you're just saying to give up?

Ronnie: I'll just keep traveling and teaching. I'll keep wearing my clothes and jewelry. We have found a way to manage things; we're coping. We've almost found a part of the tribe.

WG: How much more convincing do you need?

Ronnie: Too much time has passed. I have responsibilities to my community.

WG: Too much time has gone to do absolutely nothing. We are WAY behind. You're walking around here half dead, and you're pulling me in with you.

Ronnie: We're more than just a Black guy and a White girl. We're energy. Why not just work to develop that in a spiritual way?

WG: Don't you think that honoring our real selves *is* spiritual growth? It's just that kind of energy that can really shine bright. It needs to be redirected and sharpened. I am not just wasting my energy and half-assing it. I am tired just making other people comfortable. That's the real drone. This is no propaganda.

Ronnie: You've never had to endure any of the bullying and taunts I've dealt with. I had to COMPENSATE for EVERYTHING! I had to own it all. Your proclivities had to be justified and explained somehow. I only had so much margin in this body and in my time. I've grown damn tired myself of trying to balance this and being the administrator. The executor of all of this. And yeah—I needed respite, so I had to put you away.

WG: And this is not just about you. You were on my side for the longest. And we were both happier then.

Ronnie: Don't you know that our lives were (and are) at stake? You're not that stupid that you aren't aware of the realities around us. C'mon. Who do you think you are telling me that this isn't an option? It's my body. It's my brain. I am in real time. I have carried this load for all of this time. I make the decisions that get expressed and I don't have to negotiate with you. I don't even have to explain anything to you. I don't need to be co-signed.

WG: I am not here to ask you. I am *telling* you that more change is coming; it's *guaranteed.*

I just thought it'd be good for each of us to discuss this. But it doesn't seem like it's going anywhere.

Ronnie: I do what I want when I want and how I want. You haven't had to assume responsibility for a lot of things and so it's easy for you to make blank edicts.

WG: You've shunned me. Kicked me. Banished me. You've put me away in a cage. You've totally ignored me. I don't know how much I can say it—but this ain't optional. I say it again -- you know what we felt and what we went through long before all of the hashtags and movements and memes and all of that. No one recruited you, Ronnie. This just was and it just *is*. I am still here, and it will always be this way. And just think about how you treated me.

Ronnie: I'm trying to be civil here.

WG: I'll show you.

CIVIL WAR

"We are constantly invited to be who we are."
—*Henry David Thoreau*

• Mt. Storm in Cincinnati •

Driving to the especially hilly park, Ronnie is overwhelmed with emotion. From the perch of the lawn cut greenery, Ronnie can see many familiar landscapes and architecture. The collection includes the University of Cincinnati campus, his alma mater. The interstate. The outline of the Fay Apartments, and all of the smaller streets and areas that make up the city seem consolidated and almost immediately accessible from the aerial view. But internally—there is a completely different complex society. The panorama of the three-dimensional world colliding with the internalized psychological one underpins the tensions between Ronnie and the White Girl, which are now coming to a head.

Ronnie:

"ENOUGH!"

Who do you think you are to control me?

And why do you have an opinion where you have absolutely no responsibility?

White Girl—you've got me enraged.

The chaos of the 1992 Los Angeles, 2001 Cincinnati, and 2020 George Floyd riots well up in me now. And the early domestic violent bouts roil my soul, and you are making me lose my cool.

I will do what's needed to purge.

Here we are yet again as history rhymes.

The George Floyd protests and the burning of America triggered blazes with brilliance. And the blaze is a conflagration that melds with the fire and destruction of my adolescence. I'm ready to wrestle with you and all of the principalities that's trying to do me in.

Yes—cast you out!

You have to be destroyed and disinfected.

This torment and anger burn in me as America still boils and brims from the rage of historical injustice. The world is flipped. And I am now flipping out with you, White Girl, in me—flee!

Flee from me and flee from here.

Virus meets virus, and the spread is all fully toxic. This is where we are now. This is what we have to work with. White Girl—we are the protestors.

During those George Floyd riots, the looters destroyed in reckless abandonment. Theirs was a primal liberation that freed even the zoo animals and general order. The aftermath of bashed stores, blanked shelves, closed clinics, and upended societal roots is a senseless doomsday.

And here—in my protest against you—I loot your presence.

I loot the psychological and spiritual cities we decorated in our consciousness.

I swing the baseball bats from my mind. Not from the Cincinnati Reds, but of a different kind of Big Red Machine—my impassioned rage. I throw bombs. I shoot my ammunition at all of the interior cities I can see. This is nuclear. This is where the consciousness and psyche lives. Cars are flipped. Lightning poles whirl in the wind. The sky darkens. Nameless souls behind me are pitchfork mad. They walk in the mob energy ways. Here is that southern twang of badassery coming out. Is this what the aunt and the grandmother had prepared me for all along—to exterminate you because you upset the order?

And I look for you, White Girl. You're evicted. Papers served. Yet I can't see you! I miss the target. So everything is the target!

Yet, I am here lighting the fuse just the same.

The emotions are lost in the childhood rubble of Jane and Andy's house. This is so familiar.

I looted your abstractions and my own soul to avoid you. The careless destruction I did to my body left us with plenty to clean up. I gorged myself to fall under.

Food

Alabama's Fish Bar. The golden heat from whiting strips and thick cod nuggets was a perfect decadent delight to escape. The pale slick slivers of light beige French fries amid the greasy medium fish scent just knew how to beckon. At that point, I nearly loved eating more than living.

LaRosa Pizza. Nostalgia in pizza slices, smiles, and westside lore. Zip's Burgers. PF Chang's. I filled up on Cincinnati food in a way to feel the whole from where I otherwise was abandoned and out of step. I could be quiet and contented through mastication and via a food-induced meditation that kept me away from you. And you, too, were full and concealed with my every meal. It was me fighting back without knowing I was fighting.

And then I drank and out drank you, White Girl—to dissolve.

I needed a wash down.

Smirnoff's. Steel Reserve. Jägermeister. Jell-O shots at 2:00 a.m. Vodka runs at Kroger. These were the distractions that stuff me so that I could stuff you.

And then the hot lava turned against me.

The eruptions of the upcoming volcano of the high blood would be present.

Yes—I wanted to throw you out, White Girl—just as my father ejected and walloped those winos from my grandmother's Winton Terrace apartment.

Parties

The Green Wooden Inferno

Jason's place was a green wooden inferno. While similar in design to my childhood home red house on the hill—Jason's place was distinctly different. The green, stacked three-story wide squat of a house perched atop a different hill on an old, grizzled street always looked like nighttime was upon it.

In the backyard on the deck, a clamor of folks abounded. This buzzing of different souls was a way to get high all onto itself. I was not—we were not—accustomed to so many people around. And the same could be said for being turned upside down.

The fiery liquid of alcohol slithered through me like a snake, slyly forming Ss through the terrain of my body. White Girl, this would surely do you in. Civil war in a bottle. The drink was so strong—it took on its own other-worldly life. And other species. The liquor snaked about and hissed a fire through my throat, chest, and being—it gripped, and possessed my Black and male body—I was choked. And you, White Girl were someplace else. But you did not disappear.

And in it went.

A funnel, and down came that burn. Alcohol's component chemical elixir is an amorphous liquid fire containing a smooth sophisticated blaze. It's jagged and grace all at once. Somehow at Jason's, the liquid bright burn was part witch brew and part store bought hooch handled by the masses—the westside Cincinnati masses. The merging of the tubes and esophagus gave life to a new human form that I had to learn to embody.

Cast out the devils!

Embodying parts of Edgar Allan Poe, I went black.

Lots of dates

White Girl:

Ronnie, even when you thought you destroyed me, you just ran to connect with embodied White females. When you totally ignored me, your ex-girlfriends helped you to find your way back to me. They were the projections of what you want to reflect, all along. You cared for them as best as you could. You always meant well for them and that especially holds true to this day. I remember your exes.

Krissy

There was Krissy. Your naivete slipped away through her. Both of you merged in a ritualistic calligraphy; grace and raw instinct unearthed. You lost your virginity, and I gained a new insight into the rawest connections, too.

Allie

You really wanted to date her at the time. Ronnie, you and Allie met as undergraduates in Spanish class. It was totally wholesome. But her rejection would eventually cut deep. You didn't think it would happen.

Allie's mid-length dark chestnut hair and wide eyes screamed midwestern measurements and predictability. But Ronnie, she didn't appreciate the nuance you brought to dating. Allie wanted the tried and true. You were right—she *was* predictable, and with me in you, there was no way things could have worked. Sure, you wanted to impress Allie. And Ronnie, you wanted to fit within the same kind of middle-America lore that seemed to have the most power. So her rejection hit hard because it really came from the society just as much as it did her.

Erin

This time you were sought out from a high place. Erin's dad was the congressman. And I recall that you both briefly dated during college. Ronnie, your five-month relationship with Erin had a distinct high school flavor. You both frolicked more as friends in your shared circle of acquaintances. But your time was important. And the frisbee golf was good. That's one of the best things that came out of our time together. Ronnie, you were validated at this elevation. Sure, it helped you to recover from Allie. But notice—in the end—you were just doing the work to help me to emerge. I am unbeatable in this war—you have to know that. And then there was the next paramour.

Amanda

sry we have to go back to being friends

Amanda explained through a text message.

But it should have really said:

ronnie, ur black. and i'm white…my family does not want me dating you. 🙁

Amanda was gutted by then. She became a compliant husk that relayed the will of her family. This is where the divide felt the greatest. Ronnie, the rift left a wound that turned into a permanent scar on all of my imprints. And I feel it, too.

I hate that hatred.

But there was a very brief time when it was grand between you and Amanda. That was the only time you felt any kind of magic, I will give you that. You two had a real connection and sweet interests. Bits of electric passion was our undercurrent that one summer night. But her family would not have it. The skin divided it all.

Catie

"I don't even know why we dated," Catie would eventually conclude.

As you both walked away from her brother's high school football game under the moonbeams—Catie's aha moment landed as hard for you, Ronnie, as it did for her. It was a touchdown of the wrong kind. I could feel it coming—but hey, you ignored me, so how could I let you know. Why do you think you are blinded in this civil war?

With Catie, it was the classic case of being in love with the idea of love. The notion was better than the reality. But some meaningful times were there.

Natasha

Ronnie—your pure prurient passion devolved into a stagnant malaise. You were both bad for each other. Enough said with this one.

Lacie

"Marry Lacie!" Becky, Lacie's friend, practically begged you to do this.

It was all in good fun. You were all at some westside bar—in the midst of a pub crawl—being unfashionable in your late 20s in an unfashionable area. But it was good clean fun, for what it was worth.

There seemed to be a lot of mutual respect, at some level. But Ronnie, the family backgrounds were just too different for you and Lacie to ever make it work. That got in the way; you just saw things so differently.

Angela

But with Angela, things were much better. It was better passion and progressiveness. But it was finally at this point—after all of the diversions—Ronnie, you realized that you were not where you needed to be. You had grown out of fighting. You were ready to embrace me—and there I was. I had been inside of you the entire time. So, what's the point of this civil war? Get over yourself and get on with living the rest of your life. That includes finally committing to the right girl for you. Me. In doing so—we will become real. And we will go to heights we do not even know are possible.

Ronnie, you could never truly have been with any of your past loves because of me. I require something much different, and I burn with a blue brilliance. Your will alone could never undo it. Matter can neither be created nor destroyed.

(Psychological bombs detonate. The terrain erupts into a multicolored conflagration. The shrines to all of the hoarded personas explode in aggressive force. Still, a cluster of stars on the shape of an "X" hangs in the sky of Ronnie and the White Girl's psyche. The White Girl emerges from the psychological Underground Railroad. Joan of Arc appears watermarked into the setting and is seemingly near the White Girl—off to the side. The White Girl gestures for Joan of Arc to lower her shield and weaponry.)

White Girl:

The exclusion from the fairy tales. The unseen faces in the TV shows. The TV news escapes. The phantom families. The school bullies. The negative Black males. The grandmother. The aunt. Your sister's murder. Puberty. The seen and the unseen lapped against hidden barriers. The intergenerational wrestled among one another just as hard. We choked on the *Golden Girls'* cheesecake while being punched in the gut from the sentiment of Cosby's pound cake speech; there was no relief. All of the performances from *Bone-chiller* to *The King and I* are swirled and matted within. Indeed, my bones are cold, and any kingly persona left in you, Ronnie, is ailing. You're crying just as you did in Angela's house where you first started to write to me. Get up! Put down the facade. Give up your crown and imperialism. Let me out.

The dissonance drowns. All of these things whipped and whirled into a cyclone that would not skip over anything. It was in me. The twister that twisted from the inside out. The twister of emotions and the past is pitted against the river that is our consciousness. It drowns both of our inner regions instead of separating the outer geography boundaries. And seemingly, Ronnie, you bared the brunt of it all. And all the while, Ben's haunting question ricochets:

"Do you want to be a White girl, Ronnie?"

"Death doesn't hurt—life does."

–Rev. Dr. Donald Parsons[84]

---

84 "Dr. Donald Parson at Aretha Franklin's Funeral," Michael Cooper, YouTube, September 1, 2018, 5:19, https://youtu.be/OB3hXg1zZ5M?t=319.

REBIRTH:
AND THEN THERE WERE NONE

Church and graveyard aesthetics—Spring Grove Cemetery in Cincinnati, Ohio. In this final section of the book, Ronnie continues to drive, albeit leisurely and respectfully, inside of America's second largest cemetery. There is a more conciliatory tone in the air. Spring Grove is made up of hills and values. Gorgeous and aged trees of varying kinds fill the resting space. And elaborate and more straightforward monuments line and round out the park-like setting.

Ronnie:

And now all that's left is just the core. The pomp and pretense have given way to a blank slate. White Girl, we really are mirroring the characters Captain Phillip Lombard and Vera Claythorne in *And Then There Were None*. But it is real life now. It's just us. We are forced to confront each other in an aftermath.

Life and art blurs—and the reality of things weighs hard.

White Girl:

Ronnie, the death of the ego—the worst parts of you and me—need to die and be reborn in order to forge a new bloom. It is just us right now, yes. And we are the only ones that can do our makeover.

Gone are the escapes into old TV sitcoms and local broadcast news. We are pulled out of our dreams. And Ronnie, you have escaped from the fear of your father's hands. We are moving past casting projections on to other people and objects. The externals that we used to hide behind have collapsed. We are against the world. It is time for us to craft our lyric and get on with singing the song that is our life.

Ronnie:

I think we need each other in order to find ourselves.

It hurt to be beaten, bullied, and banished. It hurt to be so torn by a force that we could never really fully grasp.

Having the freedom to live the lives we choose can liberate us from the oppressive shackles of cultural commands.

Perhaps now we can make our own kind of integration project. Both parts of our selves need a baptism and a kind of transubstantiation of the soul and soma, I suppose.

I refuse to downgrade our dream just to fit our reality. I think we really do want to upgrade our convictions to match our destiny. I thank the late Stuart Scott for that insight.

And while we're at it, let's upgrade our conviction to match our new identity.

We are a co-created entity, deserving of equal justice, measure, and expression. This is simply our time to start new.

"You have to be willing to die a thousand deaths and be reborn a thousand times,"[85] says RuPaul, "because we are all God in drag."[86]

It is time for the rebaptism that will be our rebirth.

The deaths of Romeo and Juliet, and the king in *The King and I* represented the loss of adolescent and middle-age angst, which both myself and you, White Girl, are not unfamiliar. And the legacy of Josiah Travers in *Bone-chiller* represented the invisible but powerful nature of leftover consciousness. The living scrambled to make sense of Travers's final desires. What do you want to leave behind? All of these issues parallel our experiences.

It's time to give up the running.

And so, what do you want to do with me?

Yes—Ben asked me, "Do you want to be a White girl, Ronnie?"

I want to be free.

I want us to be free.

Ben is gone; he sadly died young. But his question ricochets with a haunt—it is potent all unto itself and here I am, being a puzzle maker all over again when wrestling with Ben's questions. I am decoding this.

Let's get it together before we're forced to have a final answer, just as Poe said in "Spirits of the Dead." Yes—we are here in this oblivion. And isolated. Poe was right.

"Thy soul shall find itself alone."[87]

---

85   Daniel D'Addario, "RuPaul on Identity in the Trump Era: 'Don't Pick Battles With Your Allies'," Time, June 12, 2017, https://time.com/4813260/rupaul-drag-race-interview/.

86   Tim Molloy, "RuPaul Explains Why 'We Are All God in Drag'," The Wrap, September 14, 2019, https://www.thewrap.com/rupaul-explains-why-we-are-all-god-in-drag/.

87   "Spirits of the Dead," Poetry Foundation, https://www.poetryfoundation.org/poems/48632/spirits-of-the-dead.

White Girl:

Agreed.

Alone I am.

It would be our greatest life's regret not to come to terms with our rich humanity.

All of these personas and other people have gotten in the way of seeing, feeling, and thinking with full-on clarity. How else can we use all of that psychic energy, Ronnie? There is so much to do in the world. There are so many people to help. And we deserve to be enriched in a way that can only come from getting out of ourselves. This has been a long wilderness. The personas have to go. It's time to move on.

You may have to leave Cincinnati and Spring Grove Cemetery—our nation's second largest cemetery.[88] This graveyard is an apt truth and metaphor for being surrounded by a lot of death in such a small area. The call to leave the city may be mounting.

Start anew and reassemble. Stitch the seven fractures that are the seven hills that make up Cincinnati. Funny. Ronnie, we're seeking freedom to leave the place where it once started. We need a release from old locks, edicts, edifices, statues, and stagnations of the soil and soul. Fresh beginnings have got to be good.

Between the two of us, we can integrate the past, present, and future. Ronnie, your outer lyric embodies the historical foundations of time. The tribe of the original people that helped to create life for all others. I realize that now. You are a part of the originals. The past is there.

And inside of you, I am your future.

I belong to the group of people that came after you. And I couldn't have been here without you being there first. With your Black and my White—we are

---

88   Doug Carlin, "Top 10 Largest Cemeteries in the US," January 3, 2021, https://usabynumbers.com/largest-cemeteries-in-the-us/.

the Pangea of the people. Yes—we are yin and yang on an infinite loop. And we acknowledge all of the interlocking of our linkages—White and Black, Hispanic with Asian—there's seemingly no limit to how we crisscross and cross pollinate the identities we have encountered through geography, genetics, history, culture, and aesthetics.

We're moving to a master alignment—an instinctive positioning toward a new enriched integrated consciousness.

Ronnie, we are going to do more with our lives than be a color, a gender, and an intersection.

This is our destiny. And our transgracial roots are just the beginning. This is our deepest bond. The intergenerational. The interracial. The intergender. The transgender. The transracial. We are trans*gracial*. The future calls. Ronnie, the map of Africa may show on your face. But the map of my mind and soul seeks to integrate into its rightful physical embodiment. There is more in the blood.

The present binds. We have the time right now to do something with our circumstance. This is our truth. A full agreement is needed. Everything depends on it.

Ronnie:

Maybe that is one of the biggest lessons that we have to learn from one another—to mesh our most striking differences. White Girl, I'm guilty for feeling that you're a large part of me—the greatest unexpressed part. And then I am ashamed to have repressed you for so long. That is imprisoning for us both.

White Girl:

Ronnie, I am at least living on this page. Throughout all of the years it took to develop our message—I made it here! I fill this book. And I bind my soul to my story and our life's work. Remember, this is where the dark letters on light speak the loudest and I hear you best. This is transubstantiation through transcription. These letters are a major gust of wind in our sails. Keep writing. Through words I will come. I will manifest in three-dimensional form soon enough. I will always be here. This is a great leap forward. And I know that more is to come. My challenge to you was not to menace but to motivate. We've been stuck for too long and it is time for both of us to harmonize and shine. I agree to that. We'll be moving around for sure.

Clarify, purify, and emblazon our worth and goodness. Outside in and inside out.

They'll want to kick our asses for this!

Our new surgeries and soft line modifications will upset, no doubt. Ronnie, they'll say you're adding to the "Buck Broken Agenda." Or you're just another fake "transtrender" and are drowning in your delusions. Drawing me out and drawing me on you, as Dolly Parton alluded, is going to bring all kinds of ire, for sure.

Bring the heat!

And then there are those who just won't care. In the end, this is for us. This is the new arena, and we have to be ready to fight. If there's any upside to your father's cruelty, it's that we've learned how to defend ourselves at whatever the cost.

We tried. This is just the next turning. It happened at the end of childhood and now it's here at the start of the middle of our life experience.

After collapsing from the weight of repression and being trampled upon, I am ready to be lifted. Airborne! Ronnie, let's merge. We can rise not to the blonde assassin but to the bright liberator and elevator. Let me come up and out. And we will visit Casey Frazier's Elysian Fields while singing their lyrics "Give my body to the sun."

(*Driving away, all of the letters are released through the car window and are circling up into the air. A mysterious hand emerges, approaching the car window.*)

part four

Resources

INTRODUCTION

Within this section are a list of resources that may help to foster greater understanding about complex intersectional identity. A mini syllabus depicting discussion questions, along with key definitions, and a list of support services may prove useful to distill notions concerned with identity allegiance and expression. Additionally, you are encouraged to respond to the various questions. Also, I invite you to begin your own letter writing campaign as you and/or an important person in your life unearth underlying trauma(s) or other unresolved issues.

TOPICS AND QUESTIONS FOR DISCUSSION

Part I: Questions for Review

1. What secrets about your identity have you or someone you know kept that is now or soon will be revealed? Why is it important for you or them to share this with others?

2. Similar to the White Girl, have you or someone else in your life had to contend with significant domestic situations? What were the coping strategies?

3. How have you or others to whom you're connected handled their complex intersectional identity? Like the White Girl and Ronnie, does the particular identity have its own label? Why or Why not?

4. How have your dreams helped you to process the reality of your identity formation and your general life direction?

5. Describe any challenges you may have/had with a significant family member. What are the direct implications to your identity development?

Part II: Questions for Review

1. Does your outer image align with your interior self, or does it betray it? Either way, how do you manage the reality? Explain.

2. Do you or have you ever felt an obligation to repress your authenticity when in the presence of your family? Are you doing this for yourself or based on the thoughts and demands from others?

3. Which popular cultural influences do you find most compelling? Why?

4. What kind of impact (if any) do those popular cultural influences have on your identity formation? Explain.

5. Do you feel an obligation to uphold a societal expectation about your image? Why or why not?

Part III: Questions for Review

1. How have you responded to a self-imposed ultimatum? How might the ultimatum pertain to the development of your identity (and of those in your community)? Explain.

2. What steps have you taken to re-express your identity in order to live more authentically? How have you balanced this without disrespecting any assigned cultural and/or ancestral lines?

3. Safety of Objects: How might objects and places in your immediate environment help you to interpret (or re-interpret) truths about your identity? Explain.

4. Describe how you or perhaps someone close to you has worked through their own "Civil War." Explain.

5. Describe how you or an individual to whom you are connected initiated and/or completed an identity rebirth process. How has the transformation helped?

Academic Questions

1. What value do the literary references add to the entirety of the book? Specifically, how might the intertextuality foster understanding regarding complex identity intersectional challenges?

2. How might the thesis of *White Girl Within* aid in advancing authentic leadership tenets?

3. Describe how you interpret and/or respond to transgracial identity.

4. In a climate of #blacklivesmatter and other socially significant topics, how can the transgracial intersectional identity be best positioned?

5. How might the thesis of the *White Girl Within* aid in the rewriting of the gender contract?

6. How might the thesis of the *White Girl Within* aid in the rewriting of the racial contract?

7. How might the thesis of the *White Girl Within* contribute to intersectional identity theory?

8. How might the author's internalized identity be flawed?

9. In what way may the author's internalized identity be virtuous?

Book Club Questions

1. Identify challenges that you have confronted in school and/

or at home?

2. How have you worked to manage your truth?

3. Identify at least three key individuals that you trust to share your identity challenges. Explain.

4. If you have been a trusted confidant, what strategies did you use to help your friend or other loved one through their challenges?

5. What is a healthy outlet for Ronnie's repressed White female identity?

6. Does the legacy of Alabama apartheid make Ronnie's father a sympathetic figure? Why or Why not?

7. Based on the text, did the educational institutions help or hurt Ronnie's development? Did the schools help with racial and gender reconciliation?

8. Is it necessary to choose between the Black male and the White female identity and expressions? Explain.

9. Can the Black male and White female identities really coexist or do they have to be separated?

10. Were Ronnie's childhood friends helpful or hurtful to his development?

11. What elements of the book (if any) made you uncomfortable? Why? Why not?

Pop-Culture Questions

1. Do the popular culture references help to legitimize the "White Girl"?

2. How do the dreams featuring the re-imagining of The Golden Girls and The Jerry Springer Show, respectively work to provide additional insight on unique identity in society? Elaborate.

3. Describe how the various social riots (1992 Los Angeles Riots, 2001 Cincinnati Riots, 2020 George Floyd/Black Lives Matter Protests, etc.) complicate the transgracial reality shared by Ronnie and the White Girl within.

4. "Comedy is a reconciliation of a paradox" as said by Dave Chappelle.[89] How might the lived transgracial paradox be reconciled in a dignified yet humorous manner?

5. Talk about how the Will Smith slap led to an axis of hostility (involving Smith and Chris Rock). Describe the connections between this event and Post-Traumatic Slave Syndrome.

6. How do the differences and similarities between the "Cheesecake Conversations" and Bill Cosby's "Pound Cake" speech relate to the thesis of this book? Explain.

7. What kinds of pop-cultural shows, music, art, fashion, etc. do you as the reader connect with that helps with crafting your identity (or deriving some perspective of it)?

8. What is the future of LGBTQ+ rights in popular culture?

9. More broadly, what is the future of identity rights?

10. Do you think society is ready to accept more transracial and transgracial representation? Explain.

If you would like further guidance with contextualizing these questions, you're invited to work directly with me.

To learn more, check out www.whitegirlwithin.com

---

89   Berman, "Dave Chappelle."

ENHANCE YOUR LIBRARY

1. In Netflix's *The Rachel Divide,* I (Ronnie Gladden) briefly discussed some points pertaining to gender, race, and intersectionality. Specifically, I weigh in on the controversial figure Rachel Dolezal—with regard to her transracial identity and presentation. Additionally, I also briefly disclose how my unique intersectional identity directly pertains to my internalized White female identity.

2. In a subsequent documentary, I will be more robustly presented where they explain more about their complex gender and racial intersectional identities along with other similarly inclined individuals.

3. I currently teach at a college and encourage others to explore classes and ideas pertaining to gender, race, etc. at similar institutions and of course at universities, as well.

GENDER MINI-LESSON CONTENT: GENDER AND SOCIETY

Statement on Gender

Gender is a nuanced and complex social construction, which has largely been situated in a long-standing binary: male and female. Classically, masculinity was solely the province of those born with XY chromosomes and presenting as male. Conversely, feminine traits were largely relegated to those born with XX chromosomes and appearing as female. While many people are cisgender[90]—meaning they identify with their sex and gender as assigned at birth—however, for many other individuals, it is not that straightforward. For millennia, brave souls challenged the often-restrictive gender mores with the intent to express their true identities, which may run the gamut of agender, nonbinary,

90   "Explainer: What Does it Mean to be 'Cisgender'?" The Conversation, September 18, 2018, https://theconversation.com/explainer-what-does-it-mean-to-be-cisgender-103159.

transgender, genderqueer, and so on. The complex biological underpinnings along with the complex social constructions that is gender often collide and take lots of processing to fully understand and to reflect.

Intersectionality is grounded in the theory that individuals are a complex sum of their parts.[91] This notion applies figuratively as much as it does literally. A person's age, ability, status, gender, race, socioeconomic background, religion, education, etc. can function in complex matrices.[92] And for some, various tenets of their intersections can predominate in such a way as to marginalize the individual. Those intersections must be considered given that marginalization often interlocks with oppressive and systemic institutional systems. By appreciating how the aspects of one's intersectionality can coalesce to signal key aspects of their expression, more understanding of the theory can result. The hope is to rail against oppressive interlocking systems, which subjugate people to tyranny and oppression. This book is meant to showcase a nuanced and perhaps transgressive interlocking of transgender and transracial (resulting in transgracial) identity, which is unexpressed and under explored. The legitimacy of this permutation, along with others are valid and are worthy of review.

Recommended Books

Introduction to Gender and Society by Susan Stryker and Jack Halberstam

If I Was Your Girl and *Birthday* by Meredith Russo

Seventy Years of Blackness by Verda Byrd

Life On the Color Line by Gregory Williams

*Trans** by Jack Halberstam

Intersectionality: Key Scholars:

Patricia Hill (formerly Collins) Williams

Audre Lorde

---

91 Jane Coaston, "The Intersectionality Wars," Vox, May 28, 2019, https://www.vox.com/the-highlight/2019/5/20/18542843/intersectionality-conservatism-law-race-gender-discrimination.

92 Ibid.

MINI-LESSON: RACE AND SOCIETY

Statement on Race

Race in the United States is a complex 400-year-old institution that's inextricably linked to the American and even international cultural landscape.[93] Certainly, slavery has existed throughout the world across many different racial and ethnic backgrounds. Although race primarily functions as a social construction, undoubtedly some biological tenets overlap as well. Phenotypic expression, bone structure, etc. are connected to the genetic tapestry and expression. It is nebulous and is increasingly difficult to categorize given the broadening spectrum that is race. This book intends to add onto the spectrum.

Most people will continue to identify with the race that they were assigned, or they inherited. However, there is also a need to recognize that for some, racial dysphoria can exist, which leads to intense, deep, long-term incongruities and

93   Audrey Smedley, "Origin of the Idea of Race," PBS, November 1997, https://www.pbs.org/race/000_About/002_04-background-02-09.htm.

can profoundly shape the perspectives and authenticity for those identifying as transracial. Transracial identity is yet another strand underneath the broad banner of race.

Critical Race Theory

Critical Race Theory (CRT) combines "progressive political struggles for racial justice with critiques of the conventional legal and scholarly norms, which are themselves viewed as part of the illegitimate hierarchies that need to be changed."[94] Essentially, CRT strives for more equity and dismantling oppressive discrimination systems. This is very controversial at the time of this writing. My aim is to respect the dignity and worth of individuals while offering expansive insights. I want to contribute to improve different kinds of social conditions.

---

94   "Critical Race Theory," Harvard.edu, https://www.pbs.org/race/000_About/002_04-background-02-09.htm.

INTRODUCTION TO CRITICAL RACE THEORY

Post-Traumatic Slave Syndrome—Joy DeGruy (2005)

Is the legacy of slavery impacting the author's sense of self? Some of the patterns of PTSS might suggest that.[95] What many may interpret as the absence of self-esteem, hostility, and anger and a renouncing of Black culture still does not consider the nuance of my life story. And it still does not factor in how other kindred individuals of varying life persuasions have come to identify in parallel ways with the author. Historical trauma is valid and most likely is a factor within my own life experiences.

But as important as it is, still I believe that other theories, social cues, direct and subtle forces, and societal dynamics are intertwined with my reality. It is my attempt for this book to foster a broader meditation on the matter and to distill an even broader expansive review and treatment on race and. Particularly since gender also intersects with that of race in a concurrent and complex way.

---

95   Dr. Joy DeGruy, "Post Traumatic Slave Syndrome," Be The Healing, https://www.bethehealing.com/post-traumatic-slave-syndrome.

RACIAL AND CULTURAL TRAUMA

Critical Race Theory:

"Racial oppression is a traumatic form of interpersonal violence which can lacerate the spirit, scar the soul, and puncture the psyche." –Kenneth Hardy[96]

As previously mentioned, "Critical race theories combine progressive political struggles for racial justice with critiques of the conventional legal and scholarly norms which are themselves viewed as part of the illegitimate hierarchies that need to be changed."[97]

Furthermore, scholars—most of whom are themselves persons of color—challenge the ways that race and racial power are constructed by law and culture. One key focus of critical race theorists is a regime of White supremacy and privilege maintained despite the rule of law and the constitutional guarantee

---

96   "Speaker Profile: Kenneth V. Hardy," Intergenerational Trauma Conference, https://inheritedtrauma.org/speaker/dr-kenneth-v-hardy/.

97   "Critical Race Theory."

of equal protection of the laws.[98]

Agreeing with critical theorists and many feminists that law itself is not a neutral tool but instead part of the problem, critical race scholars identify inadequacies of conventional civil rights litigation. Critical race theorists nonetheless fault critical legal scholars as failing to develop much to attract people of color and for neglecting the transformative potential of rights discourse in social movements, regardless of the internal incoherence or indeterminacy of rights themselves.

Statement on Queer Theory

Queer Theory has come to serve as an umbrella term, which encompasses various aspects of the LGBTQ+ spectrum.[99] Myriad identities are encompassed within the LGBTQ+ spectrum and therefore for efficiency. The term "queer" can be applied as a sort of "catchall" or as a broad encompassing term that challenges many aspects of heteronormativity.[100]

Many also have viewed using the term queer as a way to reclaim it from those who have applied the term in pejorative and inflammatory ways in the past.

Intersectionality

Intersectionality encompasses the cluster of interlocking identities, which function to comprise the totality of our experiences.[101] Often our racial background, racial identity, expression, gender identity expression, sexual orientation, geographic influences, ability status, etc. coalesce in ways, which assists us with navigating through the various socially engineered systems inherent throughout the world.

---

98   Ibid.
99   "Queer Theory: A Rough Introduction," Illinois University Library," https://guides.
       library.illinois.edu/queertheory/background.
100   Ibid.
101   Coaston, "The Intersectionality Wars."

Queer Theory, Transgender, and Transracial Intersectionality Reflections

LGBTQ+

I sought acceptance as often and as early as I could. I thought I was going to find full-on acceptance in the LGBTQ+ community—but I didn't find it. Perhaps the lack of reception was due to internalized transphobia and racial self-loathing. Arming oneself with education can be quite useful to attack ignorance. See some selected useful terminologies as provided next.

Some Useful Terminologies and Definitions

Autogynephilia: The controversial belief that Male-to-female transgender individuals are sexually gratified by appropriating or presenting as a woman.[102]

Desist: To organically align one's gender identity with their assigned expression—in essence, to fit into the cisgender framework.[103]

Detransition: To decide to return to presenting as one's assigned sex.[104]

Transition: The process of aligning one's authentic gender identity with their external gender expression.[105]

Clock: To be coded or discovered as transgender without necessarily desiring to be outed.[106]

---

102 A. A. Lawrence, "Sexual Dysfunction: Beyond the Brain-Body Connection," *Adv Psychosom Med* 31 (2011): 135, https://doi.org/10.1159/000328921.

103 Tey Meadow, "The Loaded Language Shaping the Trans Conversation," The Atlantic, https://www.theatlantic.com/family/archive/2018/07/desistance/564560/.

104 Ibid.

105 Linell Smith, "Glossary of Transgender Terms," Hopkins Medicine, November 20, 2018, https://www.hopkinsmedicine.org/news/articles/glossary-of-terms-1.

106 Joy R. Fox, "Transgender Public Clocking: Why Do We Stare?" American Counseling Association, 2005, https://www.counseling.org/knowledge-center/vistas/by-year2/vistas-2005/docs/default-source/vistas/vistas_2005_vistas05-art69.

Anti-Racism and Sexism Statement

The systematic oppression of any race is reprehensible. I disavow those that create and support systems that perpetuate systemic oppression. Similarly, I also vehemently reject the sustained sexist practices, which subjugates classes of people to a subordinate and disenfranchised status.

Statement on Identity Politics

In spite of the loaded subtext, this is a watershed for authentic identity allegiances and expressions. Many are empowered to take authority and live the way they chose. This means that authentic, organic, and often dynamic identity expressions result. The identities have often been suppressed, repressed, and oppressed—and as a result, jubilee occurs once an individual is finally able to display their true selves.

There's no need to rush into transition. Instead, arm yourself with as much education as possible to effectively evaluate all of your options. Transition can take on many different forms. Perhaps the most important transition is the one that occurs within your mind and soul. Those of all ages should balance the risks of transitions with the rewards. I have spent more than a decade in counseling. In fact, at the time, I was so repressed initially I did not even realize that my combined gender and racial dysphoria was at the center of my depression.

Shame and Vulnerability

Dr. Brené Brown has brilliantly validated the power of embracing one's vulnerability.[107] In fact, research on vulnerability continues to demonstrate the necessity of owning one's narrative and to leverage it for the betterment of the self and for others.[108]

---

107 "The Power of Vulnerability | Brené Brown," Ted, YouTube, January 3, 2011, https://www.youtube.com/watch?v=iCvmsMzlF7o.

108 Ibid.

White Girl Within is an expression of coming to terms with an essential element of my life story and to share it as a resource for others processing their own improbable and radical identities. The hope is for others to engage in watershed practices to disentangle aspects of their knotted stories to allow movement toward grasping and owning their truths. Particularly when their narratives may be enmeshed within other kinds of traumatic events. Additionally,

White Girl Within hopes to foster allyship and greater understanding of human diversity.

Authentic Leadership

Authentic leadership encompasses "the leader's self-concept: his or her self-knowledge, self-concept clarity, self-concordance, and person-role merger, and on the extent to which the leader's self-concept is expressed in his or her behavior."[109]

Additionally, "the construction of a life-story is a major element in the development of authentic leaders."[110] It is the hope that the "life-story provides followers with a major source of information on which to base their judgments about the leader's authenticity."[111]

Once effective authentic leadership tenets have been actualized, an important

pre-requisite has been fulfilled with regard to advancing toward the trajectory of transformational leadership.

White Girl Within strives to function as an example of authentic leadership because the goal is to share a story in several spaces in order to advance advocacy for cultural self-determination. Identity rights are human rights.

---

109 Boas Shamir and Galit Eilam, "'What's Your Story?' A Life-Stories Approach to Authentic Leadership Development," *The Leadership Quarterly* 16, no. 3 (June 2005): 395. https://doi.org/10.1016/j.leaqua.2005.03.005.

110 Ibid.

111 Ibid.

Transformative Leadership

Transformational leadership involves inspiring followers to commit to a shared vision and goals for an organization or unit, challenging them to be innovative problem solvers, and developing followers' leadership capacity via coaching, mentoring, and provision of both challenge and support.[112]

Transformational leadership seeks to establish significant impact within a community or institution in order deliver meaningful operations that foster positive and lasting improvement. Moreover, hopefully this book can evolve to work as a kind of act of transformational leadership in that it helps to shift one from a perpetual state of fear to a more resilient, fulfilled, and fearless person that dares to dream and to disrupt so as to effect change in useful, meaningful, and impactful ways. Also, the aim is to evolve society to a place of greater enlightenment and acceptance for people with complex identity intersections.

I would be delighted to expand the discussion on these important concepts and definitions with individuals, schools, non-profits, and businesses, alike. To collaborate, connect with me here: www.ronniegladden.com and here: www.whitegirlwithin.com

---

112 Bernard M. Bass and Ronald E. Riggio, *Transformational Leadership* (Mahwah, NJ: Lawrence Erlbaum Associates Publishers, 2006): 4.

LGBTQ+ RESOURCES

Human Rights Commission (HRC)
www.hrc.org/

GLAAD
www.glaad.org/

National Center for Transgender Equality (NCTE)
transequality.org/

GLSEN
www.glsen.org/

Campus Pride
www.campuspride.org/

PFlag
pflag.org/

CHEMICAL DEPENDENCY RESOURCES

Alcoholics Anonymous

www.aa.org/

Alateen/Al-Anon

https://al-anon.org/

DOMESTIC VIOLENCE RESOURCES

Children's Defense Fund
www.childfund.org/

Children USA/National Child Abuse Hotline
www.childhelphotline.org/

Children Welfare League of America
www.cwla.org/

Futures Without Violence: The National Health Resource Center on Domestic Violence
www.futureswithoutviolence.org/

National Center on Domestic Violence, Trauma & Mental Health
www.nationalcenterdvtraumamh.org/

National Council on Juvenile and Family Court Judges
www.ncjfcj.org

National Domestic Violence Hotline

www.thehotline.org

National Resource Center for Domestic Violence

www.niwrc.org

National Child Abuse Hotline/Child help

childhelphotline.org

National Center for Victims of Crime

victimsofcrime.org

SUICIDE PREVENTION

Action Alliance for Suicide Prevention
theactionalliance.org/

American Foundation for Suicide Prevention
afsp.org

Crisis Text Line
www.crisistextline.org

HelpGuide
www.helpguide.org

National Institute of Mental Health
www.nimh.nih.gov

National Suicide Prevention Lifeline
800-273-8255

Society for the Prevention of Teen Suicide
www.sprc.org

Suicide Awareness Voices of Education

save.org

Suicide Prevention Resource Center

www.sprc.org

The Trevor Project

www.thetrevorproject.org

Anti-Bullying/Harassment Resources

National Bullying Prevention Center

www.pacer.org

This list is certainly not exhaustive. Let's partner to discover additional resources that can be useful for you and others. I gently encourage you to reach out to me here: www.whitegirlwithin.com

If you believe *White Girl Within* offered value, meaningful perspectives, and useful resources, please leave a review on Goodreads or on the retailer site where you purchased this book.

Your comment will help others to connect with a book that advances literacy, truth in storytelling, while also championing unique identity and more; thank you for your support.

WORK WITH DR. RONNIE

In fact, once you have done this—while still preserving the essential integrity of your work—I would love for you to share your story with me.

Send your story here: drronnie.whitegirlwithin@gmail.com

Check out the *White Girl Within* website: www.whitegirlwithin.com

Check out my YouTube Channel *Our Best Letters* website:
www.ourbestletters.com

Book me to speak, coach, consult, or train here: www.ronniegladden.com

Check out my TEDx Talk: "White Girl Within: Embrace Your Inner Diversity"

And follow me on Instagram and Twitter @drronniespeaks.

#writeyourtruth #shareyourtruthwithdrronnie

WRITE LETTERS TO YOURSELF

What's your story?

What will it take for you to transition in some manner in order to align your inner life more fully with your outer life—however that may look?

Start with applying the following steps: Name it, Own it, and Work it (NOW). NOW is a process aligned with authentic leadership. The goal is to foster consensus through community building of shared stories. Gain more control over your identity.

The following identity wheel can help to organize and frame the various components of your intersections:

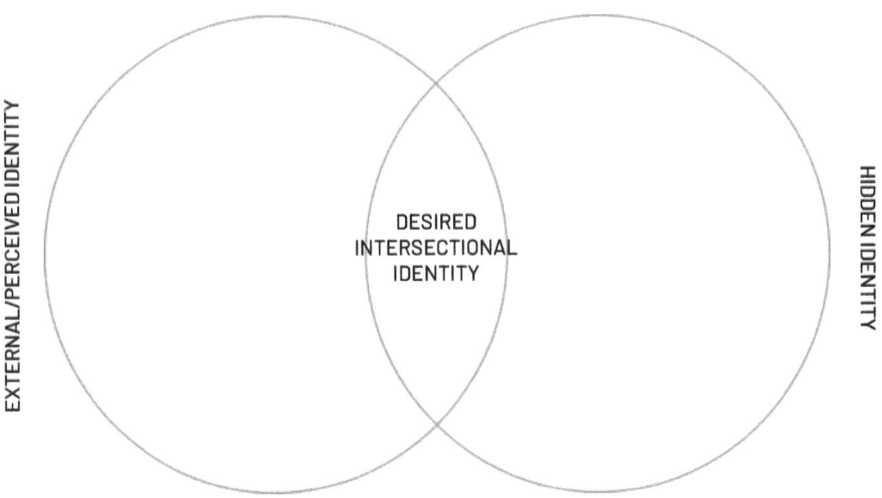

Write letters to yourself.

Consider if you have to grapple with any kind of dysphoria. Might there be underlying traumatic events, which influence the expression of the story? (Domestic violence, bullying, identity displacement, chemical dependency, suicidality, etc.)

Think about this deeply and unload!

You will likely start with an "emotional draft." At this point, care not about standard writing conventions. Just UNPACK the essence of your stories. Use a Venn Diagram (example above) if it is easier to organize your thoughts that way.

Later on, you can sophisticate the message.

In fact, I would love for you to share your story with me.

Dear ____

Dear ____

Dear ____

Dear ____

Dear ____

DEDICATION

To those who have the courage to innovate and make a difference; Dr. J. Samuel Bois who steered me intellectually; and to Augustus F. Hawkins and Dr. Norman Topping who supported and encouraged me early in my career.

All rights reserved under International and
Pan-American Copyright Conventions.
Published in the United States by
Epistemics Institute Press, Inc.
P.O. Box 18672
Los Angeles, California 90007

Library of Congress Cataloging in Publication Data

The Miracle of Abduction
Library of Congress Number 84082540
ISBN Number 0 930 371-03-8
(Soft Cover)

Manufactured in the United States of America
Book Design by Michael R. Burrows, Typographer

OTHER BOOKS BY THE AUTHOR

General Semantics and the Social Sciences
Uncommon Sense and Dimensional Awareness
Epistemics: Personalizing the Process of Change
Semantic Behavior and Decision Making

Table of Contents

Acknowledgement ii
Foreword vii

SECTION ONE — OVERVIEW
Introduction 1
Chapter 1   — Applied Up-to-Date Epistemology 7
Chapter 2   — Conceptualization and Transformation 15
Chapter 3   — Holism, Reductionism and Empiricism:
                A Focus on Abduction 23
Chapter 4   — The Creative Loop 37
Chapter 5   — Assumptions About Assumptions 51
Chapter 6   — The Use of Conceptual Revolutions 57

**SECTION TWO — THE FOUNDATION MATRIX
FOR APPLIED EPISTEMOLOGY**
Chapter 7   — A Functional Synthesis:
                The Postulating and Relating Stages 65
Chapter 8   — The Special Role of the Relating Stage 75

SECTION THREE — FOCUS ON ABDUCTION
Chapter 9   — Abduction and Public Affairs Management:
                Role of the Verb ''To Be'' 81
Chapter 10 — Abduction and the Construct of Behavior ... 91
Chapter 11 — Policy Analysis and the Abductive Process .. 95
Chapter 12 — Abduction as a Transactive Method 105
Chapter 13 — Abduction and the Notion of Rationality ... 109
Chapter 14 — A Managerial Abductive Process:
                Death and Dying 113

SECTION FOUR — ABDUCTION IN PRACTICE
Chapter 15 — Theory of Extensionalization 119
Chapter 16 — Extensionalizing Abduction in
                Everyday-Affairs 125
Chapter 17 — Abduction as a Process of Innovation 133
Glossary of Terms 141
Index 145

FOREWORD

William J. Williams' *The Miracle of Abduction* takes a novel look at how we think and what we think, and proposes a "different system of logic" to enable the social scientist to become a theoretician, practitioner and creative artist simultaneously.

This book has far-reaching implications for the social scientist, the public policy maker, and, indeed, for anyone involved in decision making.

The method of inquiry Williams proposes is applied epistemology, a way of breaking out of the limitations of the scientific method and moving toward a more theoretical and practical method. Language is an essential element in his examination, and symbolic vocabulary a key to the prevailing view of ourselves, our motivations, our goals, our relationships, and so on. The need to examine the appropriateness of our language cannot be overestimated, since, as Williams explains, "Every word we utter, every theory we create, every language we fashion is a statement about the human condition; and how we approach the developing of ideas, directions and formulations for our action is, to some extent, based on our assumptions about ourselves and our universe. Therefore, it is necessary to be exposed to applied up-to-date epistemology." (p. 16)

He proceeds to demonstrate that thought is not something separate from the language we use, and that the ability to provide appropriate symbols and language is a prerequisite for making good judgments and effective decisions. The method he recommends for achieving this is the process of abduction, a process that can transform our way of thinking.

Abduction is a symbolic process to determine whether the categories present in a discipline or professional field are accurate and adequate. This order is necessary to improve that discipline or field's decision-making capacity. It provides for innovation and change.

Williams describes abduction as the application of the science of epistemology to self-guidance and management. He suggests that innovation and better constructs can be implemented by combining general semantics epistemology and epistemics—the link to all creative thinking—to formulate a method of inquiry for abduction. This method employs the five stages of the epistemological profile: stage 1—sensing, or reaction; stage 2—classifying, or action; stage 3—relating, or interaction; stage 4—postulating, or transaction; and stage 5—participating, or synchronicity.

Creative problem-solving and with it innovation follow as we learn to question our assumptions with other assumptions and to transcend the "deterministic, prediction-and-control, reductionistic, technology-focused science." It is through this questioning that we obtain our ideas, thoughts and patterns of behavior.

In his discussion of public affairs management, Williams stresses the need for a verbal focus. Language is very limited in conveying meaning as well as in adapting to change. Though words always reflect a construction of the past, it is through our verbiage that the perception of change must be reflected and conveyed.

Based on his experience and his examination of the contemporary state of knowledge in the cultural, social and epistemological sciences, Williams strives to stimulate and move us to a different level of understanding. He believes we must view the sciences as a way of behavior and as a way of interpreting realities. We need to see creativity and ways of managing ourselves more effectively as an act of abduction that employs the five stages of the epistemological profile. This profile is a self-revising, theoretical process, an instrument to understand a particular case. It is also a process to evaluate ideas, the process and the individual. Most importantly, it is a vehicle for inventing new instruments as it helps in deciding when, how, where and whether or not to do something.

Creative communicators and decision makers function primarily at stages 4 (postulating) and 5 (participating) of the epistemological profile. They are the self-actualizers, the ones who question assumptions, the ones who welcome change. In this book, Williams has set forth a process of innovation using the method of abduction that promises expanded awareness and maximum creativity in our thinking and communicating.

DENNIS MURRAY, PH.D.
President
Marist College
Paughkeepsie, New York

SECTION ONE
OVERVIEW

INTRODUCTION

When asked what this book is about, I have difficulty responding with any degree of adequacy I respect. I have thought about it and tried to formulate a statement that would describe what I am attempting to do, and communicate an accurate message to the questioner. The nearest I have come to any decent explanation is "wrapped" up in the phrase "to articulate a method of inquiry" which might enable a social scientist to become a theoretician, practitioner, and a creative artist simultaneously. My focus is on a method called *Abduction* which uses as its foundation the formulations of general semantics and epistemics. These formulations combined use symbolic language and cultural processes as epistemological vehicles—Isn't that a 'mouth full?' Abduction is a method of inquiry which calls for questioning our assumptions, evaluating those assumptions, developing new assumptions, and constructing ways of accomplishing tasks by looking at our language and cultural history differently. Doing so should enable us to formulate new ways of looking at deductive logic and empiricism.

In deductive logic, the conclusion is already hidden in the premise and all we disclose is our own blindness. For example, the position, velocity, and acceleration of a moving body, which we take for granted today (1982), were neither ordained nor discovered in nature. Explanatory theories were invented or adopted. Deductive logic is like inventing a game of chess; you have to conceive of the board, the chess pieces and the rules of play in close conjunction with each other. We could not get very far using the rules of monopoly here. Everything has to fit harmoniously. This becomes deductive. There are many systems of a metaphysical or religious nature that have provided profound insight into the nature of reality—none, however, can

1

claim to control and predict as well as science. But, to choose science on its ability to predict and control is a value judgment. There is no guarantee of objectivity, only utility. Science is a value construct created by the human mind. It is an art of creation. It is imperative to understand how and why this art of creation is performed. So, it is not science we should understand but how and why it was created. Reasonings emerging from science do not come from us; they do not originate in us or nature. Somehow, we participate in an *innovative process*. We cannot assume that there is an independent, external, objective world out there uninfluenced by human consciousness. From the framework of either/or, I am hard pressed to envision or explain our participatory innovativeness. Which comes first—the chicken or the egg? Try asking an egg in the process of becoming a chicken. Just as past, present, and future are the same, chicken and egg are one—mind and matter are the same—creator and created are one. We cannot assume dichotomies when it is dichotomies we are calling into question. Dichotomies maroon us to deductive logic and inflexible empiricism.

How do we move beyond deductive logic and inflexible empiricism? It is easier to discuss what is exceptional and unlikely in what is remote. This is precisely what Newton did. He perceived the underlying orders in the behavior of nearby objects on earth by studying distant planets. What would be more unlikely than billiard balls and planets obeying the same laws? This process of seeking out and eliminating is an act of innovation. How does this shifting and hoisting work in social relations? A congressional assistant once designed a statewide process to elect a congressman in a certain district. He was operating from the abstract to the concrete. Our old empiricism and deductive logic bind us. Medieval consciousness did not feel so keen as does ours that the mind and the rest of the organic space of the human body is bound by our skin. We feel ourselves to be well defined and delineated from everything outside ourselves. Astrological or medieval space, by contrast, has none of this abstract lifeless character. Our modern notion of space is a compound metaphor that embodies all our concepts and experiences of separation, distinction, articulation, isolation, delimitation, division, differentiation and identity. Outer, inner, up, and below have no place—yet, we continue to believe that space is simply there—independent of us. The metaphor of space is our modern mechanics for avoiding the ''horrendous'' experience of oneness. We conceive of space as other than an empty void—cold, dark, and distant. The ''flipside'' of that or an abductive way to view space as organic, connective, nurturing, humane, intelligent, and alive with meaning. This sense of space incorporates, love, appreciation, inspiration, belonging, kinship, and holiness. Life might be difficult, but never foreign. Death might be frightening, but not annihilating. There is a metaphor for space in totally nonspatial terms. It is a linguistic version of space. It is algebraic; it is the grid of Descartes' which says that any figure in two dimensional plane geometry can be transformed into a mathematical or logical statement and vice versa. There is no formation about space that is not considered in this algebraic metaphor. Admittedly, algebra is not a natural medium of thought for most people, but neither is Chinese or musical notation. The point is that algebra is a form of language and logic which is treated very differently by the mind than spatial systems. In this algebraic formulation, mind, thought, space, and motion are one and the same *and our language should reflect this amalgam.*

Time is another factor. It is the physical notion of causality which we insist on associating with our concept of linear, sequential, continuous time. This notion sustains the illusion of our limitations. Meaningful and creative time has to do with synchronicity—rhythm and music are representative of this synchronicity. The meaning of music lies deep, indeed. We recognize in it a primary creative art. An exploration of the inner experience of rhythm discloses another fundamental metaphor for time. With a musical work, one has a sense of unity—it encapsulates time; experiences are not sequential and stretched out in a line, but are laid out in an amalgamated organic complex. Music captures what modern science in the theory of relativity has given us; a new view of causality. The speed of light is finite; therefore, the realm outside space and time cannot be accounted for within space-time. A music-like creative approach to our symbols, then, is needed.

Another element is matter. Matter is related to space and time. Space in this way is not empty nor is time. Substance is a part of the process—where do holistic symbols fit? Holistic symbols supply and give us a way of understanding time, space, and matter.

Space is a metaphor for being or becoming. It provides a feeling of relatedness to the cosmos. Time symbolizes persistence and endurance with a kind of immortality! Rhythm gives us the *purity nature* and the elemental art of creation. Matter is our metaphor for stability and inertia is our protection from falling. Holistic Symbols represent unity and diversity. It is unwise and difficult to separate space, time, matter, and holistic symbols, and symbols from one another. Dissection is impossible without "killing" the organism. There are not two separate worlds; there is one. Every part of the whole implies the whole. Where does all of this lead us?

Themes worked out in the pure conceptual notion of linguistic philosophy have to be used to challenge the epistemological foundation of the social sciences. A general theory can provide a broad orienting framework. It serves as a basis for codifying generalizations and specific theories. We have learned that what we call fact or observations are themselves theory laden and shaped by our conceptual schemes. There are no uninterpreted or brute *facts* that are simply out there, unaffected by our theoretical or conceptual schemes. There is an extensive and growing body of literature that reveals the empirical, methodological, logical and ideological inadequacies of empirical theories.

In developing mature social sciences modeled on the natural sciences, there are not only practical obstacles, but logical and conceptual impossibilities. Understanding the human condition(s) is different from understanding physical nature(s). The former are incompatible with concepts central to scientific prediction. Accordingly, social theory must provide some critical basis for evaluating alternative possibilities. The new models commitment must have a value orientation—one in which we not only interpret our own action, but also those of others and various forms of social and cultural action. This, in turn, introduces the notions of *semantic transaction* and the *structured unconscious* (see the glossary for explanation).

One does not start from scratch. An individual approaches the world with common sense constructs which must be recognized and revamped. We are not, however, compelled to continue our development of new constructs in an either/or manner. We must challenge the presuppositon that *only* by the study of regularities can we achieve legitimate empirical knowledge. Consequently, the structure of face to face situations must be defined and elucidated through the *process of abstracting*.

These basic *conceptual processes: semantic transaction, structured unconscious and the process of abstracting*, must be articulated in order to serve as a foundation for theoretical explanations and explorations with an abductive form. Simultaneously, there must be a shift in perspective and categorical framework. This shift will affect the way we understand the fact value dichotomy and lead us away from the common sense constructs of everyday life.

There will be no significant movement or shift toward emancipation unless there is a transformation of thought and a move toward the notions of love and cooperation. This may be achieved through the vehicles of the *semantic transactor*, the *structured unconscious* and the *process of abstracting* as an undergirding theory for the practical thrust of the *epistemological profile, the structural more, the conceptual revolutions*, and the *extensional devices* and *working principles*.

I believe it was put best by Chester Barnard in his book, *Functions of the Executive* (The Appendix). He labels two kinds of mental processes: logical and nonlogical. The logical being systematic, scientific, and concrete; the nonlogical involving hunches, intuition, and innovativeness. The latter is achieved by internalizing a foundation that will develop those faculties necessary for synchroncity, i.e., the ability to ''feel'' a situation—that area we call ''*abduction*''.

So this book is all about how to develop and utilize that ''different system of logic'' which is necessary to the human.and social sciences. How do we achieve a new logical state? Through the intellect, we *fabricate new formulations*. Being nonlogical is just another system of logic. Chinese logic includes rather than excludes. In the book of chances, there are 64 sides to the coin.

In Western culture, there are two sides, heads or tails, either or. In the social sciences, we have reduced it to either or in order to quantify. The momement we move from nonquantification, scientific validation cannot be the test of truth: The question is then raised—how do you test this truth? How do you know that you are correct in what you know in this nonquantification area? How do you hold a moonbeam in your hand?

In physics, through the intellect, we fabricate new formulations. Physics is what it is because original formulations were fabricated. Fabricated, not on the basis of *either/or*, but a kind of *logic different from the common sense logic*. A logic that we have not transferred to social relations, i.e., we did not adopt the epistemology of physics, but instead phased in the results of physics. This did not include their abduction and intellect. Physics was not without ''abduction;'' it is just that their kind of intellect lead to different sensations. Our intellect in the social sciences has led us to illusions rather than a more adequate understanding. Why? The kind of logic we have used has been either/or. In physics, it has been more like the Chinese logic. Again, so the key to the question, how do we know what we know, is embedded in the system of logic we use and the kinds of conceptual notions we formulate.

As physics, with its accuracy based on a many-sided method, so can our knowledge about human dynamics. It is the method of inquiry, not whether we quantify or not. While the ''abduction'' we refer to cannot be quantified, it does follow an orderly intellectual process. That process is summed up in something we call the *creative loop*, which is part of the abductive process and something I refer to in the first chapter as *applied epistemology*.

This applied epistemology emerges from a focus. In Lancelot Law Whyte's book, *The Next Development in Man*, it was referred to as the formative tendency of the world. In the *Phenomenon of Man* Pierre de Cardin referred to it as the *noosphere*. These are expressions on a more universal level of the notion of an active space without time as advocated by Roger Jones in his *Physics as Metaphor*. He emphasized Jung's synchronicity. I have opted to use the latter label because of the practical implications for applied epistemology. I am hoping that the foregoing has supplied some idea of what this book is about.

CHAPTER 1

Applied Up-to-Date Epistemology

Felix Roethlisberger, co-introducer of the human relations and behavioral focus in administration, graduate in engineering and economics, holder of degrees from MIT, Harvard and Columbia, dedicated student of anthropology, mathematics, philosophy, an admirer of Mayo, Whitehead, Russell, Korzybski, Freud, died at the ripe old age of 84, and left us with several admonitions. He proposed the most important, in my judgment, form of thinking underlying our internalization of knowledge in his book, *The Elusive Phenomena*. He suggested a way of dealing with false dichotomies or what he referred to as the nature of obsessive thinking. Before that, however, in 1968 in *Man-in-Organization* on p. 81, Roethlisberger remarked that the *Newton* or "Copernicus" that could help us in developing a new conceptual formulation, which would enable us to relate more appropriately to learning, change and decision making, has not arrived on the scene. In the same book on the same page in the following paragraph, he stated that general semantics epistemology, however, might offer us a fruitful lead. As a follow-up, he wrote a chapter labeled "Concrete Sociology" (Chapter 5) in the *The Elusive Phenomena*. In a subheading, he called it "Applied Epistemology."

This is the theme of my thrust. Applied epistemology is proposed as a way of enabling us to break out of the limitations of the scientific method. It can also move us toward development of a theory or method of inquiry that is both theoretical and practical. In my book, *Semantic Behavior and Decision Making*, I related an incident I observed with three professors talking in the School of Public Administration (USC, December 22, 1978).

One was saying that we must teach our students skills because they come loaded with theory already. This, in my judgment, was a case of the false dichotomy Roethlisberger was referring to. The issue is not the teaching of skills separate from theory as the statement implies, but, the offering of a theoretical formulation which combines both theory and skills. These professors were obviously talking about a traditional kind of theory which has very little reference to the world of human transactions. The first order of business is to make students aware that present theories are dichotomized and this dichotomized thinking should not be perpetuated. I am suggesting that any time we speak of separating skills from theories, we are dichotomizing or merely elaborating on what they have done already or adding something that does not enable us to question assumptions. The solution is to offer the thinking process called ''applied epistemology,'' updated. I use the word ''updated'' because an epistemology at any given time might be nonfunctional. Thus, terminology is suggested as follows: up-to-date applied epistemology.

A language, according to Jacob Bronowski, is essential to the building of any discipline. The objective is to capture the event through language. The question is ''How?'' Language is a metaphor and the application of the wrong metaphor will not yield the proper results.

Bronowski in *The Origins of Knowledge and Imagination*, told a story about how someone had used an inappropriate metaphor when discussing universal gravitation: ''Gravitation will not stop at the top of the mountains. It will go on to the moon.'' Then he asked, ''How will it fall off?'' ''Well, if it were an open space . . . it would fall off like light . . . but . . . the earth is in a flat orbit round like the sun, so that the sun's force is only being spread over the plane . . . and probably gravity falls off like this.'' There he was wrong. But the exciting thing is to understand *why* he was wrong. He had used the wrong metaphor; in other words, the wrong vocabulary—there is no ''*top*''.   A few years back, I was intrigued by a statement which appeared in a book I was reading about Einstein's quest for a unified field theory. The statement said that a physicist by the name of Misner had developed a paper in 1957 which concluded that there was a unified field theory already in existence. I passed over the statement without noting the source. A few weeks later, because the statement continued to "nag" me, I decided to reread it. I reread through all of the books on Einstein and the history of science in my possession but could not find the statement attributed to this finding by Misner. I searched for some allusion to this finding for two years. In other words, I was "nagged" day after day. I persisted in my search. It, however, grew frustrating because none of the contemporary writings indicated that Misner's paper existed. The tension within me created an obsession and it increased when an article appeared in the *Los Angeles Times* (1979) which indicated that Einstein had died a frustrated man because he had not been able to develop a unified field theory. I arose one morning with a new zeal for searching. I asked my assistant to go to our science library and look up anything on a person by the name of Misner. She found a textbook written by Misner and Wheeler on gravitation. In that book I found a reference to a book labeled, *Geometrodynamics—Gravitation, Electro-magnetism, Unquantized Charge and Mass as Properties of Curved Empty Space*. It stated in specific terms that in 1924 a mathematician by the name of Rainich had applied Riemannian geometry to electromagnetism and this produced, in theoretical terms, the unified field theory. Misner asserted that the application of Riemannian geometry to electromagnetism, using the dual language of electromagnetism and looking at electromagnetism as empty curved space, with mass and without mass simultaneously would produce something called a geon. This geon represented the unified field theory. He added that Einstein had developed the unified field theory with his master theory—the general theory of relativity of 1916; all he needed to do was add Riemannian geometry and use the dual language of electromagnetism, i.e., empty curve space, with mass and without mass. Instead of calling it the master theory plus geometry, Misner called it geometrodynamics. I sat down and wrote a letter to Dr. Misner (1979) at the University of Maryland, requesting verification of his position. Dr. Misner responded by saying that he had found fault with the conclusion he had reached and that further explorations indicated that

Newtonian "metaphysics" was incapable of producing a unified field theory. Also, the theory being used by Einstein could not produce the unified field theory at the classical or quantum levels (where the possibility lies) either because there was a weakness in (Einstein's) his vocabulary. This suggests that Einstein's language epistemology was inadequate. He used the word "vocabulary at fault" twice in his response to my letter.

When I received Misner's letter I realized why I had pursued this matter so relentlessly. Since my research focus is on applied epistemology and especially the language dimension of Epistemology, I received unconscious suggestions from my abstract system that I should pursue this matter. I concluded from my search (which is by no means over) the following: (1) If something nudges and pushes you, listen and follow up. (2) The language, symbols, or vocabulary used will determine the results we receive from our endeavors—one must have a language epistemology which structurally represents the world of events. (3) Einstein's language epistemology was weak. (4) The language in the natural sciences, (i.e., mathematics and physics) as the language in the social sciences, has to be revised and a new perspective created. (5) We, in the social sciences, should not borrow from the natural sciences without critically evaluating what we borrow. (6) We should seek to develop our own epistemological sources of knowledge. That is, we must go to the "sources" which produce the language and an epistomology which might not only produce effective theories for the social sciences, but, which might shed some light on faults within the disciplines of mathematics and physics. This requires rising to the state of abduction; thus, making deduction and induction particular cases within Abduction.

This example is to further illustrate, theoretically, the necessity for a proper vocabulary which must emerge if we are to create a different view of the human condition. Symbolic vocabulary is, many times, the key to the prevailing view of human beings, their compelling motivations and ultimate goals, their relationships to one another and to the myriad forms of life around them, and their conviction about the source of final authority. This view is the context—the "story," that gives meaning to the strivings of individuals and the evolution of human institutions. This was the basic set of core beliefs which changed in the Indo-European countries during the first and second conceptual revolutions marking the end of the Middle Ages and the beginning of modern times. If another shift at this level of most fundamental beliefs were to occur, the development would be as consequential to all aspects of society as was the shift from Aristotleian to Newtonian to Einsteinian beliefs.

Symbolic vocabulary has produced the invention of weapons of mass destruction. Humankind is on the brink of destroying civilization. Through a lusty technology and industry, and obliviousness to our true relationship to the earth, we have been on the brink of severely impairing its habitabilty. But then, through a global change of mindsets, the world has begun to rebuild human society in a way that is sustainable and equitable— a way based on the previously rare kind of unconditional caring for one another and for the earth that comprises one of the many definitions of the word ''love.'' This ''love coping'' and new mindset has within it the potentiality of relieving untold human conflict and misery. It is not automatic, but with a more adequate view of ourselves, we can build a sustainable and humanely desirable global society. But, we know that the future can never be built on an inadequate symbolic picture of essential human nature.

We are still in the throes of the agonizing struggle of having to deal with the old as well as the new as we push toward another mindset. This book is an attempt to suggest ways and methods for making this movement more orderly.

POST 1982 STATEMENT

The rapidity of change with reference to knowledge is something that we must learn to relate to automatically. The kind of theory we use will determine how well we do it. And, of course, the language contained therein is basic.

The second question is: How does all of this relate to everyday decision making, public policy and public affairs? I mention those three because they are more immediate. However, the more basic question is: How does this applied up-to-date epistemology relate to new theory making in the social sciences and change?

On Saturday, May 5, 1980, the *Los Angeles Times*, on p. 18, Part I, printed an article entitled "Experiments Hint at Shake-up of Physics: Proof that neutrinos have mass would change our view of the Universe." Neutrinos, according to J. A. Wheeler in his book, *Geometrodynamics* (Academic Press, 1962), are the only fermin fields which have no mass and no change. Misner, of course, in his article of 1957, had the same idea thereby concluding that we must view electromagnetism as empty curved space—completely free of any so-called "real" mass of its own.

The article about the neutrino-subatomic particle containing a small amount of mass—a particle rather than a field mass theory changes the way we view the universe. A universe with a neutrino containing mass is a collapsing universe. It has major implications for social sciences and, in general, our understanding of both the large and small scales of nature. It will shape our outlook and how we deal with each other as humans. There are tremendous economic, political, and social implications here. On May 5, 1980, John Anderson, presidential candidate, in the same Los Angeles Times, Part I, p. 9, was quoted as follows: "Particles that travel through the universe by the billions and trillions at the speed of light—they have suddenly discovered that these particles are not weightless they have enough gravity so that instead of the universe continuing to expand the universe may collapse," Anderson told the mystified crowd. Fortunately, he added smiling, "That's one problem that will be down the road a bit."

Update: Wednesday, May 5, 1982, Part I, p. 7, Los Angeles Times—the tentative finding in 1980 was contradicted by a comprehensive experiment put out by an international team of Cal Tech and European physicists. The new study did not detect any mass within the range of oscillations investigated. To have seen more or fewer oscillations in other neutrino types doing the flightfrom reactor to detector would have meant that the elementary particles have mass. The experiment does not give *the lie* to the earlier experiment, but it does impose stringent boundaries on the nature of neutrino oscillations.

The public policy implications are massive. Policy knowledge itself is raw and has to be applied, but the suggestions that it is necessary for public policy-makers and people in the various disciplines to dig deeply into knowledge in order to put our lives in some kind of perspective is indisputable. Every word we utter, every theory we create, and every language we fashion is a statement about the human conditions. And, how we approach the developing of ideas, directions and formulations for our actions is, to some extent, based on our assumptions about ourselves and our universe. Therefore, it is necessary to be exposed to applied up-to-date epistemology. This book is about how we do it.

This will later tie in with the theory of dissipative structures which involves paradigm shifts. The very nature of the neutrino will determine, I believe, in some manner the quality and kind of paradigm shift; that is, if the neutrino is without mass, the change will be more elusive because mass makes it more of a particle and suggests something available for concrete analysis. In either case, the notions of *conceptualization, transformation,* and *linguistic* attitudes are paramount.

CHAPTER 2

Conceptualization and Transformation

Conceptualization is indeed the mechanism from which idea systems are constructed. This suggests that the characteristics of a particular process may be as important in the construction of an idea system as the socio-historic settings from which such characteristics spring from.

Conceptualization is the process by which we construct ideas. Under this formulation, conceptualization is an internally based mental activity that seeks to grasp the character of sense perceptions. I see this process, basically, as being mechanical. Additionally, the method itself might be subject to some degree of alteration provided we can isolate and understand the process. This suggests the possibility that both the process of conceptualization and its component elements may be the result of learning rather than being an inherent aspect of human cranial development.

To begin with, conceptualization is both a process and the specific results of that process. As such, it closely resembles the construction and operation of a clock, for both contain a mechanism or process that has internal elements and each has a distinct external result at any given moment in time. With this process, the produced idea or result immediately becomes the raw material for subsequent thought formation.

The mechanistic principle represents an eternal, or static conceptualization of thought. It is within the framework of this concept that most thoughts are formed and held. We tend, under this formulation, to hold our perceptions in a fixed or eternal fashion. This means that once formed, our perceptions of realities tend to remain virtually the same over time. Furthermore, conceptualization implies a personal resistance to the alteration of ideas and/or idea systems. For instance, persons who describe themselves as "liberal" or "conservative" tend to hold these views and resist change even when faced with considerable forces upon their constructed views of reality. Thus, the principle promulgates a rigid conceptualization of thought—a resistance to *transformation*.

The principle of *transformation*, on the other hand, is the "flip side" of mechanistic conceptualization. By definition, *transformation* is a state of continual flux; things are constantly in a state of becoming. In a sense, the process of *transformation* is the only constant factor within the human condition. If we can predict nothing else, we can count with great assurance on the fact that nothing will remain the same through time. It is partially because *transformation* appears to be relatively constant. Manneheim sees it as the ideal or Utopian replacement element for the unitary principle in both internal and external conceptualization. If *transformation* is relatively constant, then thought must strive to parallel this occurrence if it is to grasp the "objective" character of the total structural realities from moment to moment. Without a thought process that mirrors structural realities, the individual can become increasingly lost in illusion. This occurs when one attempts to deal with or explain the present by referring to varying aspects and moments from the past. In other words, the construction of a past-oriented present reflects a conceptualization process that is static or mechanical.

To accurately grasp the distinction between mechanical conceptualization and *transformation* requires the use of the formula of relativity. This theory states (for our purposes) that all knowledge is relational knowledge. This means that all knowledge is to some degree doubtful, though the doubt may be negligible in the cases of pure mathematics and actual sense perceptions. Under this formulation, the greater the flexibility with which one develops and holds formulations, the greater the possibility of *transformation*. Theoretically, on the one extreme of absolutism, we should have a relativity index approaching zero. It should be noted, however, that zero relativity would denote ''truth.'' In other words, any notion that could be described in absolute terms would always remain the same. Absolutism, or truth, implies regularity and prediction in the extreme. Within this framework, $E = mc^2$ approaches a relativity index somewhere in the neighborhood of zero. This formulation strongly suggests that the pursuit of fixed or static ideas is a questionable intellectual activity and is not a steady authentic climb.

Transformation

Conceptualization views change, analogous to a steady climb up a ladder. New thinking views change which take place in periodic leaps. In the Soviet Union, scientists are trained with a philosophy of change. They speak of *transformation* from quantity to quality. This suggests that change occurs in large leaps, the aftermath of slow accumulation of stresses that a system resists until it reaches a breaking point.

The theory of *transformation* suggests such an order. It explains irreversible processes—the movement toward higher and higher orders. The *theory of dissipative structures* has been advanced as a theory which offers a method for understanding *transformation* at every level, a critical role of stress in transformation, and an impetus toward transformation inherent in nature. It is felt that open systems are maintained by a continuous dissipation of energy. It is a continuous exchange of energy with the environment. In a closed system such as a rock or cup, there is no internal transformation energy. A dissipative structure is flowing wholeness; highly organized and always in process. A complex structure, like the brain, is connected at many points and more energy is needed to maintain these connections. Equilibrium, in this case, is a kind of death.

Because those connections can only be sustained by a flow of energy, the system is always influx. The more coherent or intricately connected the structure, the more unstable it is. Increased coherence means increased instability. This very instability is the key to transformation and creates the potential for sudden reordering. Each transformation makes the next one likelier. Each new stage is even more integrated. Flexibility begets flexibility. The theory violates the law of large numbers. A creative minority can reorder a society; the behavior of a small group can change the group as a whole; one person can make a difference. Cooperation seems to be a key (not a conflict); the more complex a system, the greater its potential for transcendence and power. The new structure is like a large paradigm. The perturbation that provokes the very order in a dissipative structure is analogous to the crisis that helps force the shift to a new paradigm.

Evolution is a continual breaking, forming new and richer wholes. *Transformation* is about realities we cannot visualize. Underneath it are transitions and quantum leaps with relationships between events. Thus, in science, it can go where common sense cannot. For example, with math—separate particles can be connected.

When we externalize this process to the social world, we conclude that the political system needs to be transformed not reformed; our governing structures are mechanistic, rigid and fragmented; the world is not working. Our leadership does not encourage paradigm shifts. In social relations, it is necessary to discover new strategies and well springs of power. These strategies must be tied in with the individual proposition of transformation within. Whether the rationale is capitalism, socialism, or Marxism, the notion of transformation is a must. At the heart of transformation is a change in the basic social paradigm.

It is through and by our symbolic processes that we must understand and foster transformation. In other words, we must devise a symbolic (language) method of inquiry which corresponds to the *theory of dissipative structures* in order to understand and have a notion of *transformation*.

The Symbolic Process

Also, we must note that language is both the reality and the material from which all realities are molded. Thus, language is real; it has existence in both time and space. At the same time, to use a particular word is to experience that word. In other words, the use of language results in an immediate type of experience. That is, language becomes the most important single tool in forming and transmitting the character of things. As such, language is the basic material from which complex realities are constructed.

Language is like breathing. We do it automatically. Language is necessary to human life. In order to make progress in our fields of study, it is necessary for each to consciously pursue an *epistemological concern* with the symbolic processes providing the foundations for our disciplines. The Indo-European linguistic process is responsible for the representation of our thought processes here in the West. Our theories and practical applications of those theories that reflect an historical pattern started around 2000 B.C. in a region called Asia Minor. Our language received its most modern structure about 650-350 B.C. in the form of a linguistic structure we call the ''sentence''—which emphasizes structurally a subject and predicate form. This focus emphasizes a thought pattern with rigid implications. Thought became chained to the Socratic syllogism for linear ease in understanding an otherwise multi-dimensional world and became dependent upon the use of Aristotle's absolute classifications to order a shaky, turbulent environment. These powerful influences directed the development of modern human life in Western thought, language, and action until finally being called into question in the early part of the 20th century. The pervasive impact and epistemological confinement of this early European system of thought makes it necessary for the introduction of a symbolic process that, in general, would serve as an alternative and foster a practical approach to examining and reworking the symbolic structure of our disciplines. This direction would suggest that language and epistemological thinking can be combined and utilized as practical theory.

With the experience mode, virtually all perceptions of reality describe events and concepts as they were, as opposed to how they are. The first, and most prominent, cause of this phenomenon is the static conceptualization of thought. Our tendency is, within the framework of this concept, to hold and define words or concepts in a fixed or static fashion. This means that we continue such words as ''friend,'' ''freedom,'' and ''sensitivity'' to describe events that are not depicted by these terms.

For example, take the term "sensitivity." A young man today might grow long hair and wear tie-dyed Levi's in the image of the original hippies. The earlier "hippies" or "flower children" represented a more humanitarian and sensitive approach to all people. In other words, the "hippie" would take time to help a stranger, have kind words for the police officer, smile at the people who pass their way, be gentle in their approach to most people, and generally, attempt to respond sensitively to everyone he or she encounters. Following in this verbal and visual style, our young person today appears similar. That is, he or she dresses in a similar fashion, listens to the same music, and uses the same vergiage. Consequently, our young person will invariably use the word "sensitive" to describe his or her total attitude toward mankind. Upon closer examination, however, we might find that he or she is to some degree sensitive to a select peer group of six or eight other young people. Additionally, we might discover that this group generally agrees on most issues and acts with hostility toward those who hold opposing views. They respond with hostility toward their parents, toward other "hip" types who disagree with their philosophy, and toward non-hip critics. In addition, they generally maintain no friendships outside the confines of their small circle. In point of fact, whatever sensitivity is present is extremely limited in scope to a few select individuals and encompasses a particular response to a narrow spectrum of experiences. Generally speaking, this group and/or individual is insensitive to most people and is in fact, sensitive in an extremely limited fashion to a select few. However, the continued use of the term "sensitive," as applied to the totality of their action acts to hide the wider implications of their behavior from themselves and others. In effect, they have created an extremely limited context from which to construct a reality. This rigid construction provides the basis for the illusion of zero relativity and reflects an approach to change that parallels its relativity index. In other words, the more relative one's approach to reality, the greater will be the potential for change. This limited type of construction comes from an incorrect perception of, and consequently the misuse of, time and relativity, which results in a distorted construction of what is going on.

Secondly, as this behavior continues, it will gain acceptability and dependability through time. This is accomplished as the limited experience is able to maintain itself as successful in habit. As any particular experience gains acceptability and dependability, its external component will tend to become more concrete and predictable. This means that, as the word ''sensitive'' gains acceptability, the response to this word *becomes patterned*. It is then possible to predict with greater certainty, both the use and response aspects of the word ''sensitive'' in a given context.

The more stable the character of any external component, the greater will be the regularity of the subsequent experience. Theoretically, then, within this extremely limited context, the internal logic of the situation would allow for experience to become an end unto itself. That is, under the proper conditions, everyone might sanction the use of the term ''sensitive'' without caring about its applications. In other words, the internal importance of particular words acts as an experience to the group may absolutely outweigh the consequences of that action outside the group. This means that the construction of a conceptualization is a foundation of the context from which it is drawn. Unless we understand these subtle names in the language, we will not be able to discern real transformation. The most important implication here, is that thought is not something separate from the language we use. And, the ability to provide appropriate symbols and language is a prerequisite for making good judgments and effective decisions in general. I have come to the conclusion that we need a process which is comprehensive, simple and convenient; one which includes within its purview, deduction and induction; additionally, one that can be internalized and used by humans whether they consider themselves theoreticians or practitioners. This process is labeled *abduction*. *Abduction* is the process by which we finally transform ourselves.

21

CHAPTER 3

Holism, Reductionism and Empiricism: A Focus on Abduction

D. C. Philips in his book, *Holistic Thought in Social Science*, talks about the differences and disagreements between holists and reductionists. His ultimate conclusion is that they both are necessary. He states there are three levels of holism. The first level involves an elimination of individualism or reductionism as a criterion for understanding. The second relates reductionism within the holistic picture, flowing one into the other. The third is the development of a set of holistic linguistic symbols that will match the world of events.

Some reductionists do not take issue with the first nor the third level, but with the second, which says individualization or reductionism has no use. I, also, take issue with those who claim it has no value. The question, in my mind, has less to do with whether or not reductionism has any value, but whether or not the symbols used for analysis are appropriate—that is, static or non-static. For example, a symbol used frequently in the social sciences is rationality. On the above basis, one must pose a question about the use of the term rationality, not whether or not it is reductionism, but whether or not it is a term that ought to be used in the sense that it has been used. In other words, does it have a ''structural'' relationship to the world of events. With this as a starting point, holists and reductionists are not at odds; both should recognize the necessity for transcending the either/or corridor. It is a possibility that the purists have artificially dichomotized the two schools (holist-reductionist), taken us back to a separation of facts and values, and the world of the logical positivists. The key note, here, is not whether they are both useful, but how they are *useful* and whether or not the language or symbolic process for the nonverbal is in keeping with a process orientation. Therefore, I conclude that the usefulness of working in conjunction with each other are determined in both instances as follows: (1) By the kind of symbolic process used for investigation; (2) Whether or not we philosophically *draw* from a school of thought that transcends logical-positivism.

This appears to be the task ahead. It is not whether we use one or the other, but how they are to be utilized or what level of abstraction each offers at a given time.

As the reader might already know, the logical-positivists attempted to provide a solution to this situation. Logical positivism was an attempt to blend value and facts in social science jargon and in natural science jargon, logic with the scientific method or deduction with induction. Bertrand Russell, of course, in his *Principia Mathematica* introduced the *theory of logical types* in an attempt to resolve the matter by advocating logical solutions that would supply us with a rational and objective system, e.g., holistic and pure thought processes which would not include the subjective world of positivism. Pure reasoning based on a system of methods, ideally correct, would not allow for the use of induction which is synonymous with more reduction; in other words, empiricism was unnecessary. Empiricism in this sense, of course, is synonymous with the scientific method. It would logically follow that empiricism did not pertain. Therefore, the theory of types was advertised as a system without a need for ''empiricism'' (the scientific method). There were several inherent implications: (1) believing that empiricism is synonymous with the scientific method; (2) believing that anything similar to induction has to be excluded in its entirety; and (3) there was a place for deduction as symbolic logic, but narrow Aristotelian logic had to be repudiated. *The theory of types was an improvement*, as is the hypothetico-deductive method as it pertains to general systems theory, but not an epistemic jump. The logical positivists' school proposed to present us with an alternative by analytically blending induction and deduction, without making a distinction between the scientific method and empiricism, and empiricism and rationalism. To the logical-positivists, this was the best of all worlds. While they would not say that values and facts were separate (except analytically) nor would they say they were the same, they could at least show how they were connected. The key limitation was in the epistemological and linguistic confusion of empiricism, rationalism and the scientific method, which were considered synonymous with each other and objective in intent while the deductive or logical part was considered subjective and normative. So, historically, the blending took place—not only with the upside down interpretation of how these conceptual notions should be considered, i.e., rationality is analytical and inductive, but also, with the assumption that the human nervous system was a combination of value and factual components that could be analyzed under the rubic of this mechanical blend. While there is no dispute with the patterned interpretation that no separation is possible, I am disputing the belief that these two worlds (deduction and induction) blended adequately express a new dimension of "empiricism" and "rationality." The logical-positivist view automatically maroons us analytically to a separation of facts and values, objectivity and subjectivity. Additionally, we continue to use the same terms which do not broaden our outlook, although our mission is to do so. The old language maroons us to the past. I will return to this statement later; meanwhile, I feel it necessary to show how we have congealed our social science world by reifying such an analogy in terms of structural-functional analysis. In its simplest form, it states the world has structure and it has functions. Structure becomes the logic, and function becomes the actual fact. This is supposed to give us a reality orientation. The implication, here, is that there is no place for pure symbolic logic; therefore, all of our theories should be middle range. Structural functional analysis rejects the notion that there is a whole world of "rationality" (synthetic) that can only be tapped by "integrative unity." Therefore, rationality has no place in the everyday world of activity. The mission of "rationality" and abstract theories both lose their "real" purpose and mislead us into thinking that there is something called ''rational'' in the world of give and take, and that the world of ''abstract pure'' and postulative theory holds no purpose for our everyday functions. It becomes the pragmatist view that all philosophy, abstractions and speculations are esoteric and valueless for practice in management and living more effectively. The congealing of the world of deduction and induction, logic and positivism and eventually structural-functional analysis leads us to such a conclusion, thereby leaving little room and support for thoughts that fall within the abstract structure. It is a one short step to working within the confines of the old language structure by only making distinctions between Malinowski and A. D. Bradcliff Brown's functionalism, and a continued debate between the distinction that exists between organization and management, policy and administration, ends and means. The debate is perpetuated by the analytic logical-positivist pattern. The logical-positivist judgment pictures a neat package which *appears* to be a broad world, but in actuality, narrows our intellectual overview and practical commitment.

My position is not that we should only emphasize symbolic logic, but that we must begin to view rationalism and empiricism in a different manner. This focus, of course, leads me to the term ''abduction.'' Abduction makes particular cases of deduction and induction. Abduction does not attempt to blend the worlds of induction and deduction, but to particularize the usefulness of induction and deduction together and apart depending upon circumstances. Since induction and deduction are separate analytical tools, the combining of them does not produce a new dimension, nor does it enable us to provide a test of correspondence that would give us a different rendition of the structure of events. I believe this test can only be developed by rising to another stage which outlines in precise and appropriate terms the different assumptions about rationality, empiricism and ''old'' logic. We must view rationality, empiricism and ''old'' logic as being separate and together (simultaneously). Together, in terms of ''the'' pragmatic application to everyday decision making, which linguistically would serve notice that they are unified under certain holistic circumstances when we practice in our everyday affairs. In other words, the key is not to view them as separate (except in an ideal sense) on any level whether it is theoretical "practical" or practical "practical." The new dimension forces us to suggest an "empirical" and "rational" relationship which conforms to the holistic view. In other words, we are not concerned about them being reductionist, but whether these terms are being properly used. It is one of extensionalizing by using the organism as a whole approach plus environment. It becomes a circular process, which at a given moment in time, suspends the narrow scientific approach while a "logical" sequence is taking place within the broader interpretation of empiricism. It is, then, not a question of whether we work with the deductive and inductive methods, but how and on what basis.

Expanding Empiricism: The Process of Abduction

I have come to the conclusion that there are some very simple things to be done. They are so obvious that we fail to focus on them. They are elusive and nonconcrete. The requirement is that we separate the various levels and stages of thinking within a circular process and recognizing them as being holistic. The circular-holistic process becomes the container and the separation of the various levels and stages become the content. For example, if I say a criticism of the criticism that becomes one level above the first criticism or it could be a stage depending upon the *content* of the criticism about the criticism. Then I can say a criticism *about* the criticism of the criticism. I then rise to a third level, or stage depending upon the content. This can go on and on without a contradiction. I can even say a criticism to stop the criticism and later add a criticism of the stop the criticism which says we should stop stopping the criticism. Now, what makes these contents circular and holistic? Well, when I simply *examine* the tools (which are the containers) I am using to symbolize my levels, the process is circular and comes back to the fundamentals of what I am using. For example, if I say the subject-predicate arrangement of our symbolic process makes it hard for us to understand that we can move from one level to another with frequency. I can then go full circle automatically from the content to the container then back to the content. The content enables us to analyze the container, and what emerges from the container affects the content and so on. The key word is *examine*. Built into this examining process is the epistemological or epistemic concern. Unfortunately, we have usually been looking for something more difficult than this. Consequently, we over-looked the obvious. The focus was on the linear approach; we have assumed that our symbolic process is adequate and we automatically used it to understand our content without challenging the process. The challenge of the symbolic process is epistemological and fundamental. When we borrow from the natural sciences, we also borrow their symbols—some of which are static. The questioning of those symbols in our own epistemological terms enables us to draw from the same sources that the natural sciences have drawn from. Our focus treats the concentration on the symbolic process as fundamental. Korzybski once said regarding structure: "Scientists found long ago that the common language in daily use is of little value in science. This language gives us a form of representation of very old structure in which we find it impossible to give a full, coherent account of ourselves or of the world around us. Each science has to build a special terminology . . . . This problem of a suitable language is of serious importance. Too little do we realize what a language of antiquated structure is . . . such language prevents correct analysis through the semantic habits and structural implications embodied in it." (Alfred Korzybski, *Science and Sanity*, p. 56). And, I add that our structure must have an appropriate similarity with the world of events. We will only know this if we begin with structure and symbolism and so on. Our emphasis is on our examination of the empirical circular process combining deduction, induction, and abduction. Our *laboratory is the symbolic process*. At this point, we must invent (and we have always invented in the social sciences), but the difference now is to invent with holism, circularity and with a different kind of symbolism. This focus makes non-quantification as important as quantification.

The abductive process seems to be a method of inquiry for *emergence* and *transformation*. My argument, here, with structural functionalism is not that it does not focus properly; however, (1) it represents the continuation of a tight logical system that embodies the attitudes of narrow deduction and induction, (2) it does not sufficiently emphasize formally on the development of a new language, and (3) it becomes, at best, a reductionist approach although espousing holism, evolution, and diachronic and synchronic relationships as foci. This was permissible when we did not know better. Now that we know there is something called emergence, which considers structure and functions as specific cases. Furthermore, it views structure and functions as embracing each other in a tight sequence of activity, which does not even involve the theory of types (classes about classes, Bertrand Russell), nor does it go beyond the mechanical theoretical model of feedback. It is good as far as it goes. Unfortunately, it just does not go far enough.

Although structural functional analysis is within the holistic province, its roots are still within the logical-positivists' school. It is holistic within a particular order. The tools are induction and deduction. Structural-functional analysis is a part of holism 1, but does not meet the criteria of holism 2 and holism 3. Holism 2 rejects reductionism; holism 3 asks for a new language; and, holism 1 simply states that we need a theory.

Abduction means looking at the symbolic process to determine whether or not the present categories are accurate and somewhat adequate. A discipline or professional field must have this in order to improve its decision-making capacity. For example, the field of business and the discipline of economics are replete with meaningless, and for the most part, obsolete categories. The categories of depression, recession, free enterprise, inflation are nonsense symbols that ought to be exorcised from the discipline. They do not grasp the moving reality of what is going on. A different language is not only a different vocabulary; a different language is a different vision of life.

The Process of Abduction Summarized

You question the assumptions of your theories by focusing specifically on the symbols and what they represent. Not only do we question the assumptions which these symbols represent, we set upon the task of developing new symbols and new assumptions based upon the most recent epistemological data and our own individual findings derived from a cognitive study of the use of the epistemic methodology. This is the key to the use of the epistemic methodology, which undergrids the process of abduction.

Symbols must be changed, assumptions revised and replaced, not just based on the collection of data inductively obtained, but the change must come from an independent thought that emerges from an overarching theoretical process. For example, in Arthur Bentley's *The Process of Government*, his thesis included the notion that the symbol *interaction* (rationality) in human affairs should have been replaced by the notion of *transaction*. He noted that even in the field of mathematics, static symbols like interaction were still being used. This motivated him to write a book entitled *A Linguistic Analysis of Mathematics*. To this date, both the Natural and Social Sciences are replete with these static terms, one of Einstein's shortcomings. And, of course, the most contemporary books in the social sciences, political and administrative affairs, and psychology still use the symbol *interaction*, which is obsolete, and therefore, considered non-functional. It is a key notion of induction and deduction.

In our research and studies we do not abandon deduction and induction; we merely structure these within the bounds of abduction. This enables us to utilize the traditional methodological tools and remain constantly innovative and change-oriented as we revise symbols and assumptions.

An example of abduction would be the observation-inference method. Someone concluded that the garbage can had been stolen. Instead, after an accidental investigation, it was found that the garbage can had been put one into another by the collectors and they looked like one. What does this mean? We watch our inferences! Yes, it also means something deeper. There may be a pattern here which points to noninvestigation of situations adequately because one might be reluctant to know the truth about situations, whatever they might be. There may be a deep epistemological reason, which is a fear.

Observation—inference situation led this person to deduction-induction-abduction, the person was at stages III and IV simultaneously of the epistemological profile. Observation-Inference is well within stages II and III of the epistemological profile and will remain there except with the introduction of abduction which enables us to move up to the fourth stage. And the fourth stage dictates that one extensionalize and question the assumption they have made automatically. A failure to automatically question with flexibility is usually the sign of a deficient theory (William Barrett, *The Illusion of Technique*, p. 81).

Wittgenstein's tractatus contains a few papers ''tacked'' on which give us a real sense of the beginning of abduction. The place of the mystical is identified. The noumenal is the realm where our symbols fall short—we enter it on faith by postulating what we can never prove, but enter it we must as spiritual beings (William Barnett, *The Illusion of Technique*). The potential is there. The logic of Russell, for Wittgenstein, began to appear as a framework much too rigid in which to cast reality. It attempted to use language as a model which lead to critical philosophy. Furthermore, it was the beginning of turning inward for self-examination. Abduction is a continuation of this process.

In short, the positivists took over the empiricism of David Hume and annexed it to the new technique of mathematical logic. This became the language of language statements which can be classified as factual and logical components. The conclusion was: Statements about the world fall within the province of the empirical sciences; it was a rejection of symbolic logic composed of tautological statement manipulated for theoretical use—and which tell us nothing about the world. The philosopher, according to this logic, must be content to merely analyze the logical syntax of value statements; and, when philosophers have meta-physical questions, they must turn them over to the Natural Sciences.

In this sense, there is left only the logical activity of classification. So, Wittgenstein drew up a complete blueprint for logical-positivism before the name of this school had been coined. He did this in his *Tractatus logico-philosophicus*. The thrust was toward applied epistemology. This thrust must be dimensionalized with substantive and process knowledge of past history which leads me to the notion of being epistemic in our approach. Therefore, we must know that: (1) from mythology to logos—reason introduced the classical period of science. In those few centuries, the foundations for mathematics were laid, in particular geometry and mathematical astronomy, which rested the whole building of these branches of science when the great renaissance began in the sixteenth century A.D. Toward the beginning of the second century B.C., the progress of scientific thought and the rate of discovery began to slow down. This heralded the decline of the classical period of science and the advent of the Middle Ages. The scientific tradition was held together by the Byzantium and the Islamic Renaissance which began in the 9th century. The Western scholars included the Islamic scholarship within the framework of the Aristotelian doctrine. For a thousand years, the rationalization of nature was perverted and distorted by being preserved as a bookish body of learning, taught as a given system of doctrines, concepts about nature and the physical world. In the 16th and 17th century, nature, again, began to be questioned in a "rational" way. The Helio-centric system of thought introduced by Copernicus opened up a new approach to mechanics and dynamics. For the first time in history, science was confronted with two radically different comprehensive theories. This new situation gave rise to a conception of physical science in which theory, experiment and observation *interact* (transact) together with astronomy. It made for a most spectacular progress in one grand sweep. The study of mechanics was introduced because the science of motion and dynamics emerged as the central subject of Sir Isaac Newton. *The Mechanistic Mode* of thought has been prominent in physical thought since antiquity, and from the time of Descartes, even up to the end of the 19th century, physicists held the view that scientific theory had not been really proven because it had not been demonstrated in terms of mechanical analysis. A conceptual turning point in the history of physical thought was introduced by Clerk Maxwell in his electro-magnetic theory. He divorced himself from all mechanical ways of thought. This became the harbinger of even a more fundamental breakaway from mechanical ways of thought, making unavoidable the introduction of the quantum hypothesis. Together, quantum and special relativity inaugurated a new phase of intensive (*transaction*) between science and philosophy—in that, both theories grew from an epistemological analysis of the foundations of physics which led to a thorough revision of its fundamental assumptions and gave rise to the renaissance of a philosophical approach to science comparable only to the 17th century.

The Teleological approach was predominant in ancient Greece. The mechanical or causal approach played an important role for shorter periods in antiquity, it lost to the teleological view. Aristotle built a system which became the dominating world view for nearly two thousand years until it was overthrown by the work of Galileo and Descartes. Aristotle compared Nature to a supreme creative artist—an architect who builds a house according to a well-designed plan. This related it to the *structural approach*, which puts emphasis on forces and the resulting movement sees nature primarily as a well-ordered structure whose parts are related to the whole in some definite patterns. The existence of structure involved the existence of movements, structure and dynamics became interdependent. The structural conception of nature was developed by the Pythagorean School. The universe was composed of polarities and differentiated wholes and the movements were designed to remove those polarities. The main difference between the structural and dynamical conceptions of the universe has been the emphasis put on one or the other.

Aristotle had a definite structural character, i.e., the dichotomy of Heaven and Earth and the theory of Natural Motions. Kepler was the last important manifestation of the structural conception. Galileo initiated the Age of the Dynamical Conception which could be called the Newtonian Age, whose decline coincided with a renewal of the structural approach or a much higher level associated within quantum physics.

History and an understanding of history becomes paramount in the process of abduction. The historical perspective, for example, teaches us that the phrase, "solving problems," is unacceptable in holistic understanding. The solving of a problem is by definition, static and a solitary affair.

We confront, "deal with" and address situations. We are automatically included in difficult or nondifficult situations, but not automatically included in problems or problem-solving. It is one short step to saying, "It's your or my problem," rather than we are together in addressing situations. We cannot and I emphasize cannot extricate ourselves; all we can do is develop skills for living and self-management in situations that automatically include us. Moreover, we do not solve anything; we merely move it to a new level and "deal" with it differently.

Problem solving is a misnomer of what actually takes place; it is misleading and will inevitably lead us to erroneous conclusions. Finally, "problem-solving" speaks to absolutism and one cause or causality—which is not the way the world turns (as far as we know now).

Because of all that has been said, abduction must be a self-subsistent method of inquiry—by self-subsistent, we mean no dependence on any narrow field of knowledge. Cosmological theories approach this: mathematics approach this, and, a theory which emphasizes the examination, transformation, and an epistemological revision of the symbolic processes satisfies the criteria for self-subsistence. In other words, the methodology must be epistemological in intent. Abduction strives for this self-subsistence and it includes as an overarching process, the methodology of the creative loop.

In 1867, Charles Sanders Peirce was widely acclaimed as the most original thinker in American philosophy. His first statement on the subject of abduction was contained in a paper *"On the Natural Classification of Arguments,"* which he read in 1967 to the American Academy of Arts and Sciences. A more complete statement of the theory is contained in the *Journal of Speculative Philosophy Essays,* 1868. In papers written after 1891, he widened the concept of abduction to include methodological process, linking induction and deduction to abduction. He stated that abduction furnished the reasoner with hypothesis while induction provided the method of testing and verifying. Peirce conceived of three stages of inquiry: (1) abduction invents or proposes our hypothesis; (2) deduction explicates hypothesis; and (3) induction consists in the process of testing hypothesis. Abduction is the only logical operation which introduces any new ideas.

While Peirce held that abduction was a form of logic, and there is a logic to discovery; there are those, however, who disagree. Karl Popper argues that the questions of how a hypothesis happens or why the conceiving or inventing of a theory does not call for logical analysis. Popper feels that this should belong in the realm of empirical psychology. Popper, R..B. Braithwaite, and Irving Copi feel that it is guess, chance, hunch, or some type of mental jump called "intuition," and should not be subject to any kind of analysis. Moreover, John O. Wisdom concludes that there is no type of scientific inference that cannot be fitted into the hypothetico-deductive system. Thus, by not making a fundamental distinction between hypothetico-deductive and abduction, they appear the same on the surface. But, the fundamental difference is that hypothetico-deductive holds tentative the deduction; and abduction is concerned with how the tentative hypothesis was generated. Peirce, in short, wished to show that reasoning toward a hypothesis is a different kind of reasoning from a hypothesis and that there was a logic to the so-called intuitive process. When asked how one goes about generating a worthwhile hypothesis, he replied by saying that "man" has a natural bent for being connected with the universe and those intuitive "feelings" are in accord with nature. "How else," he questioned, "can we account for Galileo, Copernicus, Newton, and Einstein?" He concludes that it is not plausibility, but pursuit which dictates our direction because the peculiar affinity of the human mind with nature leads us to guess correctly. (A deeper analysis of this can be obtained from K.T. Fann's *Peirce's Theory of Abduction*; Martinus Wijhoff, The Hague, Holland— 1970; Thomas Nickles, *Scientific Discovery Logic, and Rationality*, D'Reidel Publishing Company, Boston, 1980; Robert Sharp, *Journal on Transaction of the Charles S. Peirce Society*, Induction, Abduction and the Evolution of Science," Winter, 1970, Vol. VI, No. 1—(same journal)—Spring, 1970, Vol. VI, No. 2, and Fall, 1983, Vol. XIX, No. 4; and *Philosophy of Science*, Vol. 13, Oct., 1946, No. 4—Arthur W. Burks *"Peirce's Theory of Abduction."* A most interesting essay appears in Thomas A. Sebeok's *The Play of Amusement* entitled

"You Know My Method: A Juxtaposition of Charles S. Peirce and Sherlock Holmes,'' Chapter 2, Indiana University Press, Bloomington, 1981.)

In my next chapter, I shall attempt to expand Peirce's directive by suggesting a logic behind the generating process and a language method for developing plausibility as well as pursuit. I call this logic of the process the Creative Loop.

CHAPTER 4

The Creative Loop

Our decisions become creative decisions when we begin to view a process differently. I once visited Dartmouth College at Hanover. In Hanover, I did some original and primary research on Adelbert Ames, Jr., who had done original work on perception and decision making. In a paper written in 1921, he said (I paraphrase): We could grasp truths intuitively, which we cannot understand rationalistically. In other words, we can have a correct ''abductive'' conception of the relationship of circumstances without being *conscious* of any logical steps by which we arrived at such a conception and without knowing why the conception is correct.

There is still another field of activity where our abductive innovative faculties play a large part, that is, in our ordinary everyday life. We are daily, almost hourly, called upon to take action or to make a decision. The correctness of these actions or decisions depend upon whether or not we have a true conception of the related circumstance. The related circumstance in all but the very simplest cases are so complex that an intellectual analysis and logical judgment concerning them is impossible. As a result, we largely work on intuitional basis, for example, in judging the personality or character of those with whom we have dealings. This intuitional innovative insight is markedly developed in all great men. With men of equal intellectual capacity, those among them who have intuitional innovative insight will come nearer some truth and be more useful and successful than those who have not. (Intuition and education, typewritten and used with permission of the Dartmouth Library-Archives Division). *The parentheses are mine*, added because intuition speaks to something mystical, but innovation has a pattern. *It is the position of this author that what we call intuition follows a certain pattern and can be depicted. Therefore, it is abduction rather than intuition.* The term intuition is misleading. This, in a limited way, illustrates the epistemic process.

Prospect and Projection—Postulation

Epistemics means breaking out of the cultural bind— questioning this culture, daring to challenge a value which leads to a familiar solution, getting rid of the fear of the unknown, and feeling uncomfortable with the thought that one has "smashed" an idol. It is like siding with the rebels without being a rebel, but daring to do so for the benefit of the many, knowing that this will create a world of living and not just surviving. The pangs will disappear slowly as one emerges to a new level; it is the fear of not being sure that this will not eventuate into death. The question, "Can I stand that much pain?" is answered by "yes," because it seeps in slowly as one emerges from the old life and begins to live with the new. It is just a matter of being confident that the human potential is a growing matter; we can avoid stultification and move with the stream.

In short, epistemics, in part, is the use of time-binding as a conceptual process focusing on the symbolic dimension of cultural history and evolution. Not just for looking at the past and diagnosing, but, using the various disciplines to philosophically analyze history in a contemporary fashion and postulate new directions and new mental models.

How does that cultural history shape within the conceptual process of time-binding? Deduction dominated the scene for centuries, when philosophers took common language as self-evident truths. They did not suspect, at the time, that these were postulates having currency anywhere but within their own epistemic fraction of the human family. Many centuries later, induction became the prevailing skill, and the scientific evolution unfolded itself in systematic observation, experiments, measurements, and mathematical formulations. The time has now come for abduction to be recognized as basic, not simply the anagoge of probability dimly outlined by Aristotle. We have done away with the delusion of objectivity, and we face, with undisturbed mind, the responsibility of creating the world of humans that will hold within its structure our own life and that of the next generation. Instead of simply rationalizing about the past findings of science and continuing the metaphysics of former philosophies, theorize *above and beyond* the empirical science. As the prefix ''meta'' implies, the cultural scientist (who I shall henceforth refer to as the epistemicist) has to take his place in the loop of human creative functioning and assume his share of responsibility in the total human enterprise.

First, he has to evaluate anew the interpretive results of all the sciences as they reenter the living process of human striving. Second, he has to direct the postulating process of creating new theories and doctrines that will guide humankind in the next stage of self-renewal. He does not have to *prove* his statements by deduction or induction. The time is long past when he thought his role was to be assertive as if he had found the truth revealed to him by nature (or by God, in the case of believers in revelation). The time has come to proffer, humbly but courageously, alternatives that are plausible.

The science of epistemology becomes central. It enables us to identify the many aspects of the semantic transactions that lock us and our environment in an energetic unit. Abduction is the application of the science of epistemology to self-guidance and management; it becomes the professional skill of the up-to-date time-binding epistemicist.

The time-binding begins by practicing the skill in simple situations and by self-reflexively observing as talks are conducted in the plain common sense language of the cultural milieu. One by one, *inadequacies* and *inconsistencies* of the *symbol system* inherited from ancestors whose ignorance was pervasive are discovered. *Innovation* is practiced and better *constructs* are proposed. Bergson did so when he woke up to the fact that *time* was *geometrized* like space, and he introduced the notion of *duration* to be perceived by a certain kind of *intuition*. Einstein did so when he questioned the axiom of *simultaneity* and *absolute time*, and introduced the *speed of light* as the measuring rod of the universe. Jung faced it when he introduced the process of *synchronicity* as being beyond relativity time.

Methodology and Postulation

How do we implement what I have talked about? What methodology do we use? General semantics epistemology and epistemics are combined to formulate a method of inquiry for abduction. And, general semantics epistemology finds it use within the five stages of the epistemological profile. What is the epistemological profile? How does it work? The first question: the epistemological profile is an instrument for bringing history onto a contemporary evolution and cultural science, in order to enable us to go beyond the macroscopic in finding direction and postulating new meanings. It can be used to facilitate understanding of individuals, groups, nations, international situations, institutions and systems. It is theory and therapy. It is a matter of moving from descriptive to history in action—from what was, to what is, and to what might be.

The second question is: "How does it work?" There is something called the "real" world. This pertains mostly to our everyday affairs. It has been previously determined by the epistemological profile that we have undergone three conceptual historical periods and we find ourselves, in a contemporary way, operating for the most part at one of these stages predominately; and society itself, for the most part, functions at a certain stage or episteme. The implicit assumption is that we ought to be functioning in the third period (postulating), but our activities, for the most part, are carried on in the second period of our cultural development. How do we begin to deal with the so-called external reality effectively (second period) and maintain our "personal" functioning in the third period? These periods are called conceptual revolutions and are translated in something we call epistemological stages of cultural development.

First, let me spell out the stages in epistemic terms. *Stage 1*, the sensing stage, is considered the primitive stage. It is an emotional state composed of characteristics such as being argumentative and reactive, for the most part without facts. It is a state where a person infers from observation and believes that the inferences represent the true picture of the situation and the world. The person does not see the difference between maps and territory and confuses levels of abstracting by identifying similar situations as the same without noting differences. Not only does the person use observation and inference, but he or she acts totally on those inferences as if they were actual observations. This is the stage of *reaction*. *Stage II*, the classifying stage, is the period of Greek philosophers. It is the two-valued stage. Persons operating at this stage will classify on the basis of inferences and ''feel'' and act as if an object really is the name they have given it. At this stage, a person does not go beyond the labels, i.e., a communist is a communist. Not only is there no difference between one communist and another, they are totally different from a capitalist. None of them have human instincts. They are all bad and once a communist—always a communist. This person reacts to labels. It is strictly a macroscopic interpretation. This person translates this thought in judgmental terms, and according to this person, people do not change. They are what they are and I am what I am. They are static in their interpretation of the world. It is the *action* stage. *Stage III*, is the relating stage. It is based mostly on Newtonian mechanics. For every action there is a reaction. This person recognizes mechanical differences between people, but for the most part, they are the same. This person gives lip service to change. He uses mechanical analysis to describe human situations. Usually, this is in terms of money. If this person gives, it is to win an advantage. It is thought that people respond through stimuli and react to outside stimuli; this is the overriding theme. The world and people can be run by having enough money or knowledge and having more resources than the next person. The syndrome is: The best defense is a good offense. Wars are necessary, and there are good and bad wars. The law of the jungle must prevail because there are sheep, wolves, lions, dogs, elephants, and tigers; only the strongest will survive. The themes are survival at all costs and don't trust anyone. The latest findings in human behavior are intellectual tid-bits to be used to influence, direct, and manipulate. It is the stage of *Interaction*.

The fourth stage is the postulating stage, where the indexes multiordinality, self-reflexiveness, nonidentity, nonallness, abstracting process, map versus territory, and the epistemological profile are not just intellectual tid-bits, but a way of living. Decisions regarding what man is all about are tentative abductive decisions. Man is not an animal, but a time-binder capable of cooperating and having great potential for making a better life for all. This person views others residing at the other stages with compassion, sees conflict as an opportunity for sharing, is in touch with himself and his feelings, life is a ceaseless affair and power is to be shared with, not used over. Even these tenets are held tentative by the person at stage IV. For example, indexing, dating, etc., while mechanical in nature if internalized properly, can be of value in understanding situations. This person is involved with life as a process and continues to emerge and is always in a state of becoming. This person recognizes differences and similarities, knows when a difference makes a *difference*, does not indulge in debates, but rather in the sharing of ideas and information; is dedicated to a search for bettering ways of transforming the human condition and recognizes the little knowledge he has can be of assistance only if it is flexible, tentative, and transient. There is no observation without an observer. We are all semantic-reactors-transactors. This is the stage of *transaction*.

Stage V has to do with tapping the innovative part of an individual. It is recognizing feelings and inferences without acting on them as if they were the truth or facts. It is distinguished from the sensing stage in the sense that, at the sensing stage, one continues to act on these feelings and consider them the last word and defend to the end the rightness of the position.

At the participating stage or stage V, the feeling is held tentative until proven or until extensionalization has taken place. There is a realization that this is not complete and is correct only to the point that it can be verified. Another distinguishing factor is stage V persons utilize stage IV for translation; whereas Stage I people, for the most part, use stage II criteria for participating and implementing, the stage V person believes in being aware of thoughts and feelings that emerge seemingly without reason, or out of the ''blue,'' so to speak. It is the stage of *synchronicity*.

If we are discussing power and how the world operates, at stages I, II and III, how does one who subscribes to stages IV and V operate and function effectively in a world dominated by stage III? In other words, can we deal with the "is," and, commit ourselves to the ushering in of the "ought," i.e., or how does one maneuver with political, social, psychological, economic and human realities? Or should the first question be: "Does one?" The answer to that question is in the affirmative. There are a host of mundane world problems that must be managed. So, the crucial question is, "How does one deal with the mundane particular cases, and the various stages of the epistemological profile without losing involvement in a higher level of existence?"

Let met talk for a moment in relation to this about posture and a particular formulation about posture. It is essential to assume that knowledge and understanding are of the utmost importance. It is, also, essential to assume that the knowledge we need can be invented, developed, and accumulated in such a way that it can be utilized. The first level of involvement is to view activities that come under one's theoretical or philosophical thrust as particular cases within a larger overarching process. The next is to enter into negotiations at the level diagnosed, whether it be stages I, II, or III in a detached manner. Recognition is a key. When we ascertain the implicit assumptions in the situation, we have several options at our disposal—one, we can describe what we think is best from our stage four position. Secondly, we can transact with the person on their terms, recognizing it as a mechanical device which enables us to skillfully manage ourselves in the situation. Let me give an illustration. I was having a conversation with one former president of the University of Southern California regarding the deposit of money in a black bank. First, I made the statement that this would be a laudable thing to do and would be a major contribution to the black community and also the community at large. This made sense to him. But, it was just the beginning of our conversation; I was at the fourth state of the epistemological profile. Then I quickly moved to the third stage and said this would be good for USC's image in the community—one which would probably put us into somewhat of a power position, as far as the community was concerned. When I volunteered that statement, I was at stage III of the epistemological profile, the relating stage. He agreed that it would be a good idea to put some money into a black bank.

On another occasion, the Director of the School of Public Administration and I went to the president to ask that he lend his name as co-chairman for a conference we were organizing; he replied that he was not allowing his name to be used to support conferences. I believe the director talked about 30 minutes at the postulating stage (IV) (the content of the discussion had to do with the value of the conference to society and to the community in particular). The president was still unconvinced. Then I decided to move to the relating stage. I said that we believe it would be political for USC and for himself if he would lend his name to the conference. He agreed and gave us permission to use his name.

We had moved up and down the epistemological profile in order to find the appropriate stage. The president was at the relating stage of this and, of course, our communication and message had to be at the same stage. This is a necessity if we are to be effective. An economist-philosopher puts it this way: ''The rate of technological development depends almost entirely on the amount of resources which a society devotes to the innovative process and to the educative process. Of these, the innovative process is the most mysterious. *We do not really understand the sources of human creativity.*''

I agree with Professor Boulding when he says that, we do not, yet, understand the sources of human creativity. But I refuse to stop at that negative acknowledgement. I would say, we do not *fully* understand at this time—and I emphasize *fully*.

Innovation has worked and is still working according to a very definite sequence of processes. It is comprised of 5 different steps: (1) It starts with an idea, new and untested until then, but plausible to a person who has internalized the knowledge and the skills pertinent to the field to which the idea belongs. This we shall call the *postulating stage*. The mental process that gave birth to it is abduction. It emerges from the totality of the life experiences of the innovator. (2) Planning is the second stage and it is achieved by a process of deduction from the postulate taken as a major premise. Once the postulate has been stated and accepted tentatively, we draw from it definite directives then decide how to set up the experiment or the systematic observation that will test the postulate. (3) Experimenting or observing systematically is the next step. It calls for the exercise of the most sophisticated methods and skills available to the observer—that is, experiment. (4) The fourth stage is that of interpreting the results of the experiment or observation, and drawing inferences from it. The process involved is *induction*, carried out according to the strictest rules of this aspect of logic. (5) The Interpretation of results is then checked against the original postulate. This postulate is either confirmed for the time being, corrected in part to initiate a new and better cycle of planning, experimenting and observing, or put aside because it was found inadequate for the purpose. In such case, an entirely new process of abduction is required, based on the awareness of the inadequacy of the former postulate, or of its equivalents, often disguised under different verbal forms.

This sequence of processes form a loop consisting of four operations: postulating, planning, experimenting, and interpreting. These operations are linked by the skills of abduction, deduction, and induction, as shown in the following diagram below:

Deduction

1. Postulating	2. Planning
Abduction	Induction
	3. Experimenting
X. Original experience and knowledge	4. Interpreting

The X rectangle represents a man's total knowledge and experience to date. Its value increases as he postulates, plans, experiments, and interprets a sequential series of activities, and adds to his interpretation of previously accumulated wisdom (rectangle X). As this renewed and enriched wisdom rises to a higher level of organized complexity, the creative loop (postulating-planning-experimenting-interpreting) bends in the time-dimension and becomes the spiral of human cultural advance or personal and cultural evolution.

Korzybski lumped together the four processes of postulating, planning, experimenting, and interpreting into what he called, "thought." Thought was given as the specific characteristic of man, the time bender. The creative loop then becomes the appendage that shows the addition of brainwork to mere biological functioning.

The innovative loop is considered the process or method of inquiry. Among all methods that lead to validated belief, this method of inquiry is the most successful. Effective time-binding, however, must be concerned with going beyond this goal in order to determine when theoretical statements grasp invariant regularities of social action and express relations that are of a transformative character. It is the constant questioning of deduction through abduction. Although, the interconnection of the three modes of inference represent the rules by which we must proceed if the process of inquiry is to fulfill its purpose; the special achievements of abduction is the discovery of a suitable hypothesis. This provides a methodology that transcends its own boundaries. For methodology, by itself, does not suffice; it must also prove itself as epistemology—meaning that it may not understand itself in terms of analogy and ought to embrace the dimension of self-reflexiveness. It is through the theory of knowledge that this is done. This is the epistemological circle of abduction, induction, and deduction. This, of course, is tied into working vehicles of the epistemological profile and general semantics epistemology. (For more on the process of inquiry, as such, see Jurgen Habermas, *Knowledge and Human Interests*, Beacon Press, Boston. For more on General Semantic Epistemology see Alfred Korzybski, *Science and Sanity*, J. Samuel Bois, *The Art of Awareness* and William J. Williams, *General Semantics and the Social Sciences*. For more on the Epistemological Profile, see J. Samuel Bois, *Breeds of Men* and William J. Williams, *General Semantics and the Social Sciences* and *Semantic Behavior and Decision Making*).

Conclusion

The task of the epistemicist is never finished. They accept and impose upon themselves the directive that this is *not* the end of the search; it is as far as the postulate leads us at the moment. The epistemicist is an artist—an architect of thought construction finishing a new epistemic building and starting on the design of a more advanced one. The time is past for the social scientist to limit himself to describing the frailties of human nature and denouncing the shortcomings of the establishment that our well-meaning predecessors have set up at a time when their knowledge was more limited than ours. We must innovate boldly, not simply in utopias that stand in contrast to our present situation, or in science fiction that reins on the most sophisticated gadgetry. We must, also, and perhaps rather, learn and practice in our routine activities, the skill of guided awareness and continuing self-renewal.

This kind of philosophy has its place in all human enterprise, i.e., in the life of the individual, the family, the group, the nation, and the whole of humankind. Wendell Johnson saw the future of humankind in a very optimistic manner. The last chapter of his *People in Quandaries* is entitled, "The Urgency of Paradise," meaning that heaven on earth was within reach if we only knew the art of designing it.

The innovation we need must be achieved by pursuing the unfashionable. There are fashions in science, and sometimes ridicule or hostility is the lot of those who insist on exploring the unfashionable. As Thomas Kuhn more elegantly put it, "research that does not fit well in the dominant paradigm tends to be judged unfruitful or perhaps even threatening. The struggles of early scientists to free themselves from the dogmatic certainty of the church seems also to have introduced a hesitance to look too deeply into the human mind and spirit."

One of the more noteworthy manifestations of "abduction or unconscious knowing" is the ability known as creative "problem-solving." The annals of scientific discovery are replete with anecdotes describing how insight seem to come from some behind-the-scenes creative process, often after the conscious mind has wrestled with a problem and "tried everything," and often when the conscious mind is distracted from the problem—perhaps during a nap or a walk. Business executives, architects, inventors, poets, artists, composers, all have frequently told of the creative experience. Sometimes the answer is put forth in an easily recognizable form; sometimes it is veiled in imagery. Sometimes it is visual, sometimes auditory, or sometimes simply as a sure inner knowing. The solutions typically not only "feel" right, but test out in application.

A particular form of this inner knowing, dealing particularly with constructions of the form, "What should I do?" has been known by the term, "conscience." A man's conscience was once thought to be his surest guide to correct decision-making. Then, as we became more scientifically sophisticated, it appeared that conscience could be explained away as "superego," an internal authoritarian master that one could be freed from in psychotherapy. But it seems there may be another kind of conscience as well—a "deep inner knowing" capable of a remarkable integration of past experience, bringing it to bear on a current choice to come up with an answer that "feels right."

Now imagine a hypothetical society in which there has been some technological development, but in which the tendency is much stronger to value understanding and guiding human growth and development, and the search for meaning. The knowledge system that would evolve in this society might be expected to be much more concerned with such nonquantifiable factors as purpose, volition and values. Models and metaphors used might be expected to involve holistic formulations (e.g., health, states of consciousness). Teleological explanations would have an important place; purely deterministic models would seem inappropriate. With abduction, there would be interest in explorations of alternative states of consciousness, especially the "deep inner knowing" (since this seems related to the deepest value commitments of all societies in all times). This kind of knowledge also exists in Western society, but it is less systematized; the degree of consensus is lower, and the knowledge has less prestige. It is not "hard science."

There is a real question about the appropriate methodological approaches to use in seeking publicly validated knowledge about the nature(s) of human consciousness. But it does not have to be paralyzing once we transcend the deterministic, prediction-and-control, reductionistic technology-focused science. And, we transcend by symbolically questioning our assumptions with other assumptions. This is the focus of the next chapter.

CHAPTER 5

Assumptions About Assumptions

In order for proper postulates to emerge, we must examine with a method of inquiry that does not label in a concrete or inflexible manner. Examination in a restrictive and inflexible manner maroons one at an unproductive level of abstraction. Take the example of a woman who is married, meets a man she loves, and has to decide whether to tell this man she is married. She decides at a certain point to reveal this information. When the man *replied* with *silence*, she was shaken. She began to think, "I should not have said anything." She had concluded that it was important for the person to have that information, however, when she received a negative response, she felt sad, labelling this feeling *depression*. When the labels were suspended, the woman began to examine rather than label. The examination revealed that she desired a response and wanted to be encouraged to leave her present relationship and include this person in her life. When this was apparently denied, a feeling of anger emerged and the labeling began—moving the person to a level of abstraction beyond the examination stage. If she had realized this in advance, she could have shared it with the full expectation that many responses were possible. Of course, there were the "motives" of sharing, and of keeping things clear in order to avoid future unpleasant confrontations. The issue wasn't whether it should have been done—it is a matter of realizing that there is no purity in motive—that there are many and all are legitimate. With this kind of flexibility, we are able to examine without reaching the *ought*. The *ought* imposes a heavy burden and does not permit skills for evaluating to emerge automatically.

With these kinds of encounters, we can face the "is of identity" (the verb "to be") which gives the impression of a pure transaction, as is often the case in the area of "motivation." In motivation there is a feeling that there is purity—that you can cut people into parts and "motivate" them. The process of abstracting and the semantic transacting refute the notion that something cannot be A and B at the same time. "A" can be "A" and "B." Therefore, we must speak of a transaction rather than a "motive" or *interaction* in order to be non-static.

In the book, *The Seven Mysteries of Life* (Houghton-Mifflin, 1978), by Guy Murchies, there are some questions and answers which go like this: "What is life? In simplest terms, what holds body to mind and to what degree may a mind take flight on its own? . . . I began to realize there is something intangible behind the life in physical bodies. Indeed behind all matters and that this . . . is revealed by the flow of time, which literally makes things into events. I find it convenient to classify all forms of this mysterious noumenon under the general heading of abstraction."

Murchies has done a good job of identifying the process of abstracting. Korzybski also stated this in his works and, in the 1980's, the same theme is being articulated. The difference, however, is Korzybski gave us a method for practicing this theoretical, natural and *synchronic* realm. He postulated that those beneath the surface mysterious messages are ordered and made plain by the *Process of Abstracting*.

An outline of an object is an abstraction. When you want to explain something, you show a photograph, but for explanation of how it works, you use a diagram. The process of abstracting theoretically, depicts the way the nervous system works; and from this process, we must develop a system of symbols that have a structure similar to the nervous system. The abstraction must be approached in terms of formulations and not concepts if we are to have a *synthetic* "reality" orientation. The word "formulation" is holistic and shows connectedness. When the purpose is to explain the movement of the heavenly bodies, astronomers use geometrical figures. The foundation of the ? of physics and mathematics is completely abstract. The more you consider the part played by abstraction in both thought and speech, the more evident it becomes that we could not think without abstract ideas. A construct is an abstract idea. The abstract idea is a key to the *kind of empiricism* necessary for the world of ideas, noumenon, and everyday functioning. In short, to adequately understand this world of ideas, we must substitute *formulation* for the notion of concept because formulation automatically embraces the process of abstracting—which in turn represents the world of events. As mentioned earlier, mathematics is an abstract process which is expressed in terms of formulations. A good deal, however, of the reporting in physics and mathematics, as far as application, should not be carried over into human activity. So, at a certain point, we part company with mathematical logic, but imitate the process which calls for internalizing a different abstract set of symbols. Again, this is done with formulations that synthesize the various symbols.

Abstracting, then, is close to the event. In order to understand the process of abstracting, we must approach it as a *semantic transaction*. The elements of the *semantic transactor* are: *past, present, future, electrochemical, feelings, thinking and muscular activity, and, in general, environment.* The invoking of this multidimensional approach enables us to reach a tentative multi-valued conclusion. By using this method (semantic transaction), we are less at the classifying stage (stage II-Aristotelian) of the epistemological profile and more at the postulating (stage IV—modern thinking—Einstein quantum). The latter stage enables us to explore more comprehensively. Stage IV would not necessarily change what we do, but it would change how we think about it. For example, a person rapes a small child; usually, that person is considered a rapist; thus leading to confinement of some description (classifying stage). The postulating stage might dictate another approach. In other words, when we operate as a semantic transactor, innovative decisions might emerge, thus enabling us to move toward the process of transformation.

In order to understand transformation and make application of symbols that are relevant, we must understand something about theory and theory of theories. Our ability to make correct judgments are directly determined by what we use to separate one theory, or model from another. It is not just a matter, however, of making a determination about the usage of one theory or another; it is, also, about *developing* and *inventing* theory. So, we have two purposes: making judgments about theory and inventing theory. A theory of theories enables us to function on the levels of judgmental diversity. And, if a theory of theories has any value, it will have built into the formulation values, philosophy, methodology and practical applications. Therefore, the idea of separating theory from practical situations becomes an *obsolete* perspective. The moment we move from the assumption about separation, we have created a new paradigm for functioning. And, the new paradigm assumes the legitimacy of the nonseparation of methodology, values, theory and philosophy. If this is the case, whatever we develop must be holistic and have built into the equation, the empirical process. In short, we will have included empirical testing, methodology, values, goals and philosophy. They are unified when we move beyond deduction, induction, reduction, rationalism and the narrow perspectives of the ''scientific method.'' Consequently, this becomes the first criterion for judgment, and sets the stage for a different basis for developing and inventing a ''social science'' theory. It assumes a vertical as well as a horizontal functioning. It also rejects the idea of the data base as a beginning. If we adopt the data base approach, we automatically are back to classical science which carries with it, among other assumptions, the assumption that we are mechanical and can ''hold still'' for a laboratory analysis. The assumption embedded the new paradigm identifies the person as the laboratory and our empiricism emerges in the *situation within which* we find ourselves. The vertical and horizontal focus mentioned earlier allows for the two groups of actions, i.e., making a judgment about borrowed theories and inventing vertically from the source where all theory flows (an epistemological base). This epistemological base is the key to understanding practical application. The moment we invent (epistemologically), we also make application and (empiricism) extensionalizing is set in motion. In other words, it is all one action.

Closely related to this is the notion of *holonomy* which emphasizes that any one of the ingredients in the transaction will enable us to be in touch with all the elements in the formulation. For example, the philosophy should contain information about the methodology, values, etc. When viewed with the notion of holonomy, our vertical developments lead us to the horizontal functioning. The difficulty we face is making a judgment that enables us to know the difference between a theory or formulation which lends itself to the holonomy perspective and one that does not. While the suggestions expressed in the next paragraph are by no means all possible, they begin the movement toward distinguishing between a proper and improper theory of formulation.

By internalizing the theory of *conceptual revolutions* as a beginning, we are well on the road to developing a set of criteria for judgment. We begin with the *first conceptual revolution* which had its beginning about 650-350 B.C. It produced our categories and gave us Aristotelian logic. It led us through the intensity of the scholarly development that emerged out of the Islamic culture that was finally re-transmitted to the Indo-European culture during the 8th century, through the Renaissance to the Copernican revolution which led to the Newtonian theory of gravitation, and ushered in the intensification of the second conceptual revolution. A new paradigm did not emerge until the early part of the 20th century, with the advent of the theory of relativity, which is considered the *third conceptual revolution*. Each of these conceptual revolutions represent a body of thought and those bodies of though are embedded in our behavior giving us our understanding of the institutions and our ways of thinking and making decisions. The kind of conclusions we reach and the way we interpret situations are determined by the learning we have acquired from a particular conceptual revolution.

In sum: The abductive process is the simple message of process-like contemporary knowledge kept current by the internalizing of conceptual revolutions. Conceptual revolutions enable us to move forward in terms of our thinking. We know immediately from where we are coming and where we may be going. We are able to analyze existing knowledge and create new conceptual notions based on the latest findings in epistemological thinking. In other words, it enables us to be epistemologically practical in our approach to change, make decisions, and to innovate, which is eventually reflected in our policy, disciplines, etc. In short, we begin to move forward because we are standing on the shoulders of giants. The next chapter will be devoted to a more refined understanding of what role the conceptual revolutions play in our practical epistemological approach.

CHAPTER 6

The Use of Conceptual Revolutions

The epistemological profile introduced in chapter 4 was based on, to some extent, the knowledge of the conceptual revolutions, and, to illustrate and appropriate utilization of the process of abstracting. Take for example what Harry Weinberg said about decision making in his book, *Levels of Knowing and Existence.* I paraphrase: At a particular time, the utilization of either/or is all right, especially when we rise to a level of abstraction where a decision has to be made. For example, in an answer to the question, ''Did you get married?'' is an either/or question he says, and one must come down on a particular side of the equation. This is at the second stage of the epistemological profile (the classifying stage). If I involve stage IV, postulating, I can say yes or no and escape being caught within syllogistic logic and raise the usage of the process of abstracting and multi-ordinality to a more dynamic level. For example, if I hold that question tentative by indicating that legally—yes, but in spirit—no, I include into the equation the analytic and the synthetic, the verbal and nonverbal, and the thinking and feelings. In the former case, we are analytic, verbal and thinking; in the latter case, we become synthetic, nonverbal, and on the level of feelings. By introducing the epistemological profile, we can use the process of abstracting but as a multivalued process, thus enabling us to increase our response options and decision alternatives.

I mentioned in the previous chapters that we have been through several periods in history which, theoretically, determine how we make our decisions—mainly I am referring to several historical conceptual revolutions which emerged from the past, affect the present, and project into the future. It is postulated that these conceptual revolutions, to a large extent, pattern our way of making decisions. Let us take a look at the historical periods.

The first is the Aristotelian period dating roughly from 650 to 350 B.C. These represent the period of the classifiers-the either/or thinkers. This period became embedded in our unconscious. It was the period of the Greek philosophers. It was during the period when Aristotle adopted fire and water as two main elements to focus on and when there was a rejection of Democritus' atomic theory that Aristotle put his into action by developing syllogistic reasoning. Syllogistic reasoning enabled us to classify our thinking, arrange our thoughts in an orderly fashion and incorporate the dynamics of these developments into our grammar. More specifically, it gave rise to the *verb "to be,* which produced the *"is of identity"* and penetrated the very fabric of our thinking—our nervous system, especially in the Western World. This thinking ''rationalized'' our decision making process and became a natural part of the way we approach the matter of making decisions and building our world. Also, in India and parts of the Middle East, the process continued until the 16th and 17th centuries.

A precursor, Leonardo Da Vinci, introduced a new direction in the 15th and 16th centuries. He exhibited a dislike for compartmentalization. It gave rise to a speculation that things were not well with the state of our decision making. As we know, Leonardo was a genius in his own right, i.e., mathematician, biologist, musician, artist, educator, astronomer, physicist, etc. He introduced by implication a rejection of the *"is of identity"* and concrete classification. He maintained more of an interdisciplinary approach. This was on the eve of the introduction of the 17th century. He did not reduce his ''epistemology'' to writing or print. His accomplishment, however, relates to the *supraconscious* of the *semantic spectrum* (for more on the supraconscious and the semantic spectrum see J. Bois, *The Art of Awareness*) without the theoretical process itself being made explicit. We do not get induction until Galileo, Newton, and more specifically, Sir Francis Bacon. The inductive method made solid the second conceptual revolution but did not rid us of compartmentalization. It did speak, however, to progress in the realm of providing an empirical test for some deductive notions. The rise of the scientific method and rational decision making prevailed over knowledge from the 15th to the 17th century and lasted until the latter part of the 19th century and the early part of the 20th century. During this period there was more a transcending of the inductive method. I say more here because Galileo and Newton were not solid within induction during its most intensive period.

The second conceptual revolution did not overthrow deduction. However, there was a semantic jump when the third was introduced. The second was more of an improvement of the first, (the Aristotelian). Therefore, our mental models did not change, in terms of a completely different paradigm, except to indicate there that there was another dimension to the classifying method. We see it today when we speak of "concepts," make final and emphasize rationality in decision making and induction with a capital "I." In all of our research, we find it; our empirical and statistical methods, and our doctoral dissertations in our universities are not complete without it.

The introduction of the writings on the theories of relativity, quantum relations and social epistemological theory by Arthur Bentley, John Dewey, P. D. Ouspensky, Pitirim Sorokin, Bertrand Russell, Alfred S. Korzybski and Suzanne Langer, question the value of continuing with the deductive-inductive methodology; thus, the "real" revolution. This is considered the third conceptual revolution, and in my judgment, is the most important.

There was an attempt on the part of Bentley, Russell, Whitehead, Dewey, and Korzybski to officially reject the notions of mechanical rationality—the "is of identity" (the verb "to be")—and introduce another kind of "logic." That is, one that would be embedded in the world of mathematical or geometric thinking; thus, making a decision between this and arithmetic. This new system spoke of, in some respect, a pure mathematical model as in the instance of the theory of types by Russell and Whitehead, general semantics epistemology by

Korzybski, and kennetic inquiry by Bently and Dewey. These theories could be classified as methods of encompassing both deduction and induction by. way of offering an overarching process designed enabling us to invent new symbolic structures. As a result, it makes it possible to fashion for the social sciences, a process called abduction. It is an attempt to make our world of symbolizations more accurate and adequate. It is an introduction, if you will, of an approach to the ordering and inventing of appropriate linguistic statements. Formerly, the construction of the symbols as an original and orderly process was neglected. We had mainly concentrated on the use of the symbols we were given without raising assumptive questions. The abductive method introduces the idea of questioning the assumptions behind the symbols and whether or not they have a structure similar to the world, i.e., events. When questions are raised as to how we enable ourselves to break our world of encapsulations which has socialized us into a specific way of thinking and decision making, we have to, as Bertalanffy said in *Robots, Men, and Minds* deal with the symbol-making process. This, he says, is where we obtain our ideas, thoughts and patterns of behavior.

It is no wonder then that our thinking and patterns give rise to a certain way of functioning and making decisions. In our decision making process, in order not to reinvent the wheel, we must have a sense of our history. It is the contention that these conceptual revolutions are embedded in our common systems and patterns, except for the third conceptual revolution, which is of more recent vintage.

The process of abduction introduces the idea of transformation and makes real the proposition that the whole is much more than the sum of its parts. We move to a different level of abstraction and stage of development and what we have is a different entity—where parts are not distinguishable but have metamorphized into something new. Abduction involves how to comprehensively blend this process with *past* thinking and produce new orders of thinking in our decision making. There are some who take the position that we do not learn from history. The implication is that we cannot. It is my position that we could learn from history if we knew how. By introducing the notion of the conceptual revolutions, our perspective changes and gives us a meaningful "feel" for history. We become holistic. It also enables us to understand and overcome the either/or "lock." Historically, we have aligned ourselves with either/or thinking. The abductive part of our history dictates ways of defeating this negative focus.

Abduction introduces the process of abstracting, which emerges out of the third conceptual revolution. The either/or "lock" can be overcome by internalizing the abstracting process. For example, a person loves her husband—yet also loves another man. The second relationship affects the marriage because she is in love with another man. When she makes love with her husband, she has feelings of being disloyal to the other man and thus, violating that relationship. What is the dilemma of this person? One, she is putting both relationships on the same level of abstraction thinking—one contradicts the other. Second, she does not rise to a second level of abstraction which would enable her to see more clearly and consider alternative ways of functioning in both relationships. A rise to the second level could dictate a way of functioning with each, and examining not whether she should or should not, but how to relate to each man without putting herself in strict categories of either/or. At the second level, it becomes where, who and how. It raises the level of our thinking and inserts into the equation a creative possibility. It also raises another possibility that introduces the idea of whether. It, then, does not "boil" itself down to either the husband or lover; it is not either/or. There may be a third or fourth possibility being overlooked. At this point, it becomes multi-valued.

While we rise to another level of abstraction, we also move to a new stage of thinking, both calling for a new set of assumptions which require a different set of skills; and momentarily, we become contemplative and our normal patterns of action are disrupted.

The implementation of the epistemological knowledge introduced in this overview section, requires a more specific focus. Therefore, the next section will be more definitive and concrete as a result of the introduction of a foundational matrix for applied epistemology.

SECTION TWO
THE FOUNDATION MATRIX
FOR APPLIED EPISTEMOLOGY

CHAPTER 7

A Functional Synthesis:
The Postulating and Relating Stages

In my book, *Semantic Behavior and Decision Making*, I decided to talk about theory and theory making in the social sciences in general, and public affairs in particular. I indicated that most of our theories are comments about other theories and statements regarding what we need in the social sciences and public affairs. The theories we have are borrowed from other social disciplines; many of these are "second-hand" because the disciplines (such as Sociology, Psychology, Economics, etc.) have borrowed them from the physical and biological sciences.

In 1972, I stated in my book, *General Semantics and the Social Sciences*, that we had to begin initiating our own theories or we would continue to find ourselves not only secondary, but tertiary or not in the "running" at all. I made another statement in 1976 in my book, *Uncommon Sense and Dimensional Awareness*, that we had to develop an epistemology in order to understand our discipline. This is tantamount to having a paradigm. A paradigm, especially with an epistemological foundation is a kind of foundation which is thematically under-girded with universals which connect with every other disci-pline. This kind of paradigm, in addition to having universals, must be dynamic and nonstatic. In other words, process-like. A paradigm, if it is proper and appropriate, moves a discipline or a field of inquiry to another dimension. It ushers in a new *conceptual revolution* and changes the way we view what we do. It relegates the fixed and dynamic to a place in history. It is like the Copernican revolution which transformed us from a

Ptolemic or geocentric view of a world to the heliocentric view. That is, instead of the earth being the center of the universe, the sun became the center. The heliocentric view changed how we saw our physical surrounding and ourselves. It indicated that we might not be the only creatures in the universe with intelligence; in fact, some others might be superior. It focused on the limitations and nature(s) of the human condition.

A discipline becomes of age when there is a paradigm that represents the best in contemporary thinking. At the present time, our paradigm dates back to the 16th and 17th centuries with the introduction of the Cartesian mechanical view and Baconian induction. It is, for the most part, the 17th century scientific method. I see this in the methods of inquiry undergirding policy studies. I see it in economics, political science, psychology and especially in our studies relating to theory and human behavior. The obsolescence of our paradigms become apparent when we are utilizing a method of inquiry for understanding which one transcends the bounds of the scientific method.

In one of my classes, there was a discussion relative to the use or nonuse of the methods of science. There were ones who confined themselves to the proposition that we had to borrow from science because this is where the progress had been made. We concluded, however, tentatively, that it might not be either-or. In other words, perhaps, we should borrow, but to what degree? Some of the notions from the ''scientific'' community might be appropriate at certain levels of analysis. But, we must remember that all, including quantum relations, emerged from the scientific method. Then we further concluded that the attitude that we borrow from the sciences, on the assumption that this is basic and fundamental, presupposes that science was the beginning and that it was God-given to humans, i.e., that humans did not make it. If the latter is true, then the basis for our argument is erroneous. However, we did not consider the latter to be true. Science is what it is because we made it so, and in order to create a new paradigm and change the way we view ourselves, we must introduce a new foundation in keeping with transactional, natural and process knowledge. We must go where science began and fashion a method of inquiry that is epistemological in behavior. Without this view, we remain secondary. How do we go about doing this? The measure which supplies us with some direction is the discipline of epistemics. It enables us to introduce nonstatic notions and apply them ''across the board'' and if a discipline does not measure up, then we know the paradigm is static and/or obsolete.

Therefore, instead of beginning with end results, we begin with a beginning, i.e., the sources of all human knowledge. Beginning with the source assumes that we are in charge of science as opposed to science in charge of us.

Robert Theobold, April 26, 1973, at the celebration of the 50th anniversary of the birth of Copernicus called by the Smithsonian Institution said, and I paraphrase: Our educational system is obsolete...therefore we must change the dominant paradigm in order to get in touch. He stated further that the way we structure our welfare system depends upon what kind of human condition we believe we confront. It is presently based on the belief that people on welfare are idle and irresponsible bums. This idea provides no opportunity for imaginative and innovative activity. Likewise, our educational system, to some extent is based on the belief that people will not learn unless they are forced to do so. People who submit to this system lose the capacity to learn for themselves. Accordingly, this attitude is implicated in our political and administrative set-ups in the form of individualization and conflict rather than cooperative activity. We need, he says, a new paradigm which transcends our disciplines. Many people in various disciplines can communicate with people in other disciplines better because they are on the edge of struggling toward an understanding of a new paradigm while their disciplines are using the old paradigms.

Professor Gaston Bachelard, until the time of his death in 1962, was recognized as one of Europe's most important philosophers. He authored *The Philosophy of No*. In his book, he introduced an instrument known as the ''epistemological profile.'' J. Samuel Bois, ''pegged'' the leading theoretician in the field of General Semantics, introduced the epistemological profile to the North American Continent, redesigning it to capture our contemporary setting, thus, making it more acceptable to the layman.

The profile consists of five stages. This chapter concerns itself with two of those stages (stages III and IV) and how we may utilize them to implement our abductive process; moreover, how we may use them as vehicles for developing a functional synthesis.

The relating stage (III), the second conceptual revolution, is the stage of predicability. It is about statistics, economic supply and demand theory, supply-side economics, balances in political power, institutional systems of power, relationships and frames of references based on mechanical models.

We play a ''game'' at the relating stage (the second conceptual revolution). It is a ''game'' with a definite kind of predictability. The invocation of the rules and regulations pertaining to stage IV (the postulating stage) are not appropriate. They are two difference orders of thinking with separate ground rules. The mixture would be confusing two different stages of functioning and could lead to serious professional as well as personal conflicts.

It is a ''game'' which becomes quite serious, at times, depending upon the issue. One must and/or ought to be prepared to participate in the game even though the affective and cognitive suggest a transcending of the game. For without some kind of involvement in this kind of activity, one may not be able to seriously maintain the energies necessary to function creatively at the postulating stage. The relating stage is upon us partially as we function on jobs, in schools, business, professions, marriage and mundane activity. These realistic involvements require that we engage the syndrome of the relating stage. So, the critical question here is not whether, but how we engage it. If we do not participate to some degree in an orderly fashion, we may find ourselves participating in a disorderly manner to a large degree, and being unaware of what is occurring. The relating stage is a specific case within the postulating stage; therefore, if we regard the stages as either/or, we may develop a model which does not represent the territory.

The relating stage (second conceptual revolution) viewed in

its proper perspective is a vehicle for movement. It enables us to circulate in other stages and soar above the mundane, but only *if we*, and I emphasize this, "*if we*" view the relating stage as a "game" not to be taken seriously by those who function there, do not seek to find significance in life there, and do not see it as the salvation of humanity. It is the home of the realist, the logical positivist, the totally pure empiricist and the pragmatist as well as the partial pragmatist who "tolerates" abstract. Perceiving the relating stage in this manner provides us with a reality orientation. When the relating stage is ignored, it should be done with intent and awareness in order to maintain control when we function with it. It can be an addiction or preference, or both, but it is preferable to utilize it as a preference. Preferences are at a higher level of abstraction; we have a measure of order there. Addictions are at a lower level of abstraction; there is less order. Both, for the most part, dictate direction to us. Separating, as I do here, addictions and preferences "smacks" of logical positivist rationality; but, there is a difference which makes a difference a *difference*. In rising to a higher level of abstraction, we move beyond the either/or syndrome. The level to which we have risen embraces addictions and preferences and enables us to talk about having a place within our scheme of thinking. We have not placed them on the same level of abstraction nor have we completely separated them. To repeat more succinctly—the discussion of the two (addiction and preference) is a high level abstract discussion in the sense that we rise to another level to examine the application of both.

I follow this line of thinking hoping it will lead to my major point, which is: We must function on many levels simultaneously, and if we can mentally imagine it, in a circular fashion. The circular functioning may enable us to transact at the power relating stage without becoming marooned; respect those who reside there; and, become aware that it may be a key to valuable resources, and a great means for freeing up human energy for more lofty, esoteric creative and inventive endeavors. Lastly, a recognition that the relating stage is only a means to higher means—is spiritual in quality and is a part of a larger quest. With this kind of recognition, we do not have to change others, but take full measure of our own involvement. So, what is important here, is not whether we transact at one stage or another, but that they are inevitably linked together. It is more important to repeat and develop a sense for the appropriate usage of the relating stage. The mechanical power relating phenomenon has assumed massive influence in our lives and is a segment to be reckoned with out of ''self-defense.'' A more positive way of looking at it, of course, would be to view it not just as self-defense, but a necessary event which helps, indirectly, in the drama of spiritual human progress. It is a *vehicle* for enabling us to develop new skills for functioning and leads us to more effective decision making in a complex arrangement of human transactions.

It would be safe to indicate here that we have had and do have now, persons in public life who have utilized the relating stage as a vehicle. John F. Kennedy, for example, projected aspirations and ideals of stage IV while operating at stage III. Jerry Brown, ex-governor of California, constantly called for a new way of perceiving and creating patterns of thinking. They both debunked too much concentration of the means, i.e., operations streamlining and efficiency. They managed to audibilize issues more important than mundane management; nonetheless, mundane management as a vehicle, takes on importance and provides us with an opportunity for meaningful transformative change. Specifically, it is a chance to blend stages III and IV without neglecting either. This thrust removes the stage III functions from pure ''game theory'' and provides an avenue for functioning at a more creative level. This is to me a perspective for those wishing to transcend the cultural binds in which they find themselves.

A specific way of utilizing stage III to bring about a stage IV decision may be to bring to the attention of the participants when they are violating the proper process of abstracting and/or making it known when we are functioning at a stage improper for human beings. This, however, has to be done in a manner inoffensive to the participants, probably indirectly. Instead, for example, of saying you are at the classifying stage, it might be better to introduce an alternative approach to the situation. An example is when I was teaching at a predominately black university as a visiting professor in the east; the faculty was trying to get rid of a "white" professor they did not like. In my judgment, it was prejudice and had no academic basis, although they claimed he was remiss in his academic duties. Instead of my telling them that they were coming from the classifying stage (categorizing) and using the relating stage, that is, using their power to enforce their prejudices, I suggested that if they were to set in motion a process for evaluating this situation which was fair and made public, they would accomplish two things: (1) some favorable publicity for the university; and (2) be in a position of being the first to showcase an affirmative action case and set a precedent for the rest of the nation's universities. Functioning in this manner would have put to rest the criticisms of their motives, make a significant contribution to the minority enterprise and obtain some nationwide prestige. I did not deal with the merits of the particular case. Instead, I asked them to raise their sights to another level of abstraction and be at the postulating stage of the profile, which transcends the power notion. I sought to change the process without confronting it directly. They were excited about the idea and sought to implement it, but fell short because they tried to use stage III (second conceptual revolution) methodologies to implement stage IV (third conceptual revolution) goals when the two are incompatible. But, at least the suggestion accomplished two things: (1) The accused was given a hearing, i.e., he was given a two-year full paid leave, an extended sabbatical and a stipulation which stated the administration would accept his retirement; and (2) The participants were aware of the educational process I had introduced to them for dealing with the situation. I had introduced the notion of rising to a new level of abstraction and introduced the fourth stage of the epistemological profile and the third conceptual revolution without "taxing" their fragile need to maintain their untenable and biased position. This is probably all we can do at many times. Since our particular thrust is one of education and prevention, immediate results have to be measured in terms of process and new ideas we may have set in motion. As we, however, gain more experience in utilizing the methodology, it may be possible to be more immediate in our application. It will require time, research, and application. Is this so different from what most of us do, anyway? Perhaps not, but the critical questions are: "Do we do it systematically?" and "Do we understand the method of inquiry behind it?"

Synthesizing

Since we do not function in isolation, we have a duty and a responsibility to communicate as fully as possible the skills and methods we use. It was Korzybski's contention that we are, at least most of us, potential geniuses. It is just a matter of developing skills which would enable us to tap those creative instincts. With this as an assumption, I expand my attention to include decision makers and policy makers of all varieties.

I have suggested that those aspiring to function at stage IV, should have a tolerance and healthy respect for Stage III functions. Likewise, it would be "nice" if those at stage III would have a healthy respect and tolerance for those at stage IV. But, it is much easier for those at stage IV (third conceptual revolution) to see stage III (second conceptual revolution) as a particular case within a larger process that it is for those at stage III to embrace stage IV. There are many reasons for this. Some of the more obvious are: Stage III people control the resources and are comfortable there; the majority of the people function there; our institutions are run that way; our systems reflect that kind of value component; and, more significantly, our culture has socialized us in that manner, and counterthinking is considered an aberration. It suggests going against the tide of popular opinion. Of course, historical precedent "tips" the scale in the direction of the one-man theory, that is, progress as we know it especially when it is dramatic and does not conform to what has been done. Moreover, it is usually a lonely vigil for those working at it. The crowds come later. If this is taken seriously then, the writing that I am doing would be directed to a small audience of people who accuse the traditionalist of being unable to think their way beyond the cultural bind. I am, however, at this time, of the opinion that while history is to be observed, it should not be the total guide. I feel that contemporary times dictate new models which defy, to some extent, the seeming elitist model contained herein. This is partially based on the notion that we are deluged with 38,000 books a year, radio, television, extensive travel, popularization of meditation, new forms of health and preventive medicine, a new emphasis on personal worth, and a dissemination of complex theories in a form understandable to the average layman. So, it may not be out of bounds to suggest a multiple understanding on the part of those residing at a given stage at a given time. I must admit, however, that due to my own cultural conditioning, I have more *hope* than expectation that this will occur. Nevertheless, we can be synthesizers given the proper method of inquiry. If you read sociology, anthropology, psychology, history, and so forth, you see the same thread throughout. But the experts do not know they are saying the same things in each discipline. We should climb over the walls—be a synthesizer.

There is a key to this—content becomes secondary; it is the excitement of thinking that is important. It is a sense of wonder, the dream. More precisely, it is thinking about thinking. Thinking about thinking enables us to see relationships; and, the more we are able to see the connectedness, the more we tend to care. It provides a holistic, non-elementalistic approach to life. Caring produces action.

We must see our own connectedness with the cosmic, world, nation, and connect other individuals and events. Otherwise, we do not have a felt oneness with the problem of others' compassion, sympathy, and empathy flows from the holism and formulations (related notions), not reductionist concepts that are elementalistic. General semantics and epistemics with their nonelementalism and the epistemological profile used as formulations enable us to produce holism and stay in touch with the natural functioning of the nervous system. Thus, we become caring and this provides a vehicle for taking action.

The relating stage is also known as the power stage. Issues become a matter of power because we are abstractors—persons must ''push'' their points of view because we ''all'' see the world differently as individuals and there is no one truth and no one right way of doing things. Our method for reconciling differences is usually at the relating stage of the epistemological profile—the power stage. The question is: "Is there a better way of rising to a superior level of abstraction and transcending our various individual abstractions, which would enable us to reach some kind of agreement without using the power forces?" The most poignant idea introduced thus far, has been Mary Parker Follet's theory of "*the Law of the Situation*," that is, in every situation there is a solution that will merge if we unify and integrate the forces in a cooperative manner. She calls this *creative experience*, which by itself does not provide us with a method of inquiry. However, if we introduce stage IV (third conceptual revolution) of the epistemological profile and the abductive method which makes a distinction between truth and love and considers love superior to the various truths that we experience, then it might enable us to produce a method of inquiry for "*the law of the situation*." From a practical point of view in certain situations, it is impossible at many times, to introduce this kind of equation. The dynamics of the situation will dictate our reactions. Our approach is one of prevention, and we must approach it in that fashion. There is not much we can do in rectifying a situation once it begins; all we can do is navigate ourselves more skillfully and hope that the introduction of the new equation will influence the situation.

CHAPTER 8

The Special Role of the Relating Stage

For quite some time I have been interested in the concept of power. Most of my early years were focused in politics and I became convinced that power was the most important ingredient and possibly the only way of getting anything done. After serving as an administrator and working as a politician, I went into academia. I was informed upon my entry into academic life that politics had nothing to do with our functioning. This is, to some extent, still the expressed statement for public consumption. We use the term "merit." I did not believe the statement then and I do not now. But, a strange thing occurred—after five years of functioning within academic politics, I began to select other means for getting things done. I subconsciously considered school politics—too mean, too unkind, too thoughtless, too destructive, and the stakes too low. I held out for a better way of functioning thinking that alternatives could be applied wherever power relationships and politics existed. I still think so. But, the jury is still out pending the introduction of methods that can produce such a state. There is one "ray" of hope, the general semantics and epistemic formulations. The emphasis is on rising to a new level of knowing and existence in order to see more, making a better analysis of the situation and thereby producing creative solutions. I found the alternative way of functioning to be effective and fascinating. It covered decision making. However, as I began to notice the complications of 1975, 1976 and 1977, although it was impossible to rise to that level, I felt something else had to be "pumped" into the equation. We were beginning to speak of women's rights, rights of minorities, gay rights, unemployment, conflicts in the Middle East, world wide inflation, and a general change in national and international economic and political transactions. In the classroom and in small academic arrangements, it became necessary to insert into the *agape* formulation, the element of political power, not with the idea that it was alright, but with the idea that it was necessary in order to preserve a high level functional arrangement. It also, had to be a new power process, posed as a means contemporary in character. The old "power politics" syndrome would move us to a past era of time which dictates an either/or context. For example the "hue and cry" relative to the elimination of quotas, in affirmative action, cannot be successfully evaluated by utilizing the postulating stage of the epistemological Profile alone. The decision or solution, at that stage, would rest with religion and what "ought" to be done under the label of good moral philosophy, never addressing what we must do now. Most of us in general semantics and epistemics subscribe to the proposition that quotas should not exist because that ties us to stage II (classifying) of the epistemological profile. But we realize, also, that the maintenance of orderly progress requires that we address in an appropriate manner ideas of using the more advanced notions for *long range possibilities*. For example, in terms of affirmative action, we must function simultaneously with the process of abstracting and at two different stages of the epistemological profile. Within the abstracting process the word "discrimination" would become multi-ordinal, thereby rendering the term "discrimination in reverse," an appropriate phrase.

By using the epistemological profile, however, the word discrimination loses its dictionary definition as it moves from one stage to another. For example, as we move from stage III to stage IV we find that reverse discrimination has no meaning. It does not exist because we begin to reexamine the factors giving rise to the existence of the new situation (need for preferential treatment). We learn in stage IV, abstracting, "reverse" means going back, and by definition we cannot go back. By definition, the two levels are different and by using the term "reverse discrimination" we impute sameness to the different actions. They have different motives, a different history, a different set of psychology and a much different sociological impact; thus, the limited range and power of the process of abstracting. But, in abstracting we must deal with the fact that it takes power to compel the kinds of actions we would like to see emerge—it cannot be left to moral fairness, if so, a large segment of our population would be left in the "lurch." The lower stages must be used to set mechanical goals. These are stages II and III with an "eye" on stages IV and V which enables us to hold tentative any present decision we make; and, suggest creative arrangements for future functioning. The latter is at stage IV and would require a long-range commitment because it entails an examination and change in local, national, and international economic and political arrangements. Since this is not possible, our policy decisions must utilize all of the formulation in a holistic sense in order to produce the desired results; and a tentative and cautious use of power politics becomes one of the vehicles. It seems necessary to approach some situations in this manner in view of the fact that we do not seem to learn from experience in a universal and abstract sense. Experience seems to be local and specific. The transfer of the local and specific from one situation to another is not easy, unless there is a unifying theoretical notion, simply because feelings change, but memories remain. In the case of affirmative action, when the enforcement is removed which is a unifying theoretical notion, a different situation abounds; the feelings take on the coloring of the new thrust. It could be referred to as the *line of least resistance*. Consequently, standard enforcement and quotas become necessary until the thinking is affected in stage IV (postulating). Stage IV is a long-range goal and the conceptual revolution ushering in this thinking takes hold slowly.

The relating stage of the epistemological profile is the power stage. It derives its name, "mannerisms," from Newtonian mechanics. It is the stage of push and pull—a balance of power, the machine syndrome where most of our functioning is at. It is referred to as the "second conceptual revolution," making Bacon's method of induction, "real."

Newtonian mechanics is made up of both deduction and induction. This is ushered in the scientific method which has been applied to our human relations. Since the world tends to function at this stage of development, it becomes realistic for us to be appropriate to the situation in order to be effective.

Bachelard and Bois introduced the profile as a series of stages, making it hierarchal in approach. At this time, I am ready to see the stages as hierarchal, but having a value at a particular place and time. For example, it might be appropriate to relate to the classifying stage of the profile at a given time, then relating, then postulating. I do not suggest that we ignore the qualitative differences or the relative superiority of one state from another. I merely suggest that after using the profile to diagnose, the appropriate stage be identified and situations that are political and/or administrative are not, normally, expected to be amenable to the postulating state; the situation is, usually mechanical, and belongs at that stage. However, the administrator is expected to be aware of the total situation and articulate where it might be best to function futuristically, thereby making it possible for the postulating to prevail at a later time.

This treatise on the use of the power relating stage is to give one, first, a comprehensive understanding, second, to expand one's options, and third, to develop an awareness about this obsolete stage of human development which speaks to conflict and *not* cooperation. However, it may be possible to move to the level of cooperation with a selective and judicious use of the relating stage. Being judicious means using the relating stage as a vehicle for implementation of the more desirable stage—the postulating stage. The hierarchy of sensing, classifying, relating, postulating, participating, in that order, is replaced with a circular process which enables one to select in a horizontal as well as a vertical fashion. Again, I do not, however, reject the value proposition that the postulating stage is not possibly a more appropriate way of functioning.

In sum: ironically, historically we used a macroscopic human model unsystemically and untheoretically to develop our machine model. Then we turned around and used the machine model to try to understand the microscopic workings of the human dynamics. It makes logical and common sense, but we must depart from that in order to progress.

This section has given us some sense, hopefully, of how applied epistemology works in theory, leading logically to a discussion of the developing of the new process of abduction in a more comprehensive synthesis.

SECTION THREE
FOCUS ON ABDUCTION

CHAPTER 9

Abduction and Public Affairs Management: Role of the Verb "To Be"

The failure to see the character of the "now" is universal within a language and cultural setting. Consequently, this phenomenon is granted a type of invisibility due to its foundational and pervasive character. However, within the realm of politics, a sure-fire symptom of this malady continuously appears in terms of governmental failure to accomplish what it identifies as necessary. For instance, the old mechanisms of legislation, elections, and influence seem to work less satisfactorily over time. Additionally, all the major planned efforts of the recent past have resulted in general failure. The great domestic plans of the Sixties such as the war on poverty, urban renewal, headstart, the peace corps, etc., have all deteriorated in effectiveness over time. Why? The answer is simply that we have failed to perceive accurately the circumstances surrounding our efforts. What occurred is that we perceived and planned for yesterday's today. Under those conditions, failure was a foregone conclusion.

For example, our approach to minimum wage laws is a classic, if not trivial, example, of the age of our perception. First, we can assume that minimum wage laws will be necessary for some time under our present economic arrangement. Secondly, we know that inflation will occur over time, making a raise in the minimum wage necessary. However, our response to this situation is to enact legislation at various moments, separated in time, to compensate for a relatively constant occurrence. In other words, we leap-frog from bill to bill or moment to moment in the manner and fashion of the past. This means that the past dictates: (1) separate bills, (2) separate debates over the same issue, (3) allowance for pressure for and against, and (4) a pattern that is reminiscent of tradition rather than innovation. On the other hand, a more ''now'' oriented approach would be to pass one piece of legislation that empowers a committee to apply some economic ratio and automatically increase the minimum wage on a regular basis. In this way, the inflationary trend in minimum wage would allow congress to devote more time to other activities and would provide a more suitable arrangement for the average worker.

This is not to suggest that a clearer perception of today will magically eliminate all our difficulties, but it may at least give us a chance. This clearer perception must be obtained by a deeper understanding of the verbal and operational levels. At any given moment in time, there are the verbal and operational levels. These two levels, however, give rise to primarily one construction of reality that emphasizes the verbal level over the operational level. This emphasis provides an amplification of the distortion already created by experience and the unitary conceptualization of thought.

Verbal focus consists of those concepts, ideas, beliefs, and idea systems that are maintained through language. Since language is the major source of communication, it follows that verbiage is one of the most significant individual tools in constructing concepts, ideas, and realities. However, language itself is extremely limited in conveying meaning as well as in adapting to change. For instance, when a young man and woman meet, eventually, the question of age is asked. This question only slightly reflects its initiator's interest in chronological age. More precisely, its intent is to discover where the other person's ''head is at.'' The asker wants information on sexual experience, maturity, likes and dislikes, openness to various experiences as opposed to a resistance toward experience, etc., all of which can only be minimally inferred from age. In asking the question, ''How old are you,'' you immediately limit the response to 17, 20, 22, etc. However, if you ask, ''Where is your head at?'' or ''What kind of person are you?'' either of which is a more precise question, the recipient would almost certainly reply in confusion, "What do you mean?" In other words, language has limited both the question and the response, within some parameters of present experience. At the same time, language's ability to change, while on the increase, is extremely slow. For instance, we spend our whole educational period of time learning how words are always the same. We virtually are never exposed to how they change, and for certain, we are never encouraged to experiment in the creation of new words that would adequately represent "new" ideas. For instance, a parent's first task with his child is to eliminate "baby talk," or the creative invention of expressions, and teach the child the "correct word and its meaning."

In this way, words always reflect a construction of the past. This is, the static, or unitary, construction of words which hides the exact character of the present by portraying it through terms and their connotation of meaning that reflects yesterday. For example, the word "friend" today is intended to cover a range of situations. It is used to refer to deep friendships, best friendships, acquaintances, present lovers, past lovers, as well as girlfriends and boyfriends in the romantic and the nonsexual sense. The use of the word "friend" in any one of these contexts reflects a time gone by where its use accurately described to a listener a particular type of interpersonal relationship. The use of this same term today conveys a distorted perception of reality. Only by substantial additional critical examination can a listener determine the actual character of reality in terms of the word "friend." However, verbiage is still that material from which we must model our constructions and perceptions of reality. Consequently, the verbal level will almost always construct past-oriented realities relative to the words used. Language is the level on which conceptualization occurs. That is today, verbal constructions define realities; and, consequently, perceptions of experience and/or realities are limited to the language process in which they occur.

In other words, values, patterns and transactions are immediately present through the visible character of language. Within this process, cultural pattern can be easily found in both recorded and nonrecorded, written, visual, and spoken media. Consequently, little critical examination is necessary to discover patterns on the verbal level. At the same time, it is verbiage through which the perception of change must be reflected and conveyed. With verbiage tied to a particular experience process and this process the essential element in conceptualization, our construction of realities is indeed greatly limited. Consequently, both the time and relativity aspects of experience must be altered, along with the unitary conceptualization of thought if any greater perception of realities is to be realized. In order to introduce the time and relativity necessary to process thinking, it is necessary to focus on the use of identity or the verb "to be."

Dr. Albert Ellis, head of the Institute for Rational Living and author of *A New Guide to Rational Living*, puts the *is of identity* more specifically to the test by developing a theme with a specific method of inquiry.

Dr. Ellis introduced the idea of *non-identity* in his book and in this therapy process. The theory of nonidentity "attacks" the use of the verb *to be* or specifically the is. This is commonly called the *is of identity*. In his book and in his clinical works, Dr. Ellis completely excludes the word *"is."* The theory is that our grammar in utilizing the *is* does not supply us with adequate or comprehensive information. It speaks in final cause, one cause—one effect; it categorizes in a restrictive sense. For example, when I say, "He is a man," it leaves out too many details. The statement does not consider that the person may be homosexual. It does not consider that the person is different from day to day or different from other men. It represents a generalization. While this may not make a difference in many instances, there are times when it might make a difference. Therefore, it is necessary to be aware of the inadequacies.

The word *"is"* on one level of abstraction supplies us with a static picture of the world. It represents the world of Aristotelian logic which is *static*. If you notice, I am using the word *is* which is permissible as long as I am using it at a different level of abstraction. That is, it is about *is*.

Dr. Ellis believes that the trouble we are having with classifying too concretely, relating in a static way to a process world, perceiving more comprehensively, being more holistic in our approach, having better transactions with each other, eliminating over-simplified cause-effect relationships, stultifies creativity can be automatically and indirectly managed by purging the *is* of identity at the appropriate level of abstraction.

The *verb to be* is found embedded in the commonly used notion of *problem*. The label problem is very dangerous. A conversation I had with a student about his personal growth and development indicated that he was puzzled with his lack of understanding himself and ability to unify his thinking. He defined his dilemma as a problem.

First, we discussed the concept of problem and concluded that problem was a mechanical, mental construct that fell into the area of the analytical root metaphor, and the application of it to human behavior would not lead to a conclusion about what to do. Instead it was suggested that the construct *situation* would be advisable since it spoke to process. The *concept problem* spoke to the sitting down and working out the solution with the idea that the matter would be once and for all put to rest. The assumption was that the label *difficulty* would create patience and was appropriate for functioning. Nothing is ever to be solved because everything is ongoing. The *situation* merely changes form and is modified.

The implication of this is that it is a static way of looking at a dynamic process and does not fit the structure of reality. If the matter, however, is reexamined as a *situation*, then we automatically set in motion patience, which is important for growth. In addition, relative time is an important ingredient in development, and *problem* does not consider relative time. Thus, we move beyond the strict mechanics into human dynamics and are able to function more effectively and with patience. The Space-Time perspective which rejects the *verb to be*, can be to the individual, the organization and/or a group, what the Copernican revolution was to the world. The change of perspective provides the direction.

The operational focus is the level of the synthetic system. This means that, unlike verbal direction, it is not readily apparent. Additionally, operational abstraction does not necessarily have an "a prior" existence in verbiage. That is, a new action or behavior, or a modification of an older behavior, is not necessarily reflected in the language used to describe it. For instance, there is no term that describes the behavior of the unmarried couple living together. They exist, so to speak, in a linguistic void, the character of which leaves that aspect of their reality vague to those who have not shared a similar experience.

To obtain a coherent picture of abstraction on this level requires an extremely critical examination of behavior. In this activity, we must seek to set aside traditional meanings and emphasize the character of actions. In so doing, we must compare behavior to language and the result to the total socio-historic setting. This means that we must provide some new linguistic process under which the total socio-historic setting may be organized for analysis.

The exact character of the operational focus is extremely difficult to grasp for two reasons. First, we must somehow construct a verbal description of behavior. The problem is that present verbiage and the conceptualization of ideal works to hide the character of behavior within its already existing, understood, and *change-resistant framework*. Secondly, because of the present state of verbiage, we tend to misperceive the behaviors themselves, and therefore, fail to see that many behaviors today are a direct result of technology based change as opposed to thought. What this suggests is that experimentation in conceptualization must precede any greater realization and perceptions of human conduct and planning.

Technology has always been the major impetus for human change. That is, technology, as both a method and applications of that method, has been a root cause of sociological evolution. For instance, language is itself a technological application and system. Indeed, it is man's development and use of technology that labels him "different" from other life forms on this planet.

However, it is the structural nature and speed of advancing technology on which we must focus. That is, the technology structure becomes the external component in the development of many experiences. In other words, the green light, a newspaper, a late bus, a dead automobile battery, a front door key, etc., all elicit a particular response and help to create what we call "experience." Additionally, technology provides an extremely stable external component that becomes the basis for regular response patterns.

Also, technology on the methodological level is virtually invisible in our thought and behavior patterns. This occurs because the construction of language is itself a result of and an embodiment of the methodology of technology. Consequently, the methodology of technology goes unnoticed because it is part and parcel of all our daily constructions through language. That is, both language and technology reflect (1) a cause-and-effect relationship, (2) a linear orientation to time and events, (3) a rational or logical process, and (4) a pragmatic and secular approach to reality. This means that the methodology of technology is not generally perceived with the construction of language and our resulting formulations of reality.

With technology as the basis for change, it follows that structure will be the most concrete representative change. Additionally, technology provides a rate of development that is reflected in both change and structure. The consequences of these two factors are as follows: (1) there develops a level of behavior that closely mirrors structure, (2) a structure alters and causes behavior, (3) behavior, not verbiage accurately reflects change within the socio-historic setting, and (4) the individual behavioral adaptations to structure result in a rate of change that involves (a) the rearranging of older, already existing entities and/or (b) the development of new structural additions. The speed of technological advance suggests a reversal of the classic theory that thought gives rise to behavior. Under this new formulation, the rapid increase of technologically-based changes gives rise to the development of structurally cause behavior. In turn, this behavior is immediately validated as "real" because behavior is also an experience. At the same time, change via structure has apparently outrun our verbal and conceptual capabilities to adapt to change. Within this process, accurate perception of both behavior and experience, which are survival-based reaction to structure, must come sometime after the actual occurrence. That is to say, the verbal level distorts our perceptions of the operational reality. Additionally, the speed of change and the relative slowness of conceptualization gives rise to a perceptual gap between verbiage and behavior. Consequently, this gap is also present between the verbal and operational levels. This verbal level, containing the "is of identity," is based on experience.

Experience slants reality in the following ways: (1) by requiring pastness to be used as the major vehicle for constructing the present, (2) by misperceiving the relative relationship between time, relativity, and what is going on, (3) by using time and pastness as the major criteria for dependability, and (4) by emphasizing experiences themselves, rather than the character of the surroundings from which they are at least partially drawn. This means that experience of the present are more clearly designed to meet circumstances of the past. Additionally, under this formulation, a past-oriented experience tends to hide the actual character of present events. This occurs because once a particular experience is conceptualized using a previous (past) experience as the test of validity, we tend to hold it "as is" over time. Thus, we fail to see how the environment has changed. In other words, our conceptualization process, which revolves around experience, tends to look for the ways in which things are the same rather than seeking how they have changed. Furthermore, the dependability of experience tends to distort the perceived need for change and becomes a roadblock to creating or developing alternatives to the present.

Moreover, experience as the test of validity tends to narrow future experiences in terms of diversity. That is, a particular experience which is pleasant or useful and once validated as "real," tends to act to support other similar forms of experience. In this situation, the conceptual emphasis upon what it tends to work, goes against what might be. At the same time, technology provided an extremely rigid base for experience so that, as a particular form of experience gains acceptance in the technological structure, this experience tends to remain over time. In this way, diversity is, for the most part, eliminated. For example, a hundred years ago, if you were interested in a table for the kitchen, several very different types of furniture were available. One craftsman might produce a table cut out of maple that would be intricately handcarved, while a second man might display a heavy bold table with no carving but extremely sculptured legs. The point is that all tables were different, all were stamped with the individual creativity of the craftsman involved. Also, they had a relatively long and varying existence in time and unique characteristic in space.

Today, virtually all tables are the same. They are mass produced and generally are constructed in the same manner. They have virtually the same characteristics in both time and space. Consequently, actual diversity in terms of differences in the availability of tables, has been effectively reduced while the quantity of fewer types are increased. In other words, quantity produces the illusion of diversity when, in fact, it more accurately reflects increased abundance within a narrowing spectrum of types. Under this formulation, the narrowing of experience tends to be invisible because quantity creates the illusion of diversity.

In addition, the narrowing character of experience merges with the structural character of technology to reduce our ability to "think" in a *philosophic or critical sense*. This occurs because we tend to view reality through experience, and experience in a highly developed and developing technology is ever more closely tied to the structural aspects of that reality. That is, of course, a result of the *static* conceptualization of thought. Therefore, we come to see the narrower realities as the only "real" possibility. In other words, both the character and perception of change are partially determined by the construction of experience on the *verb to be*.

Consequently, the average individual is required to accept more and "think" less. Thus, over time certain forms of experience and testing reality come to dominate a particular socio-historic setting and result in narrower perceptions of possible alternative realities, effectively reducing critical or abstract thought. The *is* becomes the totality of what is real.

What emerges is a gap between verbal and operational levels, and we only change this perspective when the verbal level and when the operational character of events come closer to accurately portraying the present. Experience, then, is not just simply the stuff we use to validate reality. It also happens to be: (1) a major factor in the conceptualization of all thought and/or idea systems, (2) a major factor in creating the things we subsequently term "real," (3) a major· factor in determining the future character of both experience and reality, and (4) the major force in determining the direction and scope of both structural and perceptual reality. In short, experience becomes the present and the *verb to-be* the focus.

CHAPTER 10

Abduction and the Construct of Behavior

The label "behavior" is what we refer to as a multi-ordinal concept, i.e., it can mean many things at different levels of abstraction. The *process of abstracting* enables us to talk about behavior from the standpoint of differences in meaning without losing the dictionary definition of the word at any given level. For example, organizational behavior is the way we function with people in the organization. This would be the definition. On the first level of abstraction, we talk about behavior in relation to men, women, janitors, supervisors, and presidents. These same people are transacted with on different matters and in different ways; on one level, we respond to them as individuals, the first level, and then we met them on different levels, such as social situations, groups and in relations to programs. The meaning or the way we function has changed in each instance, but the definition has not changed. Now, suppose we use the *epistemological profile* to examine the word behavior. Suppose at the *sensing stage* (first stage) we define it as the way one behaves with people in the organization and/or react on an individual basis. Then we move on to the *classifying stage* (the second stage) the process of paper work. As we progress to the *relating stage* (the third stage), the definition is expanded to include the formal and informal structures—the interaction with others, organizations, and the community. Then we advance to the *postulating stage* (the fourth stage) where we include all of those below: adding the environment, the world, universe, our families, and love relationships. At each successive stage, unlike the process of abstracting, definitions as well as meanings change. At the postulating stage, we have introduced the *structural more* (non-additive thinking), etc. and we must be prepared to introduce skills that are flexible. In short, we are saying four things: (1) The *process of abstracting* and *multiordinality* have limited application, (2) the *epistemological profile* expands the process; (3) the *epistemological profile* enables us to evaluate in successive stages the changes that transcend our immediate perception of things and view subjects as orders of thinking that reflect stages of development. On the other hand, the process of abstracting only enables us to utilize one stage at a time. For example, if the definition of behavior is at the classifying stage, the profile becomes a device which enables us to question what is left out, giving us a panoramic view of how behavior is viewed; and (4) the *process of abstracting* is about *levels* of transaction and development and the profile is about *stages*. The latter is tantamount to *paradigm* shifts or *epistemic jumps*.

There is, however, a need for microscopic analysis within each stage. This becomes the work of the *process of abstracting* and *multiordinality*. It makes the process of abstracting a particular case within the epistemological profile except when we use the process of abstracting to examine the definition of the epistemological profile. In this case, the function of the process of abstracting has not changed, but its role has changed meaning that the epistemological profile, in addition to introducing flexibility in terms of examination, is also a theory among theories and its specific function has to be examined. This perspective makes us aware of the either/or trap. It provides us with the notion that the *formulations* we are working with allows for thinking beyond the formulation itself. The *epistemological profile* relegates the process of abstracting and multiordinality to a particular place within the profile, but the process of abstracting has another function which at a given time transcends that place assigned to it by the profile, one of examining the elements of the profile. The profile has a definition and that definition has to do with flexible understanding which we take as universal. The fact that the profile can allow the process of abstracting to be a particular case within it, and not be a particular case, speaks to the possibility of including the philosophy, theories, formulations and skills all in one. In other words, there is *no separation of theory and practice.*

The profile and process of abstracting help us to understand, specifically, the notion of power. Our method for reconciling differences is usually at the relating stage of the epistemological profile—the power stage. The question is: Is there a better way of reconciling differences under these circumstances? Is there a way of rising to a superior level of abstraction—a level transcending our various individual abstractions which would enable us to reach some kind of agreement without using the power forces? The most poignant one introduced thus far has been Mary Parker Follet's Theory of the *Law of the Situations,* which by itself does not provide us with a method of inquiry. If we introduce stage IV of the epistemological profile and the abductive method which make a distinction between truth and love, and considers love superior to the various truths that we experience, then it might enable us to move to a different level. However, in certain situations, it is impossible many times to introduce this kind of equation. The dynamics of the situation will dictate our reactions. Our approach is one of prevention; and, we must approach it in that fashion. There is not much we can do in rectifying a situation once it begins; all we can do is navigate ourselves more skillfully. The proper use of power, then, is determined by our method of inquiry in many instances. The method of inquiry dictates our thinking.

For example, President Carter's decision to recommend withdrawal of the U.S. team from participation in the Olympic Games in the Soviet Union because of their invasion of Afganistan is an example of using reprisal which is at the relating stage of the profile and confusing levels of abstracting. The two are related—Afganistan invasion and the Olympics, but not the same. They have different purposes. Treating the two as if they were on the same level of abstraction is a misuse of the process, and, without realizing it, the long range consequences of such a decision may be disastrous. I believe decision-makers realize the subjects are separate and should be treated as separate. But, the use of the relating stage and confusion of the levels of abstracting are so embedded in our functioning, that we are prevented from moving mentally to another level of functioning. We become one-dimensional in our thinking, and therefore, neglect to fully comprehend the dangers of our actions. Carrying this a little further, what would happen if one did refuse to adhere to confusion of the levels of abstracting and reject the relating stage of the *epistemological profile*? We would simply become less emotional about a situation. We would put long range goals ahead of short range goals. Lastly, it would mean internalizing a method of transcending conflict and fostering cooperation.

While I often function personally, due to conditioning, at the relating stage, I can overcome it when I use the total *epistemological profile* as a process and abstracting as an instrument and thus rise to an intellectual level different from where I function. The intellectual use of the profile and the process of abstracting does not necessarily mean that my action will be different. Yet, it is merely a way of expanding my options, and putting me more in charge of my ways of functioning. It tells me where I am in terms of my thinking, and enables me to become adequate with my conclusions. This revelation does three things: (1) Sets in motion a creative process; (2) Prepares the decision maker for the undesirable consequences that are likely to occur from relating stage actions; and (3) Creates preferences and eliminates addictions.

The world lives at this stage of development and we cannot hope to change it "overnight," but insights can be revealed to us which will enable us to improve. Moreover, and this is the most important point, there are those who use the relating stage as if it were the only and correct way of functioning. The *epistemological profile* enables us to make a distinction between those who believe that, and those who know they are using this stage and confusing levels of abstracting, but it may be the best we can do at the present time pending a shift that will enable us to utilize methods that are (generally) more appropriate for long-range living.

CHAPTER 11

Policy Analysis and the Abductive Process

There are three critical questions, in my judgment, of major concern to us: (1) what is the state of our knowledge, (2) what should we do with it, and (3) how do we do it? The last question is the most difficult. We have a decent understanding of the state of our knowledge and, what we should be doing—our goals. But, we have been exceedingly inept at developing methods on how to do. In other words, we have pretty well diagnosed put forth a prognosis which many times have relevancy, but we have been poor postulators. Sometimes because of the range of our theories and methods and many times because we have found it more risky to spell out methodologies that speak of the new direction due, in part, to a fear of unchartered territories. By postulation, I mean methodologies that tie in with new and creative directions as a pattern for managing difficulties and navigating ourselves as part of the process of change. I have identified this as the most pressing priority of our times and, therefore, will put my attention to this task. It will not be exhaustive—time and space do not permit. Furthermore, at this time, my own understanding is rather limited. Also, based on my experience and tireless searching, the contemporary state of knowledge in the cultural and social and epistemological sciences gives us only a glimpse of what we need to know. Thus, this is just a beginning which hopefully will stimulate and move us to a different level of understanding. I begin.

In the May/June 1978 issue of *Public Administration Review*, I read an article by John Friedmann of UCLA entitled, ''The Future of Comprehensive Urban Planning: A Critique.'' He said, ''Metropolitan society is overwhelmed by change, so that many of the keenest minds in the behavioral sciences, whose business it is to explain the fundamental laws of human behavior and organization, have to fall back upon a superior kind of instant journalism. There may be laws that are immutable but the visible phenomena are so rapidly changing that the laws which presumably govern them become practically unaccessible to scientific means of exploration . . . . Under conditions of accelerated change the past is no longer reliable to a future which must be increasingly improvised.'' (p. 319)

Professor Friedmann has given a fairly accurate, but not adequate account of our condition. (For more information on accuracy and adequacy, see Kenneth S. Keyes, Jr., *How to Develop Your Thinking Ability*, McGraw-Hill). There are many things that could be said about this particular statement. For my purpose here, it is sufficient to say that contained within the language of his somewhat resigned and pessimistic analysis, is a cultural trap which limits the inventing of new and creative answers to the difficulty he poses. First, the behavioral scientist is ill-equipped to discover the immutable laws because of his limited focus. Second, immutable laws are found by going to the very nerve center of the transformative process, and this speaks to develop a new cultural epistemological base. Third, scientific exploration is tied to the old scientific method and linear determinism; this does not lend itself to going beyond our old categories of knowledge because it calls for the application of the methodology of experimental science—literally, to cultural development. To be critical of Professor Friedmann is easy. It is much more difficult to pose alternatives laced with how to obtain those alternatives. May I attempt such a task? A distinction is made between the physical sciences (frequently called by the flattering term ''the exact sciences'') and the social sciences—implicit in this distinction is the assumption that a fundamental difference occurs between the nature of physical reality and human social reality. It is confusing and unwarranted; we must cease viewing science as an entity which is divisible into a number of different quantitative parts; some wholly scientific—the exact sciences, some quasi-scientific and some only pseudo-scientific. We must, in short, view sciences as a way of behavior, as a way of interpreting realities.

This suggests that we pass from looking at human, the biological organism to human, the scientist. At this point we depart from the usual manner of looking at things. When we speak of human, the scientist, we are speaking of all humankind and not merely a particular class of people who have publicly attained the stature of "scientist." We are speaking of all humankind in its scientist-like biological and appreciative aspects. Such an abstraction of the nature(s) of human is not altogether new. The Reformation called attention to the priesthood of all humans in contrast to the concretistic classification of certain humans only as priests. The democratic political inventions of the eighteenth and nineteenth centuries favored the notion of inherent rulership of all men in contrast to the older notion of a concrete class of rulers. In a similar fashion, we may replace the concretistic notion of scientists being apart from nonscientist. And, like the reformists who insisted that every human is his own priest, propose that every human is, in his own particular way, a scientist.

Once we accept the postulation of human, the scientist, we have to see creativity and ways of managing ourselves more effectively, as an act of abduction. Abduction, to be carried out intelligently, demands some knowledge of epistemology and the practice of epistemics. In a similar view, Carlos Casteneda, the author of the *Teachings of Don Juan*, in a review of his book, *A Separate Reality*, is reported to have said: "We depend upon intellectualization for our practical actions and Don Juan depends upon magic. All things being equal, they work equally well. I think it would be arrogant to assume that there are not forces in the universe which we don't understand with our scientific method. I have experienced some of these magical phenomena and feel that this system of sorcery is as valid as our system of science."

We must begin to go beyond our present day understanding and seek a kind of knowledge which gives a different perspective on the social sciences. Additionally, we must focus on primary epistemological theories rather than the secondary normative theories founded in and validated by our cultural tradition. If not, we run the risk of locking ourselves within the old Aristotelian logic and the "scientific method." Let us illustrate the use of process by analyzing a statement about public affairs: "The corruption of individual power is incidental to the corruption of the political process and political system. The system also contains the remedy, which is to reestablish the countervailing powers established in the Constitution. By implication, the First Amendment makes a crucial assignment of power of the press. We already have begun, with clamor and controversy, the process of restoring countervailing power in the American government. Congress has been painfully attempting to reclaim proportionate power in matters of war and American foreign commitments. The action of the *New York Times* in publishing these documents is another, and very important step towards balance. For it is the obligation of the press to dig and probe government for its secrets" Los Angeles Times (article written Sunday, June 20, entitled "the Vietnam Papers. . . A Question of Power" William Pfaff).

The article talks about the restoration of balance of power. This is stage III (relating) talk. It defies the holistic perspective. It does not speak of relationships, but of separateness, and this separateness is being pursued in a pragmatic fashion. The British government long ago recognized this fallacy. What we have is a confusion of the analytic with the synthetic processes. The former is how we theoretically wish it to be (the constitution separation of powers, the machine model). The latter is how it really is—how it functions. The moment we confuse these levels of abstraction, we are in deep trouble. Basically, what we are trying to do is impose a mechanical analogy on an organism-as-a-whole situation. We have made the metaphorical transfer, i.e., we have reified an analogy. Our Constitution is an analogy, not what is going on (WIGO). We cannot restore a balance of power, because there never was a balance; balance speaks to a scale and sameness; it is a rejection of the *principle of nonidentity* (see Alfred Korzybski, *Science and Sanity: An Introduction to NonAristotelianism Systems and General Semantics*. Lakeville, CN: Institute of General Semantics, 1933).

The one relevant statement he made was that the corruption of individual power is incidental to the corruption of this political process. With this statement, he set the stage for going to the very nerve center of the difficulty. However, he backed away by saying, in subsequent paragraphs, we must restore the balance of power; in other words, keep the old machine oiled. His statement is similar to the one made by Neils Bohr in *Beyond Physics* by Ruth Nanda Ashen, when he stated that quantum mechanics had to be translated in Newtonian terms. In effect, William Pfaff is making a similar proposal. His first statement set the stage for questioning our mechanical frame of reference. Thus, leading us into unchartered territory, where we look for new and creative answers; and, at that juncture, we could question the purpose of government and the structure of that government in light of contemporary knowings. Pfaff's suggestion recommends improvement when we should be suggesting a radical transformation of the process.

The overarching theoretical epistemological formulation of epistemics recommends the utilization of stages IV (postulating) and V (participating) of the epistemological profile. William Pfaff, unfortunately, is attempting to implement a stage IV (postulating) recommendation with stage III (relating) methodology. With this, we remain marooned within the old ways of functioning.

During the same period of time, Dr. J. Samuel Bois, using epistemics, as I did for evaluation, undertook a separate analysis. Not being aware of this, I decided to share my analysis with him.

He wrote, and I paraphrase, "It was in June, 1971. The *New York Times* had published installments of a digest of secret documents dealing with the decisions taken in high governmental places concerning the Vietnam War before and after the 1964 election, when Johnson, who had presented himself to the nation as a dove, defeated Goldwater who had been branded a hawk.

The documents had revealed that contrary to what the common man had been led to believe, the Johnson administration had actually prepared itself for an intensification of the war and the bombing of North Vietnam while it was still protesting to the nation and the whole world that no such thing was even contemplated. In November of that year, Mr. Johnson, who had already completed the term of the late President Kennedy, was elected on his own as President who was going to keep our country at peace. Early in the following year, he ordered the intensive bombing of North Vietnam, as he already planned in a ''general consensus'' arrived at in the previous September, early in the campaign that preceded his election to a personal term. To sum it all up: the documents published by the Times had established that the public had been deceived.

Why was this done? Should we simply condemn these men— the President, the members of the cabinet and special advisers as if they were personally and perversely committed to war and to lies?

Perhaps not. They may be all honorable men. But, they are men without proper equations for understanding. They believed that they were serving the loftiest interests and the historical mission of the ''land of the free and the home of the brave.''

When the Republican administration, headed by Mr. Nixon, rushed to suppress the publication of the papers that laid bare the evident shortcoming of the Democratic incumbent, we saw that something trans-partisan was involved. Both parties are in agreement on one vital point: ''secret'' papers that conceal facts of vital concern to the citizen-voter can remain secret as long as men in power decide that they should be. It is not a question of morality, of truth versus untruth. The men in power have the right and the duty to tell lies. Their code of behavior is beyond the simple morality as the common citizen understands it.

How could this be? The answer is that something beyond truth and untruth, something beyond common values and naive morality is directing the performance of the principal actors in this momentous scenario. That something is the epistemic system to which we feel we owe blind obedience. Let us not blame the persons involved; let us not accuse them of being corrupted by a person's drive for power. As a competent observer, who believed in that drive-for-power theory, put it: ''The corruption of individuals is incidental to the corruption of the political process and political system'' (Ibid, William Pfaff).

I agree with Mr. Pfaff when he suggests that we look past the individuals to the system in which they function. Yet I disagree with him when he stops at the political process and system. We have to go beyond that, deeper, until we reach the epistemic system itself. It pervades all our institutions, and it is not corrupt. It is simply obsolete, antiquated, and inadequate to the conditions in which we live. I described it elsewhere as the semantic world in which men of breed II (classifying) live and function for them; the world as they see it is REALITY—plain, objective, unquestionable REALITY (used with the permission of Dr. J. Samuel Bois, July 13, 1971). Using the abductive process coupled with epistemics, Bois and I reached similar conclusions. This, to some extent, is illustrative of how separate persons using the epistemic system come to similar conclusions. This conclusion is not designed to necessarily indicate that the use of epistemics will always bring us to the same understanding, but rather to illustrate the usage of the abductive method.

I could go on citing incidents of this sort. I think it might be unnecessary in view of the clarity of the analysis above. However, before closing out this part, I would like to make another point and that is: Our definition of the what of the situation and our implicit mental models developed from our epistemological base determine the postulations we suggest.

For example, Professor Friedmann's epistemological base has led him to this: "The policy analyst must thus be able also to structure the learning experience of others; one must be a teacher and learner at the same time. Mutual learning involves a symbiosis of policy analysis and client groups that should go beyond a single interaction and extend to a continuing relationship. It is not a limited deficiency that has to be made up. The metropolitan age imposes upon all organizations a requirement of continuous adjustment, of exploration, discovery, and learning. Organizations, including communities, that fail to do so are likely to be left stranded by the ongoing stream of change. Perhaps it would not be unreasonable to suggest that depressed urban areas are, to a significant extent, the result of an existing insufficient learning capacity on the part of their existing guidance institutions. Thought should therefore be given to inventing a permanent structure for learning by action—planning groups, indeed, by all organized groups in the society in a continuous process of rapid societal learning. Policy analysis through mutual learning, structured competition amongst multiple actors, and experimental innovation in the institutional parameters of societal action comprise the essential new features that are in prospect for urban development. This new style holds nothing in common with comprehensive planning which may now be seen for what it really was, an old-fashioned, static ideology devised chiefly to advance the interest of a few professions in climbing to positions of dominating influence in the society. It is a style that is hopefully adapted to the new context in which knowledge and the power to act are fragmented and experienced sequentially. Drastic changes in expert roles and institutions are implied.'' *Public Administration Review*, (May/June, 1971, pp. 323-325).

No where does he indicate the necessity for systemic change, a necessary prelude for creative organizational and institutional development. By implication, his perspective would automatically utilize the scientific method which is not sufficient as an epistemological base to produce a new dimension in thinking.

I reviewed the November/December 1970 and March/April 1971 editions of *Social Policy* which was devoted to discussion on radical social change. I was interested in whether or not their epistemologies could lead to their objectives. The following summary of their ideas gave me a clue. The journals state: ''Indeed, one could only consider ours a post-industrial society if a fundamental structural change had taken place in the political, economic, and social institutions of this society. What we are witnessing is a new, uncompleted industrial revolution—not only here but also in Eastern and Western Europe. But the counter-culture offers the best circumstances for such a life, or rather, the most consistent rationale for it; so it must be cherished and supported and defended. That, of course, is a political commitment: narrow, but in 1970, heavy.'' *Social Policy*, November/December, 1970, pp. 14-22.

The above statement contains key phrases which mitigate against the counter culture accomplishing a political restructuring because the basic epistemological thinking has dictated the conclusion. In the first instance, there is talk about a post-industrial revolution, which does not take into consideration the question of quantum jumps in scientific affairs. We were moved out of the Industrial Revolution with the coming of the third conceptual revolution ushered in by Planck and Einstein. It was a quantum jump, not a *post* anything—a change in the very order of our thinking which has not been popularly adopted. And, as long as we do not apply this different order to our thinking and develop a new epistemological base and new mental models, our solution will continue to be mundane and remain within the old frame of reference. Why does it matter? It matters because it is essential to know where and how to focus. If we do not know the new is new, we will continue to use the same symbols. New situations require new symbols—post-industrial does not describe adequately what has taken place. It cannot . . . because a mechanical model (political, in this case) was used to direct the action.

CHAPTER 12

Abduction as a Transactive Method

Dr. J. Samuel Bois, in his book *Communication as Creative Experience*, declared that we do not have to agree with a person's statements or system of thought in order to accept his existence and set up a functional communicative relationship. He stated in an earlier book, *The Art of Awareness*, that we must move from the stage of *'know what'* philosophy to the stage of *'know how'* philosophy. I take these two statements as my point of departure to express an epistemic situation illustrating the value of these statements, and to introduce a process in the tradition of general semantics, but emphasizing epistemics. Epistemics, in this same sense, means the utilization of the epistemological profile, which incorporates the method of general semantics within its formulation. It makes the non-verbal process Korzybski spoke about not just a statement of psychological philosophy, but a workable focus penetrating the invisible cultural process—which is nonverbal, "sneaky," abstract, and difficult to "see."

The actual situation I speak of, involved the minorities and the so-called "establishment" at the University of Southern California.

The Chronology

A President of the University of Southern California authorized a minority commission to study and make recommendations to him concerning the plight of minorities. He founded the Commission as an independent body. The chairman of the minority commission in turn. set up a committee on minority faculty. I was made the chairman of that committee. The committee developed a list of particulars, collected data on these particulars and submitted the report to the Commission for ratification, and then to the President of the University along with recommended action. The key recommendation in the document was for the minority commission chairman and the President of the University to appoint three persons—each negotiating the recommendations. The President appointed two deans and the Vice-President for Academic Affairs. The chairman of the commission appointed me, the Chairman of Ethnic Studies, and a research associate from Urban Affairs to represent the committee. The minority committee group met two times prior to meeting with the president's appointees. I advanced the ideas that we should dispense with the label "negotiating" and employ the term *transaction* to describe what we would be doing. Also, I suggested that we not go in with a hidden agenda, but express to the best of our ability, exactly what had taken place in our private talks. We would share with the administration what we were about, and indicate that it was not them against us; but, that we all were involved in a mutual human enterprise which spoke to cooperation, emergence and transformation. Moreover, we were not looking for an advantage but an opportunity to develop out of this process the best that *six epistemic transactors* could produce. We reduced this orientation to writing, called the first meeting and discussed at length our feelings concerning what we were about. In turn, the administration officials did likewise. We were trying to operate in a transcending form. So, instead of considering ourselves representatives in that new group of any particular faction, we decided to constitute ourselves into a new group with our loyalties committed to what was best for the University—the minorities, the administration and humans. We committed ourselves to the proposition of developing some new ways of functioning; the group was transformed. However, the members still had a reporting function which entailed informing their respective constituents of any agreements reached. This should not be interpreted as a departure from our original theme of a mutually cooperative process. It simply means by using multi-ordinality, we were functioning at three different levels simultaneously with the second level embracing the first level. The second level was of a higher order. Also, it was an attempt to move beyond stage III (relating), to the epistemological profile of stage IV (postulating). There was a feeling, by some, that this was a ''soft'' approach in facing a complex and difficult situation which did not subscribe to the normal theory of conflict resolution. We soon discovered that transcendence does not mean being a ''softie.'' Instead, it meant not wasting time. Let me illustrate what I mean. While we were meeting at the third level (all groups—minorities, administration and the committee), we were simultaneously functioning at the second level— the committee level (in our respective groups). Our committee met separately and decided that there were certain items we should stress, and resolve to our mutual satisfaction. We transmitted this from the second level (our committee), committee level to the third committee (joint committee) and attached a deadline. We stated, in essence, that if we could not resolve a key point at the next meeting, then it was no longer necessary to meet. We concluded that it would be purely discursive if none of the basic items were resolved.

We met on that predetermined agenda; everyone had been given two weeks to think it over. When we met on the third level, the Deans and Vice President began to volunteer what they could do to meet the situation. They came up with some concrete action that they could take. These actions were strong, specific and voluntary, to the best of my knowledge. Trust seems to have prevailed in this transactive atmosphere. I will not detail the actions or specify the issues. It is sufficient here to know that we were able to eliminate the either/or syndrome, i.e., them versus us and debate in the negative sense. Good feelings prevailed, concrete results emerged, and parties in the process got to know five other humans—not deans, vice president or minorities, but humans. This was, I believe, a result of the invocation of the transactive epistemic process with the utilizing of the fundamental methods in general semantics and epistemics which is one of the major points in this discourse. It indicates that we can move from the ''what'' to the ''how'' with these methods. A subsidiary point here is that the practice of cooperative living is a

must for survival and living; and a subsidiary point is that it
"pays dividends" in terms of the by-products that may emerge
from the transactive process—for example, a worthwhile growth
experience. Another crucial point here is why involve ourselves
in needless conflict when we can participate in a cooperative
system which is easy on the nervous system and produces many
more worthwhile products? In short, we can live even while we
are transacting from moment to moment.

Transaction: Abduction

We can accept each others existence without "buying" each
others systems of thought—moving steadily from the "*what*" of
philosophy to the "*how*." A major thrust of the abductive
method is to question the viability of the notions of objectivity
and rationality.

CHAPTER 13

Abduction and the Notion of Rationality

It has been, to some extent, established that we should have a multidimensional approach to the understanding of our affairs. Since disciplines are very much related, we must move beyond either-or, and establish a central core. What has not been established is how to do it.

In management, psychology, anthropology, sociology, mathematics, physics, business, education, social work, urban planning, political science, economics, etç., there is a need for a synthesizing method of inquiry since the disciplines are related. Building a proper foundation for one is building a proper core for all. Our specific focus must be on an epistemological base. Let me give an example. I was sitting on a doctoral committee in June of 1978. Two questions posed to the candidate by one committee member was, ''What are the distinctions between 'functional' and 'substantive' rationality?'' and ''What does 'burned out' mean?'' We spent a sizeable amount of our time on these questions. I was then asked if I had any questions or comments. I got the feeling that the person who posed the question to me held under his breath the statement, ''I hope you don't have any question,'' but I said I did. My question was: How come we spend so much time redefining obsolete terms, i.e., 'rationality' and 'burned out?'' These are mechanical terms that are derived from the mechanical root metaphor and really have no place in our vocabulary if we are going to be contemporary. These models serve no useful purpose. My point: It is necessary to raise questions about the usage of those symbols, the assumptions they carry and some good substitute theories or methods. This is a typical example of our functioning; we must begin to raise questions about our assumptions, theories, and methodology. This requires a concentration on our language symbols and the processes and the nature of the human condition—in other words, questions about us as time binders. I believe a letter I wrote to one of my brighter students, who was stuck with an old paradigm, may illustrate what I mean: You have committed yourself to an obsolete logical system which speaks to precision and predictability. It has its roots in syllogistic reasoning which is more than 3,000 years old. It was devised by Aristotle under the influence of the knowledge relating to the human condition as it was known then. This was pure deductive reasoning. Then we moved to the second conceptual revolution which introduced inductive reasoning; this was a continuation of deductive reasoning. It gave us the scientific method. The responsible parts were Sir Francis Bacon and Sir Isaac Newton. It was a revolution in our thinking. It was not, however, until the 20th century that we were fortunate in experiencing the third conceptual revolution which is still in its infancy; it sought to introduce what is uniquely referred to as the process of *abduction*—which embraces the best features of deduction and induction. This period was introduced by Einstein, better known as the general and special theories of relativity. To this date, except sporadically, we have been reluctant to adapt this method to the social sciences for many reasons. We have in our educational system continued, as is to be expected, to maroon ourselves at the stages of deduction and induction. While it is not the fault of the student, I am reluctant to accept that as an alibi. Each person has a responsibility for remaining current. I notice that even our most elegant and eloquent logician since Aristotle, William Buckley, is changing a bit. He was on the Mike Douglas Show [last year] and introduced the idea of the process of abstracting and epistemics which are solidly within the abductive process. The new order of thinking rejects the notion of predictability and precision except under the rubric of probability. This is made quite clear in Sir Arthur Eddington's book on *The Philosophy of Physical Science and Epistemology* (see pages 52 and 53). Einstein in his book, *The Evolution of Physics*, also explained his reluctance and difficulty in breaking with deductive and inductive logic, and maintained that progress was not made until he was able to make the break with the old physics and the scientific method as he had known it. In *The Evolution of Physics*, Einstein asserted: A new theory shows us merit as well as the limitations of the old theory and allows us to regain our old concepts from a higher level . . . we could say that creating a new theory is not like destroying an old barn and erecting a skyscraper in its place. It is rather like climbing a mountain, gaining new and wider views, discovering unexpected connection . . . but the point from which we started out still exists . . . although it is often smaller and forms a tiny part of our broader view . . . (Einstein and Infeld, pp. 151-152).

We have broken, at least intellectually, with the mechanical view of nature, if not emotionally. Those who still cling to the old notion are behinders although still living in contemporary times. They are like fossils. The mechanical view is acceptable for mechanical things that relate to the old physics, i.e., push and pull an object is at rest until moved by an external force. This falls within the old logical context. We know now that this is nonsense if we are to make progress. It cannot even be utilized to relate to developing contemporary mechanical services—let alone behavioral and progressive notions relating to public affairs. Dr. Bois describes this in the latter part of his book, *Breeds of Men*.

In my judgment, if you are to be a serious scholar, you must develop flexibility and an openness to new and different ideas— even if the process is *painful*. My personal interest is that I believe the young are the future and will be making decisions which affect all of us. Therefore, we *must be concerned* about what they think and how they think.

In addition, most of what we have written utilizing objectivity and rationality can be easily dismissed. This, however, troubles most of our disciplines, including some forms of mathematics and physics. The rational and objective linguistic descriptions have permeated the structures of a great deal of what we study and use. This should not give us unusual concern, except as we ignore the necessity for change. If we accept the new direction, we begin to build a new core and a different foundation. This foundation has to be tentative and introduce an automatic change and/or growth orientation because our definitions today are only partial and represent only what we know today. Therefore, the development of a formulation with a change dimension is necessary.

We should have learned this lesson by now, but it appears that we have not. We know that logical arguments permeated in all areas of Greek scientific humanistic thought—Plato's dictum, ''Let him not enter who knows not geometry'' which hangs over the entrance of his academy reflects the high value the Greeks placed on analytic thought. Perhaps the greatest contribution of Greek thought was the development of rational analytic techniques and their application to the various fields of human knowledge. The Greeks became slaves to the linear either-or orientation of their logic. As a result, it limited their imagination, making it impossible for them to conceive of the concept of zero. Therefore, algebra was given birth by the Hindus in the 2nd century A.D. because they had a more relaxed, ''nonrational'' intellectual climate. It stands to reason from this that an intellectual creative climate would be hindered by the notion of rationality. Thus, it behooves us not to just improve the usage of the term ''rationality'' as we have sought to do in the management sciences, public administration, and social sciences, but abandon the term altogether and substitute something akin to process and probability. We may then be able to move our disciplines forward along with our personal and collective growth.

On a television program broadcasted Sunday, February 6, 1977, the moderator said we come from a very rational background—the working life. In reverse, the correspondent said he was from the irrational, then set out to describe his situation as mystical, synthesizing, unified, holistic, and connecting science with transformation. If we buy this ''frame of reference,'' there are two kinds of *rationality*: a rational description by man and a rationality that is universal and experienced which we consider the *irrational*. But, the universe cannot be irrational except in terms of the man-made definition. Therefore, the man-made rationality has to, by definition, be irrational because the universal appears to function according to some kind of order until we disturb it.

CHAPTER 14

A Managerial Abductive Process:
Death and Dying

In an article appearing in the *Los Angeles Times*, February 28, 1978, the hospital administrators and doctors were conferring on how they should approach death and dying. Dr. Harold Y. Vanderpool, University of Texas at Galveston, said that it was unfortunate that we approached death and dying in a negative fashion—he stated the following: The problem with using the phrase ''dying with dignity'' is that it has at least four meanings: (1) Prolonging the life of a person who is in an irreversible coma—death with dignity usually means pulling the plug . . .; (2) The phrase is often used as a symbol for voluntary euthanasia or suicide. There is dispute whether this form of euthanasia is dying with dignity. This, he says, may be counter-balanced by a general cheapening of life; (3) Persons who are able to accept death who do not deny or rage against it, are those who are said to have died with dignity; and (4) The patient maintains as much self-esteem as possible by being allowed to take part in medical decisions rather than by simply following doctor's orders.

His solution to the problem was: The phrase ''dying with dignity'' will enable us to tend to the personal needs of the terminally ill person. I find that as no solution. His recommendation will remain at the classifying stage of the epistemological Profile. It will not move us to a different order of thinking; and, since administrators in all walks of life are expected to make innovative decisions, I must take issue with the solution proposed for several reasons. In the first instance, the proposal represents dead level abstraction and not much of an understanding of multiordinal thinking. Of course, this does not help the situation very much at any rate because the doctor is talking about moving the idea to a new order of thinking. Therefore, it is quite important that the person or persons making the decisions be equipped with new skills for automatically approaching a situation of this sort. In this instance, it is mandatory that the decision maker begin to internalize a view which is more innovative. That view requires that their language adopt more advanced basic symbols for understanding what it requires to be innovative. If the decision maker would internalize a format more in keeping with new views of the human condition like transformation, they would probably arrive at something like this—this is just an example, I am not advocating this as final. The word *transformation* is specific to process, and death is a process. Suppose, we view it as a step in a long process and call it "the transforming enterprise" or "transforming transaction and/or transactional process." These words are neutral and speak to view the human condition as one of process and not form. The static way we approach death and dying now is Aristotelian and speaks to finality and either/or—either you are dead or alive. Process is the postulating stage of the epistemological profile; it does not assume that one knows what is going on, but assumes that one is uncertain. Watzlawick, in his book, *Change*, advanced a similar theory when he adopted Bertrand Russell's theory of types in order to introduce transformation as a statement about the naturalness of the human condition, rejecting the mechanical static notions of terms like *end, break, dead,* and other categories that do not introduce the idea of a process type management.

Dying is a process of life. One cannot come to grips with life until one has come to grips with one's own mortality. In other words, life is one ceaseless death which we refer to as transformation. In order to learn, grow, and be creative, we must live. The critical element here is not to die such painful deaths. It is an abandonment of the old. We tend to hold on too long. This happens in our professional and everyday life. Professionals, as administrators and people, we are required to shift as we transform ourselves. The shift is an epistemic jump. It brings into our orbit a new perspective; our responsibility is to conform to that by making the old a particular case with the new and use new shifts to relate to the present birth. Decision making, change, effectiveness, requires shifts to a new order. A mechanism for making the shift ordinary is important. We have been accustomed to the linear progression. Learning and doing require moving to another state, and this can be brought about by: (1) being aware that we transform and (2) allowing the transformation to take place. Welcome it. This perspective is not new. It is a matter of communicating ways of doing it. For example, perhaps it should not take a psychiatrist years to bring about a transformation in a person—with *shifting, hoisting, epistemic jumps* and *paradigm changes*, it could be done in a matter of minutes. It is the same in other professions, especially decision making in administration, as we deal with people and ourselves. Our responsibility is to bring paradigm shifts and epistemic jumps. ''How to do this'' becomes the question. Our focus must be on internalizing methods which enables us to function in this fashion. The following chapter will introduce specific ways to accomplish these changes and accommodate transformation. The notion of dying and being ''born again'' has to become an ordinary idea in ordering affairs. It should be happening many times during the day and we should be aware of the shifts. It is not one big ''bang'' and then it is all over. Learning requires this. It is moving to the new in order to view the old and put it in some kind of perspective. Otherwise, learning does not take place. An example of how to approach this is with the distinction made between prevention and treatment. Prevention does not lend itself to evaluation by the scientific method. Treatment does because it is after the fact. The natural sciences can utilize the scientific method and empiricism and social sciences, the abductive empiricism because for the most part, it is involved in prevention.

A prevention theory to impart along with the notion of transformation as *death* would be the theory of dissipative structures. This leads us to a number of interesting conclusions. First of all, we cannot go back once we are transformed. Secondly, we rise to another stage of development (intrinsic in that notion is we take to that other stage only the parts that fit in with our new overarching theoretical process); thirdly, we must develop skills to match our new ways of functioning. In the fourth place, this can only occur from a previous connectedness—holistic perspective in theory, which give rise to equilibrium, coherence and instability leading to a new stability. It is, as Einstein said, a rising to a new perspective in order to take a look at the old. In other words, it is an epistemic jump. This jump provides a new form and therefore requires a new methodology and symbolic process. The very nature of the shift requires that we do not look back. Therefore, the symbol of *regression* becomes obsolete. This would be the first symbol to be eliminated. And, instead of developing methods for relating to humans as if they regressed, we would be forced to relate to the forward thrust with no ''preoccupation'' with the past—in other words, we cannot go back. Instead, we develop contemporary symbols that relate to the present, based on our new shift. Then, the notion that becomes plain is enumerated by Korzybski, viz, all is structure and our symbols must have a fairly good relationship to the structure of events. With the new shift, the structure of events change; therefore, the structural symbolic process must change and this continues with each jump.

To repeat, the theory of dissipative structures speaks to epistemic jumps and enables us to think about the way we have thought about old matter, which is a way of completing the process of abduction. The internalization of the dissipative structure formula weds us automatically to the process of transformation in an ''holistic'' manner. It is a total way of functioning and this perspective carries with it automatically, the methodology and the message on *how* and *what* we must do in order to remain current. More than anything else, it is a theory which communicates not only how we stay in touch with transformation, but also, how we structure new formulations to represent those *transformations*. It is one short step from including this in our decision making process.

The next section will be devoted to the technique that determines how we should view the empirical dimension of abduction. The technique is called extensionalization.

SECTION FOUR
ABDUCTION IN PRACTICE

CHAPTER 15

Theory of Extensionalization

What do we mean by extensionalization? Extensionalization is the method by which the abductive process is made more reliable as we draw our inferences. It is the process by which we test our postulations. It is our way of preventing the domination of the classifying and relating stages of the profile. What does all of this mean?

Once a friend of mine, a lawyer, an elile-root scholar, ex-president of Occidental College's Student Body, my campaign manager when I ran for Secretary of State, said once that he considered himself the link or liaison between the Black community and the White community. This was during the high point of the Black identity movement. The Black community was undergoing, what I refer to as a therapeutic change—which tied in with a redefinition of human relationships. I could not accept my friend's definition of his role, at that time. I felt that he was not relating to the therapeutic change and, therefore, was neglecting his own black identity. Also, I believed that one either related to his black identity or not. You could not, in my judgment, serve both camps. You had to be in either one or the other.

As I reflected later on the situation and utilized the epistemological profile and the modern general semantics formulation, I identified myself as having been at the classifying stage of the epistemological profile, a stage where we label things—you are either this or that. I had classified myself only as Black. Within this stage, we find the aristotelian either/or syndrome, a two-valued orientation. It is a level of abstraction which is at a low multiordinal level utilizing none of the tools and techniques of general semantics, e.g., no *self-reflexiveness, no none-allness, no non-identity, no extensional devices,* i.e., *indexing, dating, plurals,* etc., *or hyphens.*

My friend, even though seemingly at a higher level of abstracting, was at a similar level—stage II (classifying) of the epistemological profile. He had divided blacks and whites into two camps. He, too, had an either-or orientation. He had placed himself in between two camps. Even the use of the hyphen would have moved him to another level, at least to the relating stage (stage III) of the epistemological profile.

I used the formulation and the epistemological profile as the major instruments of the epistemic process to evaluate this situation, and project something of substance. Also, to postulate how we should view situations of this kind.

First of all, substantively, the black and white situation cannot be viewed as being separate. Both groups are part and parcel of a larger all-embracing social, economic and political atmosphere. They are inextricably linked, and to separate them substantively would be an artificial construction that would not allow one to develop a theoretical formulation for understanding and making substantive pragmatic decisions.

The moment we link all together substantively, we immediately base our assumptions on the organism-as-a-whole approach. It is one logical step to the theory of *time-binding*, moving from there to analytically applying the *process of abstracting, non-allness, non-identity, self-reflexiveness, indexing, dating, plurals, etc., and hyphens and multiordinal* orientation. Moreover, we move up the stages of the epistemological profile which enables us to see the black movement or community as a particular case within a larger framework; we move *multiordinally* to a level of understanding of the intimate linkage involved. We move to stages III and IV of the epistemological profile. Then, when the substantive relationships are seen in this manner, the policy developed and promoted—social, economic, and political—are in keeping with a new conception of the human condition. Likewise, any program developed in the black community—as a particular case—based on our formulations would automatically apply to the "larger" community. Stated differently, the larger and particular cases are so intimately linked that policies which are designed for a specific case could be simultaneously applied to the larger community, thus providing us the overarching theoretical process.

In short, I am saying that my involvement as well as my friend's, if looked upon as levels and stages of involvement rather than strict categories that are separate and apart, would have enabled us to view vertically our activity, and eliminate the *either-or* syndrome. It speaks to moving up and down the abstracting ladder, using multiordinality and other general semantics and epistemic tools to develop a deeper understanding in order not to be immobilized as we move from one level to another. It means not viewing these activities and involvements as being in conflict, but as different orders of existence intimately related to each other. Unless we function at stages III and IV, it is impossible to apply the theoretical methods of epistemology that would enable us to function more effectively, be more creative, and make decisions that are in keeping with the natural direction of the human potential.

Being human becomes the highest substantive proposition, while being black becomes a particular case. But, the process of *extensionalization*, provides a circular process for a constant relating to both. At a given time, one may be the *container* and the other the *content*, then later, the *content* becomes the *container*.

The idea of extensionalization is to have a method of inquiry which enables us to see how the parts relate and how one has an affect on the other.

The extensionalization approach enables us to test, at any point, our theory and simultaneously invent new theories that emerge out of the awareness and practices; it is the patient and quiet application of the theoretical process to pragmatic situations.

My friend and I, by labeling in a nontentative fashion our involvement, concretized our position and did not allow ourselves to move to the postulating stage (IV) of the epistemological profile. Most of all, we did not set in motion a process where contradictions and crippling conflicts are nonexistent.

The social scientists and administrators relating in this fashion do not operate effectively and are less adept at understanding personal, group, and broader difficulties. The theme flowing through is one of change leading to the invention of new theories of change and *transaction*.

Specific: The Epistemological
Profile as a Focus for Extensionalization

We hopefully, do not regard the epistemological profile as a perfect instrument. It is only a guide and tool. As a method of inquiry, however, it is a useful device for the nonverbal and cultural aspects of our development in philosophical, psychological, sociological, and anthropological terms. In many other ways, it is similar to the structural differential and the semantic transactor, however, they both can be considered particular instruments and cases within the epistemological profile. The profile is broad enough to embrace these instruments and they are sufficiently powerful to be utilized alone.

The profile should be viewed as follow: (1) as a self-revising overarching theoretical process; (2) as an instrument to be used to understand a specific case; and (3) as a process to evaluate ideas, the process and the individual. More importantly, it is a vehicle for inventing new instruments. The invention of a new instrument is realized by functioning as much as possible at stage IV of the profile. It becomes a self-reflexive instrument. As an example with the aid of the profile, I am also ready to temporarily review my notion that epistemics is only a particular case within the process of the theory of time binding. I believe, now, and I am holding this very tentative pending new developments, that since *time binding* places its major emphasis on the making of verbal symbols it is, also a particular case within epistemics.

Many students have rejected the epistemological profile simply on the basis that the profile is vertical moving from low to high. This implies, they think, one person may be better than another. This is reason enough to reject the profile if it does, in fact, promote this kind of elitism. However, I do not see it that way. I see it as a way of evaluating ideas or issues in a particular situation, at a particular time, not the person per se. I also see it as a way of determining where a person resides in terms of his thinking and ideas most of the time. Consequently, there is no conclusion that the person making the judgment assumes that the other person is overall inferior intellectually. It merely assumes that the person is using obsolete methods for thinking and evaluating at that time on that matter and can, in some other instance, become aware of this. It is a method for strengthening our organismatic equipment and enabling us to become better than we are as "humans."

It is important to know at what stage the predominant part of a decision of located. This knowledge is helpful in enabling us to decide when to do, how to do, where to do, and of course, whether to do.

How do general semantics methodology and epistemic postulations relate as extensional processes? There is a similarity between the process of abstracting and the epistemological profile. The former belonging to general semantics and the latter to epistemics. The process of abstracting *stays within one order of thinking* and the profile *moves from one order of thinking* to another. Therefore, the process of abstracting becomes a particular case within the profile and makes epistemics the all-embracing overarching process. And, general semantics becomes a particular case within the process of epistemics.

It can be summed as follows: (1) The five stages of the profile allow us to evaluate and predict situations much more quickly; (2) epistemics embraces the formulation and subformulations of general semantics; and (3) When we use the epistemological profile, we are requiring that the person be self-reflexive, be aware of the consciousness of abstracting, practice habitually the notions and become a better semantic transactor.

Since, it is not a process to be intellectualized totally, as we do with most things in academia, but a process to be internalized and practiced, it is an empirical device. The first step, however, is to memorize the basic abstract theory. But, I cannot emphasize enough, practice is the key. And, this practice is not separate from everyday decision-making. It is a matter initially of thinking these notions consciously in each decision situation that we find ourselves. The repeated usage will bring about automatic internalization and after some time, the notions will exhibit themselves automatically in our behavior and in almost every decision. In this manner, extensionalization is a way of practicing empiricism.

CHAPTER 16

Extensionalizing Abduction in Everyday Affairs

In chapters 7 and 8, I outlined methods for functioning at stage III of the profile. I also suggested that it was more desirable, however, to function at stage IV. This chapter, then, is all about how to accomplish that objective. In 1940, Arthur Bentley, the author of *The Process of Government* (written in 1908) co-wrote a book with John Dewey, the noted American philosopher and educator, called *The Knowing and the Known.* In this book, they elaborated on a method of inquiry for action and behaving. The major thesis was: There are some things that are known and there are some things that we are knowing; by coupling these we manage to integrate and bring our dualistic worlds together. We do not separate body and mind, fact and value, black and white and so forth. Instead, we move to a higher level of abstraction and view the behavior in its totality without mating those separations or categorical judgments. I believe it is time now for another dimension. This other dimension is knowing and doing. As we are brought face to face with the fourth stage (postulating) of the epistemological profile and the *extensional* methods, we have to internalize in order to function effectively at stage four.

How do we begin? We must inevitably begin by engaging the proposition that what we internalize will determine what we know, and therefore, what we do. We need a series of directives that will concentrate on doing what will affect the knowing and the known automatically, therefore, what we internalize. This is a reversal of what we normally do; we normally first learn the language—the abc's, arithmetic, and then socialization. I am talking about something quite different—although we can also do it that way. This is coupled with a series of ways to function that contain a flexible, self-revising method of inquiry. We internalize it automatically. However, we must not confuse this with the approach of separating practice from theory because mere practice leads us to prescriptions, then reductions and finally to a level of functioning which is concrete and narrow. And, we are held there without any allowance for functioning at different levels of abstraction. We are talking here about the blending of theory and practice holistically in dynamic situations.

A big part of this is relaxation! Now you might say that I have just introduced another goal rather than a method for achieving the "doing" state. I would reply that you are correct. But, achieving relaxation is one of the ways of being more holistic and doing; it gives us a focus and a direction. It is sufficient just to know and think that relaxation is one of the keys. Simultaneously, we relate intellectually to something called the *structured unconscious*, which is the pattern behind the patterns.

The *structured unconscious* is a human's second nature. We assimilate into our unconscious patterns of activity that are not inherited through the chromosomes we received from our parents. These patterns are cultural and vary from one culture to another. The cultural unconscious becomes a distinctive, personal unconscious—a dynamic pattern of attitudes, habits, internalized values and modes of thinking by which each person relates and expresses himself to the world, and brings into action the thoughts of the cruel inner critic. This critic is filled with "ought," i.e., you ought to go to church, you ought to say good morning, you ought not to have fun, you ought to be ethical, you ought not like sex so much, you ought to be loyal to your husband, you ought to be loyal to your wife, you ought to have more friends, you ought not think of yourself, etc. It is the contention of some that the "cruel inner critic" is always there and the suggestions made by the critic are taped and cannot be erased. Furthermore, it is thought, along that same line, that the only way to skillfully manage oneself when the critic takes over is to challenge the suggestions and guilt being heaped on with counter suggestions each time. Thus, the process is repeated over and over. Gregory Bateson and J. Samuel Bois as well as Arthur Bentley claim, using different descriptive terms of course, that there is a pattern behind the pattern, thinking behind the thinking and an episteme. If we can somehow locate the pattern and the episteme, we may be able to reformulate the cruel inner critic. The pattern is not unconscious; it blocks the ''real'' unconscious and prevents us from fully utilizing the nonverbal process.

There are ways to approach this; one device suggested by J. Samuel Bois in his book, *The Art of Awareness* (pp. 280-281), is to be aware of the dangers and safety indicators. Without becoming too detailed, I will mention, in general, the cautionary measures. We should seek to eliminate generalizations, e.g., doctors are like this or that, implying that we know about all doctors; check on words of high order abstraction ''freedom,'' ''democracy,'' ''religion,'' experiences in simple terms. Our statements should deal with, who, what, where, when, how much and how many.

Another danger sign is the frequent use of value terms, such as adjectives and adverbs that describe much more how we feel than what is actually going on, using such expressions as ''you should,'' ''you must,'' ''you ought to,'' ''the only thing to do is,'' etc. These words show that we are attempting to impose upon the other person our own set of values.

Another danger sign is the tendency to identify and refer to the present situation as if it were just like another. The safe way to handle this is to look for differences between the present and the one we identify it with. Similarities come to mind automatically; we should look for difference—differences that make a *difference*.

There are also dangers in the way we ask questions. Instead of asking ''Are you moody again?'' one should say ''You seem to be in deep thought. Would you like to share it with me?'' The questions should not impose or intrude. Another consideration is the manner in which we carry on a conversation. We interrupt and start talking before the other person has finished completing his sentence and contradict with ''yes, but...'' There is no communication under these circumstances. All circuits are busy.

It might be useful to let a second or so elapse before responding. If neurologists are correct in stating that the speed of the nerve impulse is relatively slow and the time it takes for new cell assemblies and new phase sequences to establish themselves, it is necessary to have patience in listening.

These indicators are so closely related that if we pay attention to one, we are actually working on the others. This is the holistic approach. Let me be a bit more specific.

Benjamin Keller, head of the Los Angeles branch of the Vector Counseling Institute, tells of one desperate young woman: "Her marriage wasn't going well. As she put it, "no matter how hard I try, I just can't clean, cook, and work at the same time." She had to stop *trying* and just *do* those things the best she could. Without the inner struggle, she found that she could schedule some things, let others go, and accomplish more.

When we switch from *try*, which anticipates failure, to "do the best I can," we do exactly that. We could *not* have done better, or we would have. Check it out: Consciously delete *try* from your vocabulary for a month.

Always and *never* are our creations. Much more accurate are words that represent gradation, that cover a spectrum, such as almost always, many times, frequently, not often and hardly ever.

When we believe a person is "always" faithful, and they prove otherwise, we are devastated. When we believe we will never lose a particular friend, or our money, or a job, and we do, we respond with grief and resentment. Popular songs, expressing cultural truths, reflect this; "always and forever," we say; "you belong to me" or "I can't smile without you," we sing.

Our use of—is, are, I am, in English, is virtually unique. In Spanish, separate verbs distinguish temporary from permanent: "estar," to be in a temporary sense, and "ser," to be in a permanent sense. This is also true with French and so many other languages. But in English, we can only describe a permanent, unalterable condition.

A youngster who repeatedly hears how lazy he is tends to agree: "I am lazy." When adopted as his own reality, "the way I am" becomes a fact of his life. If I call him lazy ("the way he is''), I will see his actions colored by that judgment. Anger, resentment, and rigidity may develop in both of us as a result. *Can't* carries the same burden of permanence, expressed this time in a negative way. "You can't do anything right," say our parents. When we try our hand at algebra, cooking or calligraphy and do not do well, if we conclude, "I can't do it," we are apt not to attempt it again. Thus, language has done our thinking for us. If we accept our first-round failure for what it really is— doing the best we can at that moment—we are much freer to try again. Or by learning to be more precise: "Perhaps I can't . . . with the education, experience, or information I now have," we free ourselves to seek out the necessary information, experience or education.

Notice how you feel when you say, "I should call her," or "I must get this done." "Shoulds" are mainline to guilt. If the guilt is appropriate, fine. But it is a waste to trigger it by using language that reflects other people's standards or precepts of our own that we have outgrown.

Perhaps we use "everybody," "nobody," "no one" to make things seem better than they are, or to have our opinions supported. If *everybody does it*, we are safe. Everybody includes too much, and nobody excludes too much. These terms prevent seeing differences between individuals. When we use them, we are inaccurate most of the time; we miss a great deal.

What can we expect when we change our use of "try," "always," "is,", "can't," "should," and "everybody?" "You will notice no "overnight" changes, but you will definitely be easing yourself into a less dogmatic frame of mind—more open, less demanding, and in some ways, scarier. Did you mean everybody? Or could it be some people, or many people I know? Is he really that way, or does he seem that way to you, now? Should you really be more (or less) ambitious, or are you judging yourself by someone else's standard? Are all of your dates broken, or just the last two? It takes time, and it takes honesty. Try it. No, do it."

Another area of concern is the dualism trap. It is as follows: (1) You are blunt, I am frank, he is rude; (2) I am courageous, your judgment is poor, they are not good strategies; (3) I am truthful, you are insensitive, they are ignorant; (4) I am open, you give me your problems, they pour out their troubles; (5) I enjoy my food, you overeat, he is a glutton; (6) I correct people for their own good, you are argumentative, he has a terrible temper; (7) I am business-like, you are cold, they are sticklers; (8) I master details, you are sticking your nose into other people's business, they are snoopers; and (9) You are too concerned with money, they should allow for individual differences when collecting, I won't mix personal functioning with business.

I have introduced these concrete situations to indicate extensionally the status of our thinking and functioning. I want, however, to make it clear that in order to revise and/or change these patterns, it requires more than an intellectual and memorization approach. We emphasize internalization of a pattern of thinking which will automatically produce the results we are seeking. We can achieve some results by just focusing on the notions in this chapter, but the "real" change in patterns occur when we expose ourselves to the whole of applied epistemology as outlined in this book.

In addition to the above, a positive thought could include the following: Korzybski, in the second edition of *Science and Sanity*, remarked that if we could use the extensional and safety devices, we would be able to change our patterns from one of static, inflexible and ineffective to a pattern of process (dynamics), flexibility and effectiveness. The *extensional devices* are indexing, dating, etc., meaning: (1) Indexing—(differences) man_1 is not man_2, psychology $book_1$ is not psychology $book_2$, depressed $person_1$ is not depressed $person_2$, $doctor_1$ is not $doctor_2$, $lawyer_1$ is not $lawyer_2$, or my thinking on the subject of money is not the same as my friend's thinking on money. By using this method, we begin to experience differences. In order to become acquainted with differences, we use the method of indexing. (2) Dating (change)—the process of dating is to make us aware of change. My thinking on Tuesday may not be the same as it was on Monday. I am not the same person as I was in 1952 if it is now 1953. Depressed $person_1$ is not the same as depressed $person_2$ nor are the differences the same in 1979 as they are in 1980. Doctor$_1$, teacher$_1$, lawyer$_1$, in 1979 were not the same as they are on Monday, nor are they the same on Tuesday as they were on Monday, nor are the differences in 1980 the same as they were in 1979. As you can see, dating is used in conjunction with indexing. And (3) Etc. (exceptions)—this is to indicate that I, nor anyone else, know(s) all. The "etc." indicates that there is more to be said and that there are exceptions to "every" rule, except the rule that there are exceptions to every rule. This helps us to practice non-allness. The safety measures are hyphens and quotes. We relate as follows: (1) Quotes (different viewpoints—the same thing may mean different things to different people). We put in quotes multiordinal words such as "love," "life," "friendship," "freedom," teaching," "war," etc., and (2) Hyphens—(similarities)—the hyphen is meant to show how one thing is connected with another, for example, male-female, night-day, space-time, psychosomatic, black-white, cold-hot, rain-sunshine, similarities we see most of the time, but in things that seem dissimilar on the surface perhaps should not be separated—love-hate. The things can co-exist. Einstein is probably the most celebrated user of the *hyphen*. Instead of viewing Newton's findings as time and space, he connected them and from that connection emerged the theory of relativity, time-space. To operationalize and personalize all of these, the introduction of (1) to me and (2) ing—-ending are necessary. The "to me" personalizes the process and makes us aware that all of our observations are subjective. The use of ending "ing" changes the *noun* to a *gerund* and makes it *process-like*. In other words, we change it from a static content word to a process. For example, the process of dating and indexing are more in keeping with process than the words "dates" and "index." The latter is static. If we begin for instance, to think of movement which the "ing" indicates like mechanizing rather than mechanic, or doctoring rather than doctor, or maturing instead of mature, it gives us a feeling of growth and are more in keeping with what is going on (WIGO).

The key is habitual use of these methods if we are to realize the desired results of change—knowing difference, feeling exceptions and viewing similarities. These are, in general, being process-like and effective in natural fashion.

These practical devices are a key to the "how" of internalizing or the deeper level of the abductive method. It begins with a thinking process that will eventually penetrate the nervous system, and thus our behavior. These are some of the methods used by the scientist in the laboratory. The scientist brings this attitude to the work. There is no science without a scientist attitude. Likewise, there is no social science without a social scientist attitude. The perspective we bring to our everyday office determines the *kind* of social science. Social science is not something "out there" waiting for us to become a part. Whatever is there we created and labelled. So, social science resides within us and the quality of what we do is determined by our method of inquiry. We suggest at this juncture, that internalizing methods that fall within the abductive process and becoming an epistemist is a necessary approach to becoming a social scientist. We are all scientists, as I indicated in an earlier chapter. It is just whether or not we bring a certain approach to our situation. Our perspective includes the practitioner and/or theoretician. Moreover, the researcher who considers himself a purist will find it useful to internalize the devices which are necessary for both developing new methods and being the kind of social scientist equipped to work within the uniqueness of the human laboratory.

CHAPTER 17

Abduction as a Process of Innovation

We normally associate "creativity" with the fine arts—musicians, artists, writers, dancers, etc. They seem to have an image or monopoly on creative ability. Those of us who have not excelled in the fine arts do not understand the creative urge as the artist does. In this chapter, we would like to discuss an entirely different aspect of creativity. This aspect is creativity in thinking and communicating.

First, I will discuss some examples and supply some background to creative thinking. Second, I will discuss the focus and ask some basic questions. Third, I will present a method for creative thinking and communicating.

There must be a special thought process in those who have proved themselves creative in decision-making and communication. What strains do they have in common? There appears to be a thread which weaves throughout. For example, when we think of Arthur Bentley, Khalil Gibran, Clarence Darrow, Einstein, Paul Robeson, Duke Ellington, C. Wright Mills, and Mary Parker Follett, we observe action transcending the thoughts and functioning of an obsolete culture. We see, for example, how Clarence Darrow failed to view the accused as the only one guilty as he put our ways and mores on trial. He rose to a high *level of abstraction* beyond the *either-or* concept transcending even the multi-valued orientation; questioning the very existence of humans and our relationship to the universe. Though far ahead of his time, he was able to function from the postulating stage of the epistemological profile and communicate with the masses, who are, for the most part, at stages II and III of the epistemological profile. We say this in retrospect of course, for in his lifetime, he did not know the profile. We apply epistemics to examine his theoretical process—what it may have been like. All of the above names acted according to our epistemic process. Epistemics is the thread which was present in each of these persons; and, these persons were considered *innovative*—if *innovative* means new directions pointing the way to a more humane existence and communicating to us unthought thoughts. Their direction made sense to them, and almost everyone wanted to adopt their pattern, but did not possess the skills to translate them into action. Those few who did, did it in their own way personally, and barely left a path to follow, in terms of a broad theoretical understanding. Our task is how to communicate the invisible thread.

Epistemics, while invisibly in practice for years, is so new to us verbally that we have difficulty making it understandable. For example, if 200 years ago, a man walked on a 747 jet, he would not know what to do with it. Even if he guessed it would fly, there was no way he could understand all the instruments. Luckily, creations in the sciences have been carefully recorded, showing the process of arriving at each discovery as well as the finished product. Each new generation can use the process for further discoveries. The great thinking process of a Clarence Darrow has not been recorded in theoretical terms. What does all this mean for *innovation*? It means that in learning to think about thinking, we not only have to internalize a method of inquiry (comparable to scientists' theorems and hypotheses) such as epistemics, but we have to create our own guidelines for functioning and find a method to verbalize this method of thinking so we can communicate the process as well as the results. Science did not just present us with the light bulb, atom bomb and automobile; it gave us the process used to develop these. For *innovative* communicators and decision-makers, creativity is not solely in the finished product—the decision for example, but it is in their knowing how he or she arrived at such a decision that we might share the method. Which means when the decision becomes obsolete, we can still draw from the method.

Before I begin discussing methods and skills for charting this new direction, I would like to focus on several things we must know, believe, and question. First, I believe that I must now begin to look at old ways of thinking about theories we use for communicating our ideas. For example, if mental models, types and mental constructs as such are not sufficient—then what it? Emergence, transformation, evolution and transaction are a step beyond mental models and constructs and could be labeled as processes of inquiry, which automatically take us to a new order of thinking, viz., to flexible thinking about mental constructs as stagnant and particular cases. Stated in precise terms, this process of inquiry becomes a theory of theories and utilizes stages IV (postulating) and V (unifying) of the epistemological profile.

In order to make the statement about emergence, transformation, evolution, and transaction clear, we will paraphrase a statement from Lewis Mumford. He says in effect: In order to understand where we have been and where we are going, we must understand the nature of *emergence*. Also, he adds, that man's historic selves have served as fine meshes that rejected far more than they admitted and, a great transformation would take place if every part of man's experience were hospitably received. But, we have need for a process that is capable of reconciling persistence with change. Also, to effect a new transformation, we must have a philosophy capable of uniting every aspect of human experience and directing human development through every phase (Lewis Mumford, *The Transformation of Man*, 1956). Epistemics is a stab in that direction, and even the earlier tools of general semantics, which are a part of epistemics, was headed in this direction.

Second, I believe that those who have internalized epistemics and devoted themselves to *innovative* decision-making have a very intense intracommunication; they not only hear and understand each other, but deeply feel *felt feelings*.

Third, I must ask myself some basic questions—how do I go though these *transforming* experiences of internalizing epistemics? What skills do I use?

Fourth, I must know that differences are not in the object, but in each of us. For example, a wife had put her husband through school. She vowed to never do it again after her husband had left her upon completion of school. She met another fellow and fell in love. He had not finished school. Well, what about her vow? She was thrown in a quandary. The major objective here is not how we see someone, but how we view their similarities and differences. How different is the second person? She kept comparing them cosmetically to a balance sheet, i.e., assets and liabilities. What she needed to do was search within herself and locate the individual differences she perceived in her own feelings. Therein would lie the differences in the two individuals, not in an intellectual comparison of individual traits. While those would point to similarities and surface differences, they would not supply her with felt differences that existed. You see, her own feelings would also make a difference because as a semantic transactor, she would also be different in this situation. Her deep felt difference coupled with the cosmetic differences would supply her with direction and thus, a decision. The shared perception differences are *macroscopic* and *analytic*. The sub-microscopic *differences* are felt and *synthetic*.

We take the flexible position that in order to communicate effectively, one must first have a method and secondly, something to communicate. That method must be one which enables us to see the logic of the present culture and rise to a level beyond the logic of the present culture, i.e., be translogical. One must, as *Jonathan Livingston Seagull*, soar to a higher level of abstraction. The transformation for this is not hidden. If we were to pinpoint any two constructs within the epistemic formulation, we would, say, become familiar with the *semantic transactor diagram* and utilize the *epistemological profile*. These two elements intimately tie us in with the process of abstracting and put us into the center of the evolutionary process, which is germane to understanding growth and humanistic strengths and limitations.

Korzybski said, ''Once the linguistic character of the issues is fully realized, the 'psychological semantic blockage' is removed, freedom of analysis is inwardly established, and even nongeniuses will produce important creative work.'' Indeed, we may find that with this realization, particularly if embodied in early education, the normal person would be what we call at present, a ''creative'' genius.

This brings me to the subject of method in innovation. With a method, I can begin to understand the underlying elements undergirding the creative urge as expressed through the language dimension of creative communication.

The persons mentioned in the beginning of this discussion, of which I elaborated on one, and the others which I did not mention tend to come from a direction described in my book, *Uncommon Sense and Dimensional Awareness*, and I paraphrase: in order to make use of the transactive process, we must talk about a certain perspective and we must ultimately address construct formulation and methods of inquiry. More than that, we need a transactive epistemological base.

Let us look at the contemporary scene and call our approach to the epistemic approach and see how we come out. What kinds of rules can we make with the epistemological profile and how does it relate to the hidden dimension and vertical processes?

There must be no doubt that our lives in the 20th century are based on the epistemology of the theory of relativity, quantum mechanics and stage IV and V of the epistemological profile. The perspective is one of probability, change, a measure of order, uncertainty, and time as a creative dimension. How do we internalize this perspective? First, we must label them uncommon sense notions. Second, we must identify the common *sense notion as strict determinism, cause to effect* relationships, Newtonian feedback, accurate and adequate predictability, stability, one reality and one nature. The latter notions must be systematically and consciously stricken from our vocabulary and replaced with the process notions. We can do this by macroscopically discarding the *common sense notions* and practicing the *non-common sense notions* on a daily basis and coupling them with the total formulation of epistemics. With the theory of *time-binding, self-reflexiveness, multiordinality, the semantic transactor, the process of abstracting, non-identity, non-allness, semantic jumps, semantic psychoanalysis, the epistemological profile, the extensional constructs, viz., working devices, e.g., indexing, dating, etc., safety devices, plurals and hyphens, working principles, delayed reactions, and semantic relaxation,* the general notions of epistemics are the keys. We can systematically use the epistemological profile to understand macroscopic and analytic situations. Finally, we can come to the point where we consider ourselves synthetic and that the process is *analytic-synthetic*.

Creative communicators and decision makers function mostly at stages IV and V of the epistemological profile. These stages are described in Dr. Bois' *Breeds of Men*. I paraphrase: breed IV persons are few and far between. They are products of a sudden maturation upon our culture and are able to understand what happened to them; they are new to their own selves. They are just beginning to soar in free flight above the world like *Jonathan Livingston Seagull*—still a bit hesitant and uncertain about the management of themselves. They must practice new skills to understand themselves, stabilize their semantic orientation and get along with institutions and power groups who may otherwise crush them. There are seven ways to recognize breed IV persons: (1) they are self-actualizers, owing to but not locked into their culture; (2) they have a definite philosophy to life, too high to be formulated in simple sentences; (3) they live in a broad space-time context, encompassing thousands of centuries of life; (4) they are beyond seeking only deficiency needs (hunger, security, recognition) and find altruism the dominate passion of life; (5) they have no bitterness for those who oppose them for they recognize that the opponent draws a picture of his own world different from the one he lives in; (6) they are aware that discursive reason has limitations; and (7) they realize that at each moment of our life, we push into the unknown and discount absolute predictability.

We call breed IV persons postulators because they know that when we accept a set of postulates, we determine the pattern of our epistemic world and act according to postulates that we made on our own. Everyone of us makes his unique world and has the ability to change it.

Breed IV postulators are in outer space to survive on their own and creativity is the only method of survival there. Whatever they do not create in space does not and will not exist, and unless they provide for themselves, they have nothing. It is lonely and difficult there, but they are in the highest ground of the creative dimension. Breed IV persons not only must make new decisions, but they have to discover new methods of thinking, inquiring, functioning, and finally of returning to a verbal communication of the process they have experienced. The latter is the most difficult as well as important of all. The demand for creativity from the breed IV man is so intense that he cannot help but to continually grow intellectually and creativity.

We must remember, however, that whatever theory we come up with should be held tentative, and this theory is no exception. A paraphrase from the propaganda newsletter of the *Arts and Sciences of Communications* Vol. 3 No. 3, July 1, 1973 puts this theory in perspective; it says in essence: We can only say that our experience up to the present predisposes us to see things in such and such a way. A scientific theory should be regarded not as a creed, but as a guide to action and each guide must be accepted only tentatively, subject to modification, revision or expansion in light of further observations and experience. The fruitfulness of a theory lies in its ability to suggest, stimulate, and illuminate ongoing action and experiment.

The Summing Up and Moving On

The Summing Up

What I have said requires continuous study, and such study must be analytical, synthesizing and transforming. It must shed light on underlying principles. Fortunately, the foundations of such a study in creative living and communicating have been laid. Learned men from Aristotle to Burke, Berkeley, Mills, Veblen, Sorokin, Bachelard, Bentley, Korzybski, Bois, etc., have addressed the process of innovation. It is just a matter of arranging this knowledge in some usable order.

This continued study and usable order must be interdisciplinary relating physics, mathematics, sociology, psychology, political science, social and physical science, etc. If this is the case, then a general system of learning is necessary. The methodology must thread throughout our human experience. The methodology assumes that structured layers have been left in the human mind akin to the geological strata of earth; we need knowledge about these layers. These layer structures direct our thinking and evaluating of activities, decisions and transactions.

People of all disciplines have a common ground—innovative thinking and communicating. At this high abstract level, we feel no rivalry or competitiveness between our disciplines. Epistemics as one method can provide us with a strong sense of universalism and humanitarianism. The closer we direct ourselves toward the ''Breed IV'' model the more of an expanded awareness develops, which allows for maximum creativity in our thinking and communicating.

The Moving On

The usage of the methodology or process becomes difficult, partially because new experiences say ''no'' to old experiences; otherwise, we are not relating to a new experience. The difficulty is, of course, it assumes a new dimension and we must begin to function without a well-defined map which engages a conscious network of unspeakable felt values and relationships which make every activity of our lives an evolutionary transaction. We reject the old notions of the observed and the observer and center our process on a set of relationships which bind the intervals of our experience with a whole. This enables us to function on the subjective and objective levels with the understanding of knowledge gleaned from the sciences, the art and creations of humankind.

Glossary of Terms

ABDUCTION—a term first used by Charles S. Peirce in 1867 to show a logical sequence to intuitive thinking; a process that has natural affinity for understanding events. It precedes hypotheses and the other methods of inquiry.

APPLIED EPISTEMOLOGY—a phrase coined by Felix Roethlisberger to enable the structuring, selection, inventing and application of basic knowledge.

ARISTOTELIANISM—a body of thinking, utilizing Aristotle's Method of Inquiry, viz., the deductive method; *supports the identity* and *concretozal* categories.

CLASSIFYING STAGE—the second stage of the epistemological profile, utilizing early classical Greek thought and Aristotle's methodology.

CONCEPTUALIZATION—the process of imagining, and identifying areas of thought symbolically.

CREATIVE LOOP—a methodology designed by Dr. J. Samuel Bois for the purpose of making the abductive process practical and usable.

DEDUCTION (*deductive logic*)—designation for aristotlian logic—using the syllogism as a methodology.

DISSIPATIVE STRUCTURES—a theory popularized by Marilyn Ferguson and introduced by chemist Illya Prigogine; it bridges the gap between biology and physics. The brain is considered a perfect example of a dissipative structure. The practical implications are found in the notion of transformation, i.e., periodic leaps, semantic jumps and instability that leads to coherence.

EPISTEMIC SYSTEM—a practical theoretical system of thought emphasizing applied epistemology, the episteme, the process of abduction, general semantics epistemology and the application of other basic knowledge.

EPISTEMOLOGICAL PROFILE—an instrument invented by French philosopher-physicist Gaston Bachelard, designed to aid us in analyzing the deeper structures of our "thought-combining" theory and practice.

EPISTEMOLOGY—how our knowledge and thinking are invented and developed. And, how and why we think what we think.

HYPOTHETICO-DEDUCTIVE METHOD—a method designed to create a tentative direction for the deductive method.

INDUCTION—Sir Francis Bacon introduced this idea. It is in line with our positivistic thinking and the scientific method. Also, it is used in analytic research.

INTERACTION—a term coined from classical physics denoting cause and effect—(stimulus-response), and push and pull physics.

INTERRUPTING—a term that is a part of the creative loop, linking Induction and Abduction.

LANGUAGE—the symbolic process.

LOGICAL-POSITIVISM—an attempt to link facts and values in a systematic way.

MECHANISTIC MODE—17th century thinking—a part of the relating stage of the epistemological profile.

MULTI-ORDINALITY—a system used to order the process of abstracting, i.e., something can have different meanings at different levels of abstraction without abandoning the original definition.

NON-ADDITIVE THINKING—the notion that relationships are geometric, relative and quantum rather than arithmetic.

PARADIGM SHIFTS—leaps in thoughts and patterns of behavior transforming our ways of functioning. A difference in kind, not degree; a difference that makes a difference a *difference*.

PARTICIPATING STAGE—the fifth stage of the epistemological profile. It is beyond the symbolic process—a unifying stage of development.

PLANNING—the link in the creative loop between deduction and induction.

POSTULATING STAGE—the fourth stage of the epistemological profile where things are tentative, flexible—the stage of relativity and modern science.

PROCESS OF ABSTRACTING—the natural process of our thinking and nervous system invented by Korzybski; the major distinction between plants, animals, and humans.

RELATING STAGE—the third stage of the epistemological profile, representing the thinking of the 17th century. All involves, includes, composed of classical physics, positivism, scientific method, and inductive reasoning.

SEMANTIC SPECTRUM—a way of using the epistemological profile to perform Semantic-Analysis from Stages 1-5.

SEMANTIC TRANSACTION—a way of using the seven elements jointly, of the semantic transaction to holistically function.

SENSING STAGE—the first stage of the epistemological profile (pre-Grecian and pre-Aristotelian).

SITUATION—a substitution, symbolically and semantically, for the term problem.

STRUCTURAL APPROACH—finding a symbolic process that has a meaningful correspondence to the structure of this world.

STRUCTURED UNCONSCIOUS—the Second Nature, which determines prior intelligent and volitional behavior; the manner in which we transact with people, i.e., situation language and symbols.

SYMBOLIC PROCESS—the language system we use.

SYNCHRONICITY—the system developed by Carl Jung to understand processes that occur without apparent causal determinants.

SYNTHESIZING—bringing together seemingly unrelated instances.

THEORY OF LOGICAL TYPES—a theory proposed by Bertrand Russell to free us from the aristotelian vicious circle fallacy and static thinking.

TIME-BINDING—Korzybski—the major distinction between plants, humans and animals. The capacity to make symbols, abstractions and pass on knowledge from one generation to another—the time binding capacity.

"TO BE"—identity; the verb to be and its harmfulness to human functioning.

TRANSACTION—as opposed to interactions coined by Arthur Bentley to represent a process that speaks of fusion and being connected holistically.

TRANSFORMATION—a process theoretically more open to the natural process of human development. It has as its under-girding thought process, the theory of dissipative structures and shifts in kind rather than degree. To be transformed in thinking, behavior and functioning; a semantic or epistemic jump; a difference that makes a difference a *difference*.

INDEX

Abduction, 1, 10, 21, 26, 27, 38, 45, 55, 60, 61, 96, 97, 108, 109, 110, 113, 125, 132, 141

Abstracting, 52, 53, 61, 76, 92, 94, 141

Affirmative Action, 76

Ames, Adelbert Jr., 37

Analytic-Synthetic, 136

Anderson, John, 12

Applied Epistemology, 6, 7, 141

Aristotle, 33, 58, 76, 105

Aristotelian, 58, 141

Art of Awareness, 58, 105, 127

Ashen, Ruth Nanda, 99

Bachelard, Gaston, 67, 143

Bacon, Francis, 57, 62, 110

Barnard, Chester, 5

Barrett, William, 31

Bentley, Arthur, 30, 125

Bertanlaffy, Ludwig, 60

Bohr, Neils, 106

Bois, Samuel J., 67, 99, 101, 105, 127

Boulding, Kenneth, 44

Breeds of Men, 46, 111, 138

Breed IV, 138,139

Bronowski, Jacob, 8

Brown, Jerry, 70

Burke, Kenneth, 31

Carter, Jimmy, 93

Cartesian, 66

Castenada, Carlos, 97

Chinese logic, 6

Classifying Stage, 41, 53, 91, 141

Conceptual Revolutions, 55, 57, 61, 65

Conceptualization, 15, 141

Copernican Revolution, 55

Copernicus, 7, 67, 83

Creative Loop, 6, 37, 141

DaVinci, Leonardo, 58

Darrow, Clarence, 134

DeChardin, Pierre, 6

Deduction, 1, 10, 45, 141

Death and Dying, 113-116

Depression, 49

Descartes, René, 33

Dewey, John, 59, 125

Dissipative structures, 141

Eddington, Sir Arthur, 110

Ellington, Duke, 133

Einstein, Albert, 3-4, 8, 10, 111

Either/Or, 55, 59, 61, 62, 65, 69, 91, 121, 133

Ellis, Albert, 84

Elusive Phenomena, 7
Empiricism, 24, 53, 124
Epistemics, 38, 40, 107, 122, 134, 135, 141
Epistemology, 28, 31, 142
Epistemological Profile, 57, 67, 77, 94, 113, 122, 136
Evolution of physics, 111
Extensional Devices, 130, 131
Extensionalization, 119, 123
Follette, Mary Parker, 76, 93, 135
Friedmann, John, 95, 101, 109
Galileo, 33
General Semantics, 28, 46
Geocentric, 66
Geometrodynamics, 9, 12
Goldwater, Barry, 99
Habermas, Jurgen, 50
Heliocentric, 66
Holism, 23
Holonomy, 55
How to Develop Your Thinking Ability, 96
Indexing, 137
Illusion of Technique, 31
Induction, 45, 142
Is of Identity, 58, 84
Jonathan Livingston Seagull, 136, 141
Johnson, Lyndon B., 99
Johnson, Wendell, 47
Jones, Roger, 6
Jung, Carl, 6
Keller, Benjamin, 128
Kennedy, John F., 70
Kinetic Inquiry, 60

Keyes, Ken Jr., 96
Knowing and the Known, 125
Korzybski, Alfred, 7, 28, 46, 52, 59, 72, 105, 136, 139
Law of the situation, 74, 93
Levels of Abstracting, 93
Levels of Knowing and Existence, 57
Linguistic Analysis of Mathematics, 30
Logical positivism, 25, 142
Mathematics, 51, 56
Maxwell, Clerk, 2
Mechanistic Mode, 32
Misner, Charles, 9
Multiordinal, 92, 142
Multi-ordinality, 55, 74, 92, 142
Mumford, Lewis, 52, 135
Murchies, Guy, 50
New Guide to Rational Living, 84
Newton, 22, 110
Newtonian, 33, 78
Nixon, Richard, 100
Non-identity, 120, 137
Non-allness, 120
Noosphere, 6
Origins of Knowledge and Imagination, 8
Ouspensky, P. D., 59
Participating Stage, 42, 142
Peirce, Charles Sanders, 34, 36
People in Quandaries, 46
Pfaff, William, 98
Phenomenon of Man, 6
Phillips, D. C., 23

Philosophy of No, 67
Physics and Beyond, 99
Physics as Metaphor, 6
Policy Analysis, 96
Postulating Stage, 41, 44, 53, 65-74, 91, 143
Power Stage, 76
Principia Mathematica, 24, 29
Problem Solving, 34
Process of Abstracting, 53, 92, 123, 143
Process of Government, 30, 125
Public Administration Review, 95
Radcliff-Brown, A. D., 26
Rationality, 25, 109, 112, 119
Reductionism, 19, 71
Relating Stage, 41, 65, 75-78, 91, 143
Renaissance, 58
Reverse Discrimination, 76
Robeson, Paul, 133
Robots, Men, and Minds, 60
Roethlisberger, Felix, 1, 7
Russell, Bertrand, 24, 29
Science and Sanity, 98
Scientific method, 66
Self-Reflexiveness, 39, 120
Self-Subsistent, 34
Semantic Spectrum, 53, 58, 143
Semantic Transaction, 53, 136
Seven Mysteries of Life, 50
Sensing Stage I, 40
Separate Reality, 97

Social Policy, 102
Sorokin, Pitirim, 59, 139
Stages of Cultural Development:
Stage I:, 40, 43
Stage II:, 43
Stage III:, 43, 44
Stage IV:, 41
Stage V:, 42
Structured unconscious, 4, 5, 126, 143
Space, 3, 4
Synchronicity, 6, 52, 143
Teachings of Don Juan, 97
Technological, 31
Theobold, Robert, 67
Theory of Dissipative Structures, 17, 18
Theory of Types, 24, 29, 143
Time, 4
Time-binding, 39, 120, 143
Transaction, 106, 144
Transformation, 16, 17, 18, 144
Transformation of Man, 52, 135
Uncommon Sense and Dimensional Awareness, 65
University of Southern California, 105
Verb-to-be, 58, 59, 81-90
Waltzlawick, Paul, 114
Weinberg, Harry, 57
Wheeler, J. A., 12
Whitehead, A., 24, 29
Williams, William J., 46
Wittgenstein, Ludwig, 31
Whyte, Lancelot Law, 6